Souped Up

Souped Up

Do-It-Yourself Projects to Make Anything Better

Selected by Instructables.com, Edited by Michael Huynh

Skyhorse Publishing

Skyhorse Publishing books may be purchased in bulk at special discounts for sales promotion, corporate gifts, fund-raising, or educational purposes. Special editions can also be created to specifications. For details, contact the Special Sales Department, Skyhorse Publishing, 307 West 36th Street, 11th Floor, New York, NY 10018 or info@skyhorsepublishing.com.

Skyhorse® and Skyhorse Publishing® are registered trademarks of Skyhorse Publishing, Inc.®, a Delaware corporation.

www.skyhorsepublishing.com

10 9 8 7 6 5 4 3 2 1

Library of Congress Cataloging-in-Publication Data is available on file.

ISBN: 978-1-62087-562-9

Printed in China

TABLE OF CONTENTS

TECHNOLOGY

DÉCOR

FOOD

FURNITURE

SCIENCE

TRANSPORTATION

CLOTHING & ACCESSORIES

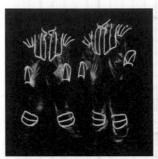

REUSE

AUDIO/VISUAL

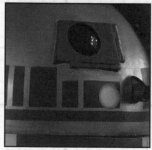

PLAY

WORKSHOP

STORAGE

Introduction

Souped up is a term used in the automotive world to describe a car that has been modified for speed, aerodynamics, or unquantifiable awesomeness. We're expanding the term to encompass material improvements made to *anything* in your life. Umbrellas, cardboard boxes, skateboards, broken televisions, and even shopping carts can be souped up for optimal performance. (Sorry to the bouillon and bisque lovers out there, we have not added turbochargers to your soup. We do have robotic cupcakes and bacon-flavored gelatin for you, though.)

The things in our life, the stuff, the various engineered objects that we use every day, are not necessarily *complete*. Our stuff is done enough; enough to sell, enough to meet most people's needs, enough to get the job done. But with a little ingenuity and some basic skills, anyone can improve or customize their stuff as well as make use of their things when they break. Not only is it cheaper than buying an off-the-shelf replacement or an even pricier custom product, there's something satisfying about bringing the stronger, better, faster mentality out of the garage and into the rest of your house.

The ingenious authors of the projects in this book are ordinary people who do not accept that their stuff is done until it does exactly what they want, looks just right, or is made unquantifiably awesome through their own efforts. These projects are excellent examples of what creative people can do to their stuff.

United under an LED-illuminated umbrella of improvements, these projects take ordinary objects and make them magnificent. So dig in, find some inspiration, and improve the things in your life.

—Wade Wilgus

Editor's note

The wonderful thing about Instructables is that they come in all shapes and sizes. Some users include hundreds of high-quality pictures and detailed instructions with their projects; others take the minimalist approach and aim to inspire similar ideas than to facilitate carbon copies.

One of the biggest questions we faced when putting this book together was: How do we convey the sheer volume of ideas in the finite space of a book?

As a result, if you're already familiar with some of the projects in this book, you'll notice that only select photos made the jump from the computer screen to the printed page. Similarly, when dealing with extensive electronic coding or complex science, we've suggested that anyone ready to start a project like that visit the Instructables' online page, where you often find lots more images, links, multimedia attachments, and downloadable material to help you along the way. This way, anyone who is fascinated by the idea of convering a car to run on trash can take a look here at the basic steps to get from start to finish. Everything else is just a mouse click away.

Special thanks to Instructables Interactive Designer Gary Lu for the Instructables Robot illlustrations!

Technology

Make your electronics excellent with these projects that convert utilitarian items into unique and customized works of art. Whether it's an old USB drive, an umbrella, or a bluetooth receiver, these projects will help you turn boring legacy electronics into new and useful works of art.

By recycling outdated technology with these projects, you're helping to prevent a mountain of electronic waste full of nasty chemicals that would otherwise seep into the ocean. For every project you complete, a dolphin receives a $5 donation to its college fund.

Do-It-Yourself USB Hard Drive

By gmgfarrand
(http://www.instructables.com/id/DIY-USB-quotHard-Drivequot/)

Using a dead hard drive, a 4-port USB hub, and a few flash drives, you will kill some time and get a few laughs from anyone seeing you use this.

Step 1: Find a Candidate
Any hard drive should do.

Step 2: Dismantle
Take the hard drive apart.

Step 3: Compare
Make sure your USB hub will fit, with the plastic case on or off.

Step 4: Expose Hub
For this purpose, I removed the plastic case.

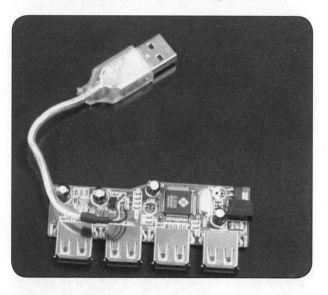

Step 5: Install
I placed the "nekkid" USB hub into the area where the platter used to be. Note: I was only placing this temporarily. If I were going to keep this mod permanent, I would glue the hub in place either using epoxy or hot glue. Also, if this were going to be used permanently, I would coat the circuit board with epoxy.

Step 6: Flash Me!
Now add your flash drives; you may have to remove the casing for some to fit well.

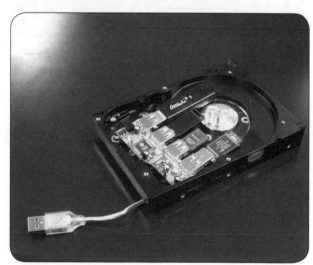

Step 7: Button It Up
Replace the cover to the hard drive and plug in! Now you will have a "new" flash drive that will be sure to get some comments. Also, there is a way to install certain flavors of Linux onto all four flash drives in a RAID configuration, assuming you have all the same capacities. Have fun!

3

Electric Umbrella

By sockmaster
(http://www.instructables.com/id/Electric-Umbrella/)

Turn an ordinary umbrella into something whimsical and magical. The Electric Umbrella will glow with many pinpoints of light. Carry the sun and the stars with you at night! This is perfect for nighttime strolls through the countryside or just being silly. It also includes a dimmer so you can adjust the brightness!!

Step 1: What You Need

The things that you need can be found in local stores, electronics parts shops, online, and by scrounging parts from old electronic junk you may have lying around.

- one umbrella, preferably light in color with a straight handle and a hollow shaft so that you can pass wires through it. It's very important that the umbrella be simple—none of that spring-loaded automatic stuff!
- 64 SMD (surface mounted device) LEDs in your color of choice. The actual size does not matter, except that the smaller LEDs will look more invisible, which is preferable, but they will also be more difficult to work with. I used size 805 (2mm wide) 3.5V white LEDs. White, blue, UV, and some greens require 3.5 volts and won't require additional resistors on each LED, but 1.8V LEDs (red, yellow, green) do (more trouble!).
- a spool of thin, single-strand, lacquered copper wire. It should be thin enough to be nearly invisible against the umbrella, but thick enough to withstand the occasional stresses and snags. This wire is what the SMD LEDs will be soldered on to.
- 3AA battery holder, preferably compact and arranged in an L shape, as the batteries will have to lie over the umbrella's shaft. 3AAA batteries would work well and are more compact but won't last as long.
- normal plastic-coated, multi-strand copper wire, preferably the type that will not break easily after repeated flexing
- one 750 ohm variable resistor with a built-in on/off switch for dimming and turning the umbrella on and off
- needle and thread that is the same color as the umbrella
- solder and soldering iron or gun
- wire cutters, wire strippers, scissors, and X-Acto knife
- drill and drill bits
- large board and small nails to be used for laying out the wires and soldering the SMD LEDs onto the wires
- masking tape and double-sided tape or carpet tape
- clear epoxy or glue
- superglue

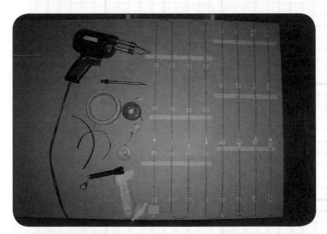

Step 2: Soldering the LEDs onto the Wires

Be prepared for some long and tedious steps. Carefully soldering 64 individual LEDs, which are not much larger than a grain of sand, onto thin and uncooperative wires takes patience.

First, measure out your umbrella and plan where each of the LEDs will go. This umbrella will have 16 spokes radiating out from the center, each spoke having four LEDs. I chose to have four different sets of LED spacing (eight of each set) to make a pattern that appears random. I set the LED spacing so they're closer together towards the outside of the umbrella in an effort to make the LED distribution reasonably even throughout the surface of the umbrella.

Get a large board that's wider than the radius of your umbrella and hammer a bunch of nails along the sides so that you can string up and stretch out your single-strand copper wires (two wires to each nail).

Place masking tape and mark off the points where you'll be soldering the LEDs. Leave some extra lengths of wire at each end in case you need some extra length once you install them onto your umbrella.

Place some masking tape under the wires to prevent burning the board in case you want to use it for some other purpose and add more masking tape to hold the wires in place as you solder. My wire was lacquer coated, so I had to first burn it off at the points where the LEDs will be added with my soldering gun and hot solder. You may try scraping it off or using a wire stripper to strip it off.

Once the wires are "tinned" with solder, try to wedge an LED between the two. Be careful to place all LEDs in the same polarity!

Time to solder your first LED! I tried to apply masking tape onto the wires so that they pinched the LED in place. This will make it easier to solder the LEDs since they're not moving around.

With a very quick, light touch, touch both sides of the LED with the hot soldering tip and the solder coating the wires, and the tip will flow into the LED contacts. If you're not sure about this step, hook up 3 volts (two AA batteries) to the wires hanging off the board and see if the LED lights up!

Once you get the hang of it, move on and do the rest of the LEDs. I soldered mine in two sets—half of the wire/LEDs on the board at one time (16 "spokes") and the other half afterwards. After all the LEDs were soldered in, apply power to the board/wires to see all the LEDs light up in their glory. This is also a good time to determine how many volts you want your umbrella to run on, and what value of variable resistor you want to use for dimming. I decided on three AA batteries (4.5 volts, or 3.6 volts if using rechargeable batteries) and a 750 ohm variable resistor.

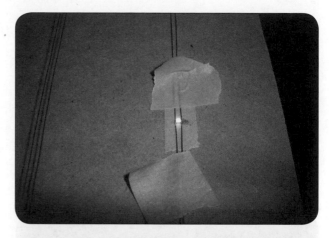

Step 3: Assemble the Central Hub for the Wires

All the LED spokes connect to a center hub near the tip/center of the umbrella. The tricky part is assembling this part outside of the umbrella first and then carefully fitting it into the umbrella between the spokes and the cloth.

I assembled it separately because it's hard to attempt on the inside of an open umbrella. I also didn't want to risk burning holes into the cloth when soldering.

Make two rings of wire. I used masking tape to hold its shape while putting it together. The masking tape also marked the spacing where each LED string would be attached. The exact size of the rings doesn't matter; you just want them to be fairly close to the center of the umbrella.

Do not solder the wires into a full circle yet. You will need these to be detached when you fit it into the umbrella later on. After you've finished assembling the rings, hold the circle together with more masking tape and leave lengths of wire long enough at one end to reach the batteries once it's inside the umbrella.

I made a mistake and used the same single strand copper wire as I used for the LED strings. Every time I opened and closed the umbrella, the wires in the hub flexed. I knew it would eventually break from the stresses. Bad, bad, bad!

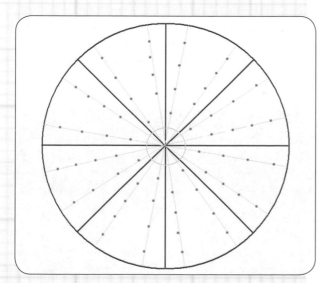

Later on I soldered additional loops of stranded wire onto the hub. These wires are much better at holding up to stresses of repeated flexing (see photos 7 and 8). The next umbrella I made used only loops of wire for the hub - see photos 9 &10.)

Cut the lengths of wire off the big board (four LEDs per length). Measure the ends/length/LED placement and start soldering the strings of wire onto the hub. Make sure you get the wire/power polarity right! You can add power to the wires to see if you're on the right track. After all 16 strings are attached you will have an interesting, glowy mess.

Step 4: Get the Wires and Hub into the Umbrella

Loosely place the hub and the mess of wires near the center of the closed umbrella. Carefully begin sliding the hub under the umbrella's spines so it runs around the center shaft and rests between the cloth and the spines. Then carefully slide the strings of LEDs under the spines until you have two strings in each ⅛th section of the umbrella.

Once everything is roughly in place it's time to secure the open ends of the hub to each other. Cut, strip, and twist the wire ends together. Once tied together, place some newspaper between the hub wires and the umbrella's cloth so that you won't burn the cloth.

Solder the wires together. Once that is finished, add tape to the new section on the hub so its shape and spacing matches the rest of the hub.

Now you should have two wires coming off the hub. These wires will go to the battery clip/power switch/dimmer. Cut little bits of double-sided carpet tape and start placing them under the hub to keep it in place.

Set it down, centered around the spokes, with two strings of LEDs between each spine. Once in place, sew the hub to the spokes and cloth of the umbrella.

Step 5: Attach the LED Strings to the Cloth

Things are finally starting to take shape. Attach the LED strings to the cloth. Carefully stretch the wires outward toward the edges of the umbrella. I used masking tape to keep them flat on the cloth.

Once the strings of wire are positioned, you may use a bit of superglue under each LED to set them on the cloth. Make sure the wires are not twisted and that all the LEDs are facing up or, rather, facing the person holding the umbrella.

Once they're all set in place, remove the masking tape and cut off the excess wire at the ends. Try adding power to see what the umbrella looks like at this stage. It's not finished yet, but this is the point you can see the lighting effect for the first time.

The superglue is not good enough to hold the LEDs in place forever. It's just temporary to keep everything in place while you sew all the wires and LEDs into place. I used small stitches—one on each LED and one on the wire halfway between each LED.

Step 6: Add the On/Off Switch and Dimmer Control

In order to add the on/off switch and dimmer control in the umbrella's handle, you need to drill some holes and run wires down the umbrella's shaft.

Drill one small hole in the shaft at the top of the umbrella that is large enough to let the fine copper wires through, but don't insert the wires yet.

Next drill out the umbrella's handle. Carefully drill a hole all the way through the handle and into the metal shaft of the umbrella. Use a drill bit that's slightly smaller than the diameter inside the shaft and drill carefully right down the center of the handle until the bit pushes through. You want the hole to be large enough to let the drill shavings that went up the shaft to fall back out again. Try to get them all out.

Next you need to drill a larger hole in the handle, just deep enough for the dimmer switch to rest inside. I used a ³/₄ inch bit for this and then drilled out one side some more for the irregular shape of the dimmer switch. Again, try to get all the shavings out of the umbrella itself.

Now it's time to run two single-strand copper wires down from the top of the umbrella and out the bottom of the handle. This part is tricky because the wires could get bunched up inside. Pull them out again if they get stuck and try again. If the wires get too bent up, throw them away and try again with new wires.

Once you get them through the handle, solder one of the wires at the top to your battery clip and the other to one of the wires leading to the hub/LEDs. The other wire from the hub goes directly to the second wire on the battery clip. At the bottom of the handle end, solder the wires to the switch and dimmer so you can fully disconnect power by turning or clicking the variable resistor counterclockwise, and so that the LEDs grow brighter the more you turn it clockwise. Once you've tested that it all works, glue the variable resistor in place with epoxy or other glue. If possible, find a nice decorative knob to put onto the variable resistor.

Step 7: Finishing Up

Finally, attach the battery clip to the shaft. I left mine tied but free to move up and down a bit—this way it can move down when you close the umbrella (farther from the tip is better as it closes up pretty tight and you don't want to add extra stresses onto the delicate wires on the LEDs), and moves up when you open it (the folding mechanism pushes the battery clip closer to the hub).

At last, you can take it out for a spin! It looks amazing but it is a bit delicate. Don't take it out in the wind; the lights probably wouldn't survive the umbrella reversing itself! Be careful opening, closing, and transporting the umbrella so you don't put too much mechanical stresses on the fine wires.

Bluetooth Handgun Handset for Your iPhone

By ManaEnergyPotion
(http://www.instructables.com/id/Bluetooth-Handgun-Handset-for-your-iPhone-iGiveUp/)

This will teach you how to turn an airsoft handgun and a Bluetooth headset into a fun, fully functional handset for your iPhone. Pull the trigger to receive calls and to, um, end them. Listen through the barrel, and talk into the grip.

I think everyone has made the thumb-and-forefinger gun-to-the-head sign when someone unpleasant shows up on their caller ID. We thought it would be fun to make an actual gun handset, and it turned out to be surprisingly straightforward—no glue or power tools were required. Even though it's not very practical, there's something so satisfying about ending a call with this handset. Pow.

Naturally, this handset works with any cell phone. You just feel like pulling the trigger more if you own an iPhone.

Step 1: Materials and Gun Disassembly
- 1 Jabra BT250v Bluetooth headset
- 1 HFC Walther P99 look-alike airsoft gun
- 1 hammer
- 1 pliers
- 1 Phillips-head screwdriver
- 1 Mana Energy Potion (that's to keep you awake)

First, disassemble the gun fully by placing the tip of the screwdriver on the pin above the trigger (not the pin connected to the safety) and tapping it

out enough that you can pull it the rest of the way out with the pliers. Tap out the rest of the pins, slide the slide back, remove the faux-striker pin cover, and slip off the top half of the gun. The gun basically falls apart after that.

Step 2: Plunger Removal
Remove the plunger from the slide assembly as well as the spring and plastic plug. Throw out the plunger. With the plunger removed, the gun can't shoot you in the ear. Replace the spring and plastic plug.

Step 3: Sear Pin Removal
Remove the sear pin assembly at the rear of the gun and throw it out.

Step 4: Prepping the Bluetooth Headset

Now direct your attention to the Bluetooth headset. There are small screws that hold it together. I opted to just pry it apart until they broke. Now cut out the middle part of the rubberized portion of the Bluetooth headset.

Step 5: Watch Your iPhone Crash

I left my iPhone synced to the headset while I prepped it, so it retaliated by crashing so badly I had to just power it down. Hopefully, you can skip this step. I recommend unpairing the headset from your iPhone during assembly.

Step 6: Insert the Headset into the Gun

Hook a rubber band over the trigger arm (see picture). Let the other end dangle out of the bottom of the gun for now. Cram the headset into the gun where the magazine used to be. Notice how the microphone portion points down (so you can talk into the handle) and it's pressed against the upper portion of the headset. The headset fits perfectly so you don't need to secure it, just stuff it in there. Make sure the rubber band stays on the trigger arm side of the gun. The pin coming off the trigger arm should be just off the call start/end button so that when you pull the trigger it operates the button.

Step 7: Insert the Earbud

Now reattach the slide of the gun. First slip the earbud into the breach of the barrel and then reattach the slide. The headphone will rest against the chamber-end of the barrel. The barrel will focus the sound into your ear. It doesn't have to be a snug fit to work well.

Step 8: Disassemble the Magazine

Take apart the magazine with a screwdriver and a hammer. Save just the butt plate and throw away the rest.

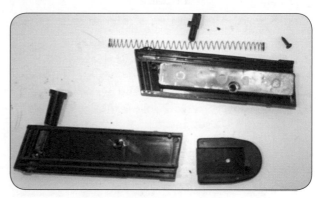

Step 9: Secure the Other End of the Rubber Band

Put the magazine butt plate back onto the grip and stretch the rubber band from the front of the butt plate across the bottom. Secure it to the back of the grip by putting it under the palm rest; put the palm-rest pin back in place to make sure it stays.

Step 10: Answer Some Calls, Take Some Photos

I was testing the phone when it rang, so I pulled the trigger and answered the call. Another trigger pull ended it, and yet a third trigger pull ended my test call. Now make some tasteless puns about ending conversations!

A little warning: Do not remove the orange tip or paint it. Word on the street has it that there are very serious consequences for this. Also, it better be obvious that this shouldn't be used in public.

Step 11: Paint It White and Bring It to the iPhone Line

Mask the orange tip, then use a plastic paint to paint the gun white. You could even made a box for it with photo paper and spray adhesive!

Do-It-Yourself Cassette Player Turntable

By araid
(http://www.instructables.com/id/DIY-Turntable/)

You always wanted to be a disc jockey. You know nothing about beats, delays, or mixing but, damn, scratching is like the coolest thing ever invented!

If this is true for you, follow this Instructable to build a low-fi DJ set and take the chance to recycle your old cassette player into a new cool instrument.

Step 1: Materials

Minimum:

- cassette player (better if it's an old one)
- wire and wire strippers
- prototyping breadboard
- soldering iron and solder
- screwdriver
- 5 9V batteries with battery holder
- some kind of variable resistor or potentiometer

Advanced:

- Arduino with its USB cable
- IRF540 Mosfet (transistor)
- 5 LEDs
- 5 220 ohm resistors (brown-red-red)
- one 1 kohm resistor (red-black-brown)
- computer cooling fan
- box or some kind of enclosure

This project is divided in two parts. By doing only the basics you'll be able to control the speed of the music without even having to touch an Arduino or write a line of code. Almost zero budget and quite fun.

If you decide to continue on to the advanced part, you'll be able to have the PC fan act as a turntable (although it won't be real scratching because the gears of the Walkman won't let you play backwards). You'll have total control over the speed of the music and can add whatever effects you like, like the LED indicator.

So, let's get started!

Step 2: Walkman Hacking

The core of this project is this: In a cassette player there's a small DC motor that spins the tape. It's powered by a battery that provides constant voltage. Our goal is to supply our own voltage to the motor—higher than the battery to speed up the song or lower to slow it down.

Start by taking off the battery. Unscrew all the screws on the back case and inside the battery place and remove the case. Do it carefully because some parts, like the volume gear, are loose, and you may have to place them again. Take a picture or remember where everything is.

Once you see the guts of your old player, you'll have to find the two wires (red and black) that provide voltage and ground to the small, round-shaped DC motor that will usually be on the right side. If you're lucky you'll see the points where they are soldered, otherwise you'll have to cut them.

To check that they are the ones we're looking for, press the play button and try to apply some volts to these wires by connecting them to your battery. If the song plays, you found the right spot! Now solder your own black and red wires to where the original ones are soldered, or cut the original ones and attach yours. Leave your wires quite long to have room to play.

We're almost done. Find a place to pass your wires once the case is closed. Many players have a hole for DC-In that's very useful for that. If yours doesn't you might have to drill yours or pass them through the space for the battery.

Finally, put everything in its place again, close the case and screw it on.

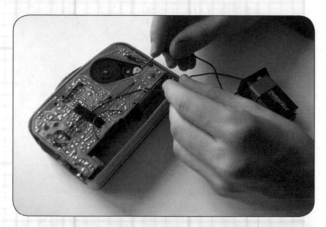

Step 3: Be Creative!

Now your Walkman is hacked. Insert your favorite tape, apply whatever voltage you want to the wires, and, if the play button is pressed, the song will play faster or slower. Be aware that there's a minimum voltage to start the motor, and a maximum you shouldn't go over if you don't want to burn the circuitry.

But the fun thing is to have control, and the easy way to do it is with variable resistors. Start with a simple slide or knob potentiometer like the one in the image. After that, you can try more interesting stuff, like placing a photocell between the positive wires of your battery and the motor (sorry, I didn't have one

to show you!). You'll probably need more power, but eventually you'll be able to play your Walkman like a theremin.

These cheap parts will change their resistance depending on different inputs and allow you to control the Walkman with a simple analog circuit.

So here's my challenge: Be creative and invent your own controllers!

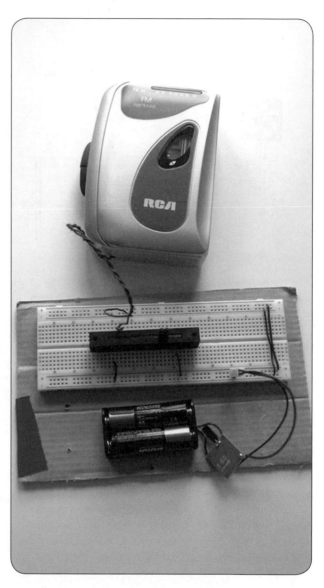

Step 4: Digital Wiring

If you, like me, are more comfortable with digital electronics, here's how I wired everything up. The fan positive wire is connected to pin A1 in the Arduino, and the negative one is connected to the ground through one 1 kohm resistor (it acts as pull-down). The Walkman is connected to the digital pin 6 of the Arduino using an IRF540 transistor.

Notice some important things:
- You'll need to have a battery holder with a jack to plug it to the Arduino. This way can we power both the Arduino and the motor.

- We're only using the red and black wires of the fan; the other is for control but we don't need it in this case. Some newer models may even have more wires.
- The fan is plugged directly to the analog pin of the Arduino, which is something you should never do because you could fry it if it reads more than 5V. I did it because I previously tested the fan and found I couldn't generate more than 2V by spinning it manually. So, if you can, test it too.

Since mine was cardboard, I fixed the cassette player and the cooling fan with their own screws, and it was easy to drill holes for the wires. It'll be more work to do this with more sturdy materials, but it will look better.

Fix the battery, breadboard, and Arduino inside of the box and wire everything up again. Plug the battery, choose a tape and make them dance!

You can now play with different tapes and see how vocals, instruments, and rhythms are distorted by the changing speed in different genres of music.

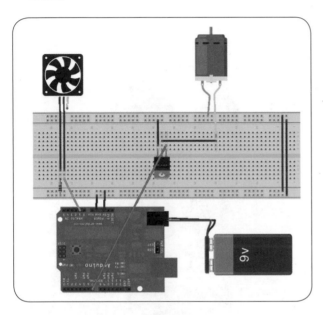

Step 5: Arduino Coding

The code basically performs one task: it reads the input from the fan and maps it to a proportional output to the Walkman. It also smoothes the readings from the fan, which are unstable.

Visit instructables.com to download the Arduino code, compile it, and upload it to the Arduino (is it your first time? check out the manual).

When testing it, you may find that you have to tweak the ranges for both the input and the output, since they will change depending on your hardware and battery. Try adjusting these three constants:

- minV
- maxV
- maxFan

Step 6: Make It Look Nice!

When everything works, you can add the LEDs for some extra eye candy. Solder black wires to their short legs and red to the long ones. Then plug the negative (black) to the ground line of the breadboard with a 220ohm resistor in between. Their positive legs should be plugged directly to digital pins 8, 9, 10, 11, and 12 of the Arduino.

Build a nice enclosure from whatever material you have available and attach the devices to it.

Double-Ended USB Flash Drive

By fungus amungus
(http://www.instructables.com/id/Double-ended-USB-flash-drive/)

I don't want to have one flash drive on hand, I want two. And if I'm going to be carrying two drives around I'd like to keep them together so they don't get lost. Thus, the double-ended USB flash drive. It keeps my files together and looks nicer than a couple of drives hot glued together.

Why not just get one larger flash drive? Good question. Even with just four gigs on each of these drives, I'm still not even coming close to capacity with the files I carry around. In fact I could get by with a 1GB and be fine. The true answer is that I just want to have a physical separation of two types of files: work and personal.

Sure sure, this could be done with two folders on one drive, but I enjoy the switching of one drive to the other as a physical reminder of what I'm working on. It's also a reminder that maybe I haven't been giving enough time to my personal projects that keep the mental fires burning. So now move on to the building of a small flash drive—let's do this.

Step 1: Design

I'm working once again in Illustrator (Inkscape is the free option), as all of the files need to be vector based for the laser cutting. Getting the basic shapes of the flash drive to be cut here is easy. Measure the dimensions of the part of the flash drive that will be inside the holder. Recreate these rectangles in Illustrator. Add a thin space around and between the drives; this will give you an H-shape for the middle layer and a rectangle for the top and bottom layer.

Step 2: Create a Design

Now for the fun part—making a design for the outside of the drive. Since the form of the drive is symmetrical, be sure to create a design that has a left and a right side. Here I created two designs: a domino and a double USB icon. On the domino it is very clear which side is which. The double USB design is a little harder to read, and form wins over function.

What you make here is totally up to you. Or you can make the outside shape asymmetrical and avoid this problem altogether.

Step 3: Cut and Sand

I cut these files out of ⅛" plywood on our Epilog 36EXT. You could easily make it out of acrylic as well. It's totally up to you. The wood is handy in that I could sand the cut pieces down to make the final item slimmer.

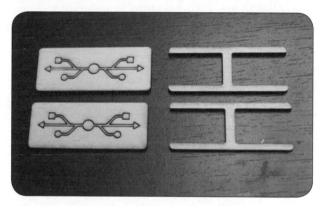

Step 4: Glue and Insert Flash Drives

Now it's just a matter of applying glue. I used Elmer's® Carpenter's® Wood Glue, then clamped it and let it dry.

The fit was so snug that I just pushed the drives in and they're staying put. If it's a little loose you can easily dab a bit of hot glue onto the end and the sides of the drives and use that to keep them in place.

So now you have a double-ended flash drive. Carry your digital life around with you and take on everything.

Privacy Monitor Hacked from an Old LCD Monitor

By dimovi
(http://www.instructables.com/id/Privacy-monitor-made-from-an-old-LCD-Monitor/)

Finally you can do something with that old LCD monitor you have in the garage. You can turn it into a privacy monitor! It looks all white to everybody except you, because you are wearing "magic" glasses!

All you really have to have is a pair of old glasses, an X-acto knife or a box cutter, and some solvent (paint thinner).

Here is what I used:

- LCD monitor (of course)
- single-use 3D glasses from the movie theater (old sunglasses are just fine)
- paint thinner (or some other solvent such as toluene, turpentine, acetone, methyl acetate, ethyl acetate, etc.)
- box cutter (and CNC laser cutter, but that you don't really need; I'm sure an X-acto knife and a steady hand would do just fine)
- screwdriver or a drill
- paper towels
- superglue

Step 1: Take the Monitor Apart

Find an old monitor that you are willing to sacrifice. Take off the plastic frame by unscrewing all screws from the back.

Step 2: Cut the Polarized Film

Most LCD monitors have two films on the glass—a polarized one to filter out the light you are not supposed to see, and a frosted anti-glare one. The anti-glare film we don't need, but the polarized one we do— it is used for the glasses.

So, grab your cutting tool and cut the films along the edge. Don't be afraid to press—metal won't scratch the glass, unless there is sand or another abrasive on it.

Then start peeling. Make sure to save the polarized film, and also remember the orientation.

Step 3: Clean the Film Adhesive

After you remove the film, the glue will likely remain stuck to the glass, so here comes the messy part.

With some solvent, soften the glue and wipe it off with paper towels. Paint thinner is more effective than OOPS. I found out that if you cover the screen with paper towels and then soak them in paint thinner you can let it sit longer and dissolve the adhesive without running and evaporating. Scrape off the soft glue with a piece of plastic or wood. Be careful not to get paint thinner on the plastic frame, because it will dissolve it.

Step 4: Monitor Test

After cleaning the adhesive, assemble everything back the way it was. Before even making the glasses, you can test the monitor with the polarized film! Notice how the upper-left corner looks clear, because it has the anti-glare film removed. That is the part we are going to use to make the glasses.

Step 5: Pop the Lenses Out

For the glasses, I used single-use 3D glasses from the movie theater, but you can use whatever you want. Pop out the lenses or take the glasses apart if you can.

Step 6: Scan, Trace, Cut

If you are going to use a CNC blade or laser cutter, scan and trace the parts. You could find a local vinyl or laser cutting service, or you could send them to an online service like Outfab.com.

I scanned the frames so I could use them as a reference for the lens orientation. Remember, this is a polarized film, so the angle is critical. Back and front also matters. If you don't have access to a CNC cutter or you don't want to wait for an online service, you can probably tape the old lenses on the film and then cut them out with an X-acto knife.

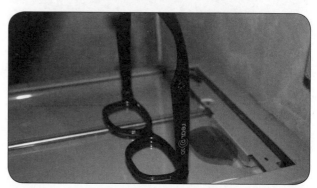

Step 7: Reassemble Glasses and Enjoy!

Finally, assemble the glasses and you are ready for some fun! People might think you are crazy for staring at a blank white screen wearing sunglasses! But I guess that makes it even more fun!

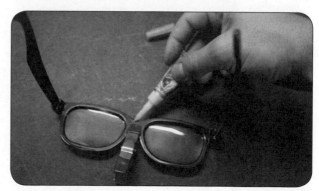

Cheap Lighter Laser Burner

By Kipkay
(http://www.instructables.com/id/Cheapy-Laser-Lighter-Burner/)

Here is the world's first BIC-style laser lighter! Butane is outdated—time to use blue-burning lasers! Watch the video and then build your own. A warning: This kind of laser can cause permanent damage to eyesight in less than a second. Never look into the beam or reflection of any laser, including this one

Step 1: What You Need

- BIC lighter (the non-electronic, standard version). You may want to get two in case you crack the first one.
- blue-laser diode and mini-housing
- mini-driver circuit
- 2 1.5V button-cell batteries
- mini momentary switch
- 4 to 4.3 ohm resistor
- 2 small magnets
- assorted wire

Step 2: Tools and Other Required Items

- Dremel cutoff wheel and small grinding stone or a similar tool.
- needle-nose pliers, small screwdrivers, snips, X-acto knife
- a small pin or paper clip
- soldering iron and solder
- heatshrink tubing
- small drill bits
- multi-meter

Step 3: Prepare the Lighter

Disclaimer for those who don't know lighters are dangerous: Lighters contain butane, a flammable liquid that can catch fire, explode, and burn you. Lasers are also dangerous: Don't ever point any laser at yourself or any living thing.

1. Remove the flint wheel by prying it out at the edges. Do not break the brackets. Once you release it, a spring and flint (and other small stuff) will pop out and fly across the room. Go get them. Keep the flint wheel.
2. Remove the shiny shield by prying it out at the edges. Do not break the brackets. Keep the shield for later.
3. Flip the lighter over and take it to a safe place. Putting on safety glasses never hurts. Stick a small pin or paper clip in the hole and it should contact the metal valve in the base of the lighter. Gently tap it with something to release the butane. You may need to tip it over to make sure all the butane is gone. You should hear something small rattling inside. That's the valve.
4. Remove the red button that releases the butane. Keep it.

Step 4: Gut the Lighter

The entire inside of the lighter has to be gutted out. There are probably many ways this could be done, but I found the best is as follows:

1. Using a Dremel cutting wheel, make two small slits in the white cover on the bottom of the

lighter. Be careful not to nick up or cut the housing or it will look crappy.

2. Use snips, pliers, X-Acto knife, or whatever you need to remove most of the plastic on the white cover. The cover is sonically welded to the housing so it cannot just be pulled out.

3. Use a sanding tool or Dremel attachment to completely remove the whole white base from the housing. This is time consuming if you want to do it right.

4. Remove the entire inside of the housing as far into the lighter as you can, in order to make room for the mini-diode housing. This is a painstaking process and you may have to resort to burning the plastic away with your soldering iron. Don't inhale the smoke or get it in our eyes.

Step 5: Final Lighter Prep

There are two main holes at the top of the lighter. One is the where the red button you removed earlier makes contact with a valve to release the butane. The other one is on the side where the flame exits. Both of these holes need to be drilled out to accommodate the switch and the mini-diode housing. Use drill bits and carefully drill the holes out. (A small bit will be needed to drill out the little valve.) Don't worry about the other hole by the center area. Stay away from the brackets in the middle because you will need those to reattach the red button later.

Step 6: Building the Circuit

This step requires an experienced solderer and a good soldering iron with a small tip. Wire the driver according to the following picture. The second picture is the other side of the driver. Be sure to add the resistor and the switch as shown in the final wiring picture. Using a multimeter set to check milliamps, put the leads between the end of the resistor and the diode. Power it with no more than 3 volts and adjust the pot on the driver to no more than 170 mA. I used two button cells harvested from an Energizer 12 volt 123 battery, taped together on the sides. I also used two small magnets to attach the (+) positive and (-) negative leads from the driver.

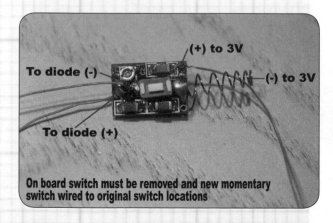

On board switch must be removed and new momentary switch wired to original switch locations

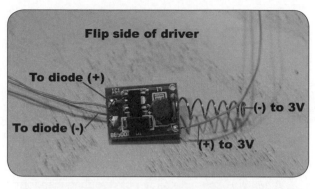

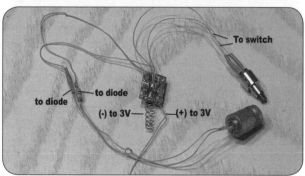

Step 7: Install the Laser Circuit

After confirming that everything is wired correctly, it's time to put everything inside the lighter housing. The diode goes on the former flame side, and the switch is pushed in on the side where the red button switch was (see the next step for details). I used hot glue to secure the switch and diode after lining up the diode to ensure that the beam cleared all areas of the housing.

Step 8: Final Assembly

Cut the original red button in half, leaving just the two small tabs that are secured in the housing holes. You will have to play around with the exact height of the switch in relation to the red button. Reattach the flame shield. As an optional step, find a small rubber stopper and cut it in half, then push it inside the base of the lighter to make sure the driver and batteries stay put. Your Cheap Laser Lighter Burner is complete! Use it responsibly!

When you combine a love of doodling with long-exposure photography, the result is light drawing! We have a large gallery of drawings on our website: www.LightDoodles.com. There you will also find a description of how we draw and a brief history of light drawing. Any light source can serve as your creative implement, but the most natural fit is something that you can hold just like a pencil, with on/off control directly under the index finger. Since you want to complete each full drawing in one exposure, you also need to be able to switch between different colored pens quickly. You'll also find that when drawing a large picture, you will need the light to be completely exposed on all sides to minimize fading around the edges.

With these parameters, I went hunting for parts at the local electronics and hardware stores and came up with what turned out to be a simple and versatile tool that results in some incredible art.

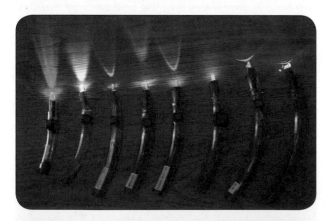

Step 1: Parts List

I'll be creating a blue light pen. Attention to voltage requirements and current draw are important, as different color LEDs have different ratings.

Here is a list of the parts used:
- plastic tubing—⁵⁄₈" outside diameter, ½" inside diameter
- plastic tubing—½" outside diameter, ³⁄₈" inside diameter
- 1 LED
- 1 normally open switch
- 1 20ohm resistor—size is determined using Ohm's law
- 3 1.5 volt button batteries
- heat-shrink tubing
- 24 gauge wire
- electrician's tape

LEDs, switch, resistors, heat shrink, and electrician's tape can be purchased at your local electronics store. The plastic tubing can be found in the hardware store. Many sizes are displayed on spools, which you purchase by the foot. The ⁵⁄₈" outside diameter clear tubing best fit our purposes. The natural curve of the tubing turned out to be ergonomic and helped keep the pens upright and stable when placed down. The switch is a "normally open" switch, which means the circuit is complete and the light is on only when the button is pushed and held down. As soon as the button is released, the circuit is broken and the light goes off. Otherwise, I chose this switch for its size and shape, not for any of its other electrical properties. Adding a resistor to the circuit is good practice in obeying Ohm's Law.

Step 2: Warning—Math Content

I picked up the basics of LED science from the LEDs for Beginners Instructable, reading not only the Instructable itself but the many associated comments. They supply a wealth of theory and important links to everything you want to know about LEDs. The back of the LED package provides the information you need to properly build the working circuit. Use this information to determine which type and quantity of battery and what size resistor to use.

The blue LED I chose requires a 4.0 forward voltage drop (Vf) to light. It will pass 25 milliamps of current (If). Three 1.5 volt batteries in series will supply 4.5 volts. Any combination of batteries that add up to the required voltage will do. For instance, AAA batteries are 1.5 volts, so three in series will give you 4.5 volts. I found these tiny 1.5 volt button batteries inside of an A23 battery (see the second picture). Three of these work nicely. Obeying Ohm's Law and using a Current Limiting Resister Calculator of LEDs, a 20 ohm resistor should be placed in the circuit.

Step 3: Put It Together

Everything in this simple circuit is placed in series, and the parts can be arranged in any order, with one exception. The LED will only light if the battery polarity is correct. Cut an appropriate length of the ⅝" OD tubing and cut a hole close to one end to accommodate the switch. Keep in mind how the pen will fit in your hand and where your finger will lie to operate the button. Since you hold this light like a pen, place the switch where you can easily push it with the index finger. Solder the LED, the resistor, and the wires in series. Remember, the resistor can be placed anywhere in the circuit. Place heat shrink over the exposed wires and heat the shrink with a lighter, protecting against short circuits. Then fold the wiring up and slide inside of a 1" piece of the smaller ½" OD plastic tubing.

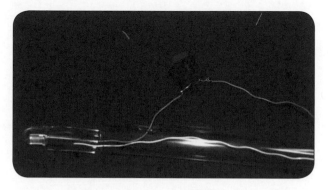

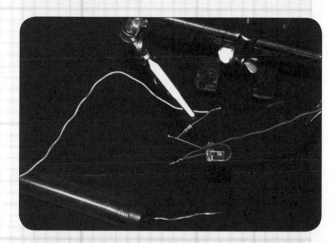

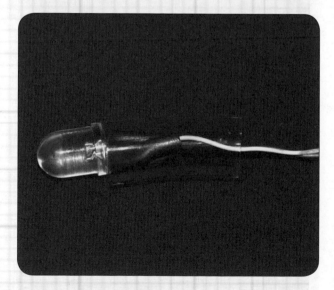

Step 4: Add the Switch

Feed the wires through the ⅝" tube, one through the hole, and solder the switch inline. Continue feeding all wires through the tube. Squeeze the switch into the cutout hole. (I bent the leads to fit.) Squeeze the ½" tube into the ⅝" tube.

Step 5: Add the Power Source

Finally, add the batteries. This is very low-tech, but I have yet to find or build a battery holder that suits my purpose. Strip the ends of the wires and wrap the bare wire and a small bit of aluminum foil together into a ball. Use the electrical tape to hold the batteries together in series (positive terminal to negative terminal) and the wire ends in place on each end of the battery stack. Polarity is important here. Test the light at this point and try reversing the connections if it does not work. (Remember that you have to push the switch while testing.) Wrap a second piece of tape around the terminal ends. Stretch and wrap the tape tightly, ensuring a positive connection. Fit the battery pack into the end of the finished pen.

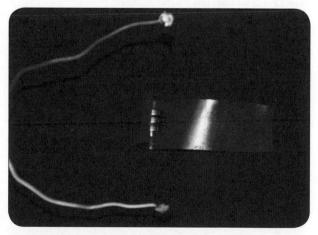

Step 6: Finished Product

It works! Now, drawing is another story.

Lego USB Stick

By ianhampton
(http://www.instructables.com/id/Lego-USB-Stick/)

Creating a case out of Legos to house a USB memory stick has been done before, but I haven't seen it done like this.

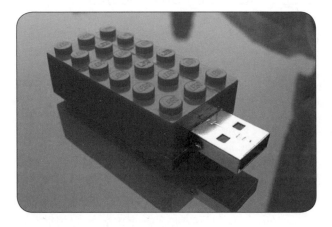

Step 1: Creating the Case

Because my memory stick was quite large (in dimensions, not in storage capacity) I had to create a 6×3 Lego brick. I chopped both a 4×2 and a 2×2 brick in half using a penknife and another brick as a guide. The pliers on the same penknife were then used to remove the inner bits of the bricks, and then the knife was used once again to remove the sides. Another 4×2 and a 2×2 brick were used to create the rest of the case. The four parts were then stuck together using superglue and a steady hand.

Step 2: Installing the Stick

A groove was cut into the case in which to place the USB connector, and, after a small amount of modification to the PCB, the stick was installed.

Step 3: Securing the Stick

I stuck an offcut of one of the bricks at the bottom of the case, as I found this made the stick sit at the right height. I then packed the whole thing full of clear silicone to make it stronger and reduce any movement from the stick. Clear silicone is important as it still allows light to shine through.

Step 4: Stick It Together and Polish

I stuck flat 6×2 and 6×1 bricks to the top of the case to enclose it all. Because of the amount of joints and glue lines some of the bricks weren't totally level, so I used some fine wet and dry sand paper to level the edges up. Two different grades of metal polish were then used to make the edges smooth and shiny again.

Step 5: Finished Product

The finished product in the second image shows the original case for the memory stick, and the final image shows the LED in action. Have fun.

Homemade Nintendo Arcade

By russm313
(http://www.instructables.com/id/How-to-build-a-Nintendo-arcade)

This Instructable will show you how to build a Nintendo arcade game. It is a bar top cabinet that plays original Nintendo games. The machine is completely self-contained, with one power switch for everything.

Step 1: Things You Will Need

- 1 sheet of 4'×8' ¼" MDF
- 1 sheet of Plexiglas
- 1 set of joystick and arcade buttons
- 1 poster board
- several cans of spray paint
- an older PC
- an LCD monitor
- 1 USB keyboard
- soldering equipment
- NES controller ports (ripped from a four score)
- DB-25 connector
- 2 cases of Diet Coke :)

Inside the cabinet is an old PC and a 17" LCD monitor. The back of the cabinet has two USB ports and two NES controller ports. You can connect regular, unmodded NES controllers and play with those or use the joystick and buttons on the control panel.

The front end is a simple Visual Basic (VB) program that auto loads when the PC boots. You never need to connect a mouse or keyboard to load your games. The VB program gives a list of games installed. Using the joystick, you can select the game you want to play.

Also, you can connect a keyboard and mouse to the USB ports in the back and use the set as a regular PC. It has wireless internet built in.

Step 2: Building the Cabinet

Draw out the arcade cabinet shape onto ¼" MDF. Cut it out with a circular saw or jig saw. Measure and cut out the remaining parts. My cabinet is 24" ×18" × 24" (H x W x D). Screw all the pieces together.

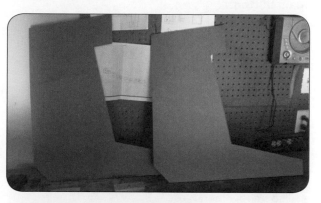

Step 3: Hack the Keyboard to Use as an Interface

Now let's work on the interface for the joystick and buttons; this is how the controls will communicate with the PC.

You can buy encoders premade and save a lot of time, or you can do it on the cheap and spend a lot of time soldering. I prefer to do as much as possible myself, without buying special parts.

Take apart the keyboard and you will find a thin, transparent piece of plastic film inside. It's actually two pieces that you must separate. After doing so, take a sharpie and mark the contacts that correspond to the keys you want to use.

I used the following keys: tab, esc, ctrl, alt, R, F4, enter, num lock, and the numbers 2, 4, 5, 6, 8— all from the num pad, which is very important. The numbers across the top of the keyboard will not work. This is because I used 2, 4, 6, and 8 as the up, down, left, and right controllers for the emulator. By turning on sticky keys, these same numbers control the mouse cursor. The num lock enables/disables sticky keys. The number 5 key is the left mouse click. If you are using an eight-way joystick, you can also

21

use the numbers 7, 9, 1, and 3 for the respective diagonals. I chose to keep it simple with a four-way joystick, since it was only going to emulate an old school NES.

Inside the emulator, you can choose which keyboard keys control what. This is what I used:

Main buttons:

- UP: num pad 8
- DOWN: num pad 2
- LEFT: num pad 4
- RIGHT: num pad 6
- START: enter
- SELECT: tab
- B button: ctrl
- A button: alt

Secondary buttons:

- Mouse Mode: num lock
- Reset: ctrl+R
- Hide/show menu: esc
- Mouse click: num pad 5
- Exit: alt+F4

Now that you have keys marked on the films, we need to trace the contacts out and see which pin corresponds to which contact. Each film will have its own set of pins. One set will be grounds and the others will be opens. The film that is the grounds will have the least amount of pins. My grounding film had 8 pins and the open film had 20 pins.

For example: Take the R key on the ground sheet and, using a multimeter in continuity mode, find out which pin of the 8 pins leads to the contact for the letter R. In my case it was pin 5. Doing the same thing for the letter R on the open field shows the R key corresponds to pin 11. Now we know that if we make those two pins touch each other that will activate the letter R. That is how a keyboard works. Repeat this for every keyboard key you are going to use, making a list of this information as you go.

Solder wires between the contact pins you need and a prototyping circuit board from an electronics store like Radio Shack. A tip: Once you have your solder point done, smother the entire thing in hot glue so no wires accidentally get pulled off. Once the interface is complete, you will wire the buttons to the prototyping boards.

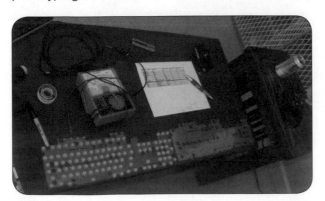

Step 4: Make the Control Panel

Now let's make the control panel. This will involve painting it, adding the joystick and buttons, and wiring these to the interface we created in the previous step.

Paint the entire board the base color of your choice. Mask out the design you want to use with painter's tape. Paint the board again with a different color. Remove the painter's tape to reveal your design. Drill the holes you will insert the joystick and buttons into.

Install all buttons and the joystick. You can also install a piece of Plexiglas over the control board to make it look more finished. You can also label your buttons if you wish. For the text, you can use rub-on letters. You can get these from the scrapbooking aisle at any craft store.

Now you need to connect the buttons to the interface. At the base of each button and the joystick is a microswitch. Wire the ground connection to the ground pin that corresponds with that button. Wire the normally open (NO) contact to the open end that corresponds.

For example: My A button corresponds to the keyboard key ALT. Looking at my matrix, I see that the alt key is ground pin 6, open pin 19. For the A button microswitch, I solder a wire from the ground to pin 6 of my set of grounds. Then I solder a wire from the NO to pin 19 of my set of opens. The A button is done; now repeat with all the others.

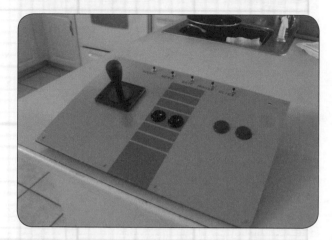

Step 5: Conceal Everything Inside the Cabinet

This step will vary depending on the size of your cabinet, your PC, and your monitor. Basically, you shove all the components into the box. I had to take my PC out of its case and mount the components into the cabinet.

There is a surge protector inside the cabinet that the PC, monitor, speakers, and marquee light all plug into. I connected this surge protector to the male power plug that sits flush with the outside of the cabinet. I also put a rocker switch that turns the surge protector on and off. This way, one switch controls everything.

Add USB ports at this point. You can use a USB extension cable by plugging one end into the PC and leaving the other end exposed for access outside the cabinet. The PC I used had an external USB control board, so I used that instead.

I made a NES controller port that works with the PC's parallel port. There are plenty of instructions available for this online. It would require another Instructable unto itself, so please look it up. Once the ports are wired up to the PC, leave the ends exposed at the back of the cabinet.

For speakers, I just took apart a set of desktop speakers. I installed them next to the marquee light, facing downward toward the screen. Be sure to drill several small holes in the wood that the speakers will be facing so the sound isn't muffled.

Connect a small fluorescent light kit and mount this behind the marquee. For the marquee design, I just printed out the logo I wanted and sandwiched it between two thin pieces of Plexiglas. Get the monitor in the exact spot you need and bolt it down.

Once all of this is done, test it out, and if you are happy with the results, install the control panel and the Plexiglas over the monitor. For the bezel around the monitor, I used a sheet of Plexiglas and spray painted the edges to hide everything except the viewable LCD area.

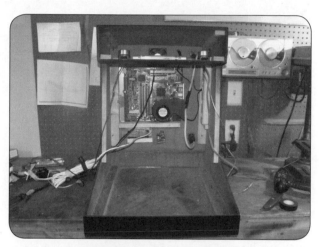

Step 6: Finished Product

Laptop Tripod

By mikeasaurus
(http://www.instructables.com/id/laptop-tripod/)

My netbook is great: It's small, portable, and has enough juice to do everything I need when I'm on the move. However, there have been times when I needed to conduct work in a specific area and there was no desk or suitable space to set my computer down and type.

Time for a laptop tripod! Whether you're in the field writing a report or stuck in an office looking for a place to set down your computer, a laptop tripod should have you covered. Depending on the type of tripod you have, there is a maximum weight and size limit it will be able to hold, so alter the dimensions and ideas here to make your own. Let's make something!

Step 1: Tools and Materials

To make your own laptop tripod, you'll need a tripod with a quick-release head. You can order extra quick-release heads for your tripod online.

- laptop
- camera tripod
- drill and wood bits
- wood saw
- hammer
- sandpaper
- pencil
- straight edge
- scrap wood (plywood, dowels, molding)
- wood glue
- extra tripod quick-release
- rubber tubing
- wood screws
- hex head bolt
- ¼" tee nut (20 thread)

Step 2: Laptop Deck

The laptop will need a solid deck to rest on when in use. This deck will also hold the hardware required to enable the quick-release head needed for the tripod and the tubing, which will secure the laptop.

Start by measuring out your laptop dimensions, then add another 50mm (2") to each side for buffer edging that will be installed later. The dimensions for my laptop were 260mm × 184mm (10.25" × 7.25"), plus the buffer, giving final dimensions of 310mm × 234mm (12.25" × 9.25"). Mark out dimensions on plywood, then cut out the deck. Lightly sand edges to remove burrs.

Step 3: Install Tee Nut

To attach our quick release to the deck, we need to install a corresponding nut of the same diameter and thread count; this is typically ¼" diameter and 20 threads per inch. If you're unsure, take your quick-release head to the hardware store and fit nuts until you find the right one.

To ensure a good bond between nut and the underside of the deck, I chose a tee nut, which has a longer neck than regular nuts. The one I found also had teeth along the edge, which allowed it to bite into the wood.

The nut will need to be located in the center of the underside of the deck. To locate the center, simply draw a straight line between diagonally-opposite corners, where the lines intersect is the center.

Next, drill an opening slightly larger than diameter of the tee nut. Do not drill through the deck, just enough to sink the nut and have the teeth bite. Apply some glue in the opening and hammer in the tee nut.

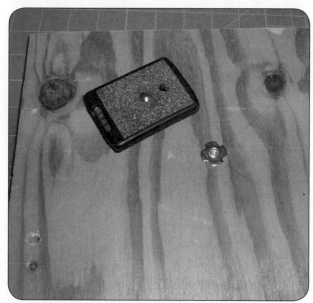

Step 4: Molding Edges

To prevent the laptop from sliding off the deck, a raised edge should be installed around the perimeter. Cut molding to the length and width of your deck, then make a 45 degree cut on each end. Lightly sand away burrs to ensure a snug fit. Apply glue to the underside of the molding and clamp it in place around the perimeter of the deck to dry.

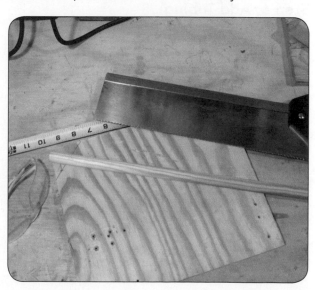

25

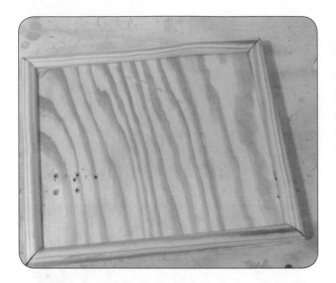

Step 5: Add Legs

Legs are added so that the base can rest on a table without wobbling on the quick-release head. A 40mm (1.5") scrap dowel was cut into four equal lengths of about 50mm (2"), then glued onto the underside of the deck, with one at each corner.

Step 6: Add Tubing

To secure the laptop when it's resting on the deck, we'll use rubber tubing, as it's elastic and won't damage the laptop. The tubing will be secured under the deck by sandwiching it between two screws.

Cut a length of tubing longer than the length of your deck (about 150mm [6"] extra). Staple one end to the underside of the deck near the edge; in the other end of the tubing, insert a bolt.

Next, pull the tubing to wrap around the deck and mark the location where the bolt meets the underside; install two screws on either side of the tubing at the location marked. Do not install the screws to be flush with the underside of the deck. The latex tube should be able to pass through the two screws so that the bolt will catch, securing the tubing taut against your laptop when it is placed on the deck.

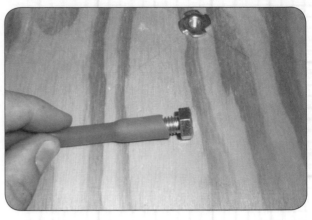

Step 7: Install Laptop

You're all done. It's time to place your laptop on the deck and strap it down with the tubing. Your laptop has a base to sit on when you're at your desk and is ready to be snapped onto a tripod for steady field work.

Simple Animatronics (Robot Hand)

By tanntraad
(http://www.instructables.com/id/Simple-Animatronics-robotic-hand/)

I made my first animatronic hand when I was about ten years old using objects I found around the house. Now I want to share with you how to easily make your own at home!

This hand is made from readily available materials and is perfect for a Halloween haunted house, scary pranks, a movie prop, or just good old-fashioned fun. It also serves as a great starting point for projects that include the use of servos, remote controlling, and more advanced animatronics.

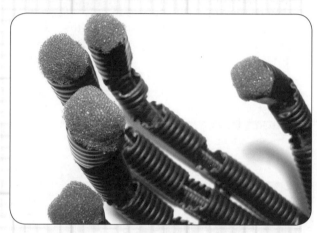

Step 1: Materials
- tubing
- string
- tape
- sharp knife
- hot-glue gun
- marker pen
- CD cases
- plastic or wooden clothes hanger

(The last two items can be replaced by other materials, as you will find out later.)

Step 2: Making the Template
First, draw an outline of your hand on a sheet of paper. Mark off the joints of each finger, including your knuckles. If you're lazy, just print out the last picture below.

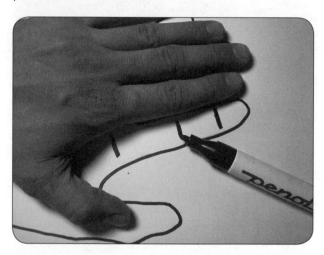

Step 3: Creating Some Fingers
For this hand I used plastic tubing that electricians use when they route wires through walls. It's easy to cut and has a nice "spring" to it. However, almost any kind of tubing will work, so use whatever you can get at the store. Cut the tube to be a length equal to the distance between your finger to your wrist; do this for all fingers. From the template, mark off the joints and then cut a V-shape in the tube at each joint using your knife. Make sure to check the angle of the bend so that it closely matches your fingers.

Step 4: Mounting the Fingers
Get your string and insert it into the tube. I used nylon string so that it doesn't frizz. Use a few feet for each finger as you can always cut it later. Tie a few knots at the end as depicted and secure it with tape to hold it all together. At the other end (wrist-side), pull and tape the string down around the diameter of each finger. This makes the next step much easier!

placing the thumb but study your hand and estimate where the thumb naturally meets the palm. Put hot glue at that meeting point, position the thumb, and hold it down until it cools and feels firm.

Step 5: Mounting the Fingers (continued)

Make use of those old CD cases that clutter your desk and snap off a piece of black plastic from the left side of the case. Cut it to the width of your traced hand and power up the glue gun. Glue the fingers to the plastic strip (just below the knuckle joints). Make sure the right fingers are in the right place!

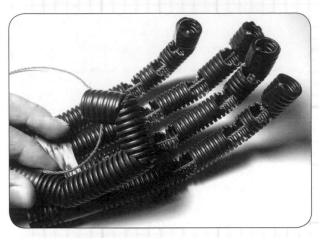

Step 7: The Wrist

Remove the tape you put around the wrist-end of each finger in Step 4. Gather and insert the hanging string from each finger into a foot of tubing (imagine this tubing to be the forearm). For support, snip out one piece of plastic from the CD case as per picture below. Glue one end of the plastic to the bottom of your wrist and then glue the other end to the top of the forearm, leaving an inch for the wires. Some extra tape might also be put in place here.

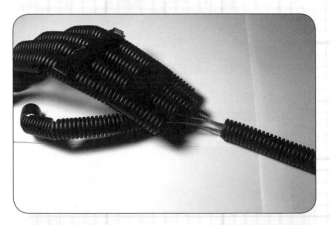

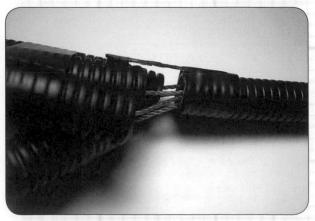

Step 6: Thumbs Up

You can tape the four fingers together before gluing the thumb in place. It might seem a bit tricky

Step 8: Controlling the Beast

To get things in motion, we need to make a bracket of some kind. A plastic clothes hanger is able to be hacked for this purpose. Make a square by taping and gluing the pieces together. Secure it to the end of the tube by using even more glue and tape. Tie loops at the ends of the strings for all fingers. The thumb is a bit tricky to control at first, but with time you'll get the hang of it. That's basically it! The next step is really not necessary; it depends on the intended usage.

Step 9: Bringing It to Life

To add a more human touch, I glued cell foam to the tips of the fingers and palm. This helps if you plan to use a glove for further realism. This is where your creativity should take over! Now, go and scare someone.

Explosive Alarm Clock

By giovannire
(http://www.instructables.com/id/Explosive-Alarm-Clock/)

The Explosive Alarm Clock is a fully-functional alarm clock made with an old beeping alarm clock.

You need:

- electronic alarm clock
- cardboard rolls
- paper packaging
- old wires
- hot glue
- electrical tape
- cutter

Step 2: Sticks

Cut the cardboard roll and made six pieces, each 20 centimeters long.

Step 3: Wrapping

Wrap the pieces with the packaging paper and fix it with transparent tape.

Step 1: Disassemble

Take apart the old alarm clock.

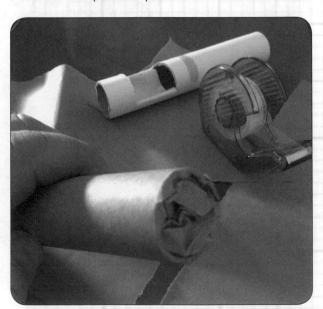

Step 5: Secure

Apply electrical tape on both sides to secure the bundle.

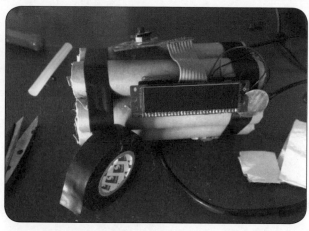

Step 4: Assemble

Use hot glue to attach the power supply to two of the pieces, then arrange the other four pieces on top and around the power supply. Tie the six pieces together in a bundle. Position the clock display in the center and fix it in place with the hot glue.

Step 6: Decorate

Twist the electric wire with a pen to achieve the desired effect.

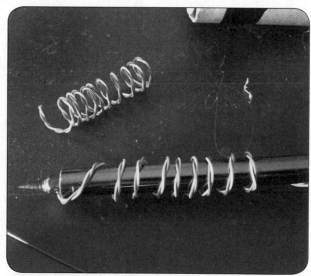

Step 7: Give!

This unique gift is ready to give to your morning-challenged friend!

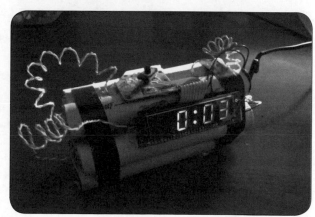

Décor

Lamps, clocks, and coasters are easy ways to customize the look and feel of your home. But buying from the same big box store as the neighbors means you're at risk of making your home unique in the exact same ways as everyone living within driving distance of said store.

Really customize your home's décor with these clever home decoration ideas. Update your garden path with some stepping stones made from concrete and an old Nintendo. Turn a beige bathroom into a rainbow-filled wonderland. Create a lamp shaped like a robot, or shaped like an alien abduction, or just cut up some of your favorite glass bottles into beautiful LED pendants.

Real customization requires equal measures of inspiration, instruction, and time. These projects will give you two out of three, a fraction that Meat Loaf tells us ain't bad.

NES Stepping Stones

By fungus amungus
(http://www.instructables.com/id/NES-Stepping-Stones/)

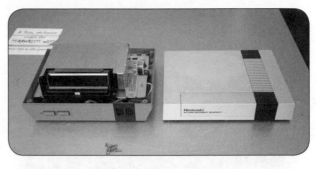

The Nintendo Entertainment System rocked the world with 8-bit goodness when it first came out, but it has faded in use as the years have gone by.

Even though I don't play retro games, I still love the old box and figured that it should be honored in some way. Thus, a concrete version would be great, since it could live on in my garden as stepping stones. Here's how to make them.

Step 1: Prep the NES—Part 1

All you need is the top half of the NES. Fortunately, it comes off easily with a Phillips-head screwdriver. After you get the top off, you'll see a few plastic posts that stick out from its underside. Cut these off with a Dremel. You now have a top half that will lie flat.

Some people are shocked to see a NES console cut up like this. Remember, the machine still works and the top can be reattached. Relax.

Step 2: Prep the NES—Part 2

The next thing to do is to make the NES as water-tight as you can so that the mold won't be able to flow through. This means going crazy with a hot glue gun. Seal up the vent on the top, the door, and any other spot you can see. To find more places that need glue, hold the NES up to the light. See a leak? Glue it! Repeat, repeat, repeat.

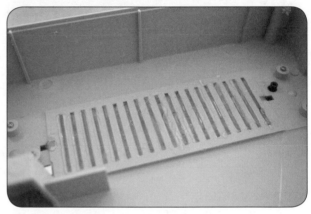

Step 3: Mold!

The mold-making here is extremely straightforward thanks to the slightly tapered rectangular shape of the NES. Glue the NES to the bottom, build a box around the NES, and coat everything with mold release. I left a ½" margin around the NES and used Smooth-On PMC-746, 1.5 qt. set for the mold itself.

Making the mold was pretty standard stuff. Mix the two ingredients thoroughly, slowly pour the set, tap to release any bubbles, and then leave it for a day. To get it out, just break apart the box, pop the whole thing off of the bottom, and slowly peel the mold off of the NES.

Step 4: Casting

All right, time to get serious! It's time for the cement. The cement I'm using here is Duracal; it mixes with a 4:1 cement-to-water ratio. Cement is tough stuff so you'll want to mix it up with incrementally larger amounts. What I did was add 400g of Duracal to 100g of water and then stirred that for a while until it was well mixed. Then I would add another 400g of Duracal and 100g of water and keep on mixing again until it was well mixed. For each stone, I used about 2.2kg of Duracal.

If you look at the first and second photos here you'll see my first attempt. Two things went wrong: the cement wasn't mixed well enough and the mold had undercuts in the vents that broke off when I pulled the mold off. The first time I mixed the concrete I tried it all in one go. It took forever to mix it up and even then it was uneven. It looks distressed, which is kind of cool, but not what I was going for. I also went over the mold with a razor blade to clean up the undercuts and got much better lines on the vent. Learn from my mistakes!

The Duracal was supposed to be able to be removed from the mold after two hours. I waited three to four hours for these two. It needs 24 hours to dry out most of the way, and I was told that it takes 30 days to completely dry out.

Step 5: Set and Enjoy!

When the stepping stones are dry, just drop them where you want them. You can paint them, seal them, or add color to the cement if you want. Personally, I like the gray look. As stepping stones, they're great, and there's an added bonus if you look down and recognize them. Other consoles that would work for this are Dreamcast, the original PlayStation, the original Xbox, 3DO, and GameCube (small stones).

Rainbow-Tiled Bathroom

By jeff-o

(http://www.instructables.com/id/Rainbow-Tiled-Bathroom/)

What happens when you combine the desires of an artist and a mad engineer into a single bathroom renovation? In this case, a soaker tub surrounded by a literal color wheel of tiles, each hand painted in one of 34 different colors.

For our basement bathroom renovation, my wife and I decided to go all-out with our color palette, and the result is gloriously bright, fun, and happy. When the sun comes through the window just right, the bathroom lights up with bright, bold colors that scream, "Draw a bath and plunge into the rainbow!"

Our design was inspired by a smattering of bathroom tiling ideas I found throughout the web, though none of those designs had gone to the extent of custom painting 34 different shades onto their tiles. The product that made this possible was the FolkArt Enamels line of ceramic and glass paint, which is scratchproof and waterproof (and dishwasher safe!) once baked.

The main focus of this Instructable will be the painting and installation of the tiles themselves, though I will go over the installation of the tub and vanity a little bit as well. I will purposefully gloss over the details of the plumbing since I am not a plumber and don't want to lead anyone astray. I'm sure I did a fine job, but a mistake made while plumbing can lead to an expensive disaster. If you're not comfortable doing plumbing work yourself, then hire a certified plumber.

Step 1: Tools and Materials

Retiling a bathroom can be pretty inexpensive. The white tiles we used were only 33 cents each at a home improvement store. The floor tiles were better quality and cost a bit more. In total, I'd estimate the tiling portion of the bathroom renovation cost about $500–$600.

Materials:

- plain white 6 × 6 inch or smaller wall tiles, quantity as necessary for the size of the bathroom
- floor tiles, as necessary, to complement the wall tiles; we used 8 × 8 inch white floor tiles
- FolkArt Enamels paints, in as many colors as you need. We basically used half the available colors, and mixed them to the right shades.
- wall adhesive
- wall grout
- floor tile mortar
- floor tile grout
- tile spacers (1/8 inch for wall tiles, 3/16 inch for floor tiles)

If you're building a bathroom from scratch, you will also need additional materials like lumber, plywood, drywall, drywall mud, concrete board, plumbing fixtures, wall paint, construction adhesives, screws, etc.

Tools:

- craft paint brushes
- ordinary kitchen oven
- wet tile saw (just go ahead and buy one; they sell for as little as $50–$60 new, which is less than renting)
- tile hole cutter and drill press (optional, depending on the fixtures you use)
- notched trowel
- putty knives
- tile float
- sponge and bucket
- shop vac for (lots) of cleanup

Again, if you're building a bathroom from scratch, you'll also need various construction tools like saws, drills, screwdrivers, levels, plumbing tools, etc.

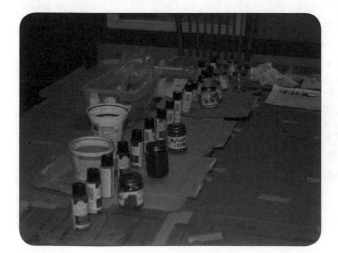

Step 2: Renovate the Bathroom

The first step is to build the bathroom itself or to renovate an existing one. Renovating will, at the very least, entail removing whatever is glued to the walls already, be it tiles or maybe an acrylic backsplash. Never ever try to glue tiles on top of other tiles! Building a bathroom is an involved process, but aside from the plumbing aspect, it isn't so different from building any other room. In this step I'll discuss renovating an existing bathroom to prepare it for new tiles (and possibly a new tub as well). Visit the next step to see how I built a new bathroom in my basement.

Demolition:

What color are your tiles now? Avocado green, perhaps? Maybe brown or orange or bright aquamarine? The '70s were not kind to home decorating. The tiles must come off. Maybe you've got an acrylic backsplash instead (installed over existing tiles? Gasp!). Well, the acrylic needs to go.

If you're planning to keep the tub in place, be sure to cover it securely so that falling tile debris doesn't scratch the enamel on the tub. If the tub will be replaced eventually, go ahead and let the tiles drop right in there. Its final purpose will be as a convenient catch basin for construction debris.

So how do you get the tiles off? Go nuts with a scraper. Hopefully, the adhesive will be old enough that it's flaking or crumbling a bit and the tiles will fall right off. There's a good chance that whatever backer board was on there will take heavy damage. Expect to replace it eventually as well. Be sure to wear gloves and eye protection when removing tiles since they can break and may have edges as sharp as broken glass. The dust may be harmful to inhale, too.

An acrylic surround can similarly be scraped off. Find an edge that you can get a putty knife under and gradually peel back the acrylic. It might help to have a friend pull as you scrape. Be prepared for nastiness hiding under the plastic. Acrylic doesn't have a good reputation when it comes to sealing out moisture and mold.

Dispose of the old tile appropriately. In some regions you can toss it in the household curbside pickup, while in other places it must be brought to the dump.

Now you'll have a room covered in rather shoddy looking walls. There's a chance that you can reuse the walls without replacing them, but I wouldn't recommend it. First turn off the water and power to the room, then grab a crow bar or demolition hammer and start peeling away the old walls. Now is a great time to check for water damage behind the walls and fix it!

Be careful when tearing out the walls close to plumbing or electrical fixtures. You turned off the water and power (right?), but you want to avoid damaging them and incurring extra time and cost to the project.

Reconstruction:

With the room reduced to stud walls, new walls can be put up. If you're installing a soaker tub with no shower, then ordinary moisture-resistant drywall is enough for the walls (but check local building codes to be sure). Concrete board should be used for the tub surround and skirt. If the bath features a shower, install concrete board all the way around the shower enclosure.

Concrete board is used just like drywall but is far more water resistant. You can cut and snap it like drywall, but I prefer using a jigsaw with a carbide blade. It's faster and easier, though it makes more dust. Cut it outside if you can.

Mud and sand the drywall with ordinary drywall compound. Use something like Durabond (it's basically plaster of Paris, for construction) for the concrete board for extra water resistance. I use a product called Durabond 90. With new walls installed, it's time to plan out the tiles!

Step 3: Build a Bathroom

When I started my renovation, the bathroom area was nothing more than an empty area in a much larger basement room, with a toilet already installed. Our little house has only one full bathroom, so I was tasked with building a second full bathroom around the existing toilet.

Construction:

The first task was to build walls around the new bathroom area based primarily on the size of the bathtub. We had bought a big soaker tub on clearance from a big box store a few months prior in anticipation of this renovation.

After deciding how much clearance would be needed on all sides of the tub as well as how much room the sink would need nestled between the tub and toilet, I marked out the locations of the footers on the concrete floor. Along these lines I screwed

pressure-treated 2×4 inch lumber. It was necessary to use PT lumber because of moisture and condensation that can form on a concrete floor—you certainly don't want your footers to rot!

Based on the footers, I plotted out where the headers should go along the ceiling. I did so by using a laser level (still the best ten bucks I've ever spent on a tool). After that, the studs were installed on 16 inch centers.

The tub surround was built according to the tub manufacturer's suggestions, though with some modification for the concrete floor. Instead of excavating into the concrete to install a drain for the tub, I decided to use something called a grey water pump. The grey water pump sits on the floor below the level of a sink or tub and pumps waste water up to a suitable waste pipe. In this case, the waste pipe was only a foot away. Since the pump must sit below the tub, I had to raise the tub off the floor a few inches to get adequate drainage. The height of the tub, the thickness of the materials, and the rise-over-run of the drain pipe must all be taken into consideration when determining the height of the surround.

The tub surround was constructed by first screwing 2×4s onto the joists that formed three of the four sides of the surround. It is extremely important that these are all level or the tub will not sit flat.

A skirt was constructed for the fourth side of the surround by framing in a two-foot-high wall with more lumber. Next, a piece of ¾ inch plywood was cut to shape to fit inside the surround. Based on measurements of the tub, a hole was cut out of the center of the plywood to accommodate the tub. On top of the plywood a layer of concrete board is required to make it waterproof. I used the plywood as a template to cut out the concrete board. The plywood was screwed onto the wood frame, and the concrete board was glued onto the plywood using construction adhesive.

Plumbing:

Plumbing comes next. I tapped into the pipes leading to the bathroom directly above and ran the hot and cold pipes along the ceiling for a bit then down the wall. I installed two valves to connect the sink, then continued the pipes to where the tub spout was to be located. With the spout temporarily installed, I connected the pipes as recommended by the manufacturer of the spout. Of course, all of this was done with the water shut off and drained. I had a section of pipe cut out of the toilet stack and a "Y" installed to connect the grey water pump. This part was done by a licensed plumber.

Electrical:

Time for electrical. I installed a moisture-resistant pot light above the tub and halogen spots above where the sink would eventually be located. These are controlled with a single switch. A second switch controls an exhaust vent located above the tub. The exhaust actually vents through the glass block window, through a specially made block. Two outlets were installed, one close to the ground for the grey water pump and one above the sink for plugging in electric toothbrushes and whatnot. Of course, the outlets are GFCI protected.

The bathroom was given its own circuit on the breaker panel. If you're not comfortable working with high voltage (a logical thing; it'll kill you without remorse if you give it the chance) then hire a professional electrician.

Drywall:

With the plumbing and electrical in place, the drywall may be installed. I used moisture-resistant drywall on the walls and ceilings. If I had installed a shower, then concrete board would have been required around the tub. Tape, mud, and sand as usual.

In my bathroom there were a few low-hanging pipes that were so low, a flat ceiling would have reduced the height of the room to less than 6 feet! So I installed drywall and mud around the pipes. I think they turned out really well.

Painting:

Prior to installing tile, I recommend painting any walls that need to be painted. The main reason is that you avoid any chance of dripping paint on the tiles or bath fixtures. But it's also necessary to help seal the walls against moisture.

The area that would eventually be tiled was painted with a coat of primer/sealer to help seal out moisture. The untiled walls were also primed then given two coats of finish coat.

So there are the basics. Again, I didn't go into details regarding the plumbing and electrical, since I'm not a professional and I don't want to lead you astray. If you're unsure about working with water or electrical, hire a pro!

Step 4: Planning and Painting Tiles

And now, for the meat of the Instructable! These tiles are what will set your new bathroom apart. Three words make it happen: custom-painted tiles. It's not a task to be taken lightly, however. It will take time, space, and patience.

Planning:

The first thing to do is to figure out approximately how many painted tiles you will need. Carefully measure the space that will be tiled and transfer those measurements to a scale drawing. We used a sheet of graph paper and drew each wall and surface that would be tiled. Since our tiles were 6 inches square, the surfaces were then divided into 6 inch squares.

My wife broke out the pencil crayons and started filling out a pattern of colors. She chose 34 different shades that formed a color wheel around the perimeter of the bathtub rim. Those colors were transferred to a master chart from which the paint colors were mixed later on.

We chose to have the colored tiles "concentrate" at the tub then taper off in a somewhat random fashion as they got farther away. As a result, somewhere between four and eight tiles of each color were required for our design. I highly recommend making extras though, since it will be troublesome later on to recreate a damaged or missing tile.

While FolkArt Enamels come in a large variety of colors, they didn't have all of the colors we needed! After choosing the colors of the tiles, my wife set to work mixing different combinations of the roughly 20 different colors we bought. Some of the colors could be used as-is, while others ended up as mixtures of three different paints. If you choose to do a color wheel like we did, you'll need to do the same. Of course, you may choose any combination of colors. Being able to paint your own tiles in the exact shade you want opens a whole new world of tiling possibilities!

Painting:

Painting the tiles is a multi-step process. We learned through a bit of trial and error, so heed these instructions if you want a good result. Do one color at a time to avoid confusion. Start by laying out all the tiles that will be painted on a flat surface. Each one should be thoroughly cleaned with 99% rubbing (isopropyl) alcohol to remove any dirt and oils that would prevent paint adhesion.

With a fine-bristle brush, paint each tile as smoothly as possible. Keep all your brush strokes going the same direction. Allow the tiles to fully dry in a dust-free environment. Try not to move the tiles while the paint is wet. For most colors, a second coat will be required. Once the first coat is fully dry, apply a second layer with brush strokes going in the same direction as the first layer. Mark each of the painted tiles with a number or color code on the back. This will make it easy to sort by color later on, especially when you have five different shades of yellow. Some colors, like Cobalt Blue, do not dry glossy like the majority of the other colors. Add a coat of "Clear Medium" to make them match the gloss.

When you are satisfied with the paint coverage, the tiles must be baked. Place the tiles in the center of a cold oven, ensuring they are not too close to the burners or the sides of the oven. We used a standard electric oven. I'm not sure if a convection oven will work the same (it'll probably be better, but I've never tried it). Set the oven to 350°F and allow it to warm up with the tiles already inside. Once the oven reaches 350°F, set a timer for one hour. Allow the tiles to bake for the hour, and then turn the oven off. Do not remove the tiles or open the oven door until the oven has cooled on its own.

Remove the baked tiles, marking each one on the back to indicate it has been baked. Again, this is to help keep track of which tiles were baked. Crucial information when you're making dozens of tiles over the span of two or three weeks! When all the tiles

have been painted and baked, they may be installed. Onwards to tiling!

Step 5: Tiling—Adhesive Time

When you go to pick up your tiling supplies, the salesperson will ask you what type of adhesive you'll need, among other questions. For the painted tiles (and their unpainted brethren), pre-mixed Flextile 200 multi-purpose ceramic wall tile adhesive was recommended. Get a big 3.5 gallon pail of it. It'll probably end up being cheaper than buying multiple smaller containers, and it's easier to fit a notched trowel inside. When tiling a floor, you'll likely end up using powdered mortar instead of a pre-mixed adhesive. Aside from needing to mix it ahead of time, the usage is the same.

Installing Tile:

The basic idea is to spread a reasonably uniform layer of adhesive onto a surface using a putty knife or the flat edge of the trowel, then use the notched trowel to scrape notches into the adhesive. The notches ensure that the adhesive is of uniform height, and when a tile is pressed into the adhesive the raised notches spread out to fill the gaps. Got it? Let's do it step-by-step.

1. Start by locating where you want to place the first tiles. It's not always as simple as starting in the most convenient corner. Sometimes you

need to work around fixtures or start in the middle so that the tiles match up with others that are already placed. If tiling a wall, start at the bottom and work upwards.

2. To avoid going off-track, use a level (bubble level or laser level) or straightedge to mark reference lines on the wall prior to placing tiles. For instance, it's a good idea to mark a vertical line on a wall being tiled so that tiles may be placed along that line. If a wall or surface is very large, multiple lines may be required so that you can "check your work" and gradually move tiles back into alignment if they're a bit off.

3. With a wide putty knife or trowel, spread a coat of adhesive onto the wall that is about 1/8 to 1/4 inch thick. If this is your first time, cover an area of about 4 to 8 square feet to start. The adhesive has an open time of maybe ten minutes, so work quickly.

4. With the notched trowel, drag evenly spaced notches into the fresh adhesive. Bare wall should be visible in the "valleys" of the notches, and the peaks should be as tall as the notches in the trowel. If they aren't, use more adhesive.

5. Grab your tiles and press them into the adhesive one at a time. Apply even pressure over the surface of the tile, wiggling it back and forth a bit to help squish the adhesive underneath. Once the tile is pressed down all the way, slide it into its final position.

6. Lay down the next tiles in the same way. You can avoid excess "squeezeout" between the tiles by first pushing down the edge closest to a tile that has already been installed.

7. With a tile spacer (or a special tool, I'm sure they're made...), clean out the excess adhesive between the tiles. The adhesive must be cleaned out before it dries or it will prevent proper grout adhesion later on. Wipe off any adhesive sticking to the surface of the tiles with a damp rag.

8. Stick tile spacers between the tiles so that they maintain an even spacing. I stick them in with only one end between the tiles—this makes them much easier to remove later on!

9. Repeat steps 3 to 9 until the surface is covered with tiles. Once you get into the groove it goes pretty fast, though it's still hard work.

10. If you need to stop before the wall is done, use the trowel to scrape any excess adhesive off the wall before it dries. Immediately seal up the tub of adhesive and clean all your tools as well. The adhesive washes easily with water when it's wet but is hard as a rock when it dries!

Of course, you will surely need to cut tiles at some point. See the next step for notes on cutting and drilling tiles.

Step 6: Tiling—Cutting and Drilling Tiles

One worthwhile investment to make before starting a tiling project is buying a wet tile saw. These can be purchased for less than $100. That's cheaper than renting one for only a few days, so it's definitely worth it. Even a cheap low-end saw will last through most tiling jobs.

If you need to tile around plumbing pipes and fixtures, I'd also recommend picking up an adjustable tile hole saw. It's pretty much the only way to drill a hole in tile.

Cutting Tile:

Using a wet tile saw is easy. Inside the saw is a reservoir of water that keeps the diamond blade cool and lubricated. It also prevents (potentially toxic) ceramic dust from flying into the air. The saw will have an adjustable guide as well as a blade guard (which protects your hands from the blade and prevents water from spraying all over the place). Most will also have a 45° pushing tool. Simply set the guide to the tile width you need and switch on the saw. With even pressure, push the tile against the blade. It should slice through the tile with minimal effort. Ease up at the end to avoid chipping the corner of the cut edge. Immediately wipe off the tile to remove excess water and ceramic "mud" from the back and front.

You can cut more complex contours with a tile saw by cutting multiple "fingers" up to the edge of the contour. The fingers are easily broken off with pliers. Alternatively, you can buy a tile cutting bit for Dremel tools that will give a smoother edge.

Drilling Tile:

Drilling tile is, in a word, nerve-wracking. In my project I had to drill holes for the tub filler faucet and sprayer— four holes in all. To do so, I first tiled or laid out all of the non-drilled tiles to get the spacing right. I then marked the exact positions and diameters of the holes on the back of the tile by tracing through the hole with a marker.

Before drilling the actual tiles, and especially before drilling a painted tile, it's important to do a few practice holes in a scrap tile. Set the proper hole diameter in the hole saw then mount it in a drill press.

Clamp the tile face-down on a block of sacrificial wood, with a piece of rag between the wood and tile. While operating the drill press with one hand, continually spray the tile with water using the other hand. There should be no puffs of ceramic dust escaping. If there are, you're not watering enough. Apply slow, steady pressure with as little force as possible. Take your time! The center hole will penetrate all the way through, but will allow the outer carbide cutter to go only about halfway through the tile.

Once you're halfway through, flip the tile around and drill it from the top. Use the center hole for alignment, clamp down the tile and drill as before,

with plenty of water. Eventually the hole saw will break through and you should be left with a little ring of tile inside of a larger tile with a hole in it.

Step 7: Tiling—Grout

Like adhesive, there are different types of grout. The salesperson will ask what the gap is between the tiles and recommend a grout based on that. I ended up with powdered white polymer-modified wall grout. You can get different colors if you like, either pre-mixed or by the addition of a color additive.

This is probably the step that frightens people the most. It's certainly what I worried about most.

The basic idea here is to take the grout on your rubber tile float and squidge it into the gaps between the tiles. A second pass using the edge of the float leaves the grout behind, and skims off all but a thin layer of grout on the surface of the tiles. That haze of grout is later washed off.

Grouting Tile:

Start by removing all of the tile spacers. You'll probably be able to re-use them, so set them aside if you've got more tiling to do. Inspect the gaps between the tiles and check for any adhesive inside the gaps or on the surface of the tiles. Carefully scrape it out or off.

Mix up a batch of wall grout. DO NOT mix up the whole bag or you'll end up throwing most of it away. I usually mixed up one ice cream container (about 2L) worth at a time, which is about as much as I was able to apply before it started drying. A professional tile installer could probably use up three times as much in the same time period. The mixed grout should have a smooth, thick consistency, though not as thick as the adhesive. If it slips easily off a trowel, it's too thin.

Start anywhere on the tile surface. Use a trowel to load up the long edge of the float with grout, then slop it on. Work the grout into the gaps by squeezing the edge into the gap. When the gap is full the grout will squeeze back out a bit. Do this for about four square feet of tile at a time.

Before the grout gets too dry, flip the float nearly onto its side and drag it along the surface of the tiles, at a 45° angle to the gaps. This step will prevent the edge of the float from sinking into the gaps, but will skim most of the grout from the tile surfaces.

Proceed in this fashion, first grouting then skimming a small section at a time. Avoid going over sections that have started to dry or the grout may pull out of the gap.

After thirty to sixty minutes (depending on the grout—read the label!) the grout will be dry enough to be wiped clean. You should be able to see a "haze" of grout on the tiles. Fill a large bucket with warm water and dampen a large, clean sponge. The sponge should be rung out as much as possible to avoid getting excess water on the tiles.

Wipe down the tiles to clean off the haze, rinsing the sponge often. Chances are you'll need to do more than one wipe-down. I found that I could drastically improve the amount of haze removed from the surface by first wiping with a damp sponge then immediately drying with a rag. The reason is that the sponge leaves behind a lot of haze unless the rinse water is totally clean.

You'll find that you can smooth and even out the grout a bit with the damp sponge. You may do this a bit, but try to avoid getting the grout wet once it has

started to dry. It will lose strength and won't last as long if it gets too wet.

So there you go. Grouting isn't as hard as you'd think.

Step 8: Tiling—Finishing Touches

In my bathroom there were a few tiled edges that did not meet in an inside corner. In cases like this, there are neat plastic and metal edging pieces that can be cut to length and placed along the tile edge, to give a cleaner look. There are different sizes available, depending on the thickness of the tile.

To use the edging strips, first cut them to length with strong scissors or tin snips (if cutting metal edges). Locate where the edging needs to go and tape it to the wall with masking tape.

Now, simply tile up to the strip, making sure that the adhesive is spread between the gaps in the edging. It's the adhesive joint between the wall and tile that holds the edging in place.

It's a good idea to apply a tile sealant once the grout has dried. After at least 48 hours, apply according to the manufacturer's instructions. The sealant I used is to be applied liberally and wiped off after five minutes. Drying time is a few hours. The sealant helps the tiles resist moisture and oil and inhibits mildew and mold growth. It does not seem to have any negative effects on the painted tiles, though I have no long-term data yet.

The corners should also be sealed with caulking to prevent water from sneaking in under the tiles. Do a test with scrap tile first, to make sure the color from the tile doesn't leech into the caulking.

- Don't walk on the floor tiles until they are totally dry.
- When tiling and grouting, start at the far corner and work towards the door.
- Painted tiles (like the ones used on the walls) are not suitable for use on floors. They will not be able to handle the severe amounts of traffic.

Step 9: Tiling—Floors

Tiling a floor is much like tiling a wall. The tiles are typically thicker and may have a rougher texture that reduces the chance of slipping when the floor is wet. Powdered mortar is used instead of pre-mixed adhesive. The grout is a bit coarser, because it typically has to fill larger gaps. Here are some things I learned while tiling my bathroom floor.

Floor Tiling Tips:

- If tiling on a concrete floor, all the paint must be removed using abrasives beforehand. Using an angle grinder, I removed two or three layers of floor paint from the floor in my bathroom. Had I know how messy this would be, I would have done it before the walls went up.
- If there are any hills or valleys, they must be ground down or filled in, respectively, before tiling. Otherwise, the tiles will be uneven and present a tripping or breaking hazard, or will just look bad.
- Choose smaller tiles if possible. It will be easier to tile slightly uneven floors because they can more closely fit the contour of the floor.
- If tiling a large area, start by tiling one long run of tiles against a reference, like a straightedge or laser line. Allow this run of tiles to dry before continuing. Once dry, this row of tiles may be used as a reference that all the other tiles are pushed against.
- Pay close attention to the edges of the tiles to make sure they are coplanar. Even if the floor is perfectly level, the tiles must also be pressed down equally so that there are no raised edges.
- Like the wall tiles, stick the tile spacers in so they are easy to remove. And, as with the wall tiles, clean out any mortar from between the tiles before it dries so it doesn't interfere with grout adhesion.

Step 10: Installing the Plumbing

After the tiling was finished I installed the plumbing, including the tub, sink, and toilet. The tub was dropped into place with a helper's assistance. The drain assembly was installed and connected to the drain pipe, then leak-tested. Once I confirmed that nothing was leaking, I ran a bead of caulking around the tub. The faucet was connected to the household water supply, and was also leak tested.

An easy way to check for leaks in the tub is to fill it up with water and close the drain plug. If everything is sealed up, there will be no water leaking from around the drain. When draining the tub, place paper towels along the length of drain pipe, especially at joints. Once the tub has emptied (and there are no obvious leaks, characterized by gushing water and much cursing), check the paper towels to see if any of them are wet.

The sink we used was a pre-fab job that came in a kit with the bowl and vanity, along with a mirror (which we didn't end up using). Due to my unique setup, I had to heavily modify the sink to accept a grey water pump. Holes were drilled for the input and output to the pump, hidden inside the vanity. The pump accepts waste water from the tub and sink, and pumps it about a foot and a half into the adjacent toilet stack. The vanity is screwed into studs on the wall, and the bowl is glued to the vanity with construction adhesive. The sink faucet came separately, and it connected via flexible hoses to the water supply valves. The sink can be tested for leaks the same way as the tub.

Prior to (re)installing the toilet, I cleaned off all the old wax on the base of the toilet and from the toilet flange. Yuck. A new wax ring was placed on the flange, and then the toilet was pressed into the wax. Resist moving the toilet too much once pressed into the wax, or the seal may break. Two bolts hold the toilet onto the flange. With the water supply hose reconnected, the toilet was leak-tested just like the tub and sink. When doing so, watch very carefully for water seeping out from between the toilet and floor. There likely won't be much water getting out, so check it over a period of a few days.

Step 11: Finishing Touches

At this point we had a beautiful, functioning bathroom! But there was a bit more to add. First up: the bathroom mirror. We found just the thing at IKEA—an inexpensive unit that included a little shelf and (more importantly) fit in the space between the lights and sink. The mirror was installed in a few minutes according to the cute little wordless instructions.

Baseboards were installed on all the walls, and the towel alcove was framed with a bit of decorative edging. Also installed were the towel bars and toilet paper holder. The towel bars are actually installed inside a recessed alcove I built into the wall opposite the tub. The alcove is a nice visual feature that helps break up the wall a bit, and it prevents the towels from sticking out into the room so much. At some point we plan to add some little pieces of artwork to the walls as well.

Perhaps you are inspired to do something similar in your own house using custom-painted tiles! Remember, you don't have to make a color wheel— you could paint a few accent tiles or restrict your

palette to only a few colors to get the look you want. In short, you are no longer restricted to the half-dozen colors available from the local tile stores!

Test Tube Spice Rack

By noahw
(http://www.instructables.com/id/
Test-Tube-Spice-Rack/)

Here's a test tube spice rack that I made to hold all of my spices. I tried to improve upon previous test tube spice racks that I've seen by using a nice looking piece of bamboo plywood and by using oversized O-rings to "float" the tubes in the rack and eliminate the base plate. Also, my kitchen is short on counter space, so moving the spices out of the cupboard and onto the wall was a bonus. I've got a lot of spices, so I made two of these racks, but the design would work well with just one or with as many as you might need to hold all of your spices. This is one of the few builds I've done where I didn't take pictures along the way, but I'll do my best to explain how I made it.

Step 1: Materials and Tools

- plywood bamboo strip approx. 2" × 16"
- glass 25mm × 150mm test tubes
- size 10 cork stoppers to match test tubes
- 22mm × 4mm rubber O-rings to match test tubes
- assorted spices
- skinny measuring spoons from Lee Valley
- screw hook to hold measuring spoons
- mini L-bracket
- hanging hardware for plaster or drywall walls
- saw to cut wood
- drill or drill press (better) to drill holes in wood and hang rack
- 1 ⅛" Forstner bit to make clean holes that are slightly larger than test tube diameter, but smaller than O-ring

Step 2: Construction

Cut appropriately sized strips of wood for your test tube rack. On a drill press, use a 1⅛" Forstner bit to create evenly spaced holes on the rack. Try to drill as straight as possible if you're using a hand drill. Slip the O-rings onto the test tubes, fill them with spices, and insert cork stopper into the tops.

Step 3: Installation

Hang the test tube rack onto the wall with small steel L-brackets using appropriate anchors or hardware for your specific wall type.

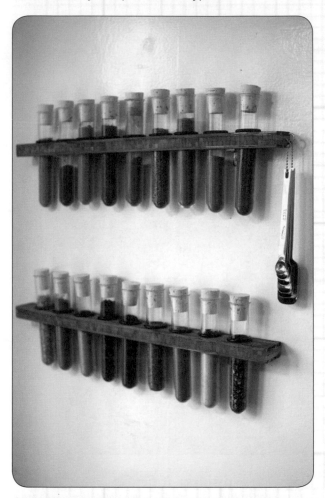

Robot Lamp

By M. C. Langer

(http://www.instructables.com/id/
Make-a-robot-lamp-using-discarded-
speakers-and-a-/)

This is my first project as Artist in Residence on Instructables. I'm just discovering how to find stuff in this city, so I started working with a small box of e-waste kept by the Instructables staff. Thanks guys!

I found a big speaker and four smaller ones with the same decoration, so I decided to make a robot lamp. I made the head with a colander found in the back alley of a Chinese restaurant (don't ask).

NOTE: Yes, I know I put the left speaker is in the right arm and the right speaker is in the left arm. "L" for "left" and "R" for "right" is so mainstream . . .

Step 1: Materials and Advice

Caution: Be careful. We will work with AC current and you know it's risky. Take all the safety measures.

I used the following items:
- 1 big speaker (Logitec) for the body
- 2 small speakers with footing (Logitec) for the arms. The footing makes a great robot hand.
- 2 small and rectangular speakers (Zenex) for the legs
- 1 plastic colander (same size of big speaker's top)
- 2 corner brace inside L (2 × ⅝ inches)
- 4 corner brace inside L (1 × ½ inches)
- 1 energy-saving compact fluorescent bulb
- 1 light socket with wires (or with screw terminals; as you wish)
- 1 on/off switch
- nuts, screws, and bolts
- iron washers
- wire
- steel cable (for the antennas)
- 6 plastic beads
- superglue (cyanoacrylate)
- plastic wheels for chairs
- weight (for balance. I used a discarded hard drive.)

I used the following tools:
- Dremel rotary tool
- tweezers
- screwdrivers
- scalpel
- pliers
- wire cutters
- screwdriver kit
- soldering iron

And don't forget:
1. If you don't have it, replace it!
2. Use protective equipment (dust mask and goggles).
3. Beware of drilled and soldered hot surfaces.
4. Work in a well-ventilated area.
5. Always have junk in stock.
6. Have fun.

Step 2: Body

Dismantle the big speaker. Remove everything inside, leaving the box inner structure. Keep the front panel, the back panel, and the speaker's power cord.

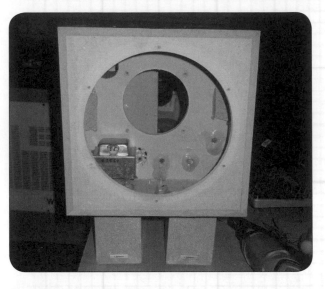

Step 3: Legs

Take both rectangular speakers, the four 1×½ inch corner braces, and the screws. With the ruler, find the center of the speaker's bottom and mark the place where the legs will be. Check stability. Now mark where the drill holes will be. Using the Dremel, drill and attach the legs to the bottom of the big speaker using the corner braces.

Step 4: Arms

Take the remaining speakers and remove the wire and the front part. The footing will be the robot claws. Screw the 2 × ⁵⁄₈ inch braces on each side (those will be the shoulders). Screw in the arms on each side, using washers for a better articulation. Check stability.

Step 5: Electrics

It's a simple circuit with the speaker's power cord, the switch, and the light socket. Arrange the power cord so it's long enough to connect to the socket wires. Insert the switch in one of the back holes and connect the wires as shown in the pictures. Solder and cover the unions with insulating tape.

Step 6: Closing the Body

Reattach the front and back panels. Add some decoration. I used as the front panel a grill from a power source.

Step 7: Head

Personalize your robot's head. Use the steel wires for antennas and the plastic wheels for eyes.

Step 8: Attaching the Head and Final Touches

Put the light bulb in the socket. Turn on and off to prove the lamp works. Attach the head to the body and you have your Robot Lamp!

Literary Clock

By mdhaworth
(http://www.instructables.com/id/Literary-Clock/)

This is a super easy project that turns a book into a clock. It's perfect for a child's bedroom—just use a storybook. It could also work in the kitchen—use a cookbook.

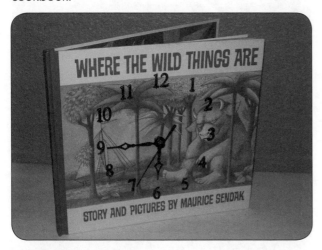

Step 1: Gather Supplies

Supplies and Tools:
- a book. It needs to be hardcover with a reasonably simple cover (not too much text). It should also be quite thin and large enough for the clock hands.
- a clock set. This is easy to find at a craft store. Pay attention to the length of the "stem" of the clock. They come in ¼ to ¾ inch lengths depending on the thickness of your book.
- spray paint (optional)
- a drill

Step 2: Remove Pages

Before you start, you may want to cut out a few pages of the book to frame to complement your clock. Imagine framed children's book art on the wall next to the clock made out of the cover. So cute! But less cute is when there is a giant hole in the pages. Also, mark the center of your book by going corner to corner with a straight edge. If you want your clock to be off center, you can freehand where you drill.

Step 3: Spray Paint

This is optional, but all the clock sets I found were in a brass color. I spray painted my clock hands and numbers matte black.

Step 4: Drill

While your paint is drying, drill a hole in the spot you marked. I used a ⁵/₁₆" bit, but you'll want to follow the instructions that came with your clock pieces. A drill press is great. A cordless drill will be fine.

Step 5: Assemble Your Clock

Follow the instructions that came with your clock parts. The only tricky part is dealing with the thickness of the book. I kept finding my book too thick for the post on the clock. In this case your options are:
1. Buy a clock with a longer post (they vary in size)
2. Make a table top clock by opening the book and inserting the clock back between the last page and the back cover
3. Cut a large, square hole in the back cover to inset the clock mechanism

Step 6: Stick on the Numbers

You may want to use glue, as the stick-um on the numbers is weak. Also, use the longest hand as the guide for where the numbers should be. If you have time, make a circle template so your numbers aren't as lopsided as mine were. Either way, start with 12, 6, 9, and 3, and then fill in the other numbers.

Step 7: That's It!

Seriously easy, right? And a great gift for a kid, or for anyone. There is a book for every hobby. Have fun!

Cardboard Cube Lamp

By lindarose92
(http://www.instructables.com/id/Cube-Lamp/)

There is not much to say except that this lamp is made entirely with cardboard! I hope I can make this Instructable easy enough for all of you to try it. I needed a lot of patience to make this lamp, but the results are worth it.

Step 1: Cut Strips

Draw many little strips 5mm × 8cm (0.19 × 3.14 inches) on a thick piece of cardboard and cut them out. I can't tell exactly how many you need because it depends very much on how thick your strips are, but you can always make more later. To obtain the effect of this lamp, you need corrugated fiberboard.

Step 2: Glue Strips Together

Take one of the strips and spread some glue on one of the smooth sides, then attach another strip to it (I used superglue). Spread glue on that one too and add another strip. Continue in this way, always leaving the wavy part on the side, until you obtain a 8 × 8cm (3.14 × 3.14 inches) square.

Try to be as accurate as possible for a better effect; keep the best edge facing down on a flat surface while you glue the pieces together. This edge will be the outside face of the lamp, and by keeping this edge facing down it will be smoother and most of the possible rough parts will be hidden inside the lamp. You will need 20 squares.

Step 3: Assemble Bigger Squares

Now take four squares and glue the edges to each other using hot glue, creating a bigger square. Arrange them so that the strips in a given small square go in a perpendicular direction to those in the small square next to it. You'll have two squares with horizontal strips and two with vertical strips. This creates more visual interest.Do the same with all the other squares until you have 5 big squares.

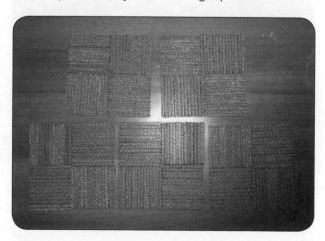

Step 4: Assemble the Cube

Take two of your big squares. Put some hot glue on one thin side of a square and position the side of the other square on it, creating a right angle. You have to create a cube, and your big squares are the sides of it. Continue gluing the big squares together at right angles to form the sides of the cube.

Now glue another square to the top to close the cube. The bottom is still open, but we will need that space for the light bulb. Put all this aside for now.

Step 5: Make the Lamp Holder Box

Take another piece of cardboard and draw the pattern that you see below. Cut it out. There are two big squares 17 × 17 cm (6.69 × 6.69 inches) and four rectangles with four little squares surrounding the left-hand big square. These little squares are 2 × 2 cm (0.78 × 0.78 inches). The rectangles are 2 × 17 cm (0.78 × 6.69 inches). The whole length is 38cm (14.96 inches).

This will be the box that contains the lamp holder, so now you have to bend it and cut some parts of it (see picture below): the red lines are the ones that you have to cut and the green lines are the ones that you have to bend.

Now glue the little squares to the rectangles as you can see in the pictures. The box is done! It should resemble a pizza box.

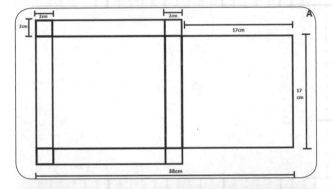

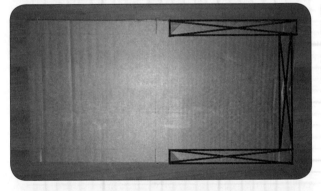

Step 6: Velcro

Cut a little piece of fabric about 8 × 2cm (3.14 × 0.78 inches) and glue one of its short sides to the inside of the box, as you can see in the picture. Take a piece of Velcro and glue it to the other side of the fabric at the other end. Close the box and glue the other side of the Velcro to the flap of the box. This ensures it stays securely closed while also allowing you to open it when needed. That this will be the bottom of the lamp box. Cut four little circles from cardboard with a diameter of about 2cm (0.78 inches) and glue them on the four corners. These will be your lamp's "feet."

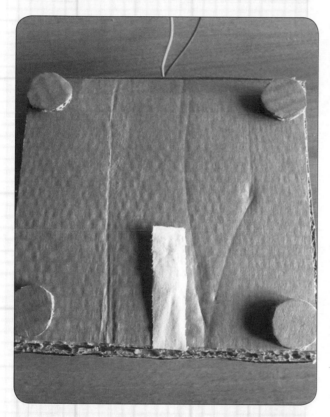

Step 7: Cut Holes

Get a lamp holder and trace the outline of it in the middle of the top of the box, then cut it out. You will need this hole for the lamp holder. You also need another smaller hole in one of the short sides of the box for the cable to pass through.

Step 8: Final Assembly

Cut two little squares from cardboard that are 2 × 2cm (0.78 × 0.78 inches), then cut them in half diagonally to obtain four little triangles. Glue these triangles on the top of the box at the angles you see in the pictures. Now you can finally put the cube structure you previously made on the lamp box, and these triangles will keep it in place.

I recommend using LEDs, or at least an energy-saving bulb, because regular light bulbs get too hot and might burn the lamp structure. Remember that it's made with cardboard, so be careful! If you use LEDs there won't be any problem.

All you have to do now is connect the cable and try it!

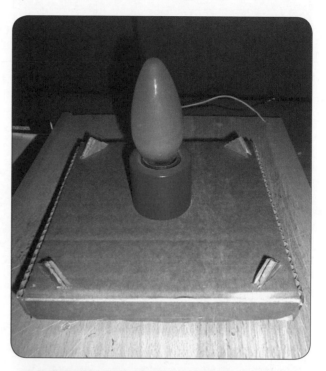

Recycled Hard Drive Desk Clock

By aloew
(http://www.instructables.com/id/Recycled-
Hard-Drive-Desk-Clock/)

This is an idea that I came up with while taking apart old hard drives for fun. It turned into a regular thing, and now I've got the process down to a science. For this Instructable, I'll be using an old WD Caviar hard drive. Drive designs differ, and some are better for this project than others.

Step 1: Tools You'll Need

- Torx-6 and Torx-8 screwdrivers
- X-acto knife
- Phillips-head screwdriver
- hammer
- drill and bits
- machinist's vise
- ¾" clock movement
- soft cloth

Step 2: Remove Screws

Next, undo the screws around the edges that hold the cover down, but don't go tugging yet. There is at least one more screw hiding under the stickers: one in the center and one off to the side. Refer to the pictures to get an idea of where they will be. Feel around and then cut through the stickers to get to the screws. Once you've gotten all the screws, you can cut through the tape around the edge and open it up.

Step 3: Disassembly

Now it's time to free up the actuator. To do this, remove the two screws securing the top magnet and remove it with a pair of needle-nose pliers. Don't try it with your fingers; it won't work. Place the magnet far away from anything electronic. Then, remove the single screw keeping the actuator retainer in place. Work the retainer up and out. The arm should swing freely now.

Step 4: Remove Platters and Motor Assembly

Now, undo the screws holding the platters down. You may have to hold the edges of the platters to keep them from spinning. Once the screws are off, turn the drive upside down on a soft cloth and the retainer, platters, and spacers will fall out neatly. Leave them in that order. Next, unscrew the motor assembly and pop it out.

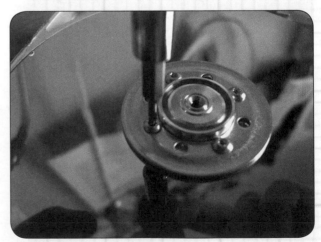

Step 5: Pre-modification

Now it's time to make sure everything is ready before beginning to make your modifications. Line the drive body up on top of the cover and mark where the mounting holes are. It's also a good time to spray paint your clock hands if you don't want them the stock color. I went with black.

Step 6: Modification

Time to break out the hammer. Place your motor assembly upside down in a vice (preferably padded) with the spinning part hanging freely. Place an old screwdriver or something similar in the center and tap it with the hammer. Eventually, the whole spin assembly will fall out. Sometimes this step takes two taps, sometimes it takes ten minutes. Be patient.

Once you've picked up your motor, place it back on the vice, this time right-side-up. Repeat the previous step, and the spindle will pop out, along with some bearings. Make sure to get all the bearings out. If the top piece (edged by some blue adhesive) stays in, don't worry about it.

Step 7: Modification

Now, take a $5/16$" drill bit and ream the motor base. Reattach the motor base to the body, and use the hole as a guide to drill straight through the circuit board on the back. Switch bits for a moment and use a $13/64$" bit to drill two holes in your marks on the cover.

Step 8: Reassembly

Now the clock begins to come together. Screw the motor base back into the body of the hard drive, if you haven't already. Reassemble the platters and spacers on the mount and screw them back in. Place your reassembled platter assembly back where it belongs, and move the actuator heads back into place. Affix a ¾" clock movement (I use Walnut Hollow) through the hole in the drive and tighten the nut.

Step 9: Reassemble and Finish

You're almost done. Flip the drive over and use two hard drive mounting screws to secure the cover (now the base) to the bottom of your clock. Make sure your clock movement is set to 12:00 and attach the hands as directed. Put in a battery, take some glamour shots, and you're done!

Want to make a unique piece of art to decorate your empty walls or to make the perfect gift for the grandparents or in-laws? Here is a simple way to make a modern and minimalistic design using just tiles, tissue paper, and a laser printer. It is time to amaze your friends.

Step 1: Getting Started
You will need:
- a nice photo
- computer
- nine 10 × 10cm tiles
- five sheets of printer paper
- five strips of 10 × 20cm tissue paper
- double-sided adhesive
- printer
- X-acto knife
- decoupage glue
- paintbrush

Step 2: Picking and Editing Your Photo
First you have to pick a nice photo. Make sure you pick a photo in which you will not cut away vital parts (such as eyes) later on. Choose which part of the photo you want to use and cut out a square. Put the square in a new document. On this new document you can change image size to 30 × 30cm, desaturate the image, and change brightness and contrast until you get the desired result. You might want use the paintbrush to get rid of unwanted details in the background. You

also might want to reverse the picture by flipping it along its vertical axis, otherwise you will end up with a mirror image of your original photo.

Step 3: Dividing Your Picture into Smaller Elements
In order to print your paper you will have to take a few extra steps. Make lines on your edited photo at 10 and 20 centimeters. This is just to make the next step easier; if you find it hard you can skip this.

Cut out the squares between the lines. You have to cut 0.5 cm away from the lines, otherwise you will end up with a distorted face in the end, as there will be a border of sorts around the pictures on the tiles. If you did not make the lines just check the ruler and make the cutting freehand. Every square will measure 9cm in each direction.

Paste the squares into five new documents, two in each except for the last one, which will have just one square. If needed, rotate the new documents to make them printable.

Step 4: Printing Your Photo on Tissue Paper
Obviously it is hard to put tissue paper into an ordinary laser printer. Here is a nice trick to make it

work. Take your strips of 10 × 20cm tissue paper. Put double-sided adhesive on the upper and lower edges. Attach it to the middle of a piece of printer paper. Do NOT use common tape as it will melt in your laser printer and make it useless (take my word for it; I have tried). Print the five documents on the five pieces of tissue paper.

Step 6: Time to Use the Glue!

Put decoupage glue on tiles and attach the tissue paper. If you want a softer look, glue them on with the printed side facing the tile. (That is the reason you might want to reverse it earlier.) For a more detailed look, attach with the printed side out. When dry, add at least two more layers of decoupage glue on top of the tissue paper.

Step 5: Cutting the Parts

No need for a longer explanation. Cut out all nine squares. Try not to cut your fingers as well.

Step 7: Finished!

Now you might want to put tiles into a frame or stick them to a board and put it on your wall. Good luck!

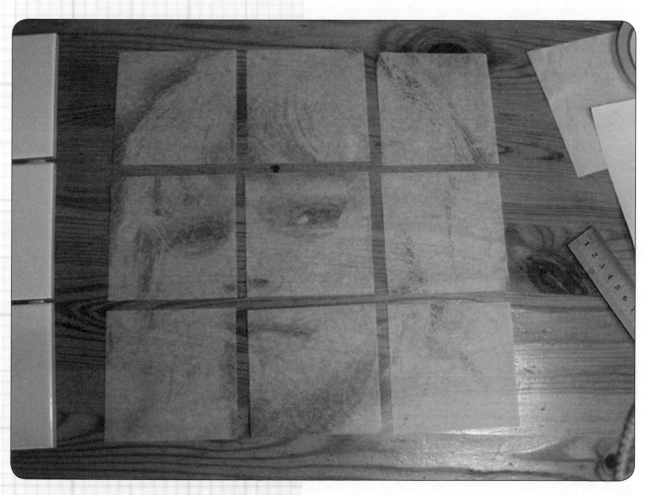

Do-It-Yourself Concrete Coasters and Trivets
By CHENG Concrete
(http://www.instructables.com/id/DIY-CONCRETE-Coasters-Trivets/)

This Instructable will show you a quick and easy way to make concrete coasters and trivets from the lids of plastic containers. The lids used in this Instructable are from plastic storage containers from the dollar store. Look for lids that are not too shallow or you might have problems with the concrete breaking. There are four steps in this Instructable: Preparing the Lid, Mixing and Pouring Concrete, Grinding and De-molding, Sealing, and Finishing.

Skill Level: Beginner

Materials:
- plastic storage container lids
- CHENG countertop pro-formula mix or equivalent
- Sakrete 5000+ Concrete or equivalent
- decorative aggregate (optional semi-precious minerals, crushed glass, etc.)
- bucket
- water
- particle mask
- rubber gloves
- soapy water/denatured alcohol
- spray adhesive (3M Super 77)
- diamond sanding pads/sandpaper
- plastic bag to cover while curing
- variable-speed polisher

Step 1: Preparing the Lid
A good lid for this project:
- coaster size = 4+ inch
- trivet size = 6+ inch
- flexible plastic
- plastic that is durable enough to be reused
- watertight
- at least ¼ inch thick
- not threaded inside (so concrete can be released from the lid without having to break it off)

- no logos
- free/cheap

Less than ideal:
- paper/cardboard
- thinner than ¼ inch
- undercuts/threads/deep logos
- thin plastic is okay for one casting, but can't be reused easily

Prepare the lid for casting:

Clean the lids with soapy water using something that won't scratch, like a 100% cotton cloth.

Decorating concrete:

Use a light mist of spray adhesive in the lid if you want to include decorative aggregate, crushed glass, or any kind of inlays. Use crushed glass and decorative aggregate that complements the color of the concrete. Rubber stamps can be fixed to the form with spray adhesive and removed after the concrete has cured, leaving the rubber stamp pattern as a relief in the surface.

Step 2: Mixing and Pouring Concrete
Mixing:

Figure out how much concrete you're going to mix. Each of these coasters weighs under half a pound. You can mix 10 pounds of concrete by hand in a 5-gallon bucket with a trowel. For larger amounts, use a wheelbarrow and a shovel. After the dry materials (concrete mix, admixtures, pigments, etc.) are combined, begin adding water gradually.

The best way to figure out how much water to add is by experience. If the mix is too wet, it will flow and pour easily but there will be excess bleed water on the surface as the concrete starts to cure. If the mix is too dry, it will be gritty with sand. Excess water will weaken the concrete. If the mix gets too wet, add more concrete. Break apart or throw away any clumps of unmixed concrete before filling the form.

Casting:

Make sure the mold is clean and free of debris. Press a small handful of concrete into the mold and pat it down to work out any air bubbles. Tapping the mold on the tabletop will further drive out any air. Remove the rocks that protrude from the top surface. If you don't have an orbital polisher, grinding them down will be very time consuming (nearly impossible). It is important that the top surface is flat and smooth to the edge of the lid. Smooth the top of the concrete by screeding it with a straight-edge or a trowel.

Curing:

Place the concrete on a level surface and cover it with plastic to cure for four days. The plastic will help keep the humidity inside; if the concrete dries out too quickly it can cause small cracks. The curing process can be sped up by using a quick-setting cement mix like Rapid Set, but this can also affect the color of the concrete. Curing should take place between 50° and 90° F, never in direct sunlight, and concrete should never freeze while it›s curing.

Step 3: Grinding and De-Molding

Grinding with an orbital polisher:

While the concrete is still in the plastic lid, grind the top flat with an orbital polisher. Keeping it in the lid will give you an even edge to grind down to. Un-ground concrete will have a uniform color without any exposed aggregate.

Grinding without an orbital polisher:

Concrete is extremely difficult to grind without the right diamond polishing tools. Even with a coarse diamond hand pad, it will take a very long time to flatten a 4″ disc. This is why it›s so important to smooth the back surface flat while the concrete is still workable. Use a lapping wheel with diamond discs. Try a coarse sharpening stone. Try a coarse wet/dry sandpaper (45 or 60 grit).

De-Molding:

You will break the coasters in half during de-molding if you haven›t waited long enough for them to cure (3 to 5 days). Pry the plastic lid off by pushing down with a flat screwdriver, working your way around the lid. Take your time and be careful not to scratch or chip the concrete during de-molding. If the concrete is really stuck, try blowing down between the edge of the plastic lid and the concrete with compressed air. If the concrete is still stuck, the last resort is to break away the plastic mold with wire cutters or scissors. These lids can be reused dozens of times, just clean

up the concrete residue with warm soapy water or denatured alcohol.

Sanding the edges:

Knock down any sharp edges with a diamond hand-sanding pad or a coarse sharpening stone.

Step 4: Sealing and Finishing

Sealing:

Concrete is vulnerable to etching and staining from anything acidic like lemon juice, vinegar, red wine, etc. Sealing isn›t necessary but will help protect the concrete from staining and keep it looking nice for a long time.

Finishing:

If your coasters don›t sit flat, you can cut thin cork backs or little cork feet and attach them with spray adhesive.

Hopefully this little project will inspire you to make something concrete. Thanks for following.

I want to show you how I converted some daily-used objects into a stylish array of four LED lamps that can be used anywhere in the house. I made mine for the kitchen table. These lights aren't substitutes for your standard bulb and only add extra mood-lighting.

Step 1: Use, Reuse, Recycle

I have tried to use only stuff that was around the house. We all want to be sustainable after all!

You will need:
- glass bottles
- phone charger
- bottle cork
- nail polish

How would you use your old phone battery charger?

Do you always recycle glass bottles?

What about wood material such as cork?

Where do people toss the nail polish that they don't need?

How many energy-saving lights do you have at home?

Answering these questions shows where my inspiration came from. I was thinking about sustainability in our daily lives. We tend to throw away items that come in shiny packaging when we don't need them.

What you may need to buy:
- LEDs (I used 32 white 5mm LEDs)
- resistors (fixed and variable)
- cables
- prototyping PCB
- switch

You also need some tools:
- screwdriver
- drill
- wood-carving kit
- soldering iron and wire
- glass cutter

Don't forget safety glasses!

Step 2: A Special Brightness Control Feature

I used a bottle cork and built a switch and a potentiometer inside. The switch turns all lights on/off, and with the potentiometer you can control the brightness. You can see the switch on the side. The lower part can be rotated clockwise to make the lights brighter and counter-clockwise to make them dimmer.

Step 3: Old Phone Charger

We are using stuff from around the house, so find your old cell phone and use its charger. Any charger that produces 5V DC can be used. Check the charger rating—it depends on the number of LEDs you use, but I think 500mA is minimum. My charger is rated at 700mA, and I used four lamps, each having eight LEDs, so 32 in total.

I mentioned sustainability above. My design is more sustainable than conventional lamps because it uses few energy resources and still gives the desired effect. Four small-size bulbs would produce a lot more light output, but at 15 times the power consumption. A typical phone charger produces 0.5 to 1.0 A current at 5V DC, which is around 2.5 to 5W—way less than any conventional tungsten light bulb.

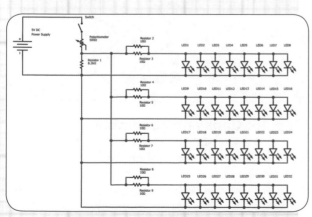

Step 4: Schematic

Look at my diagram, which explains the electrical connections.

I have eight LEDs in parallel for each lamp, in series with two 10 ohm resistors, which are in parallel. For the brightness regulator I use a 0–500ohm potentiometer and a 8.2 kohm resistor; using these I form a potential divider. I connect the LED lamps at the middle point.

If you alter the number of LEDs or the power supply or something else, you will have to measure the current through the LEDs. At maximum brightness, it is good to keep the current running through the LEDs to less than 15mA.

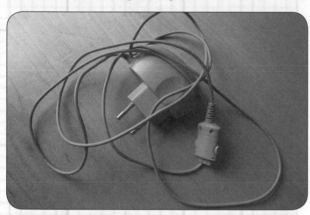

Step 5: PCB

Prepare a round piece of the prototyping board, two 10ohm resistors, and eight LEDs.

Step 6: Solder

Place the LEDs so that they form a circle. All long (or all short) legs should face to the center. Now bend the legs to form two loops—positive and negative. Do not mix short and long legs. Solder and trim.

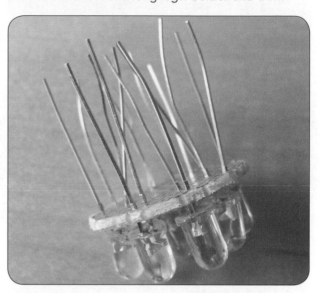

Step 7: Resistors in Parallel

Place the two 10 ohm resistors in the center and solder them in parallel. Connect one side of the resistors to the positive LED terminals—that with the longer legs. This will become the positive connection, and the resistors will restrict the current flow. Why two resistors in parallel?

$$10 \times 10 / (10 + 10) = 5$$

So the total resistance will be 5 ohms. By using two resistors that equal 5 ohms, the heat dissipation is better. The resistors won't heat so much, and they can be a smaller size and wattage rating.

Finally solder a wire and make sure all LEDs work. If none work, then check the polarity of your power supply. If only some work, then you may have soldered some LEDs the wrong way around.

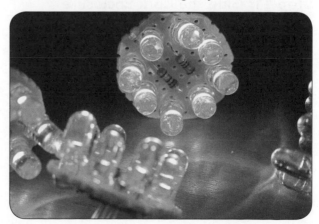

Step 8: Cork Control

Choose a switch and a potentiometer that you think will fit inside the cork. Cut off a small portion of the cork that will be the brightness control, then split the rest of the cork in two lengthwise.

Step 9: Carve the Cork

By using tools that carve wood you can make space for the switch and potentiometer inside the cork. Cork is soft, and I used a rotary tool that "eats" it rather easily and quickly. The potentiometer sits below the switch. I was able to use a two-wire cable and also made space for it in the cork.

Step 10: Potentiometer Control

Using a piece of plastic card, I made a shaft between the potentiometer and the cork. All was glued with instant glue. I would recommend using a potentiometer with bigger shaft so you won't have to do the trick with the plastic shaft.

Step 11: Glue the Cork Enclosure

Check that the switch is operating properly and then use wood glue to attach the two halves.

Step 12: Glass Cutting Preparation

Warning: Do not try this if you are unsure. Give it to someone with experience—it could be the local glass repair shop or something similar. I attempted to cut the top of the bottles using the hot/cold water method. There are numerous ways shown online, so just Google it.

Wear safety glasses!

What you need to do is scratch the bottle around the outside where you want to cut it. I used a glass cutter from the local store.

Step 13: Hot and Cold Water

Boil some water in the kettle. Now pour some hot water on the area that you scratched and rotate the bottle. Stop and repeat with cold water. Do this until the top of the bottle comes off by itself.

Step 14: Bottle Cuts Results

These photos show some of my attempts. I cut six bottles in total to get four decent-looking bottle pieces. Be careful because the edge is very sharp. At this point you can sand the edge with some sanding paper, but I did not have any so I skipped that.

Step 15: Caps and Assembly

Using a screwdriver or a drill, make holes on the caps and feed the wires through them. Place the caps back on the bottles. Tie a knot on the cables and leave the board with the LEDs hanging in the center of the bottle. If a knot does not work use cable ties or glue.

Step 17: Adding Bling Bling

I painted the edge of one bottle with nail polish. There is some glowing effect and the edge becomes very shiny. Dots also look very nice and make the lamps stand out even more.

Step 16: Operation Check

They look beautiful, right? Now it's up to you to hang them somewhere. Mine are above the dining table. They also are nice when watching TV because they emit soft light and can be dimmed easily.

Step 18: Enjoy

All that's left is to enjoy what you have made! I've added lots of photos in this step to show all aspects of the lights.

Alien Abduction Lamp

By me-again100
(http://www.instructables.com/id/Alien-Abduction-Lamp/)

This Instructable will show you how to make an alien abduction lamp.

Step 1: Materials
- 8" range replacement pans (3—2 for the UFO and 1 for cutting pieces from)
- smooth-sided tapered drinking glass
- small glass bowl
- medium base light socket
- lamp cord with switch
- small piece of plywood (about 6 × 6in.)
- small alien toy
- small abductee (Lego man, cow, sheep, etc.)
- mini CFL lightbulb
- epoxy
- superglue
- green paint
- tin snips
- file or small grinder (Dremel)
- screwdriver
- tape measure
- drill and small bit or hammer and nail
- jigsaw or small handsaw

Step 2: UFO Body
Take one of the range pans and cut a piece out in a circular shape using the tin snips. It should be a bit larger than the hole that is in the bottom of the pan. Flatten it out and drill a small hole in the center (or punch a hole with a hammer and nail). Use the file or grinder to remove any sharp edges. Epoxy this piece over the hole in the second pan. When it is dry, epoxy this pan to the third pan to make a UFO shape. The side with the covered hole will be the top of the UFO and the side with the open hole is the bottom (the small hole you drilled will allow a bit of light through to illuminate your alien). You should also have an opening at the back where your light will go in.

Step 3: Make the Base

Cut the piece of plywood into a circle about 6" in diameter. Sand it smooth and paint it green. Attach your abductee to the center using superglue.

Step 4: Assemble

Attach the bottom of the drinking glass to the bottom of the UFO using epoxy. Glue the alien to the top of the UFO, then glue the small glass bowl over the alien. I painted a black band around the bowl because I only wanted to be able to see the head of the alien, but this is optional. Finally, glue the glass to the base over top of your abductee. Try to keep everything centered.

Step 5: Install the Light

Cut two pieces from the scrap pan that are the same width as the opening in the back of the UFO, and slightly longer. Cut a small notch in the center edge of each piece. File all the edges until they are smooth. Epoxy these two pieces together so they will fit in the back of the UFO. Run the lamp cord through the hole you cut and wire it to the socket. Epoxy the socket in place on the inside of the two cut pieces. Install a light bulb and then insert the assembly into the back of the UFO. You will have to bend the ends slightly as you insert it; this keeps it from accidently coming out on its own. I also added some silicone around the edge of the hole to prevent the cord from accidentally getting cut by the metal edge (not shown in picture).

Step 6: Enjoy

Plug in the lamp, turn it on, and enjoy!

You can make anything out of cardboard! If you start a list, it won't come to an end. Cardboard has become quite popular in crafting lampshades, so I thought I'd give it a try. I always try to craft simple things and make the instructions as easy as possible. This cardboard lampshade is one of the easy ones! You can make these lampshades easily, and you can make as many as you want because they are easily changeable. So start making one now!

Step 1: Materials Needed
Things you'll need to make the lamp:
- cardboard
- white glue and superglue
- anti-cutter
- scissors
- paint and brush
- paint, marker, colored paper (to decorate the shades)
- duct tape
- lighting system (bulb, wire, holder, plug)

Step 2: Making the Base
You'll need to decide how big you want the base to be. I cut out five 6 × 6 inch cardboard pieces and cut three of them to fit the light. I've numbered each piece in the picture. You'll have to place the 1 on the bottom, glue the 2 on top of it, and glue 3 and 4

accordingly. Don't glue number 5 yet, because you'll need to paint it.

There are four more pieces to cover the sides of the base. Color the top piece of the base and the four sides. I've used black paint to color them. After the paint dries glue all the pieces together while adjusting the lighting system.

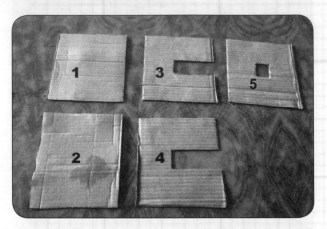

Step 3: Cutting the Shades
You can adjust the height of the various lamp shades as much as you want, but the base width is fixed. Cut a piece of cardboard, keeping in mind that it must fit into the base.

As the base I've made is 6 × 6 inches I've cut out a cardboard piece 22 inches long, which will become a shade with panels 5.5 × 5.5 inches wide) when I've folded them into a cube shape. You can also make circular-shaped shades or any other shapes, as long as you make your base to match.

Draw shapes on the cardboard piece, such as squares, stars, lines, or triangles, and use an anti-cutter to cut them out. Cut the shapes out as carefully as possible. You also need to cut out a piece of cardboard to cover the top of the shade. You may also cut out shapes on the top piece. I've made three shades, one with stripes, one with stars, and another with diamond-shaped cutouts.

Step 4: Painting the Shades

Paint the shades however you want. I've used black, cream, and scarlet paints.

You have to paint:
- Shades
- Top of the shades
- Top of the base (on which the light will be placed)
- Sides of the base

Step 5: Putting It All Together

After the paint dries, use superglue to stick all the parts together. First glue the sides of the shades to make the cube shape, and then glue on the top. Glue the corners carefully.

Step 6: Decorate the Shades

Decorate the shades however you want. I've used gold and silver glitter to decorate the black shade, paper-pieced art on the cream-colored shade, and marker to design the other one.

Step 7: Final Step!

You'll need a bulb, wire, two-pinned plug, and a bulb holder. Join one side of the wire with the plug and the other side with the bulb holder and then fix the bulb on the holder.

Insert the wire through the fifth layer (top) of the base and the wire will pass through the third and fourth layer of the base. There! Switch on to see if the light works. I think it's better to use light bulbs of not more than 40 watts, and it's even better if you use a CFL light bulb.

After you've fixed the lighting system, simply place the lamp shade on the base. You can make as many lamp shades you want, changing them when you're bored of the same shade. I hope you enjoy making it!

Do-It-Yourself Death Star Clock

By cannibal869
(http://www.instructables.com/id/DIY-Death-Star-Clock/)

When decorating my office with some sci-fi stuff, I thought, why not make a 3D Death Star myself? While I was thinking about it, I also figured, why not make it somewhat functional if I can?

Step 1: Materials (all available through Amazon and/or your local hobby/craft store):

- Lightning "Factory Second" Prostyle #1 Driver or other Frisbee; $6.48 shipped
- Clock Movement Quartz Square Straight Black Hand Shaft ¾" Kit; $12.95 (note: if I were to do it again, I would suggest going with the 1/4" or 1/2" kit instead of the 3/4")
- sticky-back foam sheets–basic colors; $9.44 shipped
- black and grey spray paint; about $4
- optional but recommended: carbon paper; about $5 for 10 sheets

Step 2: Get Your Design

To start off, I resized and printed out a photo of the Death Star. Using the carbon paper, I traced the outlines onto the Frisbee.

Step 3: Sanding

If I were to do this again, I would next use my Dremel tool and sand away the "emitter/focusing disc" portion, as well as Dremel in the curved lines. On this run I did the sanding after I put the foam blocks on and had a few missteps, which you'll see on the close-up photos below.

Step 4: Working with the Foam

Next, I used that same photo and traced the outlines onto a sheet of the adhesive-backed white foam sheet. Using a scalpel/X-acto knife, I then cut out the blocks and stuck them to the Frisbee, using the carbon-paper outlines as a guide to where they should go.

Step 5: Painting

Then I spray painted the whole thing in semi-gloss black. The paint was still wet in this image. The textural difference between the foam blocks and the Frisbee was quite a nice effect once the paint dried.

Step 6: Adding Grey Primer

I used a strip of 1/4" tape to mask the center groove/canyon area and then lightly misted some grey primer in order to highlight some of the areas and provide contrast.

Step 7: Attach the Clock

I then drilled a small hole for the clock shaft and attached the clock arms.

Here it is mounted next to my shop clock for comparison.

Step 8: Final Product

The total cost came to about $38, and the final result is hanging in my office next to the Millennium Falcon and a TIE fighter.

Homemade Gold Record

By fungus amungus
(http://www.instructables.com/id/Make-a-Gold-Record/)

Make a hit record and sell over 500,000 copies and you've gone gold. I don't play any music and will never make music that will drive music fans to the stores in droves, but I feel like I've done some cool stuff and why shouldn't I have a gold record for my own achievements? So I decided to just make one of my own. With about $10 you can do it, too. Follow these steps and live the golden life.

Step 1: Paint It Black and Gold

You can get the supplies you need at any nearby thrift store. Grab any record and a frame big enough to show it off. Don't worry about any of the colors, because with cans of black and gold spray paint it will all look perfect in just a few minutes. The record is easy enough to paint—just use lights coats and keep the can moving. Use the same technique on the frame and you'll come out just fine. The black spray paint is used to turn the backing board from the frame into a nice backdrop for the record. If you have some black foamcore lying around, then that'll work great, too.

Step 2: Add a Spacer to the Record

Instead of sticking the record directly on to the black background, I decided to float it a bit. This was done by simply gluing some foamcore scraps to the back of the record and then gluing the combined piece to the background.

Step 3: Be Careful about the Placement

Take some time to see where the record should be before letting the glue dry. Move it around a bit and check it with a ruler.

71

Step 4: Make a Label

Every record needs a label, so make one of your own! I decided to make this gold record in honor of one my favorite Instructables, the Inverted Bookshelf. Have some fun with it and make it whatever you want. Google "vinyl record label" to see lots of classic labels for inspiration.

Step 5: Make a Label for the Frame

With this label, you get to show off what the achievement is for. My Instructable has over 175,000 pageviews, so I decided that 100,000 would be a good round number to be proud of. Remember, this is your own achievement. It can be for whatever you want! Do you think some Gold Record Official is going to come after you? Have some fun with it.

Step 6: Put It All Together

The record is in place and now the label on the bottom is also in place. This label can also be floated with some spare foamcore, but once again it's all up to you. Let it dry and hang it up!

Other things you can commemorate with a gold record:

- birthdays
- graduations
- your first apartment
- getting lots of followers on Twitter
- waking up before 6 a.m.
- making a killer lasagna

Food

Drunken Gummi Bears

Watermelon Keg

Beer-Battered Bacon-Stuffed Jalapenos

Bacon Jello

Gummi Bear Surgery

Bacon Roses

Still-in-the-Shell Scrambled Eggs

Bacon Kettle Chips

Chicken 'n Waffles on a Stick

Jalapeno Popper Crescent Rolls

Fried Pickles

Gummi Shot Glasses

Chocolate Space Invaders

Apple Pie Bites on a Stick

Homemade Jello and Heart Banana

Popcorn Popper–Roasted Coffee Beans

Engraved M&Ms

Octopizza Pie

Bacon Pixie Sticks

Pig Roast

Cake Pops

Bowl of Worms

3D Dinosaur Birthday Cake

Robotic R2D2 Cupcake

Most food is boring. It's sustenance with all the excitement and creativity of filling up at the gas station.

These projects are anything but boring. Get your gummy bears drunk or simply perform surgery on them. Engrave custom messages onto your M&Ms. Like chicken and waffles? Try both at once. On a stick. Into apple pie? We'll show you how to put that on a stick, too.

Bacon is the kitchen equivalent of a turbocharger, and the bacon jello and bacon pixie sticks and bacon potato chips and bacon roses should have you and your heart racing in no time. And if bacon is a turbocharger, roasting a whole pig is like a culinary nitrous tank that will have you devouring pork fast and furiously.

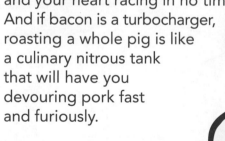

Drunken Gummi Bears

By courtnix
(http://www.instructables.com/id/Drunken-
Gummies-Vodka-Infused-Gummi-Bears/)

This Instructable will teach you how to create the most delicious alcoholic treat that will make you the life of any party. Warning: This recipe contains alcohol, so please only make this if you are of legal age in your area. Please use responsibly and legally!!!

Step 1: Prepare Materials and Get Them Soakin'!

This Instructable takes a bit more than a week to complete, but the end result is certainly worth it!
You will need:

- 1 1/2 cups of vodka (can use more or less if desired)
- 1 tub of gummy bear candies, in a plastic container with a lid (about 1kg. tub found at Walmart)
- 1 can of frozen juice concentrate, any flavor desired (I used fruit punch). You can keep the juice frozen for now, as you will not need it for a few days.

The first step is to open the lid of your gummy bears and pour in the vodka. The amount and brand is at your discretion, though I have found 1.5 cups of Smirnoff vodka to be the best. I have tried this with raspberry vodka as well, with pleasurable results. Basically, pour the vodka into the packed bears until the alcohol barely peeks over the top. Give your newly introduced gummy bears and vodka a stir and replace

the lid. Place the whole tub into the fridge. Let this sit for five days, stirring a couple of times each day.

Step 2: I've Created a Monster! I've Created 500 Monsters!

After five days, much of your vodka will have been soaked into the bears, and they may have gone through a significant growth spurt, as shown in the photo. Now is the time for the juice to be added. The purpose of the juice is to mask the strong vodka taste that exists in these candies. Place a thawed can of frozen juice into a mixing container, and add only half of the required water. Pour one cup of partially diluted juice into the tub of bears, stirring very well. Replace the lid and place the tub back in the refrigerator.

Step 3: Wait for It...

Let the bears sit in their juice and whatever vodka is left for four more days. This is essential because otherwise they will have a hard middle or will taste too much like vodka. Resist the urge to taste test! Stir twice a day to prevent sticking.

Step 4: Finally, Our Lovely Mutants!

Your gummy bears are finally finished! If there is a lot of excess juice and vodka resting in the bottom, you may drain it or leave it in to be further absorbed by the bears as they rest. Remember to return to the fridge if they are not all eaten—which rarely happens! Be ready for the rush and eat these carefully as they can be pretty potent! Please use responsibly and legally!

Watermelon Keg

By ModMischief

(http://www.instructables.com/id/
Tap-a-Watermelon-or-How-to-Make-a-
Watermelon-Keg/)

Impress your guests and enjoy a delicious drink in style! After seeing an incredible watermelon keg online, I knew I needed to try it for myself. Unfortunately, I couldn't find a similar tap and PVC adapter, so I had to modify the design somewhat.

Step 1: What You'll Need

From the hardware store:
- hose bibb, quarter turn (that's the tap)
- faucet lock nuts (those black circles)
- brass pipe nipple 1/2" (the piece with threads on both ends)
- coupling 1/2" (what looks like a hex nut)
- drill bit (optional)

From the grocery store:
- watermelon (I used a very small melon for this demo, but you'll need a big one if you want more than two drinks out of it)

- Saran wrap (or similar cling wrap)
- From your kitchen:
- paring knife
- ice cream scoop (a spoon could work in a pinch)
- large bowl
- blender
- strainer or sieve

From the liquor store:
- vodka or your poison of choice (this is optional, but there's not much of a point without it, right?)

Step 2: Cut Off the Top

Use your knife to cut the top off your melon. Try to keep the hole fairly small, but make sure it's big enough to stick your hand in. Make sure you cut on an angle (like you would if you were carving a pumpkin) so you can use the top as a lid without it falling in. You can cut a small notch out of the lid to make it easier to refill your melon after your guests inevitably finish off the original contents.

Step 3: Gut the Melon

Scoop out all of the delicious insides and set them aside.

Step 4: Make a Hole for the Tap

Using the drill bit, make a hole near the bottom of your melon. Be sure to put it on the prettiest side of your watermelon (this is, after all, what all your guests will be admiring). If you don't have a drill bit handy, a corkscrew would work. Using a paring knife, make the hole the same size as your coupling. Take your time with this step as you'll need a good fit if you don't want it to leak. Don't just shove your coupling in the hole, as a bruised melon won't be watertight.

Step 5: Connect the Hardware

Wash all the hardware.

Screw your nipple into the coupling with one of the lock nuts in between. Push the coupling through the melon. Place a small piece of Saran wrap over

the coupling and cut an opening in the middle. The plastic wrap should help prevent leaks. Screw on the tap with a lock nut between the tap and the coupling. Wrap the excess Saran wrap around the edge of the lock nut and trim it so it looks pretty.

Step 6: Blend

Throw the watermelon guts into a blender and turn it into juice. Pour the juice through a strainer to get the worst of the pulpy bits out. Add a generous helping of vodka and stir.

Step 7: Enjoy

Relax and enjoy a cool drink. Bask in the adoration of all your party guests.

Beer-Battered Bacon-Stuffed Jalapenos

By crapsoup
(http://www.instructables.com/id/
Beer-Battered-Bacon-Stuffed-
Jalapenos/)

Hot and greasy, just the way you like it!!

Step 1: Ingredients
- 2 cups flour
- 2 Tbsp. Corn Starch
- 1/8 tsp. salt
- 1/2 tsp. pepper
- 1 tsp. garlic powder
- 1/2 tsp. onion powder
- 1/2 Tbsp. cayenne
- 1 tsp. chili pepper
- 1 tsp. cumin
- 1/2 tsp. adobo seasoning
- 1 beaten egg
- 3/4 cup beer
- 1/4 cup milk
- 2 Tbsp. melted Butter (I use coconut oil)
- 4 or 5 large Jalapenos
- 4 strips diced Bacon (I use turkey bacon)
- 1/2 cup Shredded cheese (I use Havarti, Gouda, & White Cheddar)
- 1/2 cup cream cheese
- 2 teaspoons chopped garlic
- 2 quarts of oil

Step 2: Making the Batter
1. Mix flour, corn starch, salt, pepper, and all other dry seasonings together in large bowl.
2. In another bowl, mix in eggs, beer, milk, and melted butter.
3. Pour wet mixture into dry ingredients bowl and stir until well blended.
4. Let batter sit for 30 to 45 minutes, while you are preparing everything else.

Step 3: Preparing the Stuffing Mix
1. Cut the bacon into small bits and cook until browned.
2. Chop three cloves of garlic into small chunks.
3. Mix bacon, cream cheese, shredded cheese, and garlic chunks in a large bowl.

Step 4: Roasting and Stuffing the Jalapenos
1. Cut the tops off of each jalapeno and core out the insides. This can be done easily with a potato peeler (small knives work but not as well).
2. Use the stove (or a torch) to roast the peppers. The outside skin will crackle and burn, but don't worry, this is normal.

3. When all the skin is well cooked, take a knife and scrape off all of the burnt skin.
4. Carefully stuff the roasted jalapenos with the bacon mixture until they are packed full to the top.

Step 5: Battering and Frying Your Peppers

1. Heat oil in pan.
2. Place stuffed peppers in batter and coat evenly. Make sure the cheese ends are fully covered.
3. Place coated jalapenos in hot oil and fry until golden brown. You may need to flip them depending on the amount of oil used.
4. Remove from oil and let cool on paper towels for five minutes.
5. Eat them until you feel fat and happy.

Any excess batter can be dropped into the oil in heaping spoonfuls to make crispy breadnuggets. Or use it to bread up something else as a side dish, like garlic. Any excess cheese filling can be used on bagels for a tasty snack

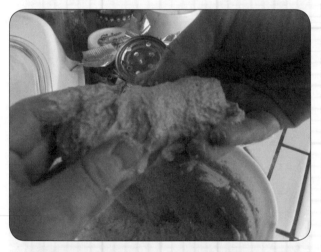

Bacon Jello

By canida
(http://www.instructables.com/id/
Bacon-Jello/)

Bacon jello. Yes, it's bacon-flavored jello that looks like you're slicing into a nice, thick slab of home-cured bacon. Think of it less as dessert and more as a surprisingly edible piece of concept art. This jello has a dairy base flavored with bacon, a mix of maple syrup and flamed and reduced Calvados, and applewood smoke. Want to get fancy? Make another batch, but change up the flavorings: breakfast (bacon, eggs, and toast layers), a BLT, or your own favorite bacon-based flavor combination.

I made this for the 2012 San Francisco Bacon Takedown and greatly enjoyed the double-takes of unsuspecting bacon-tasters who were suddenly confronted with bacon jello. While this wasn't a crowd or judge favorite (see judge Josh's reaction here), I was primarily interested in the mechanics of making my jello a) actually contain a strong bacon flavor, b) actually look like bacon in cross-section, and c) actually be edible. It was a success on all fronts.

Step 1: Tools and Ingredients

While I made a triple batch for competition, this recipe is scaled to fit in one standard Pyrex pan.

Ingredients:

- 120g fried, thin-cut bacon
- 1 quart (4 cups) half-and-half
- 17 packets (1/4 oz. each) of plain gelatin
- 1/3 cup plus 3 tablespoons maple syrup (grade B, the nice dark stuff)
- 1 cup calvados, or similarly bacon-compatible 80-proof or greater booze
- red food coloring
- 2 teaspoons applewood liquid smoke
- 5 cups boiling water

Tools:

- bacon-frying apparatus
- blender
- sieve, cheesecloth, or chinois
- wire whisk
- 8.5 × 11 inch Pyrex baking dish (listed as holding about 3 quarts or 3 liters)
- plastic wrap
- aluminum foil (optional)
- plastic bags
- rocks, beans, rice, or other small/maneuverable dry item
- tape
- fire of some type (for flaming booze)
- measuring cups and spoons

Step 2: Fry Bacon

First, fry up a pound of your favorite thin-sliced bacon. For this dish, you're going to be incorporating bacon flavor into dairy, so it doesn't have to be fried totally dry—do it however you like it, just don't burn it. I made tons of bacon for multiple dishes, so I fried some in my favorite cast iron pot and also cooked some in the oven.

Step 3: Prep Bacon/Dairy Mix

Pour the quart of half-and-half into the blender. Weigh out about 120g of bacon and add it to the blender. Blend on high for 3 to 5 minutes, until bacon is thoroughly incorporated, then let it sit for another 15 minutes. Blend on high again for 1 minute, then pour through your sieve into a bowl or pitcher to save until ready to use. This bacon-infused half-and-half is your base for all of the steps to come.

Step 4: Prep Pan

Fill your bags about a quarter full with pea gravel, beans, rice, or other similarly-weighted items. Tape or zip lock bags shut; don't tie them, or you won't get proper coverage. Arrange them flat along the base of your pan, then create a couple of channels running the length of the pan, each about a third of the way in from the sides. Cover with a layer of aluminum foil or waxed paper (optional) then a layer of plastic wrap. Tape the plastic wrap in place, especially on the edges, to prevent jello sloshing over and getting under the plastic wrap. Make sure you've left enough flexibility to follow the contours of your gravel bed!

Step 5: Prep First Layer

Measure out 2 2/3 cup of bacon infusion into a mixing bowl. Sprinkle 3 1/3 packets (.83 oz., or 23.5g) gelatin over the surface, and let it sit and absorb the liquid ("bloom") for a few minutes. Add 2 2/3 cup of nearly-boiling water and whisk until the gelatin is thoroughly dissolved.

Cool to room temperature, then pour into your prepared pan, taking care not to slop over the edges of your plastic wrap. Move carefully to the refrigerator, and allow it to set up for several hours, preferably overnight.

Note: If doing this again, I'd add maple syrup to this layer as well (probably about 3 tablespoons) to give it a bit sweeter of a jello flavor.

Step 6: Flip

Once your base layer has set fully, untape the edges of your plastic wrap and aluminum foil and gently lift it out of the pan, being sure to support the gelatin carefully. Set it on the counter and inspect your handiwork. In the fourth picture below, you can see what happens if you get jello under the containment layer—it looks pretty nasty. And worse, you've lost precious bacon jello! To avoid this, pour slowly and move your pans carefully when jello is still liquid. (I sloshed one of three when doing the transfer to the fridge.)

Now remove your rocks and wash out the pan thoroughly. Dry the pan, then reline it with waxed paper.

Set the pan upside down over the jello on your counter, then flip both pieces together, taking care to support it thoroughly the entire time to avoid any cracks. If you've done it right, the jello will pop neatly into the pan.

Finally, pull off the plastic wrap and aluminum foil, and examine your bacony ridges. Success! All of that brownish stuff you see is actual bacon residue; had I chosen to filter more aggressively, it might all be pure bacon-fat-colored creaminess, but I liked the idea of some bacon bits.

Step 8: Prep Top Layer

This one is just syrup and smoke.

Combine 1 cup bacon/half-and-half mix with 2 teaspoons liquid smoke and 2 tablespoons maple syrup. Sprinkle two packets of gelatin over the surface, and let it sit for about 5 minutes to bloom.

Whisk in 1 cup boiling water and stir until all gelatin is dissolved. Once your mix has cooled down to lukewarm, dump it over the previously-coagulated layers, and return your jello to the fridge.

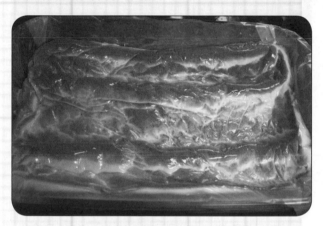

Step 7: Prep Middle Layer

This layer will be your "meat" strip in the center of the bacon. I've chosen to flavor it with maple syrup and flamed/reduced Calvados, for a nice apple-maple flavor to complement the bacon.

Place 1 cup Calvados (or high-proof booze of your choice) in a small pot and heat until the liquid starts to shimmer. Carefully stick a long match or burning skewer (or similar fire source that keeps your fingers out of the way) over the just-evaporating booze, and set it on fire. Enjoy the flames for a few minutes, keeping a wary eye on any nearby combustibles. When the flames die down, continue heating the Calvados until it's reduced to about 1/8 cup (2 tablespoons).

Combine 1/3 cup of the bacon/half-and-half mixture and 2 tablespoons flamed and reduced Calvados, then sprinkle 1 1/3 packets of gelatin over the top and allow to bloom for about 5 minutes.

Whisk in 2/3 cup hot water and stir until all gelatin has dissolved. Add red food coloring until the mix reaches your preferred bacon meat color.

Wait until the mixture cools to lukewarm, then pour on top of flipped bottom layer in the pan, making sure to fill all the crevices, and return to the fridge to coagulate.

Step 9: Serve and Store

Once the jello is fully set, grasp the edges of the waxed paper and carefully lift it out of the dish. You may need to support the middle so the jello doesn't sag or break.

Cut it in half on a clean cutting board, then decide whether you want full or half-slices of bacon. Serve by carving off thin slices just as you would with a hunk of real bacon. I found that about 1/3" was the right thickness to maintain structural integrity of the bacon slices. As you can see below, it's remarkably convincing. Just don't fry it!

To store, wrap slabs in plastic wrap and refrigerate. Food coloring will slowly migrate into the neighboring white bits of jello, but not too badly; the main image below was taken after about five days in storage.

Gummi Bear Surgery

By fungus amungus
(http://www.instructables.com/id/
Gummi-Bear-Surgery/)

Gummi bears live short lives, but that doesn't mean that they don't have health problems and won't occasionally need some care. There are times when these delicate bears will even need to go under the knife. The very substance of the gummy bears is tricky stuff and if you want to be able to identify a tumor and have it removed you need an expert. Someone you can trust. Someone who's been there. To get a better grasp of this hidden world of gummy surgery, we talked to an expert in the field who was happy to demonstrate his techniques for us. Warning: This Instructable contains graphic images of gummy bear surgeries, like the one right below. Gross, right?

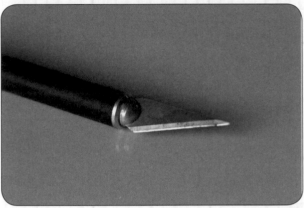

Step 1: Get Patients and Tools

For gummy surgery you need a supply of willing patients and the basic tools. Fortunately, most gummy bears are hypochondriacs, so even if they don't have a problem right away you can usually convince them to go under the knife in less than a minute. There might be an ethics problem here, but we couldn't think of it and moved on to the slicey dicey fun. Make sure you have a clean scalpel and metal tubing available. The second picture shows the exact knife you shouldn't use. Dried gummy gore should be wiped off with a paper towel, or you can replace the whole blade. Don't use your tongue to clean it! It's a bad idea!

Step 2: The Art of the Scalpel

The scalpel is the most important tool in gummy surgery. Once again, the surgeon recommends a clean blade. Push firmly into the gummy flesh and give it a little wiggle if you get stuck. Try for a clean cut. If there is too much screaming, you're doing it wrong.

Step 3: Basic Operation: Head Transplants

Like humans, gummy bears are often dissatisfied with the bodies they are given. There was once a time when all gummies were happy with the color of their flesh, but with pop culture infiltrating their sugary little heads, their desires have changed. Some insist that greens have more fun and reds are spicier. Silly little gummies. So foolish. Unlike humans, gummy bears can easily swap heads thanks to modern surgical techniques. In fact, this is the first type of surgery that happened in the gummy world, and it continues to be popular at parties. Just make sure you squish the head and body together good and tight so it sticks, okay? A falling apart gummy is a sad gummy. Sometimes you may need to use special surgical fluid to help stick the two parts together. If you don't have that, try some saliva. It's always handy and puts a little bit of you into each surgery.

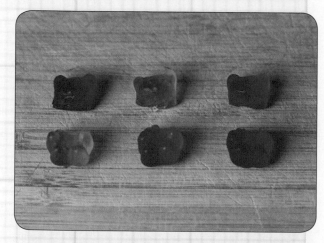

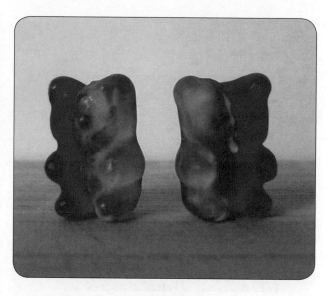

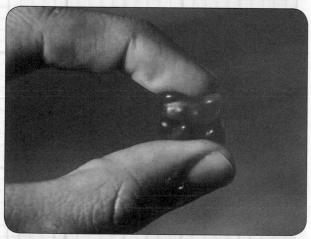

Step 5: Limb Transplants

A few quick cuts and all of a gummy bear's limbs can be removed. This is supposed to be done by consent, but sometimes a poor bear will be attacked by others desperate to sell the limbs for money. This bear paid a handsome sum to have limbs from a strong and powerful gummy bear attached to his own body. The operation was mostly a success, except that a couple of limbs got mixed up in the process. Look closely and you can see a leg brazenly placed where an arm should be and vice versa. To this date, nobody has told the bear of the mistake and we continue to let him think that he's looking good.

Step 4: Split Personalities

Soon after gummy bears realized the virtues of swapping heads, they began to wonder about swapping sides of their bodies. Combine the left side of a left-handed gummy and the right side of a right-handed gummy and it's an ambidextrous gummy virtuoso! The sad side effect is when the remaindered non-dominant halves are combined. They keep starting and stopping and mostly just fidget about. We don't like to talk about them too much.

Step 6: Heart Transplants

For some reason, the gummies decided that they wanted heart transplants, just like humans. If they were already swapping heads, then why not hearts? Surgeons weren't entirely sure at first where the heart of the gummy truly is. To be honest, they still aren't. Not wanting to give up on a willing, and paying, patient, surgeons went ahead with daring new techniques of driving metal tubes into gummy chests to extract hearts. Or they could just be extracting the bit of gummy where the heart could be. With the gummy heart out, it's a simple matter of performing a similar operation with another gummy and making the switch. Here you can see a trio of bears who made a series of swaps.

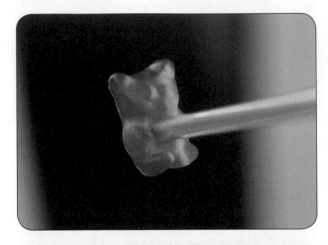

Step 7: Brain Transplants

Once the hearts had been moved about, it was just a matter of time before more drastic measures were taken. While the heads could be swapped, some bears found the process a little crude and wanted to simply swap the brains and keep the rest of the head. Here you can see pictures from one of the earliest brain transplants. The brain has a little bit of exposure to the outside, but as long as the bear doesn't think too hard it will be okay.

Step 8: Two Bodies Are Better than One

Soon after the successful split personality surgeries took the gummy world by storm, gummies wanted to try having two bodies connected, but no reputable surgeon would take part in it. This picture below shows the sad result of a back alley surgery. Notice the crude cuts and the overhanging bit of green gummy flesh. It's sad, really. The bit of hair is the most insulting part of all.

Step 9: Three Heads Are Better than One

A rough life can lead to gummy bears making terrible decisions. After hocking their original bodies, these three heads ended up sharing one weakling body.

Step 10: Any Side Up

The wealthier gummy bears can afford to buy spare parts from other bears down on their luck. This green bear has managed to amass an incredible collection of bodies from some of the finest athletes in the land. The look may be quite alien to our culture, but this little fella can do cartwheels for days.

Step 11: Freakish Experiments Gone Amuck

Sometimes the gummy bears lose all perspective and get hooked on connecting with other bears. This shocking photo shows what happens when this all goes too far. They may look happy, but this mass of gummy flesh can never stand on its own. It mostly just wiggles a bit. You can sometimes hear them crying out at night. "Join us!" they will say. "We are so sweet and sticky. Stiiiiiiicky!"

Step 12: The Land of the Lost Gummi

After a while, gummy surgeons tired of their efforts on gummy bears. They were starting to get into some freaky stuff, and the whole pile of gummy thing was getting tiresome. They thought that they should be doing more good in the world by bringing their skills to those who could not afford them. So they turned to the gummy dinosaurs. And then they put one on top of the other, for some reason. Poor bugger could barely move, and whichever one was on the bottom kept getting drooled on by the other.

Step 13: Tri-bear-atops

The surgeons' sick tendencies couldn't be held in check forever. Not even a few days or hours for that matter. No, before you knew it, the surgeons had started applying cheap bear bodies to the dinosaurs. Oddly enough, this somehow made the dinosaur more attractive in the wild, and its ability to mate improved dramatically.

Step 14: Bear Mohawk

Soon other dinosaurs came up to the surgeons and demanded bear parts. The surgeons were getting tired of being poked with gummy horns and relented. "Just this once!" they said. "Put the rest of the bear heads on your head and leave us alone!" So they did. And the dinosaurs were happy for the time being. But time will pass, and the demand for gummy surgeries will only increase and become more twisted.

Bacon Roses

By kaptaink_cg
(http://www.instructables.com/id/
Bacon-Roses/)

Flowers make a nice gift for the friend that needs a smile or for that special someone in your life. Roses are even better. But sometimes even roses don't cut it. Sometimes you need something a little less cliché and cute, something . . . extraordinary. Sometimes, you need bacon.

Step 1: Materials
- bacon—I like to use one regular pack and one thick-cut pack
- rose stems
- glass vase
- mini muffin pan
- broiler pan
- drill with bit (I used an 1/8" bit, but any similar size will work)
- gravel or marbles for vase (not shown)

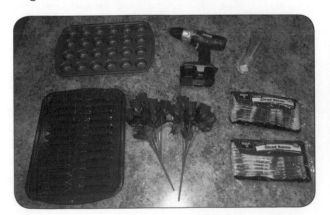

Step 2: Preparing the Pans
Drill holes in the bottom of the muffin pan. This will allow the grease to drain when cooking the bacon. Place the muffin pan on top of the broiler pan.

Step 3: Prepare the Rose Buds
Preheat the oven to 375° F. Open the bacon and begin tightly rolling the roses, one piece at a time. Start with the widest end of the bacon, with the fat edge down. I like to use a combination of thick and thin bacon so I end up with a variety of rose shapes. Place all of the bacon in the muffin pans, pushing down slightly to "seat" them. The bottoms will flare out a bit. Place in the oven and cook for 30–40 minutes. Check on them occasionally. Sometimes you will have to lift the roses so the grease will drain out of the pan.

Step 4: Prepare the Rose Stems

While waiting for the buds to cook you can start working on the stems. I found the stems that work best can be purchased at Walmart for under a dollar per bunch of seven. Pull all of the roses off from the stems. Pull the green backing off from the rose and then separate it into individual parts. Discard the petals and center red piece. Reassemble the remaining green parts as shown. Put the green piece back on the stem, but force it down so that roughly 1" of the stem protrudes. I like to tape the stems together at this point, but this is optional. Put the stems in your vase and fill with gravel or marbles to hold them in place.

Step 5: Assemble and Present!

When the bacon buds are done, remove from the oven and place on paper towel to cool. You'll now have a variety of rose buds to choose from. Pick your favorites and slide them onto the protruding stems. Arrange the roses to your liking and then present the aromatic bouquet to your favorite bacon fanatic!

89

Still-in-the-Shell Scrambled Eggs

By ATTILAtheHUNgry
(http://www.instructables.com/id/
Scrambled-Eggs-still-in-the-Shell-/)

Notice how the egg under that shell is a delicious shade of yellow rather than the typical white? In Japan this is called a golden egg. That's a nice name, but a more descriptive one would be "Scrambled egg still in the shell". This is a simple egg trick my Sensei told me about. It's easy and fun and makes a tasty hard-boiled treat.

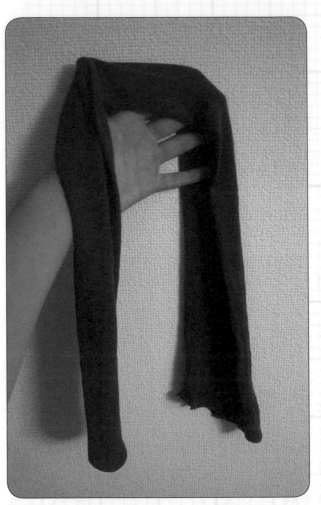

Step 1: Getting Started
All you need to make a golden egg is:
- a raw egg
- one leg cut from a pair of stockings with a low level of stretchiness

Slip the egg into the stocking leg and place it halfway between the toe and the opening.

Step 2: Scramble Time
Now we scramble! Grab the ends of the stocking, one in each hand, with the egg suspended in the middle. Begin to twist the stocking around the egg, about 20 to 25 twists. When it is fully twisted, pull the ends of the stocking apart quickly. The stocking should untwist itself, spinning the egg rapidly. Repeat about 10 times.

If you are letting the kids help, you may be concerned about handing them what are essentially flails made of stockings and raw egg. I don't blame you. But have no fear! Simply put each egg in a Ziploc bag before you put it in the stocking. Now if they smack an egg on a table top (or their sibling's head), there'll be no mess to clean up (only hurt feelings).

Step 3: Is It Golden Yet?
To check if your egg is properly scrambled, go to a dark room and shine a flashlight through your egg. An unscrambled egg will appear bright and yellow, and you may even see a shadow inside cast by the still intact yolk. A properly scrambled egg will be a much darker red color, since the yolk is now mixed with the albumen.

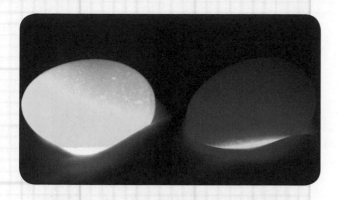

Step 4: Boil and Bubble

Of course, now that your egg is scrambled in the shell, you can cook it any way you desire. I like to hard boil them, myself.

Put the eggs in a pot of lukewarm water until they are just covered. Heat. Once the water reaches a rolling boil set a timer for six minutes. When the timer rings, turn off the heat and soak in cold water to stop the cooking (and keep your hands safe).

Hard-boiled golden eggs are harder to peel than regular hard-boiled eggs. For whatever reason, the scrambled egg grabs to the shell a bit more than usual and can make for an ugly peeled egg. (My first four eggs were hideous. Tasty, but hideous.) To solve this problem, and to produce the not-ugly egg you see in this Instructable, I used the back of a spoon to gently break the shell into small pieces, and then peeled it while submerged in a pot of cold water. It helped a lot.

Step 5: Now what?

Now that you can make golden eggs, what can you do with them? Well, just eat it. Hard-boiled golden eggs taste good by themselves, but a little

sprinkle of salt never goes amiss. Or you can chop them up and throw them over a salad for some delicious protein.

Mix it into a batch of regular boiled eggs. Like the old English tradition of hiding a coin in the pudding, whoever gets the golden egg gets good luck for the week. If it's Easter eggs we're talking about, then the golden egg can grant good luck for the whole year. This throws a whole new twist into the Easter egg hunt tradition.

Put a raw scrambled egg back in the carton as a harmless prank. The next time someone goes to make a sunny-side up they'll get a scrambled surprise.

Hollow it out. Traditionally when hollowing out eggs you must break up the yolk with a long needle before it can be blown out. Golden eggs already have scrambled yolks, so just poke two tiny holes and blow it all out.

Like I said, I usually just eat them. But I'm sure you creative folks can think of more uses for golden eggs. Go nuts!

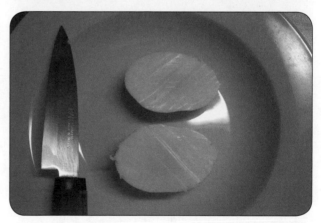

These only require two ingredients—bacon and potatoes. The simplicity is what makes them magical. They're a great snack and would be the perfect unexpected addition to a barbecue or simple sandwich dinner. They're crispy and surprisingly light, with a nice smoky bacon flavor. It's also a super way to use up what's left when you're done devouring your freshly cooked bacon!

Step 1: Ingredients and Supplies
- bacon
- potatoes
- sea salt (optional)
- knife and cutting board
- frying pan
- paper towels
- tongs and other standard kitchen supplies

Step 2: Fry the Bacon
Cook up the bacon. You won't need it, so discard it (by which, of course, I mean eat it!) The idea here is to keep as much grease in the pan as possible.

Step 3: Slice the Potatoes
You're looking for a slice that's a bit thicker than a sheet of paper. Not the thinnest slice you can make, but close to it. Peel them first if that's your preference, and by all means use your mandolin slicer if you have

one. One pound of bacon made more than enough grease to fry three potatoes.

Step 4: Fry the Potatoes
Place one layer of potatoes in the pan and fry them. You want them lightly browned. The darker they get the more likely they are to go from tasting bacony to tasting burned.

Step 5: Drain and Serve!
Drain them on a paper towel and sprinkle lightly with sea salt if you would like. Do this while they're fresh from the pan. Keep frying and draining, pretty much until you decide to stop. Serve them in a bowl, or individual small bowls if you're fancy like that!

Bonus flavor options:

Bacon Onion: Before frying the potatoes fry up a diced onion in the grease then scoop it out. The onion infuses the bacon grease with flavor.

Bacon Parmesan: As soon as you remove the chips from the bacon grease, sprinkle them with grated parmesan (the dry kind from a round can).

Flavored Bacon: Different types of bacon come with different flavor profiles—applewood, hickory, etc. Each will give you a different chip flavor.

Chicken 'n Waffles on a Stick

By Imnopeas
(http://www.instructables.com/id/
Chicken-N-Waffles-on-a-Stick/)

It's not clear who invented the first chicken and waffles, but Los Angeles institution Roscoe's opened a restaurant in the '70s that made the dish famous. When you order Roscoe's famous dish you get a waffle drowned in maple syrup topped with a piece of crispy fried chicken. The way you eat it is with knife and fork, cutting through the entire stack, making sure you get a little of everything in each bite.

To my standard, the Roscoe's version is slightly flawed because you can't eat it on the go, so I applied a little American ingenuity and, behold, Chicken 'n Waffles on a Stick were born.

This recipe will satisfy all your food cravings in one bite. It's sweet, spicy, savory, and definitely food-truck worthy.

Step 1: Ingredients and Tools
• 1 bag Trader Joe's Mandarin Orange Chicken (This recipe uses the chicken only. Discard or save the sauce packet for another meal.) You can also use your favorite fried chicken recipe.
• 2 cups flour
• 2 tablespoons sugar
• 1 tablespoon baking powder
• 1 teaspoon salt
• 1 3/4 cups buttermilk
• 1/3 cup vegetable oil
• 2 eggs
• carnival corn dog maker
• Sticks
   The waffle recipe is adapted from epicurious.

Step 2: Mix Ingredients
Combine the flour, sugar, baking powder, and salt in a mixing bowl. Whisk the buttermilk, vegetable oil, and eggs together well. Gradually pour the milk mixture into the dry mixture. Stir until the mixture is almost blended. There will be a few lumps in the batter.

Step 3: Pre-heat the Chicken
Place the chicken in a sauté pan with 1/4 cup canola oil. Heat on medium or medium-low heat for 5–6 minutes. You don't want to cook the chicken all the way through because it will dry out. The chicken will thoroughly heat when placed in the corn dog maker.

color of the waffle. If they aren't golden brown, close the machine and wait an additional 2 minutes. Repeat until you achieve desired color on waffle. Trim the edges off the waffle.

Serve immediately with syrup. Enjoy!

Step 4: Make the Chicken 'n Waffles on a Stick:

Spray the machine with cooking spray and pre-heat. You can also brush the machine with oil to prevent sticking. Use a silicone brush if you choose this method. You may have to trim some of the edges off the chicken so that they fit into the corn dog maker. Place three or four pieces of chicken onto each stick.

Once the machine is pre-heated, use a spoon or squeeze bottle to fill two of the slots with waffle batter. I found making two at a time was easiest, but you could try making four. Next, place the skewered chicken sticks on top of the waffle batter and squeeze a little extra batter on top so that none of the chicken is showing.

Close the machine and wait until the green light indicates they are ready. It takes around 3–5 minutes to get the first batch of waffles golden brown. You can open the top of the machine and check on the

Jalapeno Popper Crescent Rolls

By elewis03

(http://www.instructables.com/id/
Jalapeno-popper-crescent-rolls/)

I absolutely love making these things—they're seriously delicious. They are extremely easy to make and they are the perfect side dish. We like to eat them with spaghetti.

Step 1: What You'll Need:
- 8 crescent rolls
- 4 jalapenos
- cream cheese
- shredded cheese

Step 2: Chopping Jalapenos
First you need to cut your jalapenos into quarters. You can choose to slice up a few extra if you would like them for garnish.

Step 3: Adding the Ingredients
Now pop open your crescent rolls. (Fun fact, I'm terrified of popping those cans open! My boyfriend has to do it for me every time.) Spread the cream cheese onto the top part of the crescents, place two jalapeno slices over the cream cheese, and sprinkle some shredded cheese on top of it all.

Step 4: Bake
Roll it up and place on an ungreased baking sheet. Bake for 10–12 minutes or until lightly browned. Sprinkle more cheese on top if desired. Eat up!

Fried pickles: food of the drunk, the Southern, and the fantastic. They're one of my absolute favorite terrible for-me foods. If you've never had them, you might be questioning my taste right now, but you should really give them a try! You won't regret it.

Fried pickles make a great appetizer for a group—they're perfect with barbeque! They're also really simple to make, so you get more time eating and less time cooking. And you probably have all the ingredients on hand.

I make my fried pickles with a little cornmeal in the batter because that's how I've always had them, but feel free to change up the base recipe as you like!

Step 2: Prep the Ingredients

Set your deep fryer to 350° F or get a good amount of oil (at least 3–4 cups) heating over medium heat on the stove.

Next, drain the pickles! Then beat the eggs and milk together until no chunks of egg remain. You can add a little hot sauce to this if you like!

Add your seasonings to the flour/cornmeal. I normally add a couple teaspoons of my primary flavoring and a pinch of dill. Mix the dry ingredients with a fork and taste test to make sure you've added enough seasoning. Keep adding until you can taste the spices!

Step 1: What You'll Need:
- pickles of your choice—spears or slices
- 3/4 cup flour (all purpose is best)
- 1/4 cup yellow cornmeal
- 2 eggs
- 1 cup milk
- seasonings of choice (I did Tony's, black pepper, and dill—if you don't use Tony's you'll want to add salt)
- vegetable/canola/peanut oil for frying

I prefer thinner slices of pickle, but spears are excellent too. You might want to double bread them.

Step 3: Battering!

Plop the pickles in the milk/egg mix and let them hang out while the oil heats up all the way. Then place them in the flour and mix them around until they're coated very well. At this point they're ready to fry, but if you'd like a thicker batter dip them back in the milk and then back in the flour.

Pull them out and let them drain on paper towels. If you didn't salt your breading, you'll want to salt the pickles now before they cool.

Enjoy!

Step 4: Frying!

Shake off the excess flour and drop the pickles gently into the hot oil. Make sure not to crowd the pot, and fry in batches! Fry them until golden brown—3 to 5 minutes is perfect in most cases. Stir them around so they cook evenly.

Gummi Shot Glasses

By shesparticular
(http://www.instructables.com/id/Edible-
Shot-Glasses/)

It's always the same . . . you get drunk, you get hungry. Wouldn't it be great to have a shot glass you could snarf down as soon as it was empty?

Gummi shot glasses are shown here, but the same idea could be applied to chocolate with or without various jams as filling, or other candies (gummy-types are recommended). You can also use this mold/tray to make awesome chocolate cake shots.

Note: If you're underage and feel like getting drunk, don't—if you do, don't blame me.

Also note: The mold used here is from thinkgeek.com. It's intended for making ice shot glasses which are awesome, but not as tasty as gummies.

And one more note: If your finished shot glasses are a little on the sticky side, try a (very) light dusting of corn starch, and make sure to keep them cool if you can. Both will help cut down on the stickiness factor.

Step 1: What You'll Need
• Nifty Fred silicone shot glass mold available from thinkgeek.com
• bowl for melting gummies (microwave safe, please)
• 16 ounces gummy worms (or bears)

Step 2: Gummi Shots!
Heat your gummies in a microwave-safe dish for about 1 minute and 20 seconds or until liquefied (if you don't want brownish shot glasses, make sure to separate the red and orange from the green and yellow worms as shown here). Pour or spoon into the mold and tap on the counter to level it (make sure to fill to the top, otherwise your shots won't have solid bases and will leak). Pop into the freezer for about 1½ hours, or until the gummies have set.

hard, it's pretty hard to rip the gummy shot, but it can get a little distorted. Store in a small container in the freezer until you want to use them (this will help them to not get damaged and to stay solid). Fill with liquor of your choice. Make a toast and enjoy!

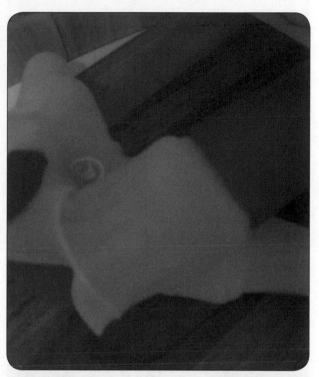

Step 3: Finishing Up

To remove the gummy shots from the mold, you'll need to basically invert the silicone of each section (as shown). Don't worry about tugging or pulling too

Show off your love for things retro and geeky with an edible armada of space invaders. This Instructable will take you through the steps of making a simple chocolate candy using a silicon mold. For Christmas last year, my better half surprised me with a spunky turquoise ice tray produced by ironic home goods designer FRED, inspired by the Taito arcade classic that we know and love: Space Invaders! After the novelty and enjoyment of freezing water, juices, coffee, and regular old liquids wore off, I set my sights on putting this gift to a higher purpose: Chocolate. That's right, after a few test runs and brushing up on some elementary chocolate-making theory, I was able to pull off in time for Valentine's day the perfect display of geek love—a chocolate 8-bit sprite.

Step 1: Tools and Ingredients

The Mold:

First and foremost, one needs to acquire a mold. I opted to use the Ice Invaders ice tray, but really any flexible silicone mold/tray could be used to shape chocolate. You could even use a clear plastic candy mold, but in my opinion silicone is more durable and easier to work with.

If you do plan on going the Space Invader route, you could try to find one locally or online. We bought ours in Japan, but I have seen them available on Amazon. The downside of these is that they are on the small side, so if you're going to make lots of chocolates you might need to pick up more than one to speed things along (there are 24 molds in each tray). They don't match the original Space Invaders sprite to the pixel, but they do get the point across rather well.

The Ingredients:

- Chocolate. I went with a Japanese dark chocolate that was available, but any type will work. Milk, dark, white—go with your personal preference. Remember, better quality chocolates will make for a better tasting Space Invader. Pictured are two 58 gram chocolate bars (roughly 2oz each). To fill the entire mold I would recommend at least three bars of chocolate, and if you're making solid chocolates, possibly four (8oz or 232 g)

- Filling. For the sake of simplicity I went with solid dry ingredients: almonds and dried blueberries. If you were to use a crème filling, caramel, cordial, or a truffle ganache, you would need to use a different method (painting a shell and so on). Since this is my first attempt at confectionery, I thought the Invaders would be too fragile to hold up as a shell. I decided to stick with fillings that would provide a strong structural center. Blending in flavorings, such as vanilla, sea salt, and chili pepper, works well, too. Be creative and adventurous.

The Tools:

Here you have plenty of freedom to improvise, but this is what I had to work with:

- cutting board (flexibility is a plus)
- sharp kitchen knife
- silicone spatula (rubber is fine, too)
- squeeze bottle (the thinner the spout the better) or pastry bag.
- stirrer (I used some disposable chopsticks)
- microwave (or double boiler) and a microwave-safe bowl (ceramic is a plus as it retains heat well)

If you have one on hand, an electric kitchen thermometer is helpful, but not really necessary.

Now that you have all of the items assembled, go find a cool, dry space in your kitchen to get to work.

Step 2: Make 'Em Melt

The first order of action is to render those chocolate bars down to a primordial soup of sugar, cocoa solids, and cocoa butter.

Shaving:

To get things started, take your knife and cutting board and begin to gently shave the chocolate bars down into flakes and chunks. Breaking the chocolate down to smaller pieces will allow it to melt more evenly and will shorten the time needed to heat it. Go slowly and don't chop or slice the chocolate; rather, push down slowly with your weight and it should come off in flakes and chunks. Run your knife through the flakes if you find they're too chunky and then transfer to a microwave-safe bowl. When you're about 2/3 of the way through with the chocolate, set aside the rest for later.

Microwaving:

Microwave the shaved chocolate on high in 30 second blasts, stirring well in between each interval so that the chocolate heats evenly. If you microwave it at longer intervals the chocolate may overheat and start to burn—be patient and things will go smoothly.

Once the chocolate gets to the point where it is melted but still chunky, continue at 15 second intervals, mixing well in between. As soon as the chocolate becomes smooth and chocolate-saucy looking you're done. You can check by dabbing a bit on your skin and seeing if it's warm (not hot) to the touch—we're looking at something around 105° F or 41°C, which is a little bit above body temperature.

Alternatively, you could do all of this in a double boiler, but if you were the type of person to own a double boiler you wouldn't need to read this Instructable, now would you?

Step 3: Watch Your Temper

At this stage we have melted chocolate, a state in which the crystalline structure (surprise! chocolate crystals!) of fat and sugar that makes chocolate so damn delectable has broken apart and rearranged itself. At this point we temper the chocolate, a process that ensures the molten chocolate hardens and sets correctly, improving the texture and melting point of the finished chocolate.

To achieve this, I opted to use a method referred to as seeding. To seed chocolate, you take unmelted chocolate to your warm, melty chocolate and have them co-mingle. Remember that extra chunk I asked you to hang onto? Add that bit into the bowl and stir it in until it is fully incorporated. Continue stirring slowly. Once the chocolate starts to thicken up a little bit and feels tepid to the touch, you are at the temperature where tempering occurs (88°–93° F depending on the chocolate, just a bit below body temperature).

The aim is to keep the chocolate at this temperature while stirring it around so that the proper crystals can form. This is difficult to do accurately without a thermometer, so I would just eyeball it and keep stirring; if the temperature drops and the chocolate becomes too thick, give it 5 seconds or so in the microwave to warm it up a bit.

In simple terms: melt chocolate, add chocolate, stir, not too hot, not too cold.

Step 4: The First Layer

Having tempered your chocolate, you can now begin to fill the molds. Make sure that the silicone mold is clean and bone-dry; chocolate and water are not friends.

First, scrape the chocolate out of the bowl into the squeeze bottle with the spatula. Work quickly and make sure that the temperature doesn't drop too much. Then, squeeze a small dollop of chocolate in each mold.

Lastly, lift the tray with your finger and let it lightly fall back to the counter so that the chocolate spreads into the cracks or the mold. Continue tapping the tray in this fashion until the bottom of the tray is covered in an even layer. Pull at the edges of the tray to stretch the silicone so that the chocolate can get into all of the corners of the mold. The legs and antennae are the most difficult parts to get filled, so if it's not working out use a toothpick to nudge chocolate in there.

If your chocolate starts to get too thick, a quick five-second burst in the microwave should do the trick.

Step 5: Go and Stuff It!

Now is the time to add your fillings. Again, work quickly to keep the chocolate from seizing up too soon. Place each filling into the mold cavity on top of the layer of chocolate, which is at the bottom. Make sure that the ingredients are small enough to fit in the mold without touching the sides or sticking too far above the tray, otherwise you won't get full coverage throughout the entire mold, and you'll end up with a mutant Invader (which is cool if that's your angle). Give it a few more taps and pokes so that the filling sinks into the center of the mold.

If you were to do a crème filling, you would take a "decorator's" brush and paint the floor and walls of the mold with tempered chocolate, chill them, repeat, and then fill the chocolate shells with your filling. I'd fill the legs and antennae with solid chocolate though, as these are the most fragile parts.

Step 6: Topping Off

Now that each mold has been filled, top off the rest of the mold with the remaining tempered chocolate. This is the messiest part, so my approach was to add a second dollop on top of the filling and then continue tapping and stretching the tray until the chocolate evened out. Keep an eye on the amount of chocolate as well—you want to have it level or slightly under the top of the tray. Once it spills over the top of the molds the Invader will start to look a bit unfinished and messy.

Continue this tapping process, while keeping the chocolate at temperature, until air bubbles stop forming on the surface of the chocolate in the mold. Lastly, wipe the surface of the tray so the edges of the mold are clear of excess chocolate.

Tip: That messy squeeze bottle can now be cleaned by pouring hot milk into it, giving it a few shakes, and squeezing out a rich hot chocolate.

Step 7: Chill Time

Now that the molds are filled and the chocolate is evenly spread and free of bubbles, park that tray in the fridge or freezer and go relax. Chocolate in the fridge? Don't freak out. It'll only be in there for about 5–10 minutes until they set up and harden.

If you have a cool area in your kitchen you can also cool the chocolates on the counter top. Either method will produce good end results. However, don't leave the chocolates in the fridge for too long or else oil will bead up at the surface and give the backs of your chocolate a sweaty appearance. (...and there's nothing appetizing about sweaty backs, am I right?)

Step 8: Breaking the Mold

Once the chocolate has hardened you can liberate your Invaders from the tray and unleash them on an unsuspecting planet. To do so, simply pull on the edges of the tray at each row and column to release the chocolate from the sides of the mold. Then gently push directly up on the bottom of the mold so that the chocolate is pushed straight out of the mold. Trying to pry them out at an angle will most likely result in a broken leg and a sorry looking Invader. However, the great thing about silicone is how stretchy and bendy it is, so with a little care they should pop right out.

Step 9: Commence the Invasion

Now that you have a finished set of Invaders you can send them out to bombard your Valentine with sweet, geeky love. Or you can eat them by yourself while playing Xbox Live. (tastes better that way!) For plating, arranging them face up in regular Space Invaders gameplay fashion is classic. For gifting, reusing boxes from commercial chocolates do the trick very nicely.

Apple Pie Bites on a Stick

By silverrock
(http://www.instructables.com/id/Apple-Pie-Bites-on-a-Stick/)

I'm all about the comfort food, and I have a crazy sweet tooth. So, naturally, I knew I'd have to make a dessert on a stick . . . and what's more comforting than a nice bite of apple pie?

Step 1: Ingredients
Main Ingredients:
- 1 large red delicious apple, finely chopped
- 1 tablespoon butter
- 1/8 cup brown sugar, packed
- 1 teaspoon corn starch
- 1/2 teaspoon cinnamon
- 1/4 teaspoon nutmeg
- 1/4 teaspoon cloves or all-spice
- 2 tablespoons cream cheese
- 1 package of refrigerated crescent roll pastry (I.e., Pillsbury)

Topping:
- 1 tablespoon melted butter
- 1/2 teaspoon cinnamon

- 3 tablespoons granulated sugar
- 1 tablespoon brown sugar

Icing Drizzle:
- 1/2 cup confectioner's sugar
- 2 teaspoon water or milk

Step 2: The Filling
1. Melt butter in a heavy-bottomed sauce pan over medium heat.
2. Once butter is melted, add in brown sugar, corn starch, and the spices. Mix well, until thoroughly combined.
3. Add the chopped apple to the sauce pan and mix well. Continue cooking over medium heat (keeping mixture on a low simmer) until the apples are tender, roughly 5–6 minutes.
4. Remove from heat and allow to cool.
5. Work on preparing your pastry for the filling.

Step 3: The Pastry
1. Remove the crescent roll dough from the packaging. With a sharp knife, slice dough log into 10 pieces of equal size.
2. Dust your work surface with flour and, one dough section at a time, roll pieces into a flat disc. (Note: When rolling into a disc, ensure that the center of the disc is thicker than the perimeter – as you do not want the perimeter to be "bulky" once you begin forming the apple pie bites).
3. Once all dough sections are rolled out, prepare to begin assembling the pie bites.

Step 4: The Assembly
1. Spread a thin layer of softened cream cheese onto a dough disc and place a heaping teaspoon of your filling into the center of the dough disc.
2. Gather up the edges. Wetting your fingertips may help the dough edges gather and stay together more easily.
3. Place on a greased baking sheet and repeat steps 1 and 2 with the remainder of the dough discs.

Step 6: Presentation

Completely optional, but adding a nice touch to the cute apple pie dessert is the icing drizzle.

1. Add water, 1 tablespoon at a time, to the confectioner's sugar. Mix well, until a thick paste forms.
2. Drizzle icing over the top of the cooled apple pie bites.
3. Skewer the pie bites and serve.
   (Note: Best if served on the same day as baked)

Step 5: The Finishing Touches and the Bake

1. Set oven to 350° F.
2. Prepare topping by melting 1 tablespoon butter and setting it aside. In a separate bowl, combine sugars and cinnamon.
3. Using a pastry brush, brush the tops of the assembled apple pie bites with the melted butter.
4. Dip the tops of the apple pie bites in the cinnamon and sugar mixture; place pie bites back on prepared baking sheet.
5. Bake for 15–17 minutes, or until the pie bites are golden brown.
6. Remove from oven and set on cooling rack, allowing the pie bites to cool completely.

Valentine's Day is one of my favorite holidays. This tutorial will show how to make jello using fruit juice and will also show you how to make heart designs in bananas. It will also show you how to use jello to fill a banana. These are meant to be eaten the first day for best appearance. Let's get started!

Step 1: Ingredients and Tools

You should plan on using more bananas than you want to make because there is a trick to getting it right. I will try and walk you through my experiments so you won't make the same mistakes that I did. I used store-bought flavored Jell-O for the jello-filled banana because it worked better.

Ingredients:
- fruit juice (I am not sure about pineapple juice though)
- Knox unflavored gelatin or Agar Agar.
- greenish firm Bananas
- lemon juice, approximately 2 tablespoons, used to help prevent browning on the bananas
- sweetener if desired

Tools:
- knife
- straw
- funnel, ladle, or spoon
- tiny heart-shaped cookie cutter
- toothpick is helpful
- ribbon
- a bowl or something to prop the banana up, as well as the banana end, as shown in the pictures.

I made some banana jello using apple juice, Knox unflavored gelatin, and the banana. I blended the juice together with the banana and followed the recipe. It tasted very good. The color was off, unfortunately, so I did not use it. I thought it would be awesome to make a banana-jello-filled banana! It tasted just like a banana only it had a different texture.

Step 2: Make Jello
Homemade jello:
- 2 envelopes Knox unflavored gelatin
- 1/2 cup cold fruit juice
- 1 1/2 cups fruit juice, heated until boiling
- 1 tablespoon sugar or sweetener if desired. I did not use sweetener because I thought it was sweet enough.

Pour cold juice into a bowl. Stir in gelatin until dissolved. Let set one minute. Add hot juice and stir until dissolved.

If you are going to make the jello-filled banana I would add 1 extra package of Knox gelatin, or if using regular jello use 1/2 the amount of water, as if you were making Jello Jigglers. My juice was not cold, so I put mine in a Ziploc bag and placed it in the freezer, and it did not take very long to chill.

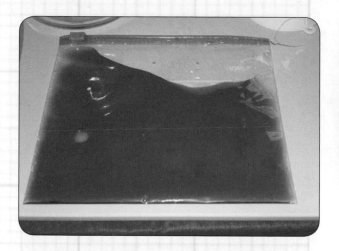

Step 4: Filling the Banana Hearts with Jello

Place the banana and the banana end into a dish to prop up the banana sections. Fill the heart shapes with jello using a ladle or spoon. Chill. When the short end is firm, dab it slightly with water and place it back on the banana, matching it to the banana section, and chill again until very firm. Tie a ribbon around it to make it pretty!

Step 3: Shaping the Banana Hearts

Wash the bananas. Cut the stem tip. Remove about two inches from the end (reserving the cut-off piece). Gently push the cookie cutter into the end piece. Carefully remove the heart. Scoop out the excess banana using a knife and straw. Re-shape the heart if necessary using the cookie cutter. Make a heart shape in the remaining banana section and scoop out excess banana and re-shape if needed. Dab the ends with lemon juice to prevent browning.

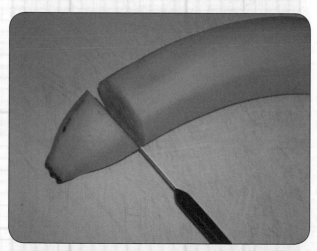

Step 5: Banana and Jello

This banana is much more difficult to make. I tried filling the entire banana with the banana jello, but it did not work because the banana peel was too limber to mold the correct shape. So I decided to remove 1/2 of the banana and fill the other half with jello. It worked much better. It is tricky not to break through the skin. It takes patience and probably a few ruined bananas, but it is worth the effort. Just take it slow and as you are using the straw do not apply too much pressure. The good news is, if you break the banana skin you can freeze the banana and make smoothies or banana bread at a later time. I did not get a picture of removing the banana with the straw using this style of banana, but I did get a picture of another banana that I tried to make.

Method:

Wash the banana. Clean up the stem as shown. Remove the end of the banana like the heart banana in step 3. Make a heart shape in the end as shown in the directions in step 3. Using the knife, carefully trim around the inside of the banana, as shown. Cut a cross shape on the banana using the knife. Remove about 1/4 to 1/2 of the banana's insides as shown, using the knife and straw. Dab the banana ends and the inside with lemon juice to prevent browning. Fill the banana with jello. Place the banana in a container that will hold it upright so the jello does not spill. Place the dish in the refrigerator until firm. When the end of the banana is firm, slightly wet the jello and place it on the banana as shown or remove the peel and then attach it. Chill until very firm. Tie a ribbon around it if desired.

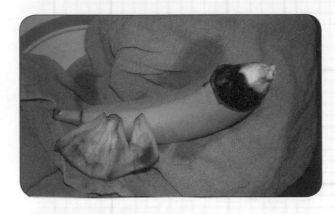

Step 6: Final Thoughts

You will notice the banana peel turned dark. I waited until the next afternoon to take pictures, and it is better to eat the banana the first day.

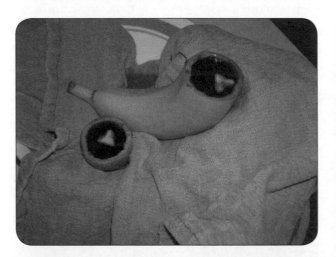

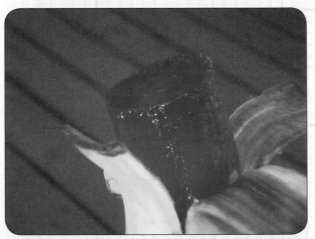

Popcorn Popper–Roasted Coffee Beans

By fungus amungus
(http://www.instructables.com/id/
Roast-your-own-coffee-with-a-
popcorn-popper/)

Enjoy delicious coffee with beans that you've roasted all by yourself. All you need is the right kind of cheap popcorn popper and some raw beans. It's really easy and totally worth it. If you grind your own beans at home and look forward to that first hit of caffeine in the morning, then this is for you. With just a bit of effort you'll be enjoying it so much more.

Warning: Doing this and getting good at it has the potential to turn you into a coffee snob who complains that coffee shops are burning their beans. Just keep it to yourself because few other people will care, okay?

Step 1: What You Need—The Basics

The core element here is the air popcorn popper. Mine is the Toastess TCP-713, but there are many others that work as well. The key is to get one that has its air vents on the side of the main chamber and a solid bottom.

If you're willing to trek through some thrift stores you might be able to find one of these for $5 or so. Otherwise, it's not too bad to get a new one for under $30. Then pick up some raw beans, which range from $6 to $8 per pound. The last thing you'll need is a couple of metal bowls or, even better, colanders. These will be used to catch the chaff and cool off the beans.

Step 2: What You Need—A Little Fancier

If you want to have more insight into the process you can install a thermometer in the lid. Drill a hole into the top, insert a flattened tee nut, and insert the thermometer. You'll want a thermometer that can go up to at least 450° F, but 500° F would be even better.

Step 3: Let's Go!

Let's roast some coffee! Fill the popper up to the max fill line with the raw beans and turn it on.

That's it; your beans are now heating up and moving in circles. After a couple minutes small pieces of chaff will start coming off of the beans. If this doesn't bother you (maybe you have a sawdust floor?), then just watch it fly. Or you can catch it with one of your bowls. Next you'll hear a cracking sound, almost like popcorn popping. Once this has happened you have roasted coffee. How much longer you leave it in for determines just how roasted it gets.

Here's the scale of roasts:
- City (426° F)
- City+ (435° F)
- Full City (444° F)
- Full City + (454° F— second crack happening)
- Vienna (465° F)
- French Roast (474° F)
- Fully Carbonized (486° F)
- Imminent Fire (497° F)

I highly recommend the City+ level of roasting. The flavors stand out and you can really tell the differences between beans. You can also see that the popular French Roast is essentially the last stop before death. A lot of the flavors are gone and it's very bitter.

Back to the roasting! When you're ready to pull the beans, turn off the popper, carefully take off the plastic lid (it's hot!) and pour the beans into the bowl or colander. Now shake the beans around and around to cool them off as quickly as you can, as they're still roasting.

Step 4: Enjoy

Now you have roasted coffee. Don't get too excited and grind right now, though. The beans will give off gas CO_2 for a little while. Let them sit in a lightly closed container for 12 hours and then seal in an airtight container. I like using old jam jars.

Grind the beans after 24 hours or so. They're good for about five days. Since you can always roast just a little more, this is a great way to enjoy fresh coffee, even if you buy several pounds of raw coffee at a time. Raw coffee is good for 6 to 12 months.

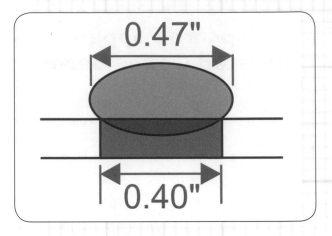

Engraved M&Ms

By JoeGadget
(http://www.instructables.com/id/
Engraved-MMs/)

Personalized candy can make for a fun gift, party favor, or conversation piece. While this Instructable shows how to engrave custom text and images on M&Ms, the same basic technique can be used on a variety of candies. Feel free to experiment with different types of candy to see how well they take to laser engraving.

Step 1: Materials and Equipment
- vector-drawing software (I used CorelDRAW)
- laser cutter (my TechShop has a Trotec Speedy 300)
- 3.5 × 3.5 × 1/8 inch acrylic sheet
- bag of M&Ms

This Instructable assumes some basic familiarity with CorelDRAW and a laser cutter.

Step 2: M&M Dimensions
In order to laser engrave an M&M, we need a way to hold it reasonably flat on the bed of the laser cutter. The cross-section of an M&M has an approximate width of 0.47" and a height of 0.24". We will laser cut a series of holes in a piece of acrylic to hold the M&Ms. We want the holes to be as large as possible (to keep the M&Ms stable), but not so large that they risk falling through. A 0.4" hole seems to work pretty well. Here you can see the cross-section of the M&M compared to the hole diameter.

Step 3: Design the Acrylic Tray
Start by drawing a 0.4" diameter circle. Use the Step and Repeat function to create four more circles spaced 0.6" apart center to center on the horizontal axis. Then use the Step and Repeat function to create four more rows of circles also spaced 0.6" apart center to center on the vertical axis. Finally, draw a 3.5" × 3.5" square enclosing the matrix of circles. This will allow us to engrave 25 M&Ms at a time.

When drawing the circles and square, make sure you set the line color to red and the line width to hairline so that the laser cutter will know you mean to cut the lines rather than engrave them.

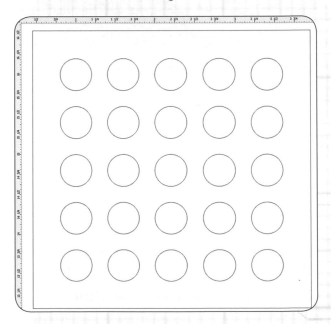

Step 4: Laser Cut the Tray
Cut out the tray on the laser cutter. I found that settings of 100 percent power and 0.7 percent speed worked well for my acrylic. Place a few M&Ms on the tray to make sure that you got all of the dimensions correct.

Acrylic works well for the tray because it is easily cleaned, so there is little worry about contaminating the M&Ms.

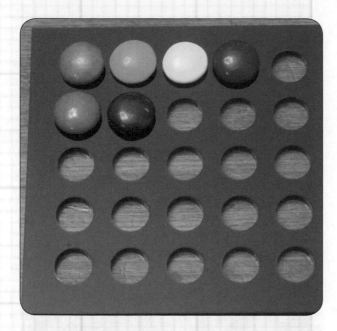

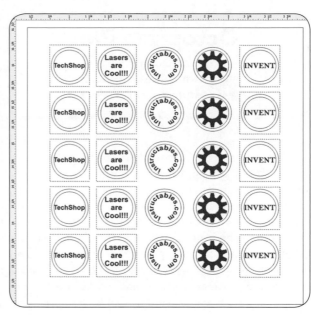

Step 5: Make an Engraving Template

Use the design file for the tray as a starting point (make a copy of the file). Add a red 0.47" diameter circle centered on each of the existing circles. This will let you see where the perimeter of each M&M is located. Now you can place text boxes or clip art over each of the M&M locations. Try to keep away from the very edge of the M&Ms as they may not engrave as well due to the greater curvature. If you are not going to fill all of the spaces with M&Ms, you want to be careful not to damage the tray. Either delete the text/image from empty spaces or keep the size of the engraving to the inner circle (so that the laser will only be attempting to engrave the empty hole).

I use black or grayscale for the text and images so that it is easy to configure the laser for engraving instead of cutting.

Step 6: Engrave the M&Ms

Fill the tray with M&Ms (logo-side down) and place the tray on the laser cutter. I found that settings of 100 percent power and 60 percent speed worked well for the text. You will likely have to experiment a little more with the settings for any grayscale images (depending upon the relative darkness of the images). Configure the laser cutter to engrave black and skip red (that way it won't attempt to re-cut the circles and square outline).

Step 7: Enjoy Your Custom Candy!

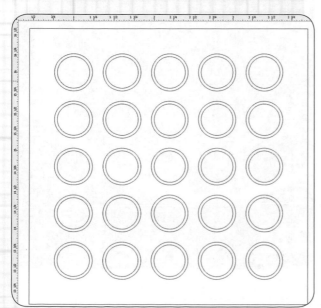

Octopizza Pie

By donedirtcheap
(http://www.instructables.com/id/Octopizza-
Pie-Gruesome-and-Delicious/)

We eat a lot of pizza. Usually that means we take a blank canvas of soft dough and apply our favorite colors—basil, tomato sauce, cheese, meats, veggies—then cut it into triangle-shaped pieces and eat the pointy ends first. But what if, this time, we changed neither the canvas nor the paints but the whole approach to eating pizza? How about dipping bread sticks in a cheesy, saucy pizza? Well, that's pretty good, except that bread sticks are boring. Then inspiration came for the Octopizza, complete with pepperoni suckers.

Step 1: Ingredients

You can use whatever ingredients you like—canned sauce, fancy cheese—as only two things are imperative to this recipe: pepperoni sticks and fresh dough.

For the sauce:
- 1 can tomato sauce (not diced tomatoes, for ease of dipping)
- some oregano, basil, fennel, garlic, onion powder, pepper, and salt
- oil to coax out the flavors

For the cheese:
- wonderful cheese

For the dough:
- 4 cups flour mixed with 1 tablespoon salt and a shot of olive oil
- 2 cups lukewarm water with a tablespoon of dissolved, foamy yeast

Step 2: Preparing the Octopizza

Mix and knead the dough for at least 10 minutes. We want big, muscular tentacles and that means kneading a lot. I like to soften and encourage the herbs in warm olive oil before the tomato sauce shows up and pushes everyone around. I call it coaxing. Try it. It makes a nice sauce and fills the whole house with nostalgia and love.

When the dough has more than doubled in size, cut off a third and use that small bit as the main crust. On an oiled sheet, stretch it out into an 8" round and peak the crust into a high sharp edge. This will keep the sauce in and ensure that the good stuff will go right up to the very cusp. Very dippable.

Cut the remaining dough into eight pieces (or more if you are overrun with offspring) and snake the ends with your palms. Tuck the fat ends under the round crust and spray or brush the tentacles with water or watery egg.

Apply the pepperoni suckers on one side of each tentacle. Pour the good stuff into the center and bake it at 350° F until it's done.

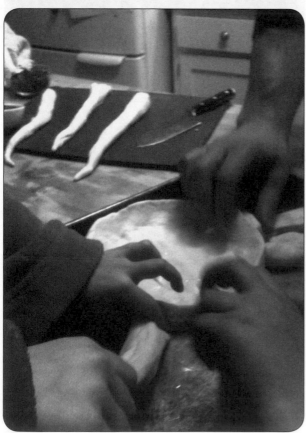

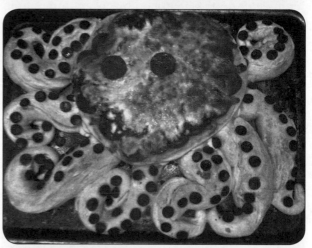

Step 3: Red Hot Lava Covered in Cheese!

Here it is! So crispy and soft and chewy and saucy. Just tear off a tentacle and start scooping pizza. But be careful to let it cool a little first because it is ridiculously hot! I did end up giving the tentacles an additional light salting, like the Olive Garden bread sticks that we all love.

The suckers cooked up cupped and were a lot of fun to talk grossly about. Then, when we had finished all the tentacles, we were left with the sauce and cheese and pepperoni–covered crust, baked golden crispy on the underside, to cut and eat.

I hope you try our unconventional pizza!

Bacon Pixie Sticks

By canida

(http://www.instructables.com/id/Bacon-Pixie-Stix-Pixie-Sticks/)

Bacon Pixie Sticks are the perfect combination of insanely awesome and totally wrong. They are, as advertised, pixie sticks—with bacon. Make these treats for your next social occasion and surprise your friends with a sweet, tart, bacon-flavored boot to the head.

And you don't just have to eat them in pixie stick form—sprinkle this amazing powder on top of fruit, salads, chocolate, ice cream, or anything else in need of a sweet, bacon-citric-acid kick.

Step 1: Tools and Ingredients

Ingredients:
- 150g well-fried thin-sliced bacon (just cook the whole pound and make BLTs with the extra)
- 310g dextrose powder (about 2 cups)
- 40g cornstarch (about 5 teaspoons)
- 25g tapioca maltodextrin
- 7.5g citric acid

Tools:
- food processor
- frying pan and splatter screen
- plate covered in paper towels
- kitchen scale
- paper or plastic straws (optional but totally good for the proper pixie stick look; plastic helps avoid grease issues)
- funnel and poking stick for filling straws (also optional; I made my own from a piece of plastic and a wooden skewer)

Step 2: Fry Bacon

Fry up your bacon until it's quite crisp and dry, though not burned. Be sure you're using thinly-sliced bacon—this is important, as you want to make sure to drive all the water off, and that won't happen with thick-cut bacon.

When done, remove from the pan (or oven, or microwave) and drain on paper towels. Pat dry to remove any excess fat.

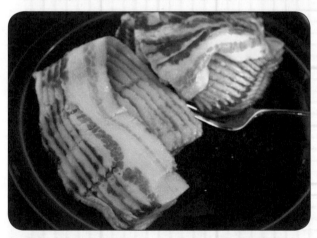

Step 3: Dextrose Powdered Sugar

First, you'll need to make your own dextrose-based powdered sugar. Normal powdered sugar is super-finely-ground sucrose mixed with cornstarch. Dextrose is slightly less sweet and provides a specific type of sweetness that's absolutely necessary for a pixie stick. It's easy enough to make your own.

Make sure your blender (or food processor) is clean and absolutely dry—you're working with powders and don't want to get them soggy and stuck.

Combine 310 grams dextrose powder (roughly 2 cups) with 40 grams of cornstarch (roughly 5 teaspoons) and blend on high for a couple of minutes. This will mix the two ingredients thoroughly and give the dextrose an even finer grind if needed. Remove from the blender and reserve.

Step 4: Combine Ingredients

For this step we'll be using a food processor, as most blenders aren't going to do a clean job with bacon powder. (I hear VitaMix blenders blend most anything.)

Dump the 150 grams of bacon into your food processor and add about half the dextrose powdered sugar.

Pulse until all the powder is incorporated, then add the 7.5 grams of citric acid and the rest of the powdered sugar and pulse some more until the mix looks like slightly clumpy greasy sand.

Sprinkle in 25 grams of tapioca maltodextrin and pulse a bit more. The tapioca maltodextrin will soak up any remaining grease, which is absolutely necessary both for proper mouth-feel and to allow you to pack the powder into straws. It should look like picture #3 below.

Check your bacon pixie stick powder. Texture: is it a fine, greaseless powder with few if any clumps? (Add more tapioca maltodextrin to absorb excess grease.) Taste: does it taste like a pixie stick with bacon in it? (Add more dextrose for sweetness, citric acid for tartness.)

If so, you're good to go. If not, adjust seasonings as needed, then proceed.

Step 5: Pack Straws and Serve

Use a plastic funnel and a skewer or chopstick to fill your straws. These are paper straws, which proved to be a strategic error as they too soaked up a bit of grease, preventing the pixie stick contents from flowing easily out of the straw. I'd recommend using slightly larger-gauge plastic straws. McDonalds makes nice big straws, and you could go even further and use the big straws intended for drinking bubble tea.

Crimp one end (folding works fine for paper straws; add a small staple to hold plastic straws) and fill your straw with magical bacon pixie dust. Crimp the other end (again, staples for the plastic straws) and get started on another one. This is a rather slow process.

Serve as soon as possible, especially if you're using paper straws! Bacon pixie stick powder is amazing, but it doesn't store longer than about a week, as its high surface area makes it prone to oxidation. You can probably put it in the freezer for longer-term storage, though I haven't run those tests myself.

This powder is tasty on its own and can also be an amazing addition to ice cream, fruit salads, or anything else you feel like sprinkling it on top of.

Pig Roast

By noahw
(http://www.instructables.com/id/
How-to-Roast-a-Pig-1/)

Roasting a pig is one of my favorite things to do, hands down. There are few other edible, legal party activities that put everyone in as good a mood and garner as much excitement as serving moist, delicious roasted pork to a large group of friends does. If you've never roasted a pig before for a party or special occasion, and are not a vegetarian or vegan, you have to read this Instructable and try it.

This pig-roasting Instructable chronicles the entire process of having a pig roast, and extends far beyond the process of strictly roasting a pig. "Having a pig roast" is a bit like "having a baby"—there's a lot besides the pig or baby to think about. As a very gross estimate, roasting a pig takes approximately one day of prep and one day of actual roasting.

To be clear—I am no expert on pig roasting, but then again, few are. I am simply passionate about the subject, having done it a number of times. I have welded my own spits out of steel and also rented motorized spits from party rental supply stores. I have roasted one pig all by itself, two pigs together, two pigs with a bunch of chickens, and some multi-headed ducks with chickens. I have learned a lot from each experience and I hope to share some of that info with you now in this Instructable.

Step 1: Preparation—Invitations

Once you've decided to have a pig roast, the first step is to send out the invitations so that everyone can know that you're having a party they should come to. Using antiquated technology like envelopes and the postal service to notify your lucky guests is cumbersome and a bit of a chore. Instead, I recommend going door to door to all the different homes of your guests and stabbing a hand-drawn invitation into their door jams, floors and porches with a fork.

Step 2: Preparation—Decorations

Next up are the pig-themed decorations (and you thought having a pig roast started with the pig). Grab some large pieces of paper and loads of crayons and make some decorations! One time we marked the house we were living in at the time with a large banner of two pigs on it so everyone could find the roast easily.

Other decorating efforts include:

- hay bales to sit on underneath some grape vines
- a pigñata—a pig-shaped piñata filled with moist towelettes and candy
- signs for the bathroom
- inspirational pig signs to get people excited
- personal expression board (for feedback and guest art)
- vegetarian personal expression board (for vegetarian feedback and guest art)

Step 3: Preparation—The Spit

The spit is what the pig is attached to while it cooks. It's best to think about how to construct the spit before the day of the event since it takes a little bit of work to build one.

The spit consists of some simple elements including:

- the spit itself: usually a simple steel pipe no more than 1" in diameter (the pipe will have to fit through the pigs body parts and size is a factor to consider)
- supports for the spit: this can be cinder blocks, steel supports with cradles or pipe welded on the top, sawhorses, rocks, landscaping, other structures and so forth—just preferably not anything that burns
- a method for keeping the spit from rotating: the pig will want to turn back-side-down unless something keeps the spit in position. A handle at the end of the spit and a bag of bricks or a clamp works well to hold the spit in the last position you set it in.
- a means of rotating the spit in a controlled manner: this can be a motor attached with a bike chain, or simply a few bricks and some string. In the second method mentioned, you rotate the spit by hand and use the weight to hold it in place.
- a method for attaching the animal to the spit: this can be bailing wire, steel rods sent through the animal, or steel prongs at the head and butt of the pig to hold it in place.
- fire pan or pit: if you can dig a fire pit in the dirt or sand, that's great; if not, it's usually necessary to put down some kind of barrier between the coals and the ground so you don't damage or stain anything with all the heat and drippings.

There are two main options when it comes to obtaining the spit. You can make one or rent a commercial one. Few people own their own spits,

but if you do, more power to you. I think making it yourself is a lot of fun, although the ease that comes from renting or purchasing a motorized spit is nice too. Your local party rental center may rent a roasting spit. Call them up and ask. If you are going to make a spit you can build something complex, or hack together a minimal but functional spit in a few minutes with a simple trip to the hardware store or metal scrap yard.

The first spit I made appears in the first photo in this step. It was a two-pig spit for a big party, with steel supports and a simple but effective handle on the end. The four positions allow you to make 1/8-turn rotations because you can chose to hang the brake (a bunch of bricks held together by steel cable) on one peg for the 1/4 turn, or on two pegs for the 1/8 turn. More on rotating later. Clamps also work to hold the spit in position, but I found the hanging weight method to be much easier and more versatile.

Another thing to keep in mind about the spit is that it should be longer than you think. The pigs' legs get stretched out in front of and behind the pig - thus making its total length longer than you'd expect. Make sure you have at least five feet of spit rod if you're roasting a single pig. If you're doing two like I am in the photos, go big.

If it's possible to construct the spit with adjustable height, that can be useful to compensate for the heat of your fire. Height adjustability is by no means a necessity, however. I have found that depending on fire temperature, you want between two and three feet of distance between the coals and the pig.

When it comes to ground protection, bricks make a great ground liner. Other things I have used include dirt, sand, cement board, and sheet metal.

Additional grilling surfaces can be nice to use for grilling side dishes. Some expanded metal welded over a steel frame works well and is pretty cheap. This can allow you to cook side dishes like corn or potatoes over the same fire that your pig is being cooked on. Having the side dishes under the roasting pig is an advantage since the tasty drippings will rain down upon your veggies.

Finally, as you'll see in the photos, I created a secondary roasting position for this roast below the main spit with three steel rods welded onto a steel plate. The rods are received in three holes located on another steel plate. Everything is held in place on the two supports. This secondary roasting area had some chickens on it once we got cooking.

The additional photos show some simpler roasting setups that are rather minimal and use simple things like cinder blocks and saw horses as supports and a very basic spit-clamping system that uses only a c-clamp.

Step 4: Preparation—Wood

Split a whole lot of wood. It takes a lot of hot coals to cook a pig. The bigger the pig, the longer it cooks. For the double pig we went through about half a bed of applewood that we got from a local orchard in a medium-sized pickup truck. Having roasted pigs over wood split from apple, almond, walnut, eucalyptus, and madrone trees, I honestly can say that I don't think the type of wood matters at all. The denser the wood, the longer it will burn. That's about all you have to keep in mind. That being said, "applewood" sure does have a nice ring to it, don't you think?

Some people like the reliability of charcoal briquettes for this step, and others, hardwood charcoal like Lazzaro. Use whatever you prefer, but I will say, for the amount of wood we burned in order to keep the fire going for eight hours, I'm glad we went with split wood over charcoal.

Step 5: Light the Fire

The first step on the day of the roast is to light a fire so that you've already got a good bed of coals burning when the pig is ready to start roasting. Teepee or log cabin method, it doesn't matter; get the fire started and start burning your wood down into some nice hot coals.

Ideally it's best to have a side fire that you can use to make coals, from which you then simply shovel coals into position while the pigs are roasting. If you don't have room, it's no problem to place new pieces of wood onto the fire, just try to keep the flames from licking at the pig, as the outside will burn long before the inside comes to temperature, by locating fresh logs off to the side of the fire pit.

Step 6: Side Dishes

Once the fire is burning outside, it's time to convert your home into a buzzing industrial kitchen and start prepping all of the necessary side dishes. Clean potatoes in the sink and dry them in the drainboard, make cole slaw in a five-gallon bucket, and start brining all of your other meats in the biggest pot you can find. Almost any kitchen that normally serves a single family can also serve 50 in a pinch. Cook BBQ sauce in soup pots or be like Kramer from Seinfeld and use the bathtub as a sink. If you are really pinched for space, you can always get creative with trash cans. Coolers with ice work well for things that won't fit in the fridge.

Sauce is always an important part of the pig roast. There are many approaches to sauce, and lot of options beyond your basic BBQ sauce.

Some sauces we've made over the years include:
- exotic BBQ sauces
- coffee
- mustard seed
- curried ketchup
- balsamic reduction
- citrus glazes with oranges and oregano
- brandy fig sauce
- cherry balsamic sauce
- peach rosemary sauce

Find your favorite recipes to support your pig roast and then get cooking. I won't go into specific sauce recipes in this Instructable, because they warrant their own extensive coverage.

Step 7: The Pig

Alright, let's get into things.

Where does one buy a pig?

Whole hogs can be specially ordered from the farm where the animal has lived, a good neighborhood butcher, or at the meat counter of your local quality supermarket or co-op. If they can't get you a whole pig, chances are they know who can, or point you to the pig farm they buy their meat from.

Pricing:

I have paid as much as $4.00/lb. and as little as $2.50/lb. for a whole pig. Organic pigs can sell for significantly more depending on the source. You pretty much get what you pay for when you buy a pig, so do a little leg work and choose wisely when ordering.

Size:

Some seasoned pig roasters will recommend about one pound of hanging-weight pig per person attending the party. I have found that ratio to be much too low. The math on that estimate yields around 6 oz. of cooked pork per person. I'm not going to say publicly how many ounces of meat I expect to eat when I go to a pig roast, but I'll tell you it's certainly more than that. I recommend doubling this sizing guideline and figuring on two pounds of hanging-weight pig per person attending the party. Roasted pork makes great leftovers and soups, so if you go a little overboard, there's no reason anything needs to be wasted.

Fresh or Frozen:

The pig may come frozen, but hopefully it will be fresh. If it's been frozen then it will need to defrost over 24 hours or so. Do not roast a frozen pig! Place it in a safe place where animals can't get to it, wrapped in plastic, and let it thaw. A big plastic tub works well as a holding vessel, as do the bathtub or a cardboard box in the garage located such that if some juices come out as the pig thaws it won't make a mess. If your pig will come frozen, order it for the day before your pig roast so you can defrost it.

If it's fresh and not frozen, that's great! Simply keep the pig refrigerated, in a cool place, or on ice in a cooler until the morning of the pig roast. Since it's so large, having a spare fridge on hand can be nice. Remove the racks from the fridge, place the pig inside, and shut the door. If your pig will come fresh,

order it for pick-up on the morning of your pig roast, and then you won't have to deal with the "where do I store a whole pig" dilemma.

Regardless of whether you defrosted your pig or not, remove it from the fridge or cooler an hour or so before you are ready to place it on the spit, since it's not proper form to cook cold meat.

Cook Time:

Roasting pigs are young pigs—usually between 30 and 60 pounds—however, they can come larger. Pigs that are used to make bacon are generally hundreds of pounds; that's not a great roasting pig since the meat is older and tougher. Stay away from anything that's over 100 pounds if you're looking for tender juicy meat. At that size, it just becomes unmanageable anyways. Better to get a second or third smaller pig for your roast.

A 50-pound pig cooks in anywhere from four to eight hours, depending on your heat source and whether you've stuffed it with anything. Some fellow pig roasters recommend around 1 hour and 15 minutes per 10 pounds of dead-weight pig. I have found that it's actually pretty variable depending on the heat from the fire, the height of the spit above the flames, whether the pig is stuffed, and whether you are using a motor driven rotary spit or rotating by hand.

In general, work backward from when you'd like to eat using the 1hr 15m guideline and add in an hour or so for carving and all the things that take longer than you've planned, just to be safe.

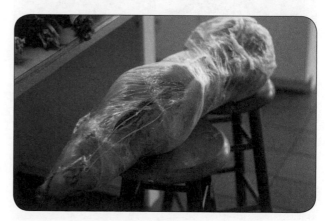

Step 8: Mount the Pig

This step is fun! First, wash all work surfaces with hot water and soap. If your surface is too difficult to wash, cover it with a tarp and wash the tarp. Remove the pig from the plastic wrap. Take the pig and insert the spit rod into one end—it doesn't matter which on most spits. Slide the rod through the pig's open body cavity and out the hole on the other side.

If your spit is much larger than 1" in diameter you might need to break the hip bones in order to slide out the back of the pig. I made the mistake of using a rod that was too thick the first time, something I won't be doing again. Better to go a little smaller on the spit rod and not have to break anything. I don't mind getting my hands dirty, but I do have limits.

Slide the pig into position along the spit until you've got it centered in place. Remember to leave room for the legs to get tied in front and in back of the pig. The photos make it all look very apocalyptic, I swear we washed our hands first and cleaned all of our work surfaces with soap before beginning.

Step 9: Stuff the Pig

With the pig in place and the chest cavity facing up, it's time to load the pig with delicious flavors. Mainstays are salt and pepper, of course.

Other flavors to consider using are fresh herbs like rosemary, thyme, oregano, and marjoram, as well as dried spices that complement your flavor pallet—things like juniper berries, bay leaves, and whole garlic cloves. There will be a marinade applied to the pig while it roasts to add flavor, as well. This is more of a rub applied inside the body cavity.

I've always thrown a few quartered onions inside the cavity and squeezed in a few fresh Valencia oranges, but I have really tried not to over-stuff the pig on my more recent. The more you put inside the pig, the more mass there is to cook, and that means there is a greater chance that the meat will dry out or the skin will over-crackle while you're waiting for the center to come to temperature.

The same theory applies to stuffing a turkey—diehard turkey roasters wouldn't dare slow cooking

times down with stuffing and risk drying out the bird. I've come to believe the same thing for pig roasting and now try to keep the stuffing to a minimum.

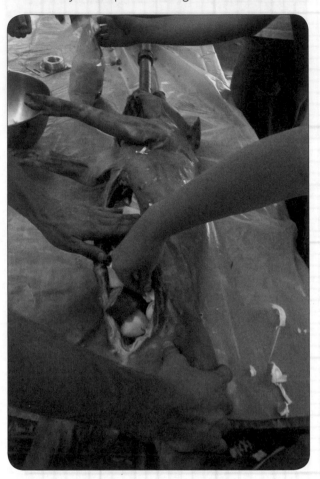

Step 10: Sew It Up

It's pretty common to use metal bailing wire to close the pig. If possible, just get regular, non-galvanized, standard metal bailing wire. Other metal wires will work as well but will likely cost more.

Start at one end and simply sew the pig shut all the way to the other end. You can use a variety of stitches to close the pig, but what's easiest to me is just to grab the two layers of skin, hold them together like a fabric seam, and stitch them together using big looping stitches.

A few words about giant sewing needles for meat: One time I was without my trusty oversized trussing needle that I made. It was pretty annoying to push the bailing wire through the pig's fatted belly skin with just a pair of pliers, or worse, by hand, as you can see in the second photo. The giant needle is the way to go for sure if you have time to make one as it really helps in the stitching step.

To make the giant needle: Get a 1/4" or 1/8" steel rod and grind the tip to a point on the grinding wheel. Then pound the other side of the rod flat using a small sledge and an anvil. Drill a small hole through the flat side and you've got yourself a freakishly large needle! The bigger the better on the needle, as pushing it through the belly skin can be a two-handed job. The more steel there is to grab when your hands are all slick and you're staring at a 60-pound pig in front of you, the better.

Once the pig is all sewn up, the final step—which is totally optional, and probably not healthy for the future of our world—is to have a small child tenderize the meat with a baseball bat.

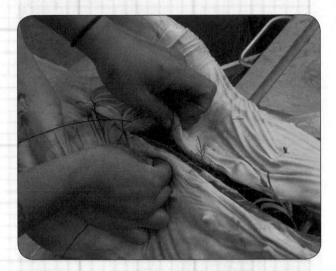

Step 11: Secure Pig to the Spit

Now there are a few different ways to secure the pig to the spit. If you are using a commercial spit then slide the retaining spikes into position around the pig's jowls and literally into the rear end, and lock them onto the pig by tightening the set screws. These, coupled with some bailing wire used to secure the trotters onto the secondary bar, are all you need. This process is shown in the first photo and is pretty straightforward.

If you have made your own spit then you'll need to come up with something a little more inventive. I chose to drill holes through my spit rod and insert additional smaller diameter steel rods into those holes. Then I used bailing wire tied around the front legs, mouth and that smaller diameter steel rod to secure the pig in place (see second photo). That way, when you rotate the spit to cook the pig evenly, the pig doesn't just flop around to its lowest point (back down, legs up).

The first time I roasted a pig I got a little overzealous and drilled several holes all along the entire spit rod. See third photo in this step. Once the pig was on I took 1/2" steel rods and skewered the pig into position hell-raiser style, in addition to the bailing wire. This was overkill, and a little scary for people to see in hindsight. Since then I've opted for simply creating a hard point on the spit rod and securing the pig's feet to that point at the front and back like the scenario I've described in the previous paragraph.

Step 12: Chickens and Ducks and Stuff

Remember the chickens that have been brining in a delicious bath of salt, lemon, herbs, and spices from step 6? Give them a good rinse and throw them onto the spit too. The chicken roasting device that I created is a bit crude, but works very well. You simply sandwich/clamp the chickens between the three rods and place it on the spit.

The key feature of the chicken roasting is to have whatever is there be basted in the juices of the pig roasting above it. Chickens roasted in pork drippings are some of the best chickens around. The second photo here shows the chickens getting secured to the spit using just a simple BBQ skewer that passes through a hole in the spit rod. There are many options here, do what's easy and exciting for you.

Step 13: Roasting and Turning

With all the animals affixed to their respective spits, it's time to put them over the fire and begin cooking. At first, watch the roasting process closely and get a feel for how hot your fire is. You don't want to burn the outside of the pig before the inside comes to temperature. Move coals away from the pig if things get too hot. Add coals with a shovel if things look like they aren't hot enough. You'll know the fire is too hot if the skin begins to crack or get crispy in the first hour or two.

If you are using a commercial spit then the motor will turn the pig constantly at a slow speed the entire time. Until recently I had only roasted animals on non-mechanized spits. The same effect can be achieved by rotating the pig every 15 minutes or so. Set a timer and remember to keep it close by. When the alarm goes off, remove the hanging weight or clamp holding the spit in place, give the pig a 1/4 or 1/8 turn, replace the weight or clamp, and go do something else for the next 15 minutes. This process sounds tedious, but it's really not. Checking back in with the pig on this kind of basis is probably a good idea to make sure everything is proceeding as planned, and if given the choice between motorized and manual rotation, I think I'd choose manual just because it's fun to hang out with the pig for a while.

Step 14: Basting

Basting the meat while it cooks is important to add flavor. I like to mix up a simple Cuban-inspired mojo of sorts made from olive oil, fresh garlic, fresh oregano, salt, pepper, orange juice, and lemon juice. Baste the roasting animals every time you rotate the spit, or even more often.

There are many possibilities on marinades here and very few rules. In general, I have stayed away from typical BBQ sauces since they are thick and don't penetrate the meat very well. Additionally, you don't want to put anything on the outside of the pig that will burn over the many hours of cooking, so it's best to stay away from sticky, sweet glazes until the very end. If you do decide to glaze, keep in mind you'll only be treating the skin and not the meat.

Instead, I usually save the sweet sugar-, tomato-, or honey-based sauces until after the pig is carved and pour them over the meat before serving, or let people serve themselves sauce as a side and just serve the meat un-sauced.

Step 15: Cook Side Dishes

As the pigs, chickens, and ducks roast over the fire and the end of the cook time starts to approach, it's time to start cooking all the other side dishes. Potatoes can be wrapped in tin foil, thrown directly into the fire, and cooked for 35 to 45 minutes, turning them from time to time. Corn can be soaked in water and then grilled in the husk over some extra coals from the fire on a wire grate.

Nice side dishes include roasted veggies, home-baked bread, beans, salads, cole slaw, and, of course, plenty of sauce for the meat.

Step 16: Remove Pig from Spit

Anywhere from 4 to 8 hours after you started roasting the pig, depending on the size of your pig and the temperature of the fire, the pig will be done cooking. The skin should be dark golden brown and very crispy. Joints should wiggle freely, juices should run clear, and when you place a thermometer into the thickest parts of the pig you should get an internal temperature of at least 140° F. What temperature to cook your pork to is up for debate, depending on what you've learned. I cook pork to around 140° F.

Remove the spit from the fire and place it back on the work surface (wash all your surfaces first). Use wire cutters to cut and remove all of the bailing wire from the front and back legs and free the pig from the spit. Remove the spit rod by sliding it out of the pig.

Take the wire cutters and snip every stitch along the pig's belly. If you pull the wire it will simply rip through the delicious belly meat and make a mess. Instead, take each stich out individually with needle-nose pliers. Pretend you are a surgeon and the pig is your patient.

A clean pair of work gloves, some clean towels, and a little patience helps a lot with this step and the next. The pig is piping hot; everyone wants to eat and the whole party will be watching your every move, so you've got to do it right.

Once the body cavity is opened up remove all of the stuffing and herbs. If juices begin to flow and collect on the work surface, place a rock underneath one of the table legs to create an incline on the table. Then take a pot and place it under the low point on the table to collect the juices.

Step 17: Carving

This step is a little tough to do the first or even second time. I've taken a pig butchering class and I still have trouble breaking whole animals down quickly and easily. The important thing to remember is that the meat will be tasty no matter how it comes off the bone, so have a drink, don't stress, work fast, and dig in.

First, sharpen a knife or two and find an extra person or two to lend you a hand. Work the knife between the shoulder and hip joints to remove the four legs from the roast. These can be treated as discreet roasts and handed off to another carver. Most meat will come off of these pieces, which include the pork shoulders and Boston butts.

You should be left with the torso of animal. This contains the belly, loins off of the back, tasty marbled meat from the neck and jowl, and also the delicious, hard to work for rib meat. Save the skin and begin to carve out the loins, as that's the most easily accessible and edible meat in this section. After that, go after everything that's left, sorting the parts into different serving platters and pots. Skin is good to snack on—people will eat it, so don't throw it away! Bare bones make a great soup stock. Dogs like cartilage and strange off-cuts not suitable for serving. The best meat should go onto platters for your guests.

It can be useful to cut the ribs with a hack saw off of the spine. If you are pulling the meat and don't want to serve "on the bone" pork, just work the meat off the bone by hand. I leave the spine relatively intact once the loins are off; there's definitely some meat along there, but it's best to pick at it with some friends rather than try to spend the time removing it.

Place a knife between two of the neck vertebrae just behind the ears and cut the head of the pig off. For some reason, everyone really likes playing with the pig head.

Once you've gotten the legs and torso carved up pretty well, serve your first round, as you can always continue carving while people begin to eat so that the meat doesn't get cold. In general, it's taken between 30 minutes and 1 hour to carve up all the pork and chicken, and people's mouths can only water for so long, so it's best to serve and then keep working.

Step 18: Serve

This is the easy part: Load up all the side dishes and meat platters on a big table and ring the dinner bell!

Step 19: Party

Once all the meat is carved up it's important that, as the host, you remember to enjoy yourself. At the roasts I've put on, my friends and I have been working literally all day, so by the time everyone is eating and the music starts up I always try to remember to put the pig parts down, wash my hands, grab a cold beer, and have some fun.

Step 20: The Head

For some reason people are really fascinated with the pig head. No one wants to eat it, but everyone wants to play with it and wear it as if it were their own head.

There's surely more to say about roasting pigs, but this is a good start. Best of luck on your pig roasting adventures and be sure to invite me—I'll be looking for the fork in my door.

Cake Pops

By scoochmaroo

(http://www.instructables.com/id/
Cake-Pops/)

Made famous by Bakerella and ubiquitous by Starbucks, cake pops are the latest trend in dessert culture. Here I walk you through the steps to make your own cake pops at home! Whether you use homemade or store-bought cakes and icing, you can still customize these adorable treats to your heart's content. Decorate them for any occasion! The process may be time consuming (be patient!), but the rewards are well worth the effort.

Step 1: Materials
Tools:
- mixer
- baking pan
- Silpat or parchment
- cake pop sticks
- cake scoop
- chocolate melter (optional)
- cake pop baker (optional)
- cake pop stand or Styrofoam

Ingredients:
- cake mix (or homemade)
- frosting (or homemade)
- candy melts (I prefer Merckens and am thrilled by the color selection you can get!)
- colored sprinkles
- colored icing tubes
- other stuff for decorating, like fun shaped sprinkles and candy eyeballs

Step 2: Bake a Cake and Mash It Up

Either make your favorite from-scratch recipe or follow the instructions on the box. I chose strawberry as I thought pink would be cute. Next time I'm sticking with chocolate.

Once your cake is cooled—really cooled—crumble it up into a bowl. Stir in your jar (or homemade) frosting, a little at a time. Once it reaches a nice consistency that will cling together when you roll it in a ball, you're there. Stick it in the fridge.

Step 3: Ball It Up

Once it's nice and cool, you'll want to start rolling it into balls. This is really baker's choice—how big, what shape, and how to make them.

I don't have one of those little melon-baller gadgets, but I might get one for the next round. My hands seem incapable of rolling a sphere—they all come out like footballs. It took some work to make the beautiful spheres you see here.

Roll your cake mash into ball-like pieces. Mine were about 1¼" in diameter. Next, stick 'em in the fridge.

Step 4: Melt the Candy Coating

These candy melts are super easy to use. Following the instructions on the package, I put them in a bowl in the microwave on 50 percent power for 1½ minutes. Then I stirred them and zapped them again at 50 percent for 30 seconds. Repeat until nice and melty, then repeat once more for superior dipping quality. I melted up some pink, yellow, and white.

Step 5: Dip Your Pops

Get those cake balls outta the fridge! Get your lollipop sticks ready and dip them slightly in the melted candy before inserting them half to three-quarters of the way into each cake ball.

This is where I would say, "Stick it in the fridge!" but when I did so at this step, I think it worked against me. So don't. Or, try it without sticking them in the fridge at this point, and if it turns out to be a hot mess, then, well . . . stick 'em in the fridge.

Dip your newly-sticked cake pops into the candy coating and rotate to ensure even coverage. Stand the dipped pops into cake pop stand or Styrofoam to let them drip dry.

Step 6: Decorate Your Pops

Now it's time to get creative. If you had any pops that didn't turn out so hot, practice on those.

I don't have any pictures of my decorating process, but I just used what I had in terms of glitter and confetti and such. The ducks' noses and wings were more melted candy coating, and the feet were little orange stars that came in the confetti mixture. The eyes were dotted on with the tube decorator icing. The eggs were made by using the decorator icing and glitter/confetti.

Step 7: Share!

Trust me: These babies are not to be eaten on one's own. They are potent sugar-bombs! Bring them into work or to the next party you have. Share them with your friends! Bet someone a dollar they can't eat a whole one in one bite! Then go call your dentist.

over the straws and squeeze them out or you can hold the straws over warm water. The worms will slip right out.

Bowl of Worms

By cpacker1
(http://www.instructables.com/id/
Bowl-of-Worms-Anyone/)

Create tasty, edible worms. This recipe is simple and great for Halloween, April Fool's Day, or anytime you feel like snacking on wormy goodness! If you can make jello, then you can make these cool-looking worms.

Step 1: Ingredients

- 2 packs (3 oz.) raspberry jello
- 1 package unflavored gelatin (for extra firmness)
- 3/4 cup whipping cream
- 3 cups boiling water
- 15 drops green food coloring
- 100 flexible straws (or enough to fill your container)
- tall container (1 quart or 1 liter carton of milk)

Step 2: Directions

1. Combine gelatin and jello in bowl and add boiling water.
2. Let it cool to lukewarm and then add the whipping cream and 15 drops green food coloring.
3. Gather your straws (don't forget to flex them out) and put them in the container. It's important that the straws have a tight fit so the jello stays in the straws. For this reason, a 1-liter carton may be better; you will probably get longer worms since there is a tighter fit. If you have a bigger container, a rubber band around the straws is helpful. Or you could just add more straws to fill the container.
4. Add the gelatin mixture to the straw-filled container and let it set until firm.
5. There are multiple ways you can remove the worms from the straws. You can roll a rolling pin

Two nine-inch round cakes, frosting, decorations, and an unquenchable thirst for adventure are all you need.

Step 1: The Raw Materials

For this Instructable, you will need two nine-inch round cakes. Cakes made from scratch will be denser and stronger than a cake mix, but you love the Duncan Hines don't you—just be forewarned that the time you save using a mix will be spent cursing during the frosting crumb coat.

You'll need two batches of frosting. We did a butter cream with 50/50 butter/vegetable shortening. Dye one batch green. Keep half of the second batch white and dye the other half blue.

Next you need rolled fondant. We don't know what this stuff is, but we were darn sure we weren't going to make it. We found some multi-colored fondant at Michael's, a big-box craft store. Buy the non-stick mini rolling pin while you are at it.

As for decorations, you'll need cinnamon red hot candies for the eyes, candy corn for the tail spikes, chocolate chips for toenails, and toasted coconut for the prehistoric grass.

You'll also need one cardboard cake board, half-sheet size, and frosting pipe tips and bags. Use a star tip. Yes, this makes a difference, so don't skimp here. Really. Also, maybe find a partner. Not required, but it could speed things up during frosting or at least help pass the time.

Step 2: The Body

Bake the cakes and cool completely. Take out of pan and find the center of one cake. Cut the cake in half with a bread knife. Put the two halves together with cut edges aligned, and place on a work surface as pictured.

Step 3: The Appendages

Ever heard the advice, "Measure twice, cut once?" Unless you are a blackbelt paleolithic pastry chef who can think in three dimensions of cake, you will probably want to make a paper template to design the head, legs, and tail. I drew the template below, and you will generally want to cut the paper in the same shapes I used. Cut a nine-inch circle of paper and lay it on top of the second cake. Draw the tail and head in one half, the legs in the other. Cut out the paper pieces and arrange them on your body segment to see how they look. Tweak and repeat as necessary. When you are feeling lucky, carve 'em and stack 'em. Oh, and you may want to affix the head to the body with some toothpicks, just in case the birthday party gets a little rowdy. Move all pieces to the cake board. Use white frosting to join the body halves together, then join the appendages to the body. Trim the corners and square edges off the feet and shoulders if you like.

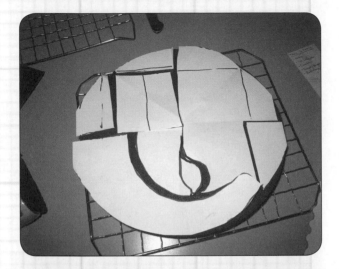

the plates with a toothpick to give them a scaled texture. Spread a thin layer of green frosting over the cake. This is called the crumb coat—and for good reason, as much of the crumbs pull away and get mixed up in the frosting. Use a very light hand on the cut surfaces of cake.

Did you use a cake mix instead of making one from scratch? Are you cursing now? Tip: crumb coat one half. Have a partner start piping with the star tip while you finish crumb coating the other half. Use a star tip to pipe on green frosting, then blend in blue for an accent. Stick fondant diamond plates into back. If the frosting does not hold the plates well, stick a toothpick into the plate and then stick it into the cake.

Step 4: The Skin

Roll the fondant out so it's 1/8 inch thick. Hand cut the fondant with a small knife into some diamond shapes for the plates on the dinosaur's back. Detail

Step 5: The Final Touches

Spread a layer of white frosting on your cake board and toss some toasted coconut around for grass. Add any other finishing touches you like— candy corn for spikes on the tail, cinnamon candies for the eyes, and chocolate chips for the toes. We made palm trees using tube cookies with fronds of parsley—this was the first thing every kid wanted, so make a small forest if you do it. Grab the camera and enjoy!

Robotic R2D2 Cupcake
By RollerScrapper
(http://www.instructables.com/id/
Robotic-R2D2-Cupcake/)

I'm going to show you how to make your cupcakes move! I started with R2D2 as my main idea, but part of me was inspired by the shape of the bottom of the cupcake to do a quick and dirty R4 A22, as well. Please note that I used food-safe markers on this project; do not draw on your cupcake with regular markers!

Step 1: Make Marshmallow Fondant
First gather your ingredients:
- 8 oz. Powdered Sugar
- 4 oz. Marshmallows
- a few drops vanilla extract
- 1 tablespoon minus a few drops water
- food scale (this is helpful if you want to make a smaller quantity like this)
- Silpat mat (very important so things don't stick!)
- coconut oil or Crisco (not pictured. if you don't have the Silpat, or even if you do, using about a

spoonful of this can help grease your hands and work space so stuff doesn't stick)

Weigh out the ingredients. This makes it easy to determine the quantity. Note: when reading a scale, you need to calibrate the scale to zero and also weigh the ingredients by looking from the same point of view. These measurement photos look off because I took the photo at a different angle than I was at when I weighed the ingredients.

Microwave the marshmallows and a few drops of vanilla in a tablespoon topped off with water for 30 seconds and then add in ¾ of the powdered sugar and stir with a spatula.

Turn this out on to your work surface, which should be liberally sprinkled with powdered sugar. Knead until you get a soft playdough-like consistency, which pulls and stretches but does not tear. Put this in a plastic baggie and refrigerate overnight to one week.

Step 2: Bake Some Cupcakes (the Next Day)
Gather your ingredients for your cupcakes:
- eggs, water, oil and cake mix
- pretzel sticks to hold these little robots together
- white chocolate and vanilla crème wafers for the legs (unless you can find some of those elusive white Kit Kats)
- frosting to hold on your fondant
- blue gel dye
- silver shimmer dust (optional; I used this because I had it but felt it didn't add a whole lot of silver color.)
- toothpicks
- cornstarch and coconut oil for kneading the fondant
- a tomato sauce can cut open on both ends and cleaned

And most importantly:
- a hex bug. This is a small robotic bug. Get the original one that looks like a lady bug. I found mine for $10.99 at Michaels, but I got it for $5.50 with my 50 percent off coupon!

Before I made the batter I used some mini oranges to shape some aluminum foil into dome-shaped molds. You might need to use a tangerine or something else round.

Prepare the batter according to your favorite cake mix. You will be making regular cupcakes, mini cupcakes, and some dome-shaped cupcakes. I put 3 tablespoons of batter in the regular cupcakes, 1 tablespoon in the mini cupcakes, and 2 tablespoon in the dome-shaped aluminum foil molds.

Bake the minis for 15 minutes and the regular and domes for 19 minutes, or until a toothpick inserted in the center comes out clean. Put these on a rack to cool completely.

Step 3: Cut Up the Cookies for the Legs

Using a sharp serrated knife I cut up the wafer cookies. Since these break easily, my method was to make four cuts near the four corners and then cut out the middle thinner part of the leg. Once you've cut out the thin part, shave off the top two corners; this makes that round "shoulder" part, the other part the foot.

Nuke your white chocolate for 30 seconds on half power, and keep doing this until it starts to get shiny and you can stir it around. I added coconut oil, which made it easy to dip, but unfortunately it melts very easy. I think I ended up making magic shell. If anyone has any suggestions of how to make the chocolate harder (I suspect I needed more chocolate) it would be greatly appreciated. Dip the pieces in one by one and use a fork to fish them out and put them on your clean Silpat. Then stick them all in the freezer. Use a sharp knife to trim off any wonky bits.

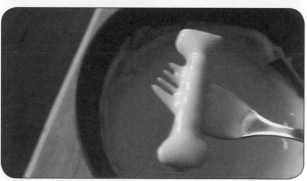

Step 4: Dye the Fondant

Using a toothpick or skewer, as I did, put a liberal amount of blue dye in the center of a warmed and kneaded fondant blob. Keep folding and kneading. I think I had to add dye about three times to get the right amount of blue. Just note, this blue fondant seemed stickier than the white because it had more moisture; this will make it more challenging to roll out properly. I rolled it up into some saran wrap and stored it in the same baggie as the white fondant.

Step 5: Roll Out Your Fondant

This is where you need a non-stick rolling pin, a Silpat mat, and additional cornstarch, because as everything warms up, it gets sticky. Make a long piece for the body and a round piece for the head.

I used a pizza cutter to cut strips of blue for the decoration. On the blue curved part at the top of the head I was able to make many strips by cutting at opposite angles and then flipping the shapes.

Some notes about fondant: I washed my hands a lot while taking photos. Make sure you are 100 percent dry. Any wet fingers will make this stuff incredibly sticky, which is not good. Also, do not store them on top of each other; use layers of Saran wrap. I didn't think about this and had to repeat this step, which was a bit frustrating.

Step 6: Cut Your Cupcakes to Size

Cut your cupcakes to size using the tomato paste can. It is easiest if you flip them upside down before cutting. Use three pretzels to join two of the three layers together. The third domed one will be added once you have frosted and put on the fondant.

Step 7: Frost and Add Fondant

I find frosting the cupcakes the most frustrating part, but this has to be done or, alas, the fondant will not stick. Add a layer of frosting and drape the fondant over the dome-shaped cupcake. Use a sharp knife to trim the excess. Put frosting around the edges of your cylinder and roll the thinner piece of fondant (which I trimmed to the proper height) around that. Use a domed cupcake to make an R2D2, or an upside down mini cupcake for the R4 A22.

I included pictures of putting fondant on both tops. This is the point at which I put the edible silver dust on the dome. I think I'd skip it next time, as it didn't give that much of an effect, but it was worth a try.

Step 8: Assemble Robot and Begin Decorating

Carefully place the head on the body and begin decorating. If your fondant has dried at all you can add a drop of water to the back of it to stick it on, but be careful as the dye can smudge. Also at this point I used food coloring markers that I got at Michael's (but have also seen in the regular grocery store in the frosting section). I looked at a photo of R2D2 and an R4 A22 and went to town. Note that I used fondant for R2D2, but used a marker for the R4 A22, so you can see the difference. I'm also not the best artist, so it was a little messy, but you get the point.

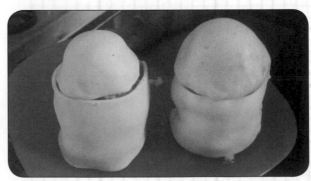

Step 9: Attach the legs

Now you can decorate it with legs. Basically use some of your left over "magic shell" white chocolate and use that as glue. Smear some on a leg and put it on a droid, stick it in the fridge. For the second leg it is a little harder, since you have to lay it on its back. I used a few food coloring markers to prop it up.

Do not refrigerate this for too long, as fondant's not supposed to be refrigerated once decorated due to condensation.

Step 10: Make It Move!

Here's where the magic happens. Take your hex bug, break off the pointy ends of one side of three toothpicks, and attach them to the hex bug in its crevices. Then gently slide your R2D2 onto the toothpicks. This is what takes a bit of care as if it's too far forward or back it will topple over. Then, test it out! I put it on a baking sheet and had it walk on that, but it would be cool to have it walk up to the birthday girl or boy!

Enjoy!

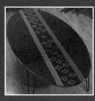

Furniture

Sliced LACK Table

IKEA Shelf Hack

Raised Bed with Storage Bookshelves

Pallet Desk

Bean Bag Sofa/Bed

Aquarium Coffee Table

Duct Tape Hammock

Skateboard Table

Ladder Bookshelf

Hang .10 Coffee Table

Modular Bookshelf

Adjustable Standing-Desk Conversion

By its very nature, furniture is utilitarian. It keeps things off of the ground. Butts, books, and boxes are all kept elevated by various types of furniture, and by and large that furniture is very dull or very expensive.

With these 12 projects, you can make furniture that you can show off. Coffee tables, desks, chairs, and bookshelves are among the easiest pieces to customize, and these pieces will look so good that you'll be hard-pressed to put anything on them once you're done. And you won't break the bank in the process.

Sliced LACK Table

By BrittLiv
(http://www.instructables.com/id/Sliced-LACK-table/)

I am going to show you how to make a LACK table from IKEA stand on only two legs. Even though this is a rather simple mod, it is going to get you quite a few puzzled looks. I originally wanted to make the table stand on one leg, but I was afraid that it could break should somebody lean on it. I finished it up by sealing the surface to prevent wear.

Step 1: Materials and Tools

- LACK side table, 55 x 55 cm (from IKEA)
- plywood or MDF board 1 x 55 x 55 cm
- cheap rug (mine is 80 x 140 cm)
- double-sided tape
- wood filler (spatula or something else to apply it)
- paint (and paint brush)
- rectangular block of wood, 4.5 x 4.5 x 36cm
- newspaper
- wood glue
- long screws
- sanding paper
- primer (optional)
- masking tape (optional)
- drill
- saw
- hammer and chisel

Step 2: Supportive Legs

The legs of the LACK table are hollow and will not be able to hold up the weight unless you stabilize them. I used a hammer and chisel to break through the bottom of the leg, as shown in the first picture. To fill the leg I used a rectangular block of wood, which I glued to the inside.

Step 3: Sliced Legs

Use the saw to remove a piece from the middle of two of the legs. You can either make a straight cut or an angled cut like I did. Then fill the legs with newspaper and a top layer of wood filler. Afterward I sanded the cuts and primed and painted them.

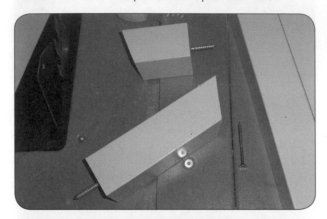

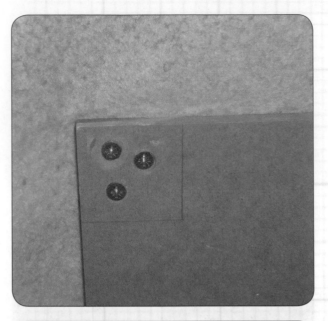

Step 4: Assembly

In order to assemble the table, drill holes in the MDF or plywood plate for the screws and stick it to the underside of the carpet with double-sided tape.

I removed the carpet fibers directly underneath the legs in order to get better stability.

Screw the legs to the table and then to the MDF plate (make sure the screw heads don't stick out or they will scratch your floor). Make sure that the two long legs support the table and then attach the two shorter legs.

IKEA Shelf Hack

By randofo
(http://www.instructables.com/id/
IKEA-Hack/)

The nice thing about IKEA furniture is that it is cheap and easy to hack. Let's say that you were to buy two cheap $30 GORM shelving units and assemble them, only to discover that one was crooked. Well, it would be really easy to spend an afternoon converting the crooked one into a solid, stylish, and symmetrical bookshelf bench. As you probably just guessed, this Instructable will show you how to convert a GORM shelving unit into a bookshelf bench. With a few extra pieces of hardware and a couple of basic power tools, you can be on your way to relaxation and organization, all at the same time.

Step 1: Go Get Stuff
You will need:
- GORM shelving unit
- 2" x 4" piece of wood
- 92¾" x 12" x ¾" piece of plywood
- 16 cross dowels that are 3/8"
- 16 bolts that are 2½" (to fit cross dowels)
- 8 two-inch woodscrews
- 50 feet of rope
- tape measure and pencil
- circular saw
- sanding block and/or sandpaper
- power drill, 3/32" and 3/8" drill bit
- assorted hand tools
- fabric, foam, and stuff for a cushion
  (see step 13)

Step 2: Assemble Your Crooked Bookshelf
Assemble your GORM bookshelf and realize that two out of the four posts are crooked. Stare at it in displeasure. Resolve to take drastic action.

Step 3: Cut a 2x4 into Four Pieces
Cut four 12¼" lengths out of the 2 x 4.

Step 4: Drill Holes

With a 3/8" drill bit, drill holes in the ends of the 2 x 4 so that they are ¾"in from each edge (top, bottom, left, and right). Also drill holes on the flat surface of the board that are 2" in from the end and perfectly aligned with, but perpendicular to, the hole you first drilled. In other words, this hole should intersect at a 'T' the holes in the end.

Step 5: Take Apart Your Bookshelf

Disassemble your horribly crooked bookshelf. Select the two prettiest and straightest beams to cut up for use as the supports for the bench. You will be able to make six supports with these two beams. Using the two ugly beams, you should be able to get one support from each.

Step 6: Cut the Beams

Cut one of the nice-looking bookshelf beams to a height of 18.25 inches, starting from the bottom edge (edge that used to be on the floor).

Then take this piece you just cut and line up its holes with the holes on the new bottom edge of the board. Make a mark on the longer board at each end of the first cut beam.

Using the two lines you just drew as cutting guides, make two cuts. You should now have a second beam. Now use the first beam to line up to the holes on the opposite end of the board and make cut marks as appropriate so they are all the same size.

Cut at these markings. You should now have 3 beams. Repeat this process on the second pretty-looking beam.

Next grab the two ugly-looking beams. Measure in from either the bottom or top edges (whichever edge looks best) of both ugly beams and make one cut on each to produce two more 18.25 inches beams. You should now have eight 18.25 inches beams with all of the holes lined up.

Step 7: Sand

Sand and smooth any rough edges you may have from sawing and/or drilling the 2 x 4 or bookshelf beams.

Step 8: Insert Cross Dowels

Insert cross dowels into the four holes drilled through the surface of the 2 x 4 sections. Depending on the tolerance involved, this step may require driving the cross dowels into the holes with a hammer.

To push it in beyond the surface of the board, place a screwdriver or chisel atop the cross dowel and slightly tap it with the hammer. Make certain that the slots on the cross dowels are all facing the same direction inside the board.

Step 10: Fasten the Seat

Flip your bookshelf bench upside down so that it is perfectly aligned over the top of your plywood. Drill two 3/32 inch pilot holes in each of the 2 x 4s, such that it goes all the way through into the piece of plywood.

Using your woodscrews, fasten the plywood to the 2 x 4. Make sure you apply a lot of pressure downwards while drilling so that the two surfaces are fastened tightly flush together.

Step 9: Build the Frame

Using the IKEA hardware, attach three shelves to the lowest holes in the bookshelf beams. Next, using your 2 ½ inch bolts and cross dowels, attach the 2 x 4 sections to the topmost holes of the boards.

Step 11: String It Up

Thread rope through the extra screw holes in the boards to serve as bookends and to keep books from falling off.

Basically, on the two ends, you should tie a knot and pass the rope through to form a rectangle. Once all the way through, pull it tight and tie the rope together so that the rectangle is closed. The middle sections are slightly trickier.

You use the same method, but rather than closing the rectangle by tying it shut, you pass it through again from the back to form another rectangle.

Once that's finished, you pull it tight and tie the end of the rope to the knot at the beginning. This step will create two sets of two parallel ropes and two vertical lines in the front, which will aesthetically match the two ends.

Step 12: Add Books

Arrange your books on the bookshelf. You may want to consider placing larger books towards each end to make sure the rope doesn't accidentally let smaller books slip through.

Step 13: Make a Cushion (optional)

Make yourself a nice comfortable cushion and enjoy your reading bench!

Raised Bed with Storage Bookshelves

By ripflash

(http://www.instructables.com/id/
Raised-Bed-with-Expedit-Bookshelves-
for-Storage/)

I created underbed storage using IKEA EXPEDIT bookshelves. This is a super easy project with no sawing required. And, surprisingly, the bed is completely stable. Since I already had a bed and frame, it cost about $400.

Step 1: Supplies

- 3 EXPEDIT bookshelves ($90 each)
- 2 IKEA OBSERVATOR Cross Braces, 393 Version ($5 each; be sure to select the 39 inch version, not the 28 inch queen-size mattress)
- queen-size bed frame or 80 x 58 5/8 inch sheet of wood
- IKEA LEKMAN boxes (optional; $12 each; 8 fit in each bookcase)
- 3 mat shelf liners sized at least 15½" X 59" ($5–8 each)
- drill
- Phillips-head screwdriver

Step 2: Build the Bookshelves

Build the bookshelves as IKEA instructs. Space them evenly on the floor as shown.

Step 2: Install Cross Braces

On the two end-unit bookshelves, drill and screw in the IKEA OBSERVATOR 39" cross brace as shown. This will keep the bed from swaying left to right. Just with one cross brace, the bed was stable. I added a second one to be careful. I chose to install the cross brace at the foot of the bed on the inside (under the frame) so that it would not interfere with reaching storage from the outside. At the head of the bed (touching the wall), I installed the cross brace on the outside so that it would not interfere with reaching the storage under the bed.

Step 3: Place Frame and Bed on Top

To protect the shelves from scratches and provide some grip, consider placing a mat liner at least 15½" x 59" on top of them (mine are 16" x 62", so I had to cut a few inches off the end). Then place the bed frame or 80" x 58 5/8" sheet of wood on top of that. For this project, I lined up four narrower sheets of 80" x 14 5/8" wood. That's it!

Because the bed is around 3½ feet high, kids and those under 5'10" will need a chair or stool to climb into it. But if you need the storage, this provides lots of organized space.

Pallet Desk

By pierrevedel
(http://www.instructables.com/id/
Pallet-desk/)

This is a simple way to create a desk using a pallet and some IKEA table legs. The pallet allows one to double the desk surface and to get a lot of storage.

Step 1: Materials List
You need:
- 1 pallet (or 2 if you plan to make the top surface with pallet wood)
- 5mm plywood to make the bottom surface
- wood floor board with interlock (to make the top surface)
- 4 IKEA VIKA legs
- some nails (10mm) and screws (at least 40mm)

Usually, pallet dimensions are 120 x 80cm, and you should select plywood and floor board according to your pallet size.

I have used two plywood boards of 60 x 80cm (perfect fit!) and five wood floor boards of 16cm width (another perfect fit!)

Advantages of wood floor are: cheap, robust, and clean

Tools: You may need a wood saw, a metal saw, a hammer with a nail puller, and a screw gun.

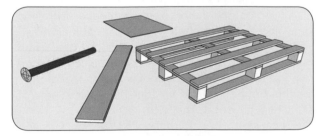

Step 2: Dismantle the Pallet
There are two ways:
1. using a nail puller (very time consuming)
2. using a metal saw and sawing between the two parts to dismantle them (faster) Images

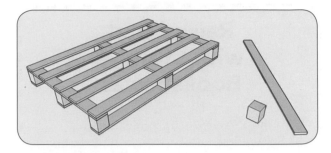

Step 3: Assembly
Cut the floor boards to fit the pallet board length. Adjust the plywood boards to get an overall surface equal to pallet board × cross board.

Now you have every part at the right size, so let's build up the desk!
1. nail the plywood into the three bottom boards
2. screw the pallet blocks through the bottom boards
3. screw the pallet block through the cross boards
4. screw the floor board into the cross-boards
5. screw the leg into the bottom boards

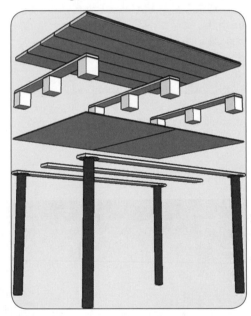

Step 4: Option: Secret Access to Hidden Treasure
If you have chosen the floor board with interlock, you can create a secret access by sliding boards.

Bean Bag Sofa/Bed

By dan
(http://www.instructables.com/id/bean-bag-sofa–bed/)

I started out thinking about building a bean bag, but being the prototypically exuberant man's man that I am, I thought, "I am going to go huge! Why make a bean bag just like everyone else? I'll make the biggest, baddest bean bag ever!"

Well, in the end I did make the biggest, baddest bean bag ever, but I think any practical assessment would say that it is too large to be convenient (e.g., it is hard to get through doorways and tends to fill all available floor area in room). But I learned enough through this effort that I can advise you, dear reader, how to build a most useful and practical bean bag sofa should you want to do so.

Summary: looking for that plush bean-bag chair comfort, but in a sofa size? Bean-bags are easy and inexpensive to make (as furniture goes). The bean-bag sofa can be easily formed into a form-fitting bed as well.

Step 1: Materials and Tools
- bean bag beans
- spool of sturdy cloth
- about 3 feet of Velcro
- a sewing machine
- a 4–6 inch diameter cardboard tube about 2–3 feet long
- shop-vac (optional)

Step 2: Choose Your Sofa Size

Sofa Model	Diameter	Length	
pea	3 feet	3 feet	(standard bean bag chair)
garden slug	3 feet	8 feet	(recommended)
banana slug	4 feet	10 feet	(bad! Diameter is too big!)
centipede	3 feet	30 feet	(around-the-room sofa)
earthworm	1.5 feet	8 feet	(back rest only)
millipede	3 feet	1000 feet	(block party sofa)

The size of your sofa determines how much cloth you need. Where a standard bean bag chair is a sphere (ball), the bean bag sofa is a cylindrical shape. There are several possible sizes of sofa you can make:

It turns out there is also a jellyfish sofa. The jellyfish is what you get when you don't have enough beans in the bag for it to keep its shape and it just squooshes out all over the floor. The problem with the banana slug that I built—and the reason I don't recommend it—is that when it is filled enough to not be a jellyfish, it no longer will fit through a doorway. Plus it tends to envelop everything else in the room.

Your spool of cloth must be as wide as the diameter of the sofa. For the recommended garden slug sofa you'll need a spool 3 feet wide and 32 feet long. Use something sturdy! I made mine out of corduroy. There's a good selection of fabrics for $4 to $8 per yard at the local fabric store.

Step 3: What about the Beans!

You'll want to fill the bean bag at least 80 percent full of beans. A normal bean bag chair is not this full, but the sofa will not hold its shape unless it is nearly full. For the earthworm type used as a backrest, you may want to pack it 100 percent. Calculate the volume of the sofa (a cylinder): pi × radius × radius × length. So the garden slug is 56 cubic feet (3.14 × 1.5 × 1.5 × 8). Beanbag beans are sold by the cubic foot, so you'll need about 50 cubic feet of them. You will need a lot of beans, so the best thing is to find a local Styrofoam (eps) products manufacturer. Try the website epsmolders.org to find a list of eps manufacturers around the country.

Getting the beans will be a fun excursion unto itself, as you can see below. The technical term for what you want is "expanded polystyrene beads" or "eps beads" for short. Usually they will have both new beans ("virgin beads") and used beans ("regrind"). Virgin costs about ten times as much as regrind, usually more than you'll want to spend on some lunatic project you read about. The fancy places online that sell bean bags will tell you that virgin beads have a better feel in the bean bag, but my sofa seems perfectly nice with the regrind. Remember: regrind = recycling!

How do you find a Styrofoam products maker? Look under "packaging and shipping materials" or whatever else they might be making out of Styrofoam, such as architectural trim.

It took some effort, but I was able to wedge about 120 cubic feet of beans into my minivan after I took most of the seats out.

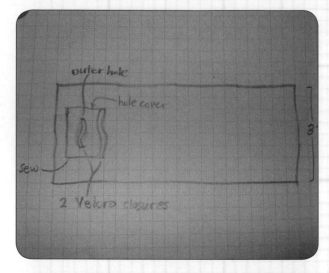

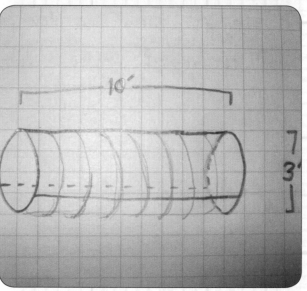

Step 4: The Plans

We're making a basic cylinder out of cloth. Of course I made the banana slug model. Cut two circles of fabric three feet in diameter—these will be the ends of the cylinder. Cut three rectangles three feet wide and as long as you want the sofa (eight or ten feet long). These three will form the tube of the cylinder. Cut a two-foot square; this will cover the fill-hole.

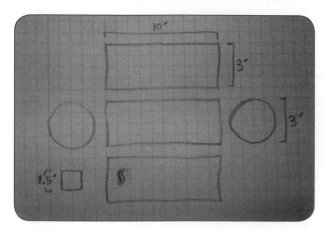

Step 5: Make the Double-Sealed Filling Hole

Whether you are making a slug or a centipede, surely nothing can be more important than a huge gaping maw to swallow up your kids and never let them out again! The filling hole is how you will get the beans into the sofa. I made a double seal to ensure that no beans can escape by accident! The double seal also reinforces the Velcro closures so that you'll be able to jump all over the sofa without fear of it opening up. This banana slug is proof! Cut a one-foot slit in one of the 3 x 8 foot fabric rectangles, about one foot from the end. Put Velcro on each side of the slit so that you can close it up. This is the outer seal. Sew the two-foot fabric rectangle onto the 3 x 8 foot piece so the middle of it covers the one-foot slit. Sew it only on three edges; on the fourth edge attach Velcro. This is the inner seal. Of course, do this on the "inside" side of the 3 x 8 foot fabric.

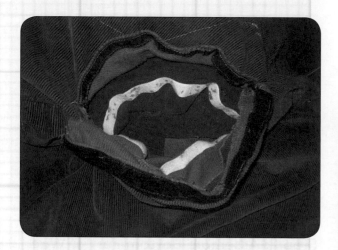

- Attach 6-inch-diameter cardboard tube to your bag of beans.
- Insert cardboard tube into sofa mouth.
- Pour in the beans.

Step 6: Sew the Sofa!

Sew the three big 3 x 8 foot rectangles together along their long edges, basically making an 8 x 9 foot sheet, then fold the sheet in half and sew its eight-foot edges to make a tube (do it inside-out). When you are done, you'll have an eight-foot-long tube with open ends. Go over all seams twice for strength. Keep the tube inside-out. Sew on one of the end-cap circles (also inside-out). Remember the circle circumference is a teeny bit larger (9.4 feet) than the tube circumference (9 feet). If you are a perfectionist that means you'd actually want your circle to be about 2.9 feet diameter, not 3 feet diameter. Sew on the other end-cap circle, inside-out.

Step 7: Flip It! Fill It!

It is time to pull the entire sofa out through its mouth (where you made the double seal), to make it right-side-out.

Once it is righted, the fun starts! How are you going to get all those beans into it? The most important thing to remember is that no matter how you do it, you'll be finding beans all over your house (and probably your neighborhood) for the rest of your life, so you might as well have fun trying.

Shop-Vac Method 1:
- Put mouth of sofa over the head of the shop-vac.
- Suck the beans out of the bag from whence they came!

Shop-Vac Method 2 (the bean cannon):
- Turn shop-vac into blower-mode.
- Put shop-vac head into bean supply (careful not to clog it).
- Point nozzle at unsuspecting passersby. When bored, point nozzle into sofa mouth to fill it.

Leaf-Blower Method:
- Just like shop-vac method 2, but with a leaf blower.

Boring Method:
- Hold mouth of sofa with the rest hanging down a staircase.

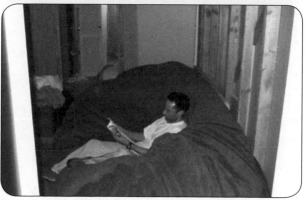

Aquarium Coffee Table

By x86Daddy
(http://www.instructables.com/id/
Aquarium-Coffee-Table/)

Build an aquarium coffee table for a fraction of the cost of ready-made models using supplies found mostly at your local superstore. Ten gallon and twenty gallon models are easily possible.

Step 1: Gather Supplies

You'll need:

- 20 gallon long gank
- 24 inch fluorescent fixtures (2)
- black foam board
- power strip
- light timer
- 1 inch chair end caps (2 4 packs)
- 36 x 14 inch wire shelving unit
- glass table top
- 100 watt heater
- 20 gallon internal filter
- glass vase marbles or beads 120 oz.
- two-prong, three-way power splitter

10 Gallon Alternate parts:

- 23 x 14 inch shelving unit
- 10 gallon standard tank
- ½ inch chair end caps
- 18 inch fluorescent fixtures
- 50 watt heater
- 10 gallon filter

Tools you'll need:

- mallet
- bolt cutter
- zip ties

If you don't already have these parts, I've estimated the costs of the ten-gallon and twenty-gallon models at $115 and $180 respectively.

However, this is where an old glass-top coffee table, spare wire shelving, or extra aquarium equipment can dramatically reduce the cost. Even if you go out and buy every item you need for the project, note that ready-made coffee-table aquariums appear to start at $500 before shipping.

Disclaimer: I'm not an engineer, but the shelving used is rated for more weight than what would be added by a full aquarium of the sizes discussed, so I feel quite safe with the choices made for this project. Do read the packaging on the shelving you buy to ensure your structure will support the approximate 10 lbs./gallon guideline.

Step 2: Assemble Bottom Part of Wire Shelving Unit

Either size of wire shelving unit includes four posts, which usually split in half for smaller packaging. Some of the 36 x 14 inch shelving units have posts that split into uneven lengths, with a top segment that is roughly 18 inches tall. This would be the best kind to find, as a short segment like that would provide appropriate legs for your table. If you cannot find such shelves, use of a hacksaw or other implements of destruction will be required. Add the first shelf at a height that will allow you to stow your light fixtures and power strip beneath it.

Step 3: Zip-Tie Fluorescent Fixtures and Power Strip under the Bottom Shelf

Consider cable routing before securing the zip-ties in place; for example, where is the best place for the power cable to stick out? If using two light fixtures, use the power splitter with your light timer. My arrangement leaves enough clearance for me to unplug the timer and pull it out to change the time settings, as well as plug and unplug the aquarium's filter and heater.

Step 4: Add Aquarium

At this point, put the aquarium in and verify that the heights and clearances are to your liking. I have sufficient space above the edge of my aquarium to reach in and drop food without removing the glass top.

Step 5: Cut the Shelving Wires from Top Shelf, Leaving Only the Sides

Having two "shelves" adds stability and good looks to your new coffee table. Using bolt cutters is a quick and easy way to remove the internal shelf area for your top-middle stabilizing shelf. Although I was too impatient, using a Dremel, file, or other deburring instrument on the remaining stubs of the cut wires would make the upper shelf safer. I recommend doing so if you have kids around who may put their hands on that part of the table. After placing that shelf, you can complete the support structure by placing rubber-chair end caps on the posts.

Step 6: Add in Aquarium Components and Decor

You're almost finished! Test your lights and power and position the table exactly where you'll want it at this point; once you add even ten gallons of water, moving the table will no longer be easy. An internal power filter in a corner of the tank is an unobtrusive, yet highly functional way to provide filtration. Likewise, a standard submersible heater will be needed if you're keeping fish that require a temperature other than that of standing water in room temperature. Route the cables down a corner of the tank, through the bottom shelf, and to the power strip. Zip-tie in place as needed.

Usually, it is highly advised to not power these devices until they are under water, so don't plug them in until you've added water. I used a suction cup and a glass-tube thermometer mounted diagonally inside the aquarium so that it would be readable while I sat beside the table. I used a very thin layer of colored, flattened glass marbles as substrate, but any translucent substrate would work. As there is not a top directly over the aquarium in my configuration, and I plan to add a species known to jump, I did not fill it to the very top. Instead I'm leaving 3 to 4 inches of "wall" at the top of the tank. Research

your desired species or consider an acrylic or glass inset for the top of the tank. Another option would be to configure your shelf height or post length so that the glass table top would be placed almost directly over the aquarium. Leave some space for airflow though!

Step 7: Fill and Add Top Glass

Cut the foam board into strips appropriately sized for wedging vertically under the bottom shelf. They will be used to conceal the components and the extra light. You're done! Now you can cycle the aquarium to establish the needed bacteria colony and then add fish suitable to your quantity of water.

I've had mine running for months now, and I must say it's very enjoyable. The only complication I've encountered is that when vacuuming the gravel, the standard siphon effect is pretty weak given that the bottom of my bucket, resting on the floor, is only about four inches lower than the bottom of the tank. It's still good enough to do the job, but I've considered buying a battery powered tank vac.

Duct Tape Hammock

By Dadzilla

(http://www.instructables.com/id/
Duct-Tape-Hammock-1/)

This red, white, and blue hammock is the perfect place to relax on the Fourth of July!

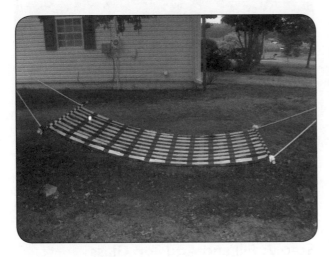

Step 1: The Pieces

3 rolls duct tape
2 wooden dowels (48" x 1")

Step 2: The Set-Up

Since this hammock is woven and duct tape is as sticky as, well, duct tape, a rigid set-up is necessary. I used a wooden table I had built and screwed 2 x 4 scraps (12" long) to the sides, then attached the dowel with another screw. The distance between the points of attachment of the dowel will be slightly more than your hammock width. My final width was about 34 inches.

Step 3: Long Loops

Roll tape out sticky-side up. Run under dowels on each end.

Step 4: Folding Over

Press tape down onto itself on one side, then roll out enough tape to complete the loop and press the loop together.

Step 5: Lots of Long Loops

Continue making loops, close but not touching, until full width is reached. Stagger tape joints to keep the hammock strong.

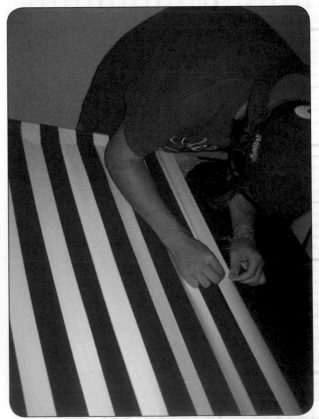

Step 6: Marking for Weaving

The important thing to remember before starting to weave is that the side facing up is the bottom. Take a ruler and mark where the tape edges go on the outer two loops of each side of the hammock. To duplicate my pattern, start on the outside with a mark about two inches from the end, then make a mark every 7½ inches. Move to the inside loop and make a mark 5¾ inches from the end, then make marks every 7½ inches.

Step 7: Weaving

I used a piece of half-inch PVC (you could use a broom handle) to separate my loops, then used the ruler as a shuttle to pass between them. Making these loops is the same as before, sticky-side up and then fold over. Be careful not to pull the outside loops in when you fold over.

Step 8: Weave Set-up

Be careful when weaving duct tape, as it will hang up given half a chance.

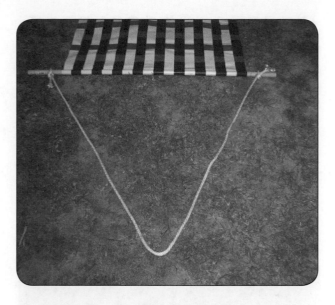

Step 11: Securing the Hangers

You wouldn't want the ropes to slip, so secure them with—wait for it—duct tape! Tape over the dowel and the knot on all sides.

Step 12: Enjoy!

Find some suitable trees, hang the hammock, and relax!

Step 9: Bottom Side of the Weave

When weaving is finished it will look like the photos. Remember, at this point the bottom side is still up. Only the top side of the loop is woven. The bottom side (visible here) is stuck down all the way across. Also notice how the weaves shift up and down. This is because I have an even number of long loops. With an odd number it would shift inside and out.

Step 10: Attach Rope

Make a triangular rope support for each end of the hammock. The length of the rope will be approximately ten feet and it should be tied to the hammock on either side.

Skateboard Table

By wilgubeast
(http://www.instructables.com/id/
Skateboard-Table/)

For those of you who were told not to skate in the house as a child, here's a Lazy Susan coffee table that rotates on skateboard wheels. Think of the possibilities: Play board games where nobody has to look at the board upside down. Bring the remote within reach without getting up from the couch. Epic tea parties.

Step 1: Design Inspiration
I wanted a table that met the following constraints:
- less than $100
- made from wood and parts that are easily available
- requires minimal power tools
- easy to assemble

I spent around $70 for everything but the glass top. The glass put me over my intended budget by around $60. I purchased only from Anytown, USA stores: Home Depot, Ace Hardware, Amazon, and Pier 1 Imports (for the glass). No specialty shops. No exotic lumberyards. Nothing fancy. Just deck planks, a couple of cheapo complete skateboard sets, and miscellaneous fasteners.

I used a power drill, a miter saw, and a palm sander. After cutting and drilling, assembly is more or less IKEA-style—inserting dowels into slots and then some screwing.

Step 2: Materials
Parts:
- two redwood boards (2 x 6 x 8)—$14 each
- dowel pins—$2 (12-pack with channels in the side for extra glue hold)
- dowel centers
- Simpson strong-tie T-shaped strap—$4 (6" x 6"; screws to install on the bottom)
- two Krown Rookie Complete Skateboard—$44 (you can save the decks for future projects)
- wood glue
- semigloss polyurethane
- eight 1" wood screws

Tools:
- miter saw
- palm sander
- drill with brad point bits at 5/16" and something tiny for your pilot holes
- speed square protractor
- a band clamp (you can also use any ratcheting tie) with brad point bits at 5/16" and something tiny for your pilot holes
- rubber mallet
- sponge for applying polyurethane

Step 3: Saw
Cut your 2" x 6" boards to length. The length of the radial portions on the top of the table base may vary. Customize it to your space. Make sure each board end is absolutely square by trimming the last inch or so from each side of the 2 x 6 prior to working with them. Not every cut at the mill or the lumberyard is going to be to your specifications.

154

Here's what I did for a 36" diameter table:
- Radial boards for the top of the base: 18 inches
- Leg boards: 14 inches

Check that everything is square and the proper length before you move on. Making exacting cuts only to discover that the end of your board isn't square feels terrible.

marks as exact as possible. Use the speed square. Use a ruler. Check with a protractor. Then cut.

Step 4: Saw 2

Now that all of your boards have been cut to length, it's time for the hard part: that central joint. You'll need to know where to make the cuts to get a beautiful set of 120 degree pointed boards, and that might require some math. I've broken it out into three options for you.

For students of the humanities, use a protractor to mark a line from the center of the end of the board. Draw a line along the 60 degree mark from that midpoint to the side of the board. That'll give you a lovely line that you may cut along.

For those of you who fully trust the angles along the bottom of the miter saw, mark the midpoint of your board, then set the saw to 30 degrees, align with the midpoint, and cut.

For those of you who are comfortable with trigonometry, just puzzle it out. [Hint: x = .5(width of the board) •tan(30)]

For my table, the measurement from the end of the board came out to around 1 17/32", but do this part for yourself to ensure that everything lines up properly.

Now that you know where to make the cuts, get to it. I cut a few practice pieces to get a feel for the new saw, figure out the size of the kerf, and because I am on the obsessive side of cautious. I also struggle with simple math. Things to remember— make your

Step 5: Treat the Wood

You can save this step until last, but I like my pieces to be finished before I assemble everything. If you are unsure of your polyurethaning abilities, you might want to do that step just before installing the skateboard parts. I chose polyurethane because it has protective qualities and a matte finish. The semi-gloss is good for my needs and hides mistakes better than a full gloss. You will be fine with oil or wax if you want to go that route. The Minwax tung oil gave me the same look as the semi-gloss poly. (It was also approximately easier to apply.)

For the brave and/or foolhardy, let's put on some polyurethane. First, follow the directions on the can. **Then:**
- Use a matte finish to avoid having a tiny mistake force you to start over.
- Use a disposable sponge brush (or just a sponge, like I did) and don't over-do it, as it'll create bubbles and drips.
- Follow the grain.
- Allow plenty of drying time.
- Hand-sand between coats (the palm sander moves too fast and will melt the finish).

However, if any of that sounds too hard, just use oil or wax. I used two coats, hand-sanding with 220 paper after each coat. I could have gone for a finer grit, but I like the ever-so-slightly unfinished look of the 220. Play with it. It's your table, after all.

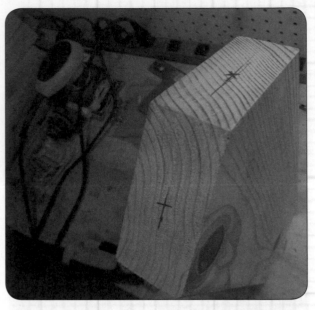

Step 6: Joint

Now that everything is cut to size, it's time to mark our holes for doweling. Refer to the images for this step, as many of these ideas are easier to convey visually than with text.

You'll need dowel centers for this. (If you don't have any, a thumbtack should do in a pinch.) They will help you align your holes after drilling. Your drill likely has some wobble and may travel a bit as you drill out your holes. The dowel centers allow you to mess up a little bit on your initial hole placement by letting you use the existing hole to mark where to drill on the next board.

Mark your drill locations in the following places:

- Each side of the pointy bit on the radial supports
- Two equidistant marks on the underside of each radial support
- Two equidistant marks on the top of each leg

Using the dowel centers means that you don't need a doweling jig for this. It does mean, though, that you will need to keep track of which boards fit together. Each dowel joint done this way is slightly different, so label your boards (on a spot that'll be covered) in such a way as to be able to know which radial support fits perfectly with which leg. This is important.

Use a brad point bit. It will make this easier. If you don't have one, drill pilot holes then use your normal bits. You shouldn't need to buy anything special for this. Be sure to wrap your bit so you don't end up drilling too deep.

Measure twice, staying away from the edges of the wood so you don't split your board. Take a deep breath then drill perpendicularly to the face you are working on. Use the dowel center to mark the drill location for the board you will attach to the board you just drilled into freehand.

Step 7: Glue

Put a small dab of wood glue on both sides of your dowels. Insert them into the holes you made in Step 6. Then align the corresponding boards together. You'll have to glue and push in all three boards at once for the interior joint. Once you've pushed everything together to your satisfaction, put the strap clamp around all three pieces of wood. Tighten it to the point that everything is pushed together, but not so tight that it starts to pull your joint apart. Then wait for it to dry.

A helpful tip: Screw the T-strap onto the base of the joint after the glue has dried. I don't fully trust the dowels, so using the metal T-strap ensures full stability.

Then glue on the legs. Clamp them in place with something—a clutch-lock bar clamp or something similar.

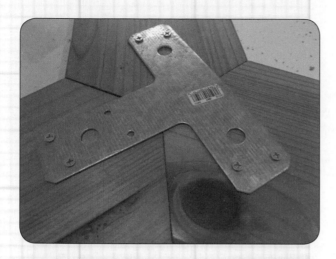

Step 8: Attach Trucks

Your trucks may vary in size, so I'll give approximate directions for attaching your skateboard apparatus. Center the trucks on the board.

You'll want your outermost wheel to be even with the edge of the radial board. Measure carefully! Mark the center of the holes with an awl, pencil tip, or something else thin and pointy.

Use the same technique as before to create drill stops with tape, using the length of your screws as a guide. Then drill each mark that you made. Go in as straight as you can to keep the screw heads parallel to the radial boards. It'll be prettier that way. Put on all the trucks facing the same direction. Look at the pictures. Then screw them on.

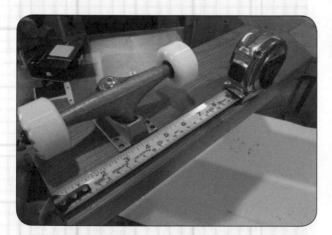

Step 9: Tabletop

Glass tabletops can be pricey. Check for cheap ones at thrift stores, garage sales, and flea markets, or repurpose one from another table.

I got mine from Pier 1. It was worth the slight mark-up to not have to dig through trash for a day looking for a single item.

Put the glass on top of the skateboard wheels. Centering the table is a bit of a challenge, so I decided to just eyeball it to get it as close as I could. You're welcome to experiment with the placement of the glass, the bearings, or the glass size.

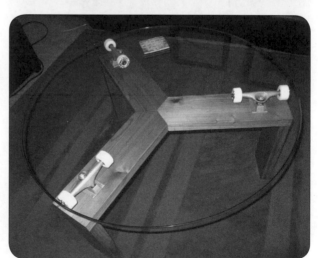

Ladder Bookshelf

By action pig

(http://www.instructables.com/id/Ladder-Bookshelf/)

I found this amazing, dingy old ladder in the trash around the same time I discovered half-price bookstores. I can't bring myself to buy those canned, pressed-wood, department-store bookshelves anymore, and I need space for my Lemony Snicket collection. Hence this project!

Step 1: Materials and Equipment
- ladder
- wood for shelves (I used ¼" thick red oak planks, backed with ¼"–½" thick red oak for support)
- wood for cross bars (I used ½" x 1½" red oak)
- shelf brackets (1½", to support cross bars; you need 8)
- shelf braces (look for "mending plates"—straight brackets to support cross bars; you need 8)
- wood glue
- sandpaper
- wood finish (I used 50/50 tung oil/mineral spirits)
- ½"–5/8" wood screws
- jig saw
- sander
- drill

- level
- T-square
- measuring tape

Not having a table saw or planer, I used craft wood that had already been squared and nicely planed. I chose oak. This project could be built for much less money if you have the ability to cut and plane your own boards!

Step 2: Prepare the Ladder

I wanted to see what was underneath all of the grime and paint. I sanded with 60, 100, and 150 grit and discovered some lovely oak pine. This part was time consuming.

Step 3: Add the Braces

I decided to make the shelves so that they would sit flush with the steps. Metal braces are used to support cross bars that support the shelves.

The straight braces are screwed to the underside of the ladder steps. You might notice that when the ladder is oriented so that the back rails are perpendicular to the floor, the steps are slightly slanted. In order for the wooden shelves to be level, the metal braces need to be bent until they are level.

The square brackets are screwed to the inside of the back rails. The cross braces will be screwed into both sets of brackets.

Step 4: Cut and Install the Cross-Bars

I used ½" x 1½" red oak for the cross bars. The cross bars sit flush against the back of the steps and extend to the back rails. Unfortunately, this ladder was not built to be especially square—when the ladder is oriented correctly, the right-hand cross bars (looking from the back to the front) need to be longer than the left-hand cross bars.

To cut with a jig saw, measure the distance from the side of the saw to the blade. Set up a rail that is this distance away from your desired cut to guide the cut. For instance, my jig saw has 1½" between the blade and the side of the saw. To cut 3", I clamp a piece of wood at 4½" This is where the T-square comes in handy. If your rail is slanted, your cut will be, too!

Screw cross bars into the braces. Use pilot holes before drilling—it turns out that ½"-thick boards have a tendency to split.

Step 5: Cut and Reinforce the Shelves

I bought craft wood ¼" thick in widths of 4" and 2" (I think I used 12 feet of 4" and 8 feet of 2"—it takes a lot more than it looks).

The steps of the ladder are about ¾" thick. When the ¼" thick shelves sit on top of the ½" cross bars, the shelves sit flush with the wooden steps.

I cut and glued supports (¼" x 2" oak) to the underside of the shelves. The supports keep the shelves from sliding off the cross bars and prevent bending from the weight of the books.

Step 6: Assemble and Finish

I sanded the shelves and applied a 50/50 mix of tung oil and mineral spirits to everything. In order to apply a proper finish, rough up the surfaces lightly with #0000 steel wool, wipe off woolly bits, apply finish (wear gloves!), wipe off excess finish, and allow it to dry. Repeat until satisfied.

The final product is meant to be disassembled—the shelves are not glued in and the cross bars can be unscrewed, allowing the ladder to fold.

Happy building!

Hang .10 Coffee Table

By CraigRJess

(http://www.instructables.com/id/
HANG-10-coffee-table/)

The Hang .10 Coffee Table is a think-outside-the-box design. The name comes from the two racing stripes made of Canadian dimes and the option to hang it on the wall if you so choose, hence the name Hang .10. Since I used a surfing term as the name, it would only make sense to shape it like a surfboard. The dimes were laid with one stripe having all "heads" showing while the other stripe was showing the "schooner." There are two keyhole slots routed in the back. These slots allow the table to be hung on the wall if you get tired of its original purpose.

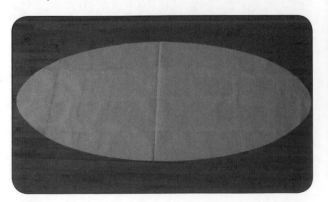

Step 1: Make a Template

I used free online drawing software to make the ellipsis the size I wanted. Then I printed it out. Since the printer cannot print out a shape this big on one sheet, it will break it down into smaller pieces I call tiles. Once the tiles were printed out it was simple enough to lay them down and tape them together. Once it was all taped together, I cut out the elliptical surfboard shape. This template is what I used to make the top of the table.

Step 2: Make a Jig

Take your paper template and trace its shape onto the wood that you will use for your jig. I used ½" MDF, but you can use ¼" MDF, Masonite, or plywood.

Use your jigsaw to cut out that shape from the MDF. Once it is cut, take a belt sander and clean up all the edges around the jig. This construction will be your main jig now. This jig is what the router bit follows to cut out your perfect ellipse.

Select the wood you'd like for your table. I chose pre-finished birch. Now put the wood template onto the wood you've selected and clamp it down. Proceed to route around the jig with the router bit riding against the jig. I used a 1" pattern bit with a ball bearing. This bearing is what rides against the edges that I smoothed out earlier.

Once the main shape was routed out, I switched to a 22.5° router bit and routed around the edges once again. This gives me a 22.5° bevel on the edges. Now your table top is ready for your design.

Step 3: Paint

I masked off the edges and painted only the top black. I left the edges to show the different plywood layers as a design element. I laid out the location of the coin stripes with painter's tape.

Now you can throw down some dimes! I used white glue and Q-Tips. The type of glue doesn't matter because the whole table will be getting covered with epoxy resin later.

Step 4: Decorate

I removed the painter's tape in order to lay out my chrome maple leaf decals. I originally tried to cut them out myself with a X-acto knife but it wasn't very neat. I had a professional cut out 50 chrome maple leaf decals for me on the computerized cutter. I then laid out all the decals in the pattern I wanted.

Step 5: Coat with Epoxy Resin

Now it's time for the epoxy resin coating. You will need enough for a minimum of two coats. I mixed my epoxy in a 1:1 ratio. This may be different with other brands so be sure to read the instructions carefully. I poured the epoxy and waited ten minutes for all the bubbles to come to the surface.

Now take your plumber's torch and wave it around the surface of the table, popping all the bubbles. Keep the torch moving at all times and about six inches away from the surface to avoid burning the epoxy. I waited overnight and did a second pour of the epoxy. You have to try your best to avoid airborne dust and grit from getting onto the top.

Step 6: Adding Legs

You should wait about four days for the epoxy to cure, then you can move the table around and finish it off.

I attached nice 13" powder-coated hairpin legs. These legs seem to be really popular right now. I used a keyhole router bit and routed out two keyhole slots. These slots will allow me to hang the table on the wall if I tire of this as a coffee table or want to display it as art. They are spaced 16" on center to allow hanging onto wood studs.

And finally to finish it off I made a customized nameplate using a military dog tag. I think that finishes it of nicely.

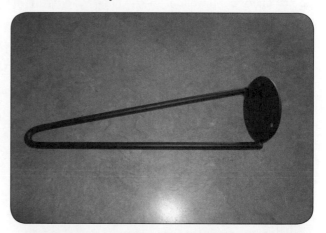

Step 7: Enjoy

And you have the final product. Hang10 everyone!

Modular Bookshelf

By Luegg

(http://www.instructables.com/id/Modular-bookshelf-1/)

I wanted to build a good-looking and practical bookshelf for our new apartment. Since the apartment is on the top floor, the ceiling is angular, and the bookshelf had to be fitted to the wall. I decided to design it in a modular way so it can easily be adapted to different circumstances. It took some thinking and tweaking, but I came up with a solution that works rather nicely.

There are some big advantages to a modular bookshelf (in my opinion):

- You can rearrange the whole thing whenever you get tired of looking at it.
- It's easily expandable (by either rearranging or building more modules).
- It creates a "living" wall of books (and/or other things).
- The modules are very light and easy to move around, plus they take up very little space (for example, in a moving van).

Step 1: Design

The modules come in different sizes (either quadratical or oblong). The width is in every case a multiple of the height (up to 5:1, in my case), so the modules are stackable. There are three different module-heights to accommodate paperbacks, hardbacks, binders, big books, and so on. The different sizes of books and binders demand different depths for the modules, as well, which gives a really nice look to the complete bookshelf.

The longer modules (3:1 and more) need a middle panel to distribute the weight of the modules on top of them evenly. To combine all these different heights and widths, I had to build two customized modules with different sizes (to adjust for the height), but besides that, everything is standardized.

I wanted to build the modules to be as low-key and sleek as possible. There is almost no hardware needed, since all the joints are glued. The mitred joints allow for a very elegant construction (although it's harder to build) and keep the whole design very simple. To assemble the whole bookshelf, I made aluminum clips out of a U-profile. Lined with textile tape, they clamp the modules together, making the whole bookshelf stable and sturdy.

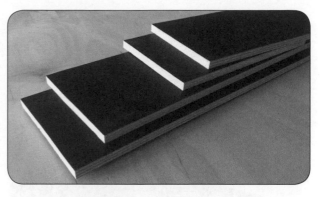

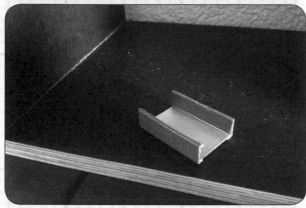

Step 2: Materials and Tools

For my bookshelf, I chose a 9mm phenolic, resin-coated, birch plywood. This coated plywood has a very robust and nice-looking surface, but is rather expensive (about $48 per square meter). Plywood offers the advantage of constructing the bookshelf with quite thin material (9mm), and there is no real need for the coated surface besides the look.

Since I don't own equipment to cut the big boards down to size, I had the material ordered as strips of the three different depths I needed. Clean and nice cuts are really important, since half of the edges are visible at the end.

So the needed materials are:
- plywood strips (widths depending on the measurements for the modules)
- aluminum U-profile (to produce the clamps)
- felt pads for the bottom modules

The tools used for this project are:
- a halfway decent circular saw bench (with the ability to tilt the saw blade to 45°)
- a calibrated try square
- a measuring tape
- lots of abrasive paper
- a very well-sharpened chisel
- 1-K PUR wood adhesive (it has to be a really strong adhesive, since the surface of the connections is quite small)
- plenty of plastic adhesive tape

Step 3: Cutting

The first step is cutting the plywood strips to the required lengths. To achieve very clean cuts, I use a piece of thick plywood as a base on which I cut the miter joints (and even joints for the middle panel). This way I get close to no chipping at the edges. It is very important to use arrestors so that the corresponding pieces have the exact same length. I tend to check the lengths after every second cut, just to be on the safe side.

The angle of the saw blade is crucial, since even a half degree off can result in joints that don't fit properly. I use surplus wood to test that angle very carefully until the pieces fit perfectly. Always take care to use the safety devices as specified, even if it means slower progress.

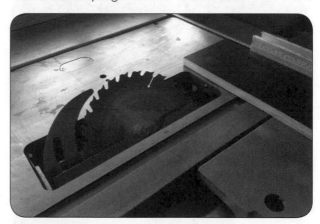

Step 4: Sanding and Preparing for Assembly

The surfaces of this coated plywood don't need to be sanded, but with other materials, now would be the time to get a nice smooth surface. To get the edges nice and smooth, I take several pieces of the same width and pinch them together with wooden bar clamps. It's easier to work this way and ultimately, it's a lot faster.

After sanding all edges like this (a very important step), I chamfer the edges very subtly. I prefer sharp edges, but they still should be a bit chamfered. When all of this is done, the pieces should be cleaned. All the dust needs to be removed as to not affect the quality of the adhesion.

All the joints (inside and outside) need to be prepared with plastic adhesive tape. This technique will take a moment, but the time it saves after the adhesive has cured is substantial. Align the tape very carefully on the very edges (inner and outer edges) and do this wherever there will be adhesive (as seen in the pictures). Do the same for all middle panels by measuring precisely where they will be and then taping around the adhesive surface. The overspilt adhesive will cure on the plastic and can then be removed very easily.

Step 5: Assembly

Now it is time to assemble the parts by means of plastic tape. Place the pieces in the right order on a flat and clean surface and tape them together on the outside. It's very important that the outside edges are perfectly aligned so the miter joints will fit. When everything is taped together on the outside, it has to be flipped, which can be quite tricky. Now it is possible to "fold" the whole module and check if everything fits nicely. I always do this before I apply any adhesive!

After this check, I apply the adhesive. The adhesive I use expands while curing, so not much of it is needed in these joints. If there is excess adhesive, don't bother wiping it off. PUR-adhesive is really nasty before curing and can much easier be removed mechanically after curing.

After applying the adhesive, I "fold" the pieces together and fixate both "open" ends with more plastic tape. I use a try square to check the angles and to check all the corners carefully, because the edges can sometime shift a bit.

Since the plastic tape is also applied where the middle panel is planned, it is convenient to insert this panel at this time. I apply the adhesive on the panel's edges, spread the module a bit, and put the middle panel in-between. It's easy to adjust its position because of the plastic tape, and to be sure I check it again with the try square.

When all the angles are checked again, I put some weight on top of the module so that the middle panel receives the needed pressure, check all the angles once more, and let it cure for at least three hours (depending on the adhesive).

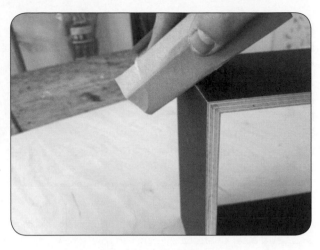

Step 7: Finished Product

I've had some practice in producing these modules, since I wanted to fill the whole wall with this modular bookshelf. It sounds like a lot of work, but by producing multiple modules at a time, it becomes quite efficient. To produce a single module takes about one hour (besides the curing process). Producing ten modules will take maybe five hours, and the more modules are made side by side, the less time it takes.

I enjoy this project a lot because it's practical and beautiful. Working on it is very satisfying, since all the time spent for preparations really pays off in the end.

Step 6: Finishing Touches

After curing, all the plastic tape can be removed, which should get rid of almost all the excess adhesive. The adhesive residue on the edges and in the corners needs to be removed very carefully with a well-sharpened chisel. The traces of adhesive on the edge need to be removed by sanding, so that the miter joints look nice.

I chamfer the now-joined edges a little bit and retouch them with a black marker. This leaves no trace on this material, but needs to be tested with every other material.

I always test the modules by trying to pull them apart, but they are really sturdy. After checking all the edges, I decide which side looks better and mark the less perfect side so that I know which way to assemble the whole thing at home.

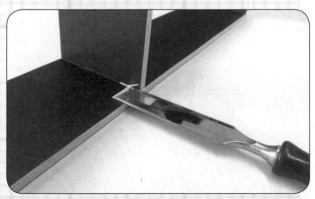

I recently switched to a standing desk at work and used a set of affordable and simple screw jacks to raise my desk to the proper height. Fully adjustable from 11" to 17 3/4", these jack stands will raise any normal desk to standing desk height for people between 5' 3" and 6' 1", depending on your body geometry.

Now, let me be clear—while these are adjustable jack stands, they are not really something that you'd want to change on the fly throughout the course of the day. This is no substitute for someone who wants both a sitting and standing desk. For that, you've got to shell out the big bucks and buy a motorized system. This DIY solution is more for someone who wants to commit to a standing desk, but wants the ability to dial in the perfect height for comfort and ergonomics.

For anyone who is thinking about converting to a standing desk, take a tip from someone who already has: You want to raise your whole desk up, not just your monitor and keyboard. Sure it's easier to simply raise your monitor on a stand or arm and buy a small platform that your keyboard and mouse can rest on at the proper height, as many DIY standing-desk conversions online suggest, but then you lose access to all the good stuff on your desk besides your computer. Where do you put your coffee, paperclips, obscene-but-thoughtful hand-drawn Christmas cards from coworkers, and the 800 cords for your iPhone, camera, SD card reader, and external hard drive? Having the whole desk at standing desk height sacrifices nothing (except your chair) and gives you easier access to all your stuff.

Step 1: Purchase Jack Stands, Four Nuts, and Four Washers

I'm testing a number of different jack stands to convert a normal sitting desk to a standing one, but I thought I'd start with the simplest and cheapest solution first—these Husky aluminum screw jacks from Amazon for $36. Go to the hardware store and pick up four ¾" standard zinc-plated nuts and four large zinc-plated flange washers.

Step 2: Assemble

The jack stands are pretty darn stable on their own, but since they come with only one nut that just "sits" in the base, I thought it'd be best to eliminate any rocking or shaking and lock the threaded rod onto the base with a second nut and flange washer so that everything is held tightly in place.

To accomplish this, first slide the threaded rod that comes with the jack stand onto the base. Then place the flange washer over the bottom of the threaded rod and follow it with the second nut.

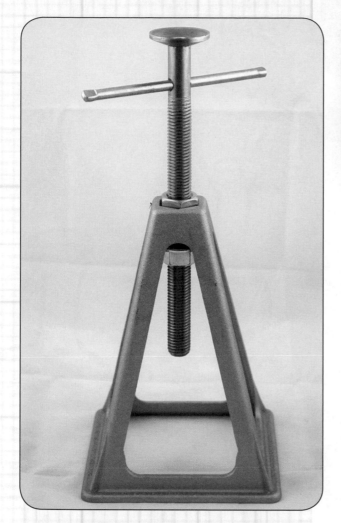

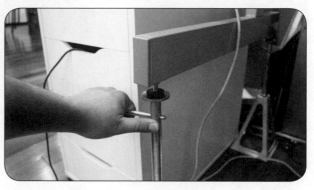

Step 4: Level

Level the desk once you've got the proper height adjusted. It's nice that all four jack stands can be adjusted independently, since the floors in our office are actually quite sloped.

I used the original leveling feet on the desk to dial in the level, but it's really six of one or half a dozen of another whether you choose to turn the jack screws or the leveling feet.

Step 3: Slide under Desk and Adjust to Proper Ergonomic Height

With some help, lift your sitting desk up around 15" and slide the four jack stands underneath your desk. Most desks have leveling feet of some kind—that's right where you want to place the jack stands. If your desk has some other kind of foot system, it's easy to use a small piece of wood to create a platform for the desk leg to rest on that simply sits on top of the jack stand.

You can get a vague idea of how high you'll need to jack up your desk by using a simple standing desk height calculator. That way, you can adjust the jacks most of the way before you put them under your desk, so you only need to do some fine-tuning once they're in place. It's a whole lot faster to feed several inches of threaded rod through the nuts before you plop your desk on top of them than once the heavy desk is in place.

Fine tune the height using the leveling feet and then the threaded rods. Even though this is really beyond the scope of this Instructable, my monitors had to be raised to the proper height as well. I bit the bullet and went to IKEA for some steel feet and a black wooden shelf to accomplish that.

Step 5: Secure

If you happen to live in an earthquake-prone area, like San Francisco, it's not a bad idea to affix your desk to the wall. This will also reduce any minor shake or shimmy on the desk that may occur from simply the vibration of your hands upon the keyboard. The jack stands do not shake; it's actually the surface of the desk (at least on mine) that is moving.

Screw an L bracket onto the bottom of the desk and into the wall, which will really help lock everything into place. Don't want to screw into your wall because it's made of brick and you are scheduled to be moving to a new office soon? Use a wooden shim slid between the desk and the wall to put some tension on the system and hold everything in place. I'm not too proud of this solution, but until the move, it works just as well as a screwed-in bracket to reduce any shaking. Earthquake proofing . . . not so much.

With this configuration of jack stands and the wooden wedge, my desk doesn't move at all, can be adjusted to the exact proper height so that my arm forms a right angle at my elbow, and can easily be changed should I come into work wearing high heels one day but flip flops the next.

Science

There is boring high school science, and then there is mad science. These projects fall between the two extremes. You can make your own diamonds in the microwave, but they're a little on the small side. You can create a solar death ray with a recycled Fresnel lens, but you'll need several before you can take over the world with them. You can grow your own crystals, but few will contain enough kryptonite to incapacitate any superheroes from Kansas.

If you're not a budding Brain/Doofenshmirtz/Frankenstein, you can still demonstrate scientific principles in spectacular ways. Magnetic silly putty is a great way to learn about magnetism while playing with a blob. Wave pendulums are the most soothing way to learn about amplitude and frequency without drooling into a physics textbook after falling asleep.

Magnetic Silly Putty

By mikeasaurus
(http://www.instructables.com/id/magnetic-silly-putty/)

Thinking Putty (also known as Silly Putty) is a silicone polymer children's toy. Silly Putty is fun because it has some unique properties. It is viscoelastic, meaning it can be stretched and shaped and mashed back together again, as its apparent viscosity increases directly with respect to the amount of force applied (read: it can be torn or shattered with impact). Also, it bounces. Okay, enough science. I'm sure we've all played with Thinking Putty in our youth, but how about magnetic Silly Putty?

By adding a ferrous component to an already wacky toy we can keep all characteristics of the original putty but now also have the dimension of magnetism! I've seen magnetic thinking putty for sale on other websites, but I'll show you how you can make your own for a fraction of the price and in about 20 minutes.

Enough talk, let's make some magnetic putty!

Step 1: Tools and Materials
Tools:
- disposable gloves (latex or other)
- disposable face mask
- disposable work area (paper plate)

Materials:
- Thinking Putty ($2.00 or less)– any color
- Ferric iron oxide powder (artist supply stores)
- Neodymium magnet

The secret ingredient that makes the putty magnetic is an iron oxide powder, which is ferric (magnetic). Ferric iron oxide is a fine powder used as black pigment and can be found at art stores. If your local artist supply store doesn't carry it, you can always purchase it online.

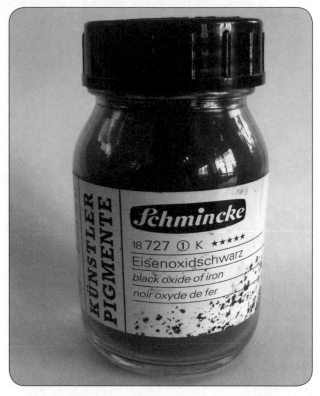

Step 2: Prepare Putty
Start by clearing a space to work, making sure it is well ventilated. Iron oxide powder is very fine and inhaling it is not such a good idea. Put on your gloves and face mask before you begin.

Open the putty and remove from the container. Work the putty in your hands to warm it up, then stretch it out like a sheet and lay it on your disposable work surface (sheet of paper or paper plate).

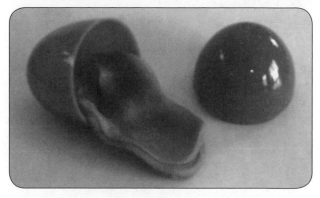

Step 3: Add Iron Oxide
Thinking putty comes in different sizes, depending on where you purchase it. I found mine in

a local toy shop; it comes in an egg-shaped container and is about 24 grams (0.8 oz.).

For this size, I used about a tablespoon of iron oxide; you may require more or less depending on your putty size and amount of magnetism desired. Carefully spoon the iron oxide into the center of the putty sheet, then close the lid on the iron oxide powder to reduce excess iron dust escaping.

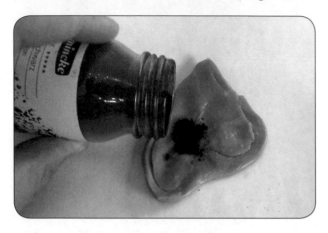

Step 4: Work It

Gently fold the edges of the putty sheet into the center and work the powder into the putty. Go slowly, as the powder produces lots of dust. After a minute of massaging, the putty will lose its color and begin to look black as pitch. Keep massaging putty for about three to four minutes.

Step 5: Experiment and Have Fun!

That's it, you're done! Grab your magnet and start experimenting with your new magnetic putty. You can stretch out a strand and make it follow your magnet, you can polarize your putty to work as a magnet itself, and then there's the classic of placing the magnet directly on the putty and watching it envelop the magnet. There's plenty of fun to be had.

Caution: Putty has been known to leave a residue on some surfaces, even more so with the iron oxide powder. Use caution when playing with your magnetic putty.

If you get magnetic putty stuck to fabric, you can try placing the magnet on top of the fabric and the putty may work its way out (wait 24 hours). Alternatively, you can apply rubbing alcohol to the area and work out the putty, but try a concealed test area first. WD-40 may also work. If all else fails, take the fabric to the dry cleaner and tell them it's a silicone-based stain.

What are you waiting for? Get going and make your own magnetic putty! Have fun!

How to Make a Synthetic Diamond

By mrcrumley
(http://www.instructables.com/id/How-to-Make-a-Synthetic-Diamond/)

My ten-year wedding anniversary was coming up, so I thought I'd make my wife something special. A few months ago I saw a show on TV where they demonstrated how companies were now making "cultured" diamonds in the lab. There are a few different methods, but the simplest is something called chemical vapor distillation. The process is pretty straightforward. Basically, microwaves are used to create a slurry of graphite plasma, which, when rapidly cooled, forms a crystal structure. The best part was that everything I needed was pretty common in the typical household. So, I rounded up the necessary supplies and began imagining how great life would be once I'd cornered the international diamond market.

Step 1: Materials
Here's the surprisingly short list of materials I used:
- standard home microwave oven
- 2 coffee mugs
- 3 pieces of 3mm graphite pencil lead
- few drops of extra virgin olive oil
- 5" piece of 100% cotton thread.

Step 2: Prepare the Olive Oil
As I mentioned above, the theory behind this project is using microwaves to heat the graphite into plasma. In general, pencil graphite is not reactive enough to microwaves. So, thin oil is used to concentrate the heat in a specific area of the graphite. Also, as the oil heats up and begins to burn, it chemically separates the binder in the pencil lead from the graphite. Place a few drops of olive oil onto

a plate and lay the thread in the oil. The thread will absorb some of the oil.

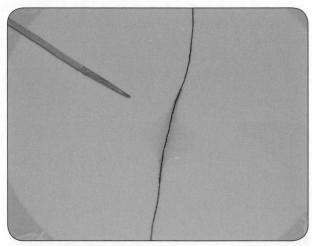

Step 3: Transfer Oil to the Graphite
Lift the oily thread and tie a knot in it. Don't pull the knot all-the-way closed! Carefully slip a piece of graphite through the knot loop and lay both the thread and the graphite on a plate. I used two halves of a toothpick to keep the graphite suspended above the plate. This helps keep the oil confined to a single spot on the graphite. Pull both ends of the thread until the knot has closed around the graphite. Wait about 30 minutes for the oil to soak into the graphite.

Step 4: Setup (i.e., Clean) the Microwave Oven
While the oil was soaking into the graphite, I cleaned the microwave. The sites I'd read that a clean microwave would yield better results. Maybe, maybe not, but it sure looks better.

Step 5: Remove the Thread
Clip off part of the thread as close to graphite as possible. Then, gently tug on the other end of the thread and pull the knot undone. Try not to slide the thread up-and-down the graphite. Remember, it's important to keep the oil concentrated in one spot.

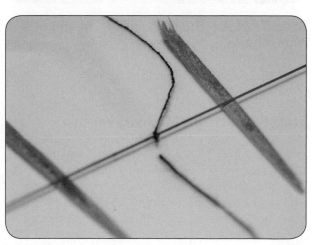

Step 6: Set the Graphite on the "Crucible"

Here's the ingenious part of the project. Turn one of the coffee mugs upside-down. (I used a slightly larger one as the base.) Set 2 more pieces of graphite (non-oiled) on the upturned mug, parallel to each other. Lay the oiled graphite across the other 2 pieces. Place the other coffee mug over all of it. Presto! It's a makeshift crucible!

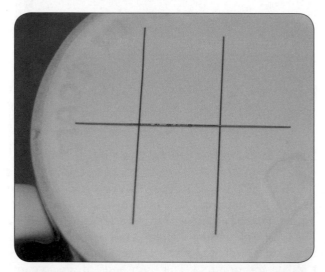

Step 7: Place the "Crucible" in the Microwave

Place the stacked mugs in the microwave. In my setup, the large bottom mug required that I remove the glass tray.

Step 8: Start the Microwave

Set the microwave for its maximum cook time at the maximum power setting. In my case, that was 99 minutes and 99 seconds, which turned out to be long enough. Be advised: The microwave will spark a bit where the oil has soaked into the graphite. This is normal, as the oil is bonding with the binder in the pencil lead. It should stop sparking after a few

minutes. After the microwave is done, let the mugs cool completely before removing them. Remember, if done correctly, you've generated 1,200+ degrees inside the crucible. Be safe.

Step 9: Admire the Finished Product

After the mugs have completely cooled, remove them from the microwave. The oiled graphite will be broken. The others should largely be intact. You'll also find a small lump, slightly larger than a grain of sand, where the oiled section was placed. Congratulations! This is the product of your labors, a genuine diamond. I took the raw diamond to a jeweler I know and had her test it. She confirmed that underneath the scale material, there's a tiny bit of diamond material. She said that its quality was pretty poor, but it did fluoresce like a "real" diamond. Now, admittedly, this homemade synthetic diamond is too small and too filled with inclusions to be made into jewelry. But it technically qualifies as a diamond, and I made it, so that's pretty cool.

Step 10: Make It Into a Keepsake

Obviously, this falls a bit short of what we think of when we hear "diamond." But I came up with a pretty cool way to preserve my achievement. I filled a small washer with clear epoxy and dropped my diamond into it. After it hardened, I strung it on a chain to make a diamond necklace. My wife was impressed. After all, how many women can wear a diamond that their husband actually made?

Giant Fresnel-Lens Deathray

By DrSimons

(http://www.instructables.com/id/
Giant-Fresnel-Lens-Deathray-An-Experiment-
in-Opti/)

So you don't have access to your own rail gun or military space laser, but never fear—we'll use the 1000 Watts/m2 of free sunlight in your backyard! But how? A 13 square foot magnifying glass! Seriously. A solid glass lens that size would be silly, but instead we can use a 4ft.-wide Fresnel lens. You know, those clear, flat things with the ridges you find on overhead projectors and the rear windows of some buses? The idea is pretty simple: A Fresnel lens is just a normal curved lens chopped into thousands of little rings, but just as effective.

The project: This Instructable chronicles my progress over the last month or so on this Fresnel-lens deathray. Each step was figured out in real time, but the general idea is this: Once you have your giant Fresnel lens, all that remains is to build a frame to keep it straight and hold it perpendicular to the sun. While you can stop here and enjoy the blinding energy of the nickel-sized spot you get at

the focus, I went further and attempted to collimate the light into a straight beam. I ordered a focusing lens online and constructed a scaffold to hold it in place, but ultimately found the Fresnel lens to have imperfections standing in the way of proper functionality.

Disclaimer: This device is extremely dangerous and will instantly set things on fire! It's extremely cool, but I'm not responsible for anything that happens if you decide to ignite yourself, your house, the forest, or anything else. Also, if you decide to skip the eye protection step, I hope you like braille.

Giant Fresnel Lens

Step 1: Acquire the Lens

For many future scientists, the destructive power of magnifying glasses provides hours of fun in the backyard (although I do not believe in burning living creatures, whatever the size). But everybody already has a magnifying glass. Where are we going get a 60-inch Fresnel lens? They can be found online, but only for substantial piles of cash (from $80 to $150 on eBay), which is why few people ever enjoy these devices.

Traditionally, the actual lens is by far the biggest cost in a project like this, with lumber and hardware being almost nothing if you already have the tools. And now, I will impart to you the ultimate source of free giant Fresnel lenses: rear projection TVs. Every rear projection TV uses a Fresnel lens the exact size of the screen to focus the image. The screen has several layers: outer cover (optional: some TVs have a clear layer on the very outside. Keep it, as it could be useful in another project); lenticular lens (this is the hideous outer screen with 1000s of vertical lines. The purpose of the lines is to spread each pixel outward so you can see the screen from the side. It will probably rip apart as you separate the layers); and the Fresnel lens (this is the innermost layer and is clear with millions of circular ridges on one side—the crown jewel of the TV).

Two excellent sources of free rear-projection TVs:
1. Craigslist! Go to the free section on your local Craigslist community and you'll probably find dozens of massive, usually broken, projection TVs being given away. Say Billy has a TV from about 10 years ago, and when it breaks, Billy decides to upgrade to a newer technology. Big-screen TVs usually weigh 200–400 pounds, so all Billy wants is someone to make it disappear. If you have a truck and at least one strong friend, this is a great option, especially if you don't like option 2.

2. The dump. If your local dump recycles TVs, you may be fortunate enough to find a pile of TVs sitting around there. My dump doesn't allow scavenging, so we just made sure there was no one around and helped ourselves to the front parts of TVs and scored three giant lenses.

Once you have your TV screen, peel the layers apart (you may need to cut some tape along the top) and extract the precious Fresnel. Admire your plunder, and dispose of/recycle the TV carcass.

Step 2: Build a Frame

The first thing you'll notice about your lens is that it flops around and refuses to stay straight. The lens absolutely must be flat in order to work right, so we need to build a frame. This will also prevent it from being bent or cracked. Note: the ridges on one side of the lens are extremely delicate and scratch easily. A few scratches won't affect performance, but will look terrible. Try not to drag the lens against anything.

Materials Required:
- at least 15 feet of lumber (I recommend 1" × 2" boards of plywood or miscellaneous scrap wood
- 20–40 wood screws
- power drill
- tape measure
- pencil

Holding the Lens:

The goal here is to secure the lens in a frame. The most elegant way to do this is to cut a groove down the length of each piece of wood so the lens fits into the slot. By lowering the table-saw blade so it only stuck up about half an inch, I was able to cut perfect grooves down the boards.

Cutting the Frame:

Once you have your grooved beams, you'll need to cut them to be just long enough to come together with the lens nested in the grooves. Make sure the grooves are all on the inside, and after measuring exactly how long each side should be, cut the sides at 45° angles so the corners look nice. I used a miter to get the precise angles here.

Assembly:

Once the frame pieces are positioned around the lens, you can pull everything together. We sandwiched each corner between two pieces of plywood and put screws through all three layers, but there are lots of options for this part. It's a little complicated, and the method varies depending on what tools you have available. If you don't have a table saw, there are other ways to make a groove, or you could trap the lens with multiple boards. If you have any kind of workshop you should be able to rig something up. I don't advise screwing directly into the lens though, because it might crack. Once your frame is done, you can move the lens around safely.

The light spots these lenses can produce are literally as bright as the sun. On that note, be extremely careful where you put this lens. If it's sunny out, the thing shouldn't even be left outside. You never know when it might decide to focus and set your house on fire! Once again, I am not liable for anything, including forest fires, so use your head.

Step 3: Eye Protection!!!

This is such a good idea, I decided to make it a whole step. Throughout this project you will spend a lot of time playing with this device, and you'll want to look at the focus a lot to see the results. However, you will find that after a few seconds, spots linger in your vision when you look away. The center of your retina will become more and more desensitized until it starts taking permanent damage, and then you won't be able to see anything. When you're looking at this spot, it may not seem so bright. That is because your eyes are already being desensitized. Thus, you have to wear at the very least some dark sunglasses. With welding goggles, you can't really see anything except the focal point, so I recommend glacier glasses (used in mountain climbing so you aren't blinded by the sun reflecting off of ice).

Step 4: Measure the Focal Length

Rather than proceeding with building the rest of the device, at this point you need to measure your lens' focal length. This is the distance from the lens to the spot of light it will produce. This distance will only be correct when the light rays hitting the lens are parallel to each other, and perpendicular to the lens. In other words, the light has to either be sunlight or two parallel laser beams, and has to hit the lens dead on. Unless you live at the equator, with the sun straight up, measuring the focal length is actually quite difficult. After a lot of frustration I decided to use lasers.

Materials Required:
- 2 (or more) laser pointers
- a level
- some flat ground
- T-square
- tape measure
- large, rigid screen

Laser Setup:

We want to find the point in space where parallel light beams bending through the lens intersect. This is the focal point, and it will be straight out from the center of the lens. To set up our parallel beams of light, put your two laser pointers on either side of a book or something so that they're parallel. The goal is for the lasers to be perpendicular to the lens, so make sure they're on a level surface. Turn them on and aim the whole setup straight at the lens. Meanwhile, have someone hold the lens straight up, using a T-square to make the lens perfectly vertical. You'll get two weird diffraction patterns on the wall behind the lens.

Finding the Focus:

Now, with your tape measure extending out from the base of the lens, hold your screen up so the two lasers hit it. Move it back and forth until the two spots converge. When they do, see how far from the lens your screen is. This may sound confusing, but the pictures should help. I recommend trying several times, maybe moving the lasers around, so you can see whether your results are consistent. For my lens, the focal length was about 40 inches (about 100cm), which is average for especially large Fresnels.

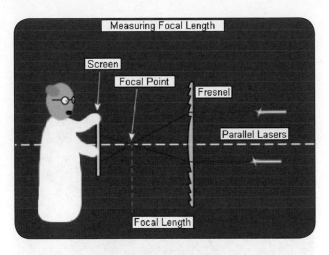

Step 5: Acquire Focusing Lens

Now that you know the focal length of your Fresnel, it's time to get a diverging lens to bend the light into a beam. This will be placed right at the focal point, so you can get as small a beam as possible.

Benefits of Creating a Beam:

Objects don't have to be right at the focal point to burst into flames! The beam can be further manipulated—magnified, reflected, put through a prism, whatever floats your optical boat. Ridiculously intense light beams are like lasers.

Optics Refresher:

In optics, the strength of a lens is measured by its focal length (stronger lenses have shorter ones). To cancel the converging effect of the Fresnel lens, we need to either diverge the light before it gets to the focal point (use a diverging lens with a negative focal length) or converge it after the light spreads out beyond the focal point (using a converging lenses like a magnifying glass)

Diagram 1: When two lenses are far apart, it's useful to think of light in terms of geometry and angles: the focusing lens has to be strong enough that its focal length is small so that the light spreading out from the Fresnel's focal point is completely captured by the second lens. From basic geometry, we know that the second lens has to have at a ratio of diameter to focal length at least as big as the Fresnel lens in order to capture all the light. This means if the second lens has a focal length fB, it has to have a diameter of at least dB = fB (dA / fA), where dA and fA are the diameter and focal length of your Fresnel (use the larger width since the Fresnel is not a circle).

Diagram 2: With a strong enough lens (the one I got had a focal length of 35mm), you put the lens 35mm (or whatever) past the Fresnel's focal length. The light will then be bent inward, forming a beam. Of course, this will only be approximate, so you'll have to move the lens back and forth until you find the correct distance. You can find lenses in lots of random places online, and the closer the focal length is to your measurement, the better. Also, bigger lenses are preferable because giant Fresnels typically don't create a very small focus spot (between 1 and 2 inches wide) so you'll need at least a 2" wide lens to capture all the light. I should also mention that you want a glass lens, as plastic simply won't do for this intensity of light.

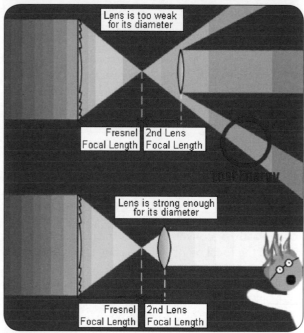

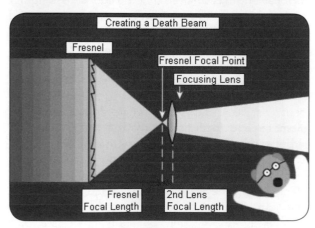

Step 6: Lens Scaffold

Now that we have a set of focusing lenses, we need to devise a scaffold to hold them in place out in front of the Fresnel lens. After a good deal of thought,

we conclude the easiest way is to use thin (1" × 1") wooden stakes held together by plywood gussets.

Materials Required:
- 4 1" × 1" stakes
- scrap plywood
- woodscrews drill
- countersink (if available)
- 2" × 4" plank
- 2" hole saw (or larger)
- several right-angle brackets

Basic Structure:

Odds are you're going to do this your own way if you try it, so I won't go into too much detail about the construction. I assembled the sides first (minus the 2 × 4s) by cutting the stakes with a miter saw to get the necessary angles, then cut plywood gussets to hold these together. We used two right-angle brackets (inside corners) to attach these gussets to the plywood crosspiece that will eventually hold the lenses.

Note: A very important thing here is the orientation of the Fresnel lens. I found out the hard way that when the flat side of the lens is facing the sun, it doesn't work right (but well enough that you might not notice). So make sure the ridges are facing out, away from the scaffold, which means they'll be facing down if you build this with the lens on the ground. After the sides are completed, two long plywood gussets secure them onto the side of the frame. Since we want the whole device to rotate about its center of gravity (somewhere between the Fresnel and the small lenses), we need a strong beam that passes through that point (hence the 2 × 4s in the diagram), so we screwed the 2 × 4s onto the necessary gussets, providing a substantial increase in strength.

Finding the Center of Gravity:

To find the center of gravity of this whole scaffold (it will be along the centerline of the 2 × 4), you and a friend each grab one of the 2 × 4s and see where the thing balances. You'll want to choose a point closer to the Fresnel (so the Fresnel wants to hang down), because the lens assembly hasn't been installed yet. Finally, drill 1/4" or 5/8" holes (depending on the carriage bolt in the next step) through the points you choose. Note: When using wood screws in the small wooden stakes, you definitely want to pre-drill/countersink holes, because wood this thin is very easy to crack.

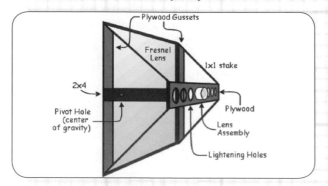

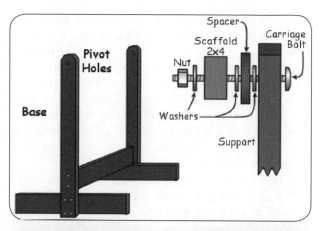

Step 7: Support Base

The lens scaffold we now have needs to be able to rotate around so it can aim up at the sun. To accomplish this we came up with a super simple, super sturdy base made from five blocks of wood.

Materials Required:

- 1 8-foot 2" × 4" board
- around 8 feet of 2" × 6" board
- 8 medium lag bolts
- 2 big lag bolts
- 2 carriage bolts and nuts
- 6 washers
- 2 wood spacers (use the lightening holes you cut out for the scaffold)

The Design:

You can see the basic design from the diagram. The planks are held together with large lag bolts. To use these, drill clearance holes through the first part (as wide as the part of the bolt without threads) and a pilot hole through the second part (not as wide, so the threads can bite into the wood). Then screw the bolts in with a ratchet. It's very tight and very strong. A few of these should hold each part together. You'll want to measure the lens scaffold first, then slightly overestimate the width for the base so you can get it between the two supports easily (the spacers will take up the rest of the width).

Mount the Lens Scaffold:

We want to put a couple of holes at the top of each support and insert a spacer, washers, a nut, and a carriage bolt (see the diagram). Once the pivot is together, you can use a wrench to tighten the bolts and lock the scaffold in position.

Step 8: Lens Mount

Clearly, our deathray is missing something. If you swivel the lens up so it's perpendicular to the sun's rays, you'll just get a spot of bright light on the piece of plywood at the focus. Once you do this (yes, I recommend it—but don't let the thing catch on fire), you'll know just where to put the focusing lens.

Materials Required:

- 2" PVC expansion joint
- your favorite epoxy
- miter saw or hack saw
- sand paper (60 and 150 grit)
- lens tube

The easiest way to set up the optics here is to mount the main focusing lens on the end of a tube around 2" wide. This will do exactly what this Instructable does—collimate the light into a smaller beam. In a sense, the entire device is already doing this with the sun's parallel rays, but we want the smallest beam possible. Up until now, I was troubled and lost as to what I would use for this part. What was needed was essentially two tubes inside each other, with the inner one allowed to telescope in and out easily while staying put. Then, while wandering the aisles of Home Depot, I found the perfect part: a PVC expansion joint for 2" conduit pipe. It consists of two pipes, the inner one having two O-rings and a lot of silicon lube, allowing it to slide in and out of the outer pipe beautifully. It also happened to be a perfect fit for my 57mm focusing lens.

Preparing the Tube:

This was fairly straightforward—the inner tube had a rim sticking out past the ridge where the lens wanted to sit, so I made quick work of it with a miter saw (a hack saw would work equally well, just take it slow and rotate the tube as you're cutting). After a quick sanding, the tube was ready for the lens.

Epoxy:

I rifled through the adhesives toolbox, found something appropriate for both glass and plastic (Duco Cement), and glued down the lens. A day later someone knocked the tube over and the lens popped off, so I decided to use epoxy to seal the lens in. This worked better (the specific epoxy isn't that important, just pile it up around the sides of the lens to keep it in). Note: Since diverging light is entering this lens, we want the least-curved side of the lens (assuming your lens isn't symmetrical) facing out so the angle of incidence is lower, minimizing loss of light by reflection. Imagine a stone skipping off a pond versus a stone dropping straight down (which is what we want in this case).

Step 9: Installing the Lens Mount

One morning I woke up and found the sun was actually out. So I ran out, put on my glacier glasses, and pulled the tarp off the device.

Aiming:

A simple way to aim at the sun is to rotate the device until its shadows are parallel to the supports on the ground (if the ground is flat). This means the sun is directly forward. Then all you have to do is rotate it so the lens is closer to the sun, and an intense spot of light should form on the lens scaffold. Even in the middle of winter at this latitude, a 1" charred spot formed in a few seconds. It wasn't exactly in the center of the plywood beam, meaning the device wasn't facing perfectly towards the sun.

Lens Mount:

I didn't expect the light spot on the plywood to be so small. This meant that the focus was right on the plywood—farther than I expected. And since the lens assembly can only extend forward (towards the Fresnel), I had to recess the tube past the plywood. We accomplished this with a primitive housing made of 2" × 4" beams and plywood sides. The 2 × 4s were ripped to a width slightly less than that of the lens tube, so the plywood sides squeezed the tube in place. If you decide to mount the lens this way, be careful not to accidentally crack the tube. But, even better, think of a better way to attach it and make the lens scaffold stick out at least four inches past the focal point.

Step 10: Testing

Despite it being December 22nd, Winter solstice, the shortest day of the year, I proceeded to test out the completed lens system. But even with the least possible sunlight to work with (several hours before noon, at 37° latitude, we got a very satisfactory spot of blinding energy at the focus. When the device was aimed so that this spot fell on the secondary lens . . . nothing happened.

Failure Analysis:

Despite moving the lens tube back and forth through the focal point, no beam of light formed beyond the lens mount. To find out why the light wasn't cooperating, we decided to do a beam visualization by blowing dust to reflect the light. We first used flour, but then switched to water mist (from a sprayer) since it's not as messy. The light funneled into a highly concentrated point, as expected, but then basically fizzed out.

If your Fresnel deathray is doing this, most likely the Fresnel lens is backwards and the flat side is facing the sun, rather than the ridged side. Getting this right is essential to getting a good beam profile (which we'll see in the next step). Since the secondary lens is convex, i.e., it bends light inward, the incoming light has to be diverging in order to form a straight beam. Since the light from the Fresnel seems to disperse randomly past the focal point, almost no light even entered the secondary lens. Other Fresnel lens devices on the Internet demonstrate good beam shapes, such as in this picture.

Step 11: Let's Burn Something!

I flipped the Fresnel lens around so the ridges are facing the sun, and found a dramatic increase in lens performance. The secondary lens still isn't working right, but I was able to upgrade from melting zinc pennies to liquefying solid copper ones and destroying nickels!

First Test:

Inspired by similar Fresnel experiments floating around the 'net, I decided to try melting a penny. On winter solstice, I found that a zinc penny melts within a minute when held in the focus. Solid copper pennies (from 1982 or earlier) wouldn't melt, but probably would during summer. Copper's melting point is almost 2000° F compared to Zinc's 790° F.

See the first row of images for these tests.

Round Two:

With the Fresnel lens oriented correctly, I had another crack at melting those coins. The second row of images shows my results. MUHAHAHAHA!!! Note: Copper's melting point is about 2000° F, but nickel's is 2600° F, so it's highly possible that only the copper in the coin (75% copper, 25% nickel) melted, resulting in the mutilated pitted surface.

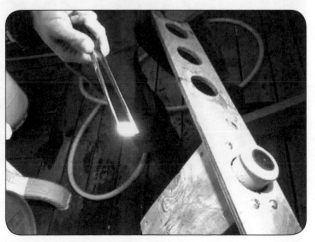

Step 12: Conclusion

Clearly, a giant Fresnel lens with an area of about 1.2m2 is a powerful asset. Assuming the maximum available solar energy hitting the ground is around 1000W/m2, this lens could theoretically concentrate 1200 watts of power into a square centimeter. Of course, at this latitude and time of year, around half of the maximum sunlight is available so this would make an excellent summer project. But even during winter, the fact that I could easily melt solid copper and make a nickel red hot is pretty damn cool.

Additional Information:

There are a good number of websites about the joys of giant Fresnels. Perhaps the most valuable thing you can get out of this Instructable is the source for these giant lenses. There are loads of them heading for landfills, or recycling, or god knows what else, so reclaim these things and put them to use! Note: You may think, as I did, "Gee, I bet I could make a super-efficient solar panel with one of these." But that isn't a very good idea and could ruin your expensive solar panel. You could certainly power a small heat engine though, by trapping all the light in a black container thermally connected to the boiler. A company working on this technology, but using reflectors instead of lenses, is Stirling Energy Systems.

I hope you enjoyed this project!

Magic Crystal Tree
By mik3
(http://www.instructables.com/id/Grow-your-own-Magic-Crystal-Tree-or-any-other-sha/)

If you found an ad for this Instructable in the back of a comic book, it would read something like: "Amaze your friends by growing a crystal tree out of common table salt and a few other ingredients available from the grocery store."

Step 1: Gather Your Materials
Gathering the ingredients is probably the most difficult step.

To grow your Magic Crystal Tree, you'll need:
- Mrs. Stewart's Bluing
- table salt
- household ammonia (the kind with no soap added)
- cardboard (not corrugated)
- bowl
- water
- measuring spoon
- food coloring (optional)

The bluing is the hardest item to find but can be found in the cleaning section of many grocery stores. You can find the ammonia close by. The cardboard I used came as packing material from a new shirt, or the backing from a paper notepad. Cereal box cardboard might work, but it's thinner and has printing on one side. Depending on the temperature and humidity of your location, the ammonia is optional, but it does speed up the crystal growth—the tree in this Instructable started "sprouting" in less than an hour. Without ammonia, it may take a couple of days to start.

Step 2: Cardboard Shapes for the Crystals to Grow On
For this Instructable, I made a tree formed out of two cardboard triangles, roughly 2" at the base and about 3½" high. Cut a slot from the top to the middle in one piece, and from the bottom to the middle in the other. The slots allow the two pieces to be assembled into a 3D shape. Make sure that whatever shape you create can stand by itself.

Step 3: Color the Tree (Optional)
If you like, you can add a little color to your shape by putting drops of food coloring on the edges. The food coloring will soak into the cardboard.

183

Step 4: Adding the "Magic" Solution
Mix together:
- 1 tablespoon water
- 1 tablespoon salt
- 1 tablespoon bluing
- 1/2 tablespoon household ammonia

I put everything into a small bottle that could be shaken to mix the ingredients. Again, the ammonia is optional, but I'd recommend it. Find a place where you can watch your magic tree grow undisturbed for a few days. Put the tree into the bowl and add the solution.

Step 5: Wait...
Wait. . . . Wait a little longer . . . more waiting . . . (First sign of growth showed up at around the one hour mark.)

Step 6: Time Passes
This picture shows the tree after 12 hours. You can keep your crystal shape growing indefinitely by adding more water/salt solution to the bowl.

Step 7: What's Going On?
The salt solution is wicked up into the cardboard tree via capillary action. Water evaporates from the surface of the tree, forcing the salt to crystallize out. Mrs. Stewart's Bluing is a colloid—tiny particles suspended in water (think of glitter in a snow globe, but much, much smaller). The tiny particles make it easier for the salt crystals to form. The ammonia helps speed up the evaporation process, which makes the crystals grow faster. There's a more detailed explanation available from Mrs. Stewart's Bluing at http://www.mrsstewart.com/pages/explanation.htm.

Step 8: Filming the Crystal Tree Growing
I set up a Canon PowerShot A40 with remote capture software to take one picture every minute. The halogen desk lamp overhead is an attempt to provide a consistent light source, as well as warming things up a little to speed up evaporation.

Wave Pendulum

By SargentPepper

(http://www.instructables.com/id/Wave-Pendulum/)

The holiday season is anticipated by people of all ages. It's a time for good food, family, vacation, and fun! But it's also a time to figure out what to give people, which can be a difficult task. I'll have great ideas for gifts throughout the year but when the season comes I can't think of anything to give people, especially my dad.

This year his Christmas list consisted of dress socks, ties, and books. Boring, boring, boring! That got me thinking, What if I make him something? He has a large desk at his office, and I wanted to make him something he could display. I thought of a Newton's cradle but that was too simple. I wanted the Wow! factor.

After searching on the web, I came across a YouTube video of a simple pendulum. Harvard's Science Demonstrations' website also gave me some helpful information on the apparatus so I could build it!

So that was that—I was going to make him a wave pendulum! It's a unique gift, a perfect conversation starter, and would look great on my dad's desk. It's also a cooler gift than a pair of socks.

Step 1: Materials
- titanium epoxy (or any type of glue that bonds two metals together)
- thread (it needs to be thick so the weight of the ball bearings doesn't break it. We used fishing thread and it worked well)
- 15 ball bearings (or any other type of semi-heavy ball would work. I think marbles would work as well)
- 15 gold brads
- 15 nuts (as small as you can get them so when they are attached to the balls they don't take away from the sophisticated look)
- hot glue

- wood glue
- drill
- straight edge
- MDF wood for the base (this is a type of compressed wood, but you can use whatever you would like for the base)
- basswood for the legs and top of the structure (4 ½" × ½" pieces and 2 ½" × ¼" pieces)
- saw to cut the wood (preferably one with fine teeth so you get a more even cut)
- black acrylic paint for the base (or you can choose to stain it, or paint it a different color, whatever your artistic heart desires!)
- wood stain for the rest of the structure

Step 2: Preparing the Base

For the base, cut a piece of MDF (compressed) wood, or any type of wood you choose, to these dimensions: 9½" by 22½". These measurements will give you a broad "viewing window" through which to admire the wave pendulum effect when you are finished.

Once you have the properly sized base, you need to drill holes for the four legs of the structure. To ensure that the legs are evenly spaced, measure ¼" from the edge of the board on each side and place a mark with a pencil. Use a straight edge to connect all of your marks, giving you a ¼" border around the entire base. Where the lines cross at the corners (see second photo below for clarification), pencil in a large dot. That point is where you will drill a hole for the legs of the structure.

Before drilling the holes, place a scrap piece of wood beneath the base. If you accidentally drill through the wood base entirely, you don't want to hit cement and dull your drill bit. Keep in mind that the legs of the structure are ½" by ½", and you don't want a hole so big that the leg will be swimming in it. I made that mistake and it caused some assembly headaches, so go for a snug fit! Don't drill all the way through the wood—1cm to 2cm deep will be sufficient. Make sure you are consistent for each hole. Measure after you drill and make the holes as close to the same depth as possible so your structure is even!

Step 3: Preparing the Legs and Top

The Legs:

Using a fine tooth saw, cut the ½ inch by ½ inch bass wood dowels to 18.5" long for the legs of the structure.

The Top:

- The top consists of three pieces. They are created using the ½" by ¼" basswood. Cut two 8" long pieces of the basswood to connect the two side legs together.
- Cut one piece of wood to be 21" long. This piece will connect the two sets of legs together lengthwise.
- The longer piece of basswood is what the balls hang from, so you need to drill 15 evenly spaced holes in the top. Choose a drill bit that is slightly smaller than your brad size to ensure a snug fit. My holes were approximately 1½" apart.
- When drilling the holes, put a scrap wood board beneath your top piece. This time you are drilling all the way through the wood, and you don't want to dull your drill bit!

Step 4: Assembling the Wood Structure

First, you will put the legs of the structure into their pre-drilled holes. Fill each of the four holes with wood glue and then set the legs into the holes. To help stabilize these legs while the wood glue dries, you can use a dab of hot glue (comes off readily) on a piece of wood and glue it to both the base and each leg (see second picture). You will take this piece of wood off once the wood glue dries.

Next, (this can be done before the wood glue dries as well), glue the two smaller top pieces into place. This will also help ensure that the wood legs dry straight and the proper distance apart. Once the wood glue has dried for the most part (not necessarily completely, but has stabilized enough), glue the long top piece into place.

Once that is completed wait for 24 hours until the wood glue dries completely. Be sure you keep an eye on this structure; if you notice a leg tilting use more wood or a string to stabilize it. Don't underestimate the importance of the structure's stability.

Step 5: Assembling the Ball Bearings

While you patiently—or not so patiently—wait for the wood structure to dry, you can begin creating the ball pieces of this pendulum. First, mix a small bit of your epoxy. You don't need much epoxy as the nuts are super tiny and that stuff is pretty strong. Please be careful when using this! Do not get it on your hands and don't lean in too close and breathe in the fumes.

Once you mix the epoxy you have about five minutes to assemble the ball bearings before the it doesn't work anymore. I would recommend doing this step in stages. Make about five balls at a time and then mix up some new epoxy for the next batch. Using a pair of tweezers, pick up a small nut and dip it into the epoxy, then set the nut onto a ball bearing. Be sure to place the nut on the ball bearing so that the nut is vertical and not at an odd angle.

A helpful way to ensure that the balls don't go rolling all over the place is to use Styrofoam! By indenting a piece of Styrofoam, you create a place to set the balls down so the epoxy can adequately dry. Once the epoxy dries, pick up each of the ball bearings by the nut and ensure that the bond is strong. If the nut falls off, try again with a little more epoxy.

Let these set overnight.

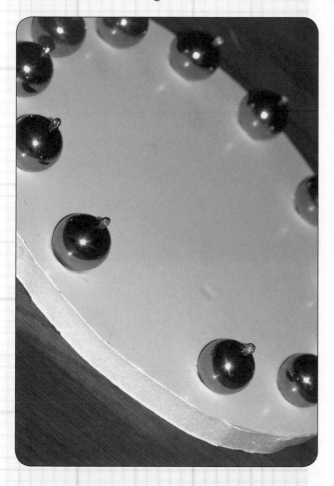

Step 6: Finishing the Structure (Assembly)

The next step is to fill in the holes where the legs are inserted into the base. Using wood filler, fill in each of the four leg holes. After setting up the wood pieces, sand it down to become as smooth and level with the rest of the base as possible. This will make the finished, painted product much cleaner.

As you can see in the pictures, I put the strings and the balls on the structure before I painted it. I would not recommend doing it this way. It is far easier to paint without the strings and balls on the structure.

After you fill in the leg holes you are ready to paint and stain.

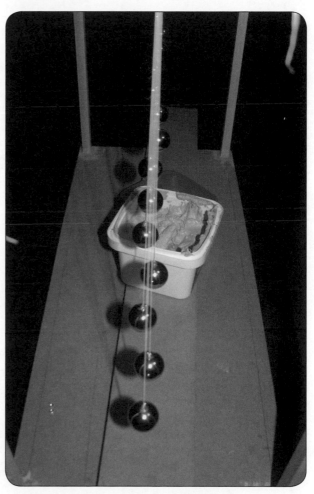

Step 7: Painting and Staining!

It's best to stain the piece before painting the base. (Painting over stain looks better than attempting to stain over paint.) To stain the base you need two cloths: one to apply the stain and one to wipe the excess stain off. This method will give you an even stain coating and a nice finish.

Once you have stained the piece it should dry for 24 hours. After it's dry, paint the base. I used acrylic paint, but spray paint would work as well. If you use spray paint make sure that you tape the legs and top of the structure really well!

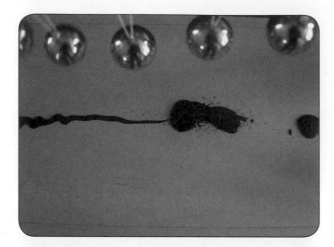

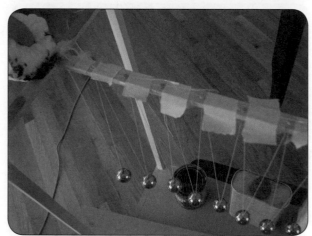

Step 8: Timing and Final Product

Now attach the strings and balls to the structure with the gold brads. Below are the necessary lengths of string to achieve a one-minute period for the entire wave effect. Essentially it's timed so that each ball has one oscillation more than its neighbor. For example, the longest string achieves 51 oscillations in one minute, the next longest string achieves 52 oscillations in one minute, and so on. The shortest string achieves 65 oscillations in one minute. I imagine that as long as you ensure each string has one oscillation more than its neighbor you are fine (the number 51 will ensure that you'll achieve a wave effect lasting one minute. The

shorter the beginning oscillation is, the shorter the wave period will be.

Here are the approximate lengths from the longest string to the shortest one:

- 33.0cm
- 31.3cm
- 30.4cm
- 28.9cm
- 27.2cm
- 26.5cm
- 25.3cm
- 24.6cm
- 23.6cm
- 22.7cm
- 21.9cm
- 21.2cm
- 20.8cm

Now keep in mind that these are rough estimates and it may take further tinkering to perfect. This process is very tedious, as the smallest adjustments can make a huge difference, and can take hours, so be patient! Your patience will be rewarded.

My dad loved the pendulum! It works great on his desk, and I find the wave effect to be calming and transfixing.

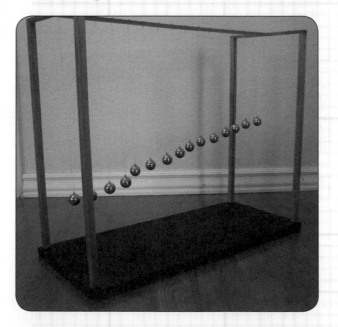

Transportation

Cart Bike

Night Bike Set!

Leaf Blower Engine Bicycle

Bamboo Bicycle

Homemade Leather Bike Seat

Camping Hot Tub

Bicycles are the easiest mode of transportation to soup up. There's no internal combustion engine, easy access to all of the mechanical components, and many people learned to operate them as small children. There is so much room for improvement that these projects don't even begin to scratch the surface of what can be done with a bicycle.

But they will get you started on creating a speedy, safe, light, or comfortable two-wheeled conveyance. And you can relax in a riverside hot tub when you're done riding (or building) for the day.

Cart Bike

By zieak
(http://www.instructables.com/id/Cart-Bike/)

Combine a derelict shopping cart with a bicycle for a ride with ample cargo capacity. This is a nice way to reuse a shopping cart and a bike that might otherwise end up in a landfill. It is quite the head turner, but not a good corner turner. Any mention of this project needs to mention www.zieak.com with credit to Ryan McFarland. Thanks Ryan!

Step 1: Gather Materials
- bicycle
- shopping cart
- socket set
- hex key set
- Dremel tool
- utility knife
- zip ties
- screwdriver

A note on shopping carts: Please don't steal them. This one happened to be floating around our downtown area for over a week before I grabbed it. The bicycle is almost ten years old and still works fine, but I just bought the bike shop in town so I suddenly have access to plenty of cycling materials.

Step 2: Remove the Handlebars and Shopping Cart Handle

Use the hex key set (probably number 6) to loosen the stem bolts on the bicycle. Use the socket set to remove the shopping cart handle. Ideally the diameter of the cart handle is close to the handlebar center. I was able to just bolt the handle right in as a replacement. Remove the front wheel. You also can remove the front brake.

Step 3: Install the Brakes

In order to attach the brake, I had to cut off the plastic handle. I used a rotary tool to cut a line down to the metal and then used a chisel and utility knife to peel back and cut off the plastic handle. I then used a screwdriver to pry open the brake lever and gear shifter just enough to slide it on. I also slid the handle grip on, since the end had already been cut off for the bar ends.

Step 4: Stabilize the Forks

The bike needs to articulate a little for the irregularities in the road. Leaving the forks hanging free makes the bike prone to leaning over when you turn. Just using a few zip ties to connect each fork to the shopping cart frame helps stabilize the bike and prevents it from falling over. I would like to find a more permanent solution that allows the fork to swing forward and back but prevents too much side-to-side sway.

Step 5: Test Ride

The front brake lever won't be useful unless the shifter is attached to it. I will modify the left handlebar for the shifter when I find one without a brake lever attached. On test rides it does not corner well. Steering requires very wide turns, and sometimes the cart teeters on two of the wheels on one side. I'll definitely be playing around with the details. This will make a great rig for making trips to the post office for the bike shop. The cart bike will be a great addition to our town parades.

Gas is too expensive and is not ecofriendly, so I like to bike wherever I can. Unfortunately, that means a lot of biking back from work at night. This always makes me a little nervous. How much can you trust drivers going 45 miles per hour right past you? I mean, a little dinky bike light can only do so much.

After too many close calls to count and a lot of weekend TV watching, I was inspired by a commercial to create a better bike for night riding.

After doing a little bit of research, I found that there were some super glow in the dark paints that were better quality than your typical craft store stuff. In fact it's called phosphorescent paint, which can glow for up to 12 hours, is substantially brighter than simple glow in the dark paint, and only takes ten minutes to charge up!

I must say, after creating this bike I feel much safer riding in the dark, as cars are able to spot me from quite a far distance. I've even gotten a few compliments on the cool style of the bike! Safety and style—it's a win win!

So thus begins my Instructable—a glowing bike that will not only amaze friends and onlookers, but will also be extremely safe for riding in the dark.

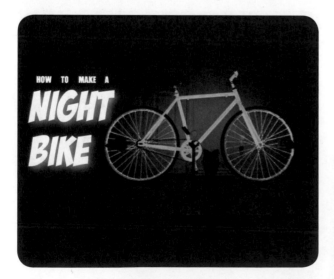

Step 1: Phosphorescent Paint

Now I want you to know that when I say this bike glows, it really glows. Back when I was a youngster and was fascinated by glow in the dark paint, I was always disappointed by how dull and short lived the glow was. The typical craft-store glow paint is zinc-sulfide based in an acrylic medium, and if it is colored,

pigments are used. The problem with using pigments is that these colors absorb most of the light, and thus the glow isn't as bright.

Instead, phosphorescent paint (used for this bike) is strontium based and glows ten times longer and brighter. Impressive! The paint works only after it is exposed to an energy source, like the sun, black lights (which work really well), or regular lights. The paint absorbs the light energy, and the little electrons get excited and jump up a few energy levels, sort of like climbing a few steps on a ladder. This is not a stable state for the electron (eventually you have to come down the ladder), and once it falls back down to its "ground state" it emits light, in the color of your paint. It turns out that strontium aluminate is more efficient and better at this than craft store glow paint.

Step 2: Time to Start!

What you need:

- bike (preferably a fixed-gear bike, because it is much easier to paint with fewer parts to keep track of)
- bike assembly/disassembly tools
- Y Allen wrench (if you ever need just one tool to disassemble a bike, this is it! It was really useful.)
- nylon string
- masking tape
- paint brush
- spray paint primer (at least 2 bottles)
- spray paint white flat (at least 3 bottles)
- phosphorescent paint (at least 8 ounces total for the bike, but you can choose more than one color if you'd like—for example, I used 4 ounces of green for the frame and 4 ounces of blue for the tires)
- spray paint high gloss clear overcoat (got to protect what you already painted! You don't want your hard work to go to waste.)
- helmet (always wear a helmet when riding a bike; this is about safety after all!)

Step 3: Disassembly of Bike

Essentially, take everything off of the bike that you can. I recommend first sitting on the bike and adjusting the seat and handlebars to your desired height. Place some tape there (with the top edge of the tape at the desired height), so that when you paint, you will only paint the exposed metal and leave the rest paint-free so it will more easily be put together.

Then just start the disassembly and take pictures along the way so you know how to put the bike back together! Trust me, those pictures are life savers!

Tips:

- When you take off the seat, place all the nuts and bolts in a Ziploc baggy labeled "SEAT." You don't want to have spent forever painting your bike only to be frustrated that you lost that one little screw you needed.
- Unless you have a special tool called a crank puller, you won't be able to take off the crankshaft. It doesn't really matter, though; it is just as easy to paint the frame with it on.
- Unless you have a special tool called a chain tool (really creative name there . . .) you won't be able to take off the chain. But this is easily solved by taping the chain.

Step 4: Preparing for Primer and Paint

First tape up all of the parts you don't want painted; I wanted to keep all the silver parts silver. Also ensure you tape the threaded parts of any screws or other parts you want painted. If you paint the threads, good luck reassembling! Tape the chain if you didn't take it off.

Now tie string onto every piece you want to paint. This is so you can hang it wherever you will be painting but make sure that wherever you paint there is good ventilation. If you do it in your garage, keep the garage door wide open.

When you tie string onto the bike parts, make sure that you make a large enough loop around the part so you can maneuver it well while painting. Then make the rest of the string rather long so you won't have to use a ladder to reach it to paint. Also, try not to go all gung ho with the string tying—keep it one or two strands per piece. This way the string isn't covering too much of the bike, resulting in more unpainted sections of the bike.

Step 5: Prime and Paint

Once you have hung up all your bike parts you are ready to prime and paint your bike! After you prime the bike, let it dry for 24 hours and then spray paint it white.

Be sure to put enough coats of white paint on your bike to really make it white. The phosphorescent paint dries clear and glows better on a very white background. So basically, the whiter and neater the better, because that is what your bike will look like.

Remember:

- Primer isn't meant to cover extremely well. It is merely a first layer, so don't get discouraged when you've run through two cans and can still see that fire truck red peeking through—this is what you want! The white spray paint will then cover up everything.
- Shake the cans really well before you begin.
- Ventilation, ventilation, ventilation!
- Don't put on too heavy of coats, and keep that can 6–12 inches away. Read your paint

instructions. You don't want drip marks, so multiple lighter coats are preferred.

• Your patience will be rewarded!

24 hours later . . .

After the white spray paint has had adequate time to dry, you are ready for phosphorescent paint!

Using a paint brush, apply the phosphorescent paint in very even coats. Please, please be patient—this will take many, many coats to ensure an even, bright shine. I didn't realize that uneven painting resulted in uneven glowing, so I had to put on more coats. After you let the phosphorescent paint dry for 72 hours after the final coat, apply your clear protecting coat.

Tips:

• Lay it on thickly for the spokes, as imperfections won't be seen while riding. The thickness on the spokes makes the bike look even cooler while glowing.

• If painting in the garage, it can be hard to see the phosphorescent paint on white, since it paints on clear. So you can turn off the lights to double check if you missed any glaring sections.

• Allow plenty of time for the phosphorescent paint to dry between coats; this takes much longer than the normal coats.

Step 6: Assembly/Finish

Use the pictures you took as an aid to reassemble your bike! Be sure to add a front and rear light. The bike can't be too bright after all. Charge it up and then you're ready for a night ride!

If you want to make the bike even brighter and last even longer, you can invest in black light LED strips to place on the frame of the bike. Now that would be really cool, and you wouldn't have to worry about the glow fading!

Additional Information:

• I bought my paint at glonation and it worked fairly well. A better choice (for brighter glow) may be gloinc, as they advertise their paint is three times brighter than their competitors. However, it is pricier than glonation. You could also do a little Google search on super phosphorescent paint and you will find a few other places to purchase the paint. You can't buy it in a typical craft store (at least to my knowledge).

• The paint is not radioactive, so you don't have to worry about that.

• We used eight ounces total, four for the frame and four for the wheels. We had to put on many layers since it is hard to get even coverage with a paintbrush. There is not a spray glow phosphorescent paint on the market yet, and the paint is creamy, so it doesn't really work for an airbrush.

• Be careful when you purchase the paint and be sure to read the advertising. For instance, glonation states that orange only glows for 15 minutes while green (though it dims) glows for 12 hours. Gloinc states that their green glows for 24 hours.

Leaf Blower Engine Bicycle

By Jnkyrdguy
(http://www.instructables.com/id/
How-to-Strap-a-Leaf-Blower-Engine-to-a-
Bike-and-Go/)

This was one of those projects I couldn't get out of my head. I had seen, on the Internet and in person, the small two-stroke-engine-powered scooters that were becoming increasingly popular. Naturally I wanted one, but I'm not the type that would just buy a commercially available scooter that will work well and last for years and be happy about it: I would have to build my own. This was also a project that kept changing. I kept redesigning as I went along, tweaking the bike for more reliable usage. In its current condition it is quite effective at moving someone around and makes for a quick and easy to build project.

My initial build lasted about eight hours over one day. When I hopped on the thing and went flying down the road at speed, I was very thrilled and surprised to have gotten that much of a result out of one day of bodging. While you view this project, please keep in mind that some major improvements could be made to my design to fix various safety and performance issues. If you plan on building a similar design, make sure to check out the lessons learned step before you build.

Step 1: Design

First, a quick disclaimer about the design: Since there is a lot of variation between different bikes and small engines, this design will likely need to be adapted to fit your equipment. It's important to figure out what you have before you commit to an engine or bike, since some types won't work very well. The design was constrained most by the motors available to me at the time and my lack of welding capabilities. I wanted to use my all-terrain-style 12-inch-tire scooter along with a clutch, but I couldn't come up with the necessary equipment. Mounting the motor without welding also posed a challenge, since that was the efficient and obvious way to fix everything all together. When I couldn't get a motor with a clutch, I got frustrated enough to improvise a spindle-driven design for my fifth-grade bike. The bike is quite small for me, but still allows pedal starts and has coaster brakes, which frees the handle bars for the gas and kill switches. I decided to make it front-wheel drive for ease of construction: There's a lot more free room up front.

For the engine, I used a small 26cc McCullough engine that came from a hand-held leaf-blower. It is a half-shaft motor (only one side of the crankshaft is supported) without a clutch, but it had a threaded shaft that allowed for easy attachment of the spindle, so I was happy. I initially went very simple with the design: I just made some brackets and bolted it on. That worked for a few miles until the engine mounts loosened up and the spindle stopped transferring power. I eventually modified the bike to include a spring tensioning system to keep the motor firmly on the tire.

Step 2: Attaching the Spindle

The 1¼" spindle with a threaded hole that I used on my bike is a peg that came with my all-terrain scooter. The shaft was already threaded, so the spindle was easily tightened onto the shaft and secured with two more nuts. In a spindle-driven design, the diameter of the spindle is the only factor that can change the effective gearing of the bike (the tire diameter doesn't matter.) A 1¼" spindle works well on this bike as a nice middle ground between top speed and acceleration. It would still be interesting to try out some other sizes.

Step 3: Strapping on the Engine

My engine came completely encased in plastic shrouds. Once the engine was free from its casings it was possible to lay out a pattern for the engine mount. I rough-cut the holes for the flywheel and coil so I could lay out the pattern of the screws. This engine has a cast bracket perpendicular to the shaft, which made it easy to screw to the ¼" plywood plate. The thinness of that plate was my first mistake. Thicker plywood would have been much better for this purpose for reasons I will explain farther down the page. Mounting brackets with the engine screwed securely to the plywood, I continued by making brackets to connect the plywood to the bike's front fork. These brackets bolt around the front fork, through the plywood, and to a set of flat brackets with 5/16" bolts. The brackets are able to tighten down on the fork so there is enough tension to hold the spindle to the wheel.

First Test Run:

At this point, I took the bike on its first test run, which didn't last very long at all. Actually, more accurately, it never started. The ¼" plate tended to bend rather than engage the tire. I couldn't get enough traction to kick over the engine. Hence why thicker ½" plywood or, even better, ¾", would be much more effective. To stop the plywood from bending without starting over, I used more aluminum strapping bolted to the face of the plywood. Amazingly, this worked! With some furious pedaling I kicked the bike over and the motor started, rocketing me to the end of my street. This was very surprising and quite exciting to me, since most of my poorly thought out, frustration-ridden second attempts tend not to work out.

Step 4: Adding the Spring

I was able to ride the bike at this point, but I didn't get very far: After a few miles of high-speed bumps and vibrations, the motor brackets loosened up. After a bit of time thinking up solutions, I ended up buying a spring from a local hardware store. I rigged up a wire hook to a hole on the bike's fork and a brass hook on the far end of the plywood plate, between which the spring can be tensioned. The spring allows for changes and movement of the engine while keeping plenty of traction between wheel and motor.

Step 5: Throttle

All of the parts for the handlebars were scavenged. The gas lever was originally a brake pedal on a free bike I found during one of my yard-sale searches. The irony of using a brake for the throttle should not go unnoticed. In fact, it's a borderline bad idea considering this bike has coaster brakes and I'm used to quickly squeezing brake levers for panic stopping. That could be a nasty surprise. The brake levers originally slipped over the ends of the handle bars. Since I couldn't slide the lever into its new position, I instead cut a section of the lever's clamping attachment. It still allows for a tight fit without having to remove the handle bar grips. I was able to use the original cable from the brakes of the donor bike, which was plenty long. The end of the cable was secured to the engine in the same way as the original throttle cable. To attach to the throttle lever, I crimped on an electrical terminal with an eyelet and used a small 4-40 screw to bolt the terminal to the lever.

Step 6: Killswitch

The killswitch is very handy. For example, you can let the engine cool down when it starts overheating and pinging. It can also let the engine assist with braking, which is a helpful safety feature. I used a simple, momentary, normally closed switch with a flush-mount housing and basic copper wire for this task. The wiring just connects to the two terminals on the coil to allow the switch to interrupt the spark when pressed. The switch is mounted into a piece of plywood and fixed to the handle bars with an aluminum bracket and a single bolt.

Step 7: Results

Starting Procedure:

To start the bike, I use the standard priming and choking procedure. This usually includes priming until the bulb fills with fuel, followed by a quick pedal start with the engine fully choked until it kicks over. Once the fuel is in the lines, I open up the choke to the middle setting. The motor starts when the bike is pedaled to around 8mph, which can take some furious pedaling but isn't too bad. The bike is even easier to start when it's hot. At about 12mph the bike has enough power to start accelerating up to speed.

Performance:

Acceleration is very sluggish at low speeds, but over 15mph the bike zooms along with adequate acceleration. According to the bike odometer I have attached, it has hit about 29mph on a slight downhill. It can go up significant hills and still hold 15mph. Average speed riding around the neighborhood is

about 18mph. If you think of the machine as a bike with a power-assist rather than a mini-bike, it is very reasonable. With a little gas it is effortless to cruise at 20mph, a speed barely attainable on a downhill when pedaling this bike. Since your rear is near the ground, it feels even faster than it is.

Is it worth it?

With all of the frustration that comes with keeping the machine running, the question you have to ask yourself is: Is it worth it? Well, as long as you enjoy hot exhaust blowing on your leg and the wind in your hair while flying down the road at obscene speeds with a small two-stroke between your legs screaming at 7000rpm, it is definitely worth it.

Step 8: Lessons Learned

Overall, the bike could have been built better. With modifications, it does an adequate job, but a bit more forethought would have helped make a better bike with fewer headaches. The bracket system is not a bad method for attaching an engine without welding, but using a tensioning mechanism is essential. A better mechanism than the spring that I used (I've been thinking about using a turnbuckle) and a sturdier mount for the engine would show the greatest improvements in usability, reliability, and safety. In many ways this project should be used as much for how not to build a motor bike as how to build one. Here are some things I would do differently next time:

- Use at least ½" thick plywood for the plate (¼" thick aluminum or steel would be even better it you can cut it)
- Add a tensioning mechanism from the start. There is definitely a bracket geometry that would work better.
- A stiffer setup that connects on the other side of the wheel would make for a much stronger and more stable platform.
- The rims that came with the bike are not nearly strong enough to take the 25 plus miles an hour the bike can achieve. Mine have come out of alignment and been bent a few times already. Steel brackets would be better to attach the motor plate for added strength and safety.
- One of the aluminum brackets I made broke at one of the bends. A set of store-bought U-bolts would probably be the best solution, and they would be even easier to use as long as you can find the right size.

Bamboo Bicycle

By ben_k

(http://www.instructables.com/id/Build-a-Bamboo-Bicycle-And-Light-it-up/)

If you have ever wanted to build your own bicycle frame but can't afford a framebuilding class or the materials to braze a frame, building one out of bamboo and carbon fiber is a great and relatively inexpensive way to get started. In this Instructable I will explain in detail how to build a great looking bamboo frame. After that, you will learn how to make some LED spoke lights to go along with your DIY bike, or any other bike you want to put them on.

Warning: If you are not comfortable with being stopped by strangers and answering their questions about your bicycle, this is not the project for you. And definitely do not build the spoke lights.

Step 1: Gather Your Tools and Materials
For the bicycle frame:
- bamboo: I used 1 7/8" diameter for the down tube, 1 3/8" for the top and seat tubes, 15/16" for the seat stays, and 1 1/16" for the chain stays. All values are approximate, and anything close to those should work.
- carbon fiber tow: I got 5000 meters of it off eBay for $50. I have enough left over to build at least four more bikes.
- epoxy: I used West Systems 105 resin and 205 Hardener.
- old bicycle frame: I chose to cut apart an old frame for the lugs rather than buy new ones. Using an old frame also lets you get away with not building a proper jig.
- propane torch: for heat-treating the bamboo.
- basic hand tools: saws, a decent knife, a drill, a rotary tool

- electrical tape: for compressing the carbon fiber while the resin hardens.
- aluminum angle bar: for making a simple stand to hold the frame in place.
- threaded rod and nuts: for holding the dropouts in place in the stand.
- spar varnish: for finishing the bamboo.
- paint remover: for stripping the old frame.
- sand paper: for sanding, of course!
- rubber gloves: for working with epoxy. Apparently, you can develop a nasty allergy from too much skin exposure to the hardener. You will need at least 50 pairs of these.

For the lights:
- 4 square wooden dowels
- drill and 1/16" drill bit
- 80 LED's: I used 3mm orange ones
- Two 9V battery clips
- resistors: to run the orange LED's off 9V, I needed 20 × 30 ohm resistors
- electrical tape
- soldering iron

Step 2: Preparing the Bamboo
I cut down my bamboo green, so I heat treated it with a propane torch to remove some of the water and harden the bamboo. Heat treating also gives the bamboo a nice golden color.

To start, use a long metal pole such as a gardening stake to punch out all the nodes. If you do not, the heat can cause the nodes to explode. Light your torch and begin heating the bamboo, one node at a time. You will know when you have heated it enough because the green will suddenly turn tan or brown. Obviously, try not to actually burn the bamboo or you will weaken it.

After you have torched the bamboo, it is probably best to let the poles sit for a month or so to let the rest of the water escape. Once my bamboo was dry, I sanded it down past the outer skin. In my opinion, the bamboo looks much better this way, as it has a beautiful golden color under the skin. I sanded down the nodes to be even with the rest of the bamboo as well.

Step 3: Building a Stand

I did not want to build a full jig, but I still built a stand for the frame. This helped enormously with wrapping the carbon fiber and aligning the dropouts.

I screwed two pieces of aluminum angle into a 6" wide plywood board to hold the bottom bracket shell in place. To hold the rear dropouts, I used a threaded rod bolted to the wooden base.

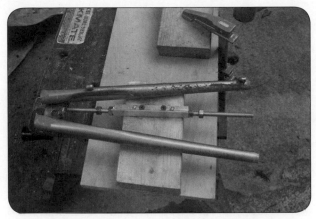

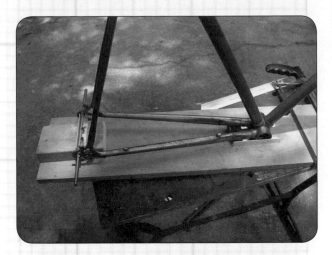

Step 4: Preparing the Donor Frame

Having a donor frame to cut apart makes it possible to build the frame without building or buying a jig. If you can find one for free or at a garage sale, it also cuts down on costs because you do not have to purchase a head tube, bottom bracket shell, or dropouts.

To get the frame ready, strip the powder coat off the head tube, BB shell, and dropouts using paint stripper. Beware, this is pretty nasty stuff. Use it outside, and try to keep if off you.

To avoid using a jig, the order in which you remove the bike's tubes is very important. You have to be able to retain the bike's geometry for everything to align and for the bike to track straight. I started out by removing the chain stays. By removing them first, the dropouts are still held in place by the seat stays and no other part of the frame is affected.

Step 5: Adding the Bamboo Tubes

The first tubes I replaced were the chain stays. I used quite wide diameter bamboo to avoid flex in the BB area. Before replacing the tubes, I built up the dropouts with carbon fiber so that they fit snugly inside the bamboo tubes. I then sanded the metal to help the epoxy grip, and fit the bamboo in place, tacking it in place with epoxy. As you can see, the bamboo is heavily sanded on the outside.

Step 6: Adding the Bamboo Tubes, Part Two

After the chain stays, I added the bamboo top tube, seat tube, and seat stays all at once. I started out by mitering the top tube on the head-tube side. I then cut the original top tube off to figure out the correct length of the new bamboo one. Once the top tube was cut to the appropriate length, I removed the seat tube and chain stays. The bamboo seat tube was mitered to fit around the BB shell, the top tube was mitered to fit the seat tube, and the seat stays were mitered to fit the seat tube. If you have them, you can use a hole saw and a drill press to do the mitering. I do not, so I used a Flexcut woodworking knife. Once all the tubes were cut and mitered, I tacked them in place with epoxy. Alignment was done by eye: I used the down tube as a reference. An easy way to hold everything in place while the epoxy is drying is to wrap it in electrical tape. It may not be the most elegant approach, but I found it works quite well.

Step 7: Adding the Bamboo Tubes, Part Three

Before replacing the down tube with bamboo, I had to strengthen the seat cluster with some carbon fiber. If I had not, the joint may well have cracked apart when I inserted the down tube, because I had to bend the frame slightly to fit it in. I will go into more detail about wrapping the carbon fiber in a later step.

I chose to use really wide diameter bamboo for the down tube. I really like how it looks, and it adds a lot of stiffness to the frame. The down tube was mitered and tacked into the frame just as the other tubes were.

Step 8: Wrapping the Joints

Now that your frame is tacked together you need to strengthen the joints with carbon fiber. This is easily the most time-consuming part of the frame-building process, at least if you choose to use carbon-fiber tow rather than cloth.

To start out, mask off your frame. This makes cleaning up the tubes much easier, but be sure not to wrap over the tape at all, or it will be impossible to remove.

Wrapping the carbon fiber is best done a little bit at a time. I found that the easiest way to wrap was to paint some epoxy on the joint, wrap one or two layers of carbon around the joint, and then paint more epoxy on top of the carbon. Repeat these steps until

the joint is too soft to wrap much more. When you have finished with the carbon fiber, wrap the entire joint in electrical tape, sticky side up, to compress the joint as it dries. Once the epoxy is dry, remove the tape, sand the surface of the joint lightly, and add another layer of carbon. Continue this process until the joint looks sturdy. When you are wrapping, be sure that you have fibers going in all directions. If you just wrap circularly, the joints will only be strong in one direction. This can lead to cracks or even joint failures later on. To fix this, I cut lots of short strips of tow and laid them lengthwise on the joints before wrapping circularly around them. I alternated one lengthwise layer and then one layer around. I have no idea how much carbon fiber is necessary, but it is better to have really thick joints than too-thin joints.

Once the joints are strong enough, sand them down to a smooth surface. This step is not necessary, but it makes the joints look infinitely better.

Warning: Epoxy dust and carbon-fiber dust are not good for you! The carbon fiber will irritate your skin and eyes (and probably your lungs), and epoxy is just not nice stuff, so be sure to do all your sanding outside, preferably while wearing long sleeves and a breathing filter.

Depending on your frame's geometry, you may want to add a chain-stay bridge to stiffen the frame. Also add a brake bridge and cable stops if you need them. For both these parts, I cut the tubes out of thin bamboo, and wrapped them heavily with carbon fiber.

While you are wrapping, occasionally check to make sure you have clearance for your back wheel's cassette. I found that I had to remove a significant amount of bamboo and carbon to get them to fit.

If you are going to have a derailleur or rear brake on your bike, you can attach cable stops with carbon fiber as well. To make the cable stops, I cut short segments of very thin bamboo and glued a metal cable cap into the bamboo. I then glued the assemblies to the bamboo frame on the down tube and wrapped carbon fiber around them. For the brakes, I decided to run housing all the way along the frame, so I did not use cable caps. I just cut short segments of bamboo to guide the brake cable and glued them along the top tube.

Step 9: Touching Up the Joints

There are almost certainly going to be some pits or ridges in your joints that would be too difficult to sand out. To fill these imperfections, I made my own epoxy filler out of carbon dust. When mixed in with epoxy, this forms a black, tar-like glue that can be used like putty to fill in the gaps. I made the carbon dust by filing down a piece of burned wood. I then used a super fine strainer to filter out all but the very smallest particles. Once you have made the thickened epoxy, spread it generously on any imperfections in the surface. Once it has dried, sand it down to the level of the carbon fiber.

Step 10: Finishing the Bamboo

Once your joints have been sanded down, you can simply paint a thin layer of epoxy over them to make them shiny and beautiful. The bamboo, however, requires more careful treatment.

First of all, sand down the bamboo and remove any epoxy that might have gotten on the tubes. To finish the bamboo, I chose to use varnish. I thinned the varnish with mineral spirits and applied about ten thin layers of it. Other people have used tung oil to finish bamboo instead. I have only used it on wood, but, while it looks very good, it does not provide a hard coating like varnish does.

Step 11: Making a Head Badge

This step is far from necessary, but making a nice head badge is a great way to separate your bamboo bike from all the others. I made mine out of a segment of steel tubing cut from the donor bike. Once I came up with a design, I drilled the rough shape out of the steel using a fine drill bit. Then I fixed the edges with a reinforced Dremel cutting disk. I cut the lines into the badge with the cutting disk as well. To get the lines to pop out, I colored over the entire badge with a Sharpie marker and then wiped it off with a rag. The ink stayed in the crevices, giving the design some clarity. I then put a clear coat of polyurethane over it and epoxied it to the head tube.

Step 12: Build Up Your Bicycle

If you have managed to build yourself a bamboo bicycle frame, you should be able to do this part yourself. I won't go into too much detail about how it is done.

I built mine up with a mixture of new and vintage parts. I bought a new carbon fiber fork from Nashbar on sale for $52. I highly recommend you get a carbon fork simply because they perfectly match the carbon on the frame. I got my brakes on eBay for $24 for the pair. I already had the wheelset, bars, shifters, derailleur, and cranks, and I got cables and housing from my local bike store.

Step 13: Light Up Your Bike

Because simply having a bamboo bicycle is not unusual enough, you may want to add some lights to it to garner even more attention. I built these simple wheel lights, which are based off a very simple circuit. Each one is composed of ten sets of four LEDs and a resistor in a series, in parallel. I chose to use 3mm orange LEDs.

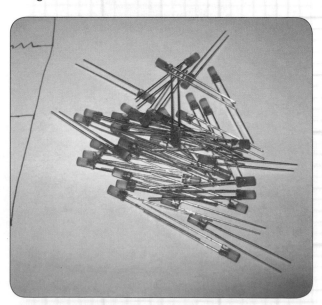

Step 14: Building the Lights

I used four thin, square dowels to make the frame of the lights. Drill forty 1/16" holes close together along the length of each dowel. They must be spaced so that an LED's leads can fit into every pair of holes. To space the LEDs evenly, drill the holes in sets of four—one LED on each side of the dowel per set. Then fit the LEDs through the holes, alternating sides. Make sure that the LEDs are oriented positive to negative through each hole. Solder each pair of LEDs together positive to negative. Also join every two pairs of LEDs the same way. For every four LEDs, solder a resistor to the positive lead of the first resistor in the chain. Four LEDs and one resistor in a series make one node of the lights. Each dowel has five nodes in parallel, and each set of lights has two rods in parallel.

Step 15: Building the Lights, Part Two

Next, you need to wire each LED node together in parallel. When doing this, try to keep the wire as close as possible to the dowel so it does not get in the way. Once you have wired together each dowel, connect each one to the 9V battery leads, with a slide switch to shut off the circuit. Then wrap each rod in electrical tape to insulate the circuits. To attach the lights to the circuit, first fix the 9V battery to your wheel's hub using electrical or duct tape. Then fix the rods to the spokes using zip ties or more tape.

Step 16: Light 'Er Up!

Now, flip the switch and go on a bike ride!

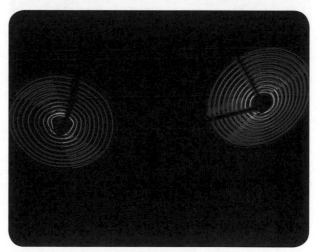

Step 17: To Conclude

This project was a great learning experience. Although I think it turned out quite well, there are a number of things I would do differently if I were to build another bamboo frame. First of all, I would coat the insides of all the tubes with a thin coat of epoxy for protection. Also, I would try starting without an old frame so that I can tailor the fit to my body, rather than going with what I had. I would also like to experiment with tube shape, i.e., building a TT-type frame with bladed tubes and a rear-wheel cutout.

Homemade Leather Bike Seat

By thearchitect
(http://www.instructables.com/id/
Cover-your-worn-bicycle-saddle-with-
real-leather/)

Wanting to fix myself a cheap recycled bike to get around, I found a stray bike that had a decent Selle Italia saddle on it. However, its vinyl cover was completely shot. Fortunately, the foam was intact and in good shape, so I decided to refinish the saddle with some natural-looking leather. I got the leather pieces from eBay. If you search for leather at hobbies and crafts section, you'll find plenty of them at very good prices. Try to get a thinner (1–2mm) leather since it is easier to work on.

Step 1: Materials

For this Instructable you need:

- a saddle in bad shape
- scrap leather large enough to cover it
- impact adhesives (i.e., Evo-Stick for U.K.)
- scissors
- a ballpoint pen

Below are the original saddle and the new and improved version. There are not many hazards or risks with this job. Watch out what you are cutting with scissors. Impact adhesives are mostly solvent based, so I advise you to do this job in a well-ventilated area or you may get high. Seriously, don't forget that these adhesives are carcinogenic.

Step 2: Remove the Saddle from Old Cover

This is not so hard. Your aim is to achieve a clean base for your work. I had to dry mine under the sun for a few days, since the foam had absorbed rainwater. Clean it thoroughly, since we will basically glue the leather on it. Peel all glue remnants off. Use some rubbing alcohol to clean the inner edges; we will glue the leather there.

Step 3: Measure Twice, Cut Once

Now you have to measure the leather to the saddle size and mark it for cutting. Tightly wrap the leather over the saddle and mark the edges. Then draw a 10mm (about ½") offset around the saddle edge marks. Finally I added a longer edge for the nose since my saddle has a screw there, which can be used as an extra fastener for the leather. Cut the leather using scissors. I used pinking shears (zig-zag scissors), as the cuts look very cool and professional. Zig-zag cutting may also help folding the concave edges, and the edges won't crumble too much.

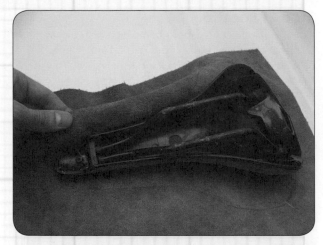

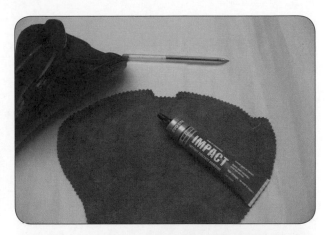

Step 5: Stick the Leather on the Saddle

Start from the nose. In my case there was a screw hole where I could attach the longer nose edge of the leather. Stretch it towards rear and glue the rear edges. Then move towards the front piecemeal on both sides and meet up at the nose. Impact glue is a wonderful thing. It holds strongly immediately, but also is very elastic. Put the plastic pieces and screws back in place (i.e., the rear and nose pieces in my case). Adore your final product. One note, though: I found out that my leather was not waterproof. Even worse, it sucks water like a sponge. Thus, I have to keep it covered with a plastic bag to save it from rain.

Step 4: Glue the Leather and Saddle Edges

Impact adhesives need to be applied on both surfaces. Use a thin coat of adhesive on both edges and spread it evenly using your fingers. Let both sides dry for something like ten minutes. For a better adhesion, repeat the application and wait another ten minutes. Please read all the instructions and warnings on the adhesive packaging! They are important, and there are good reasons why they are there.

Camping Hot Tub
By player2756
(http://www.instructables.com/id/Camping-Hot-Tub/)

Sitting around the campfire at a lake has left us too hot on one side and freezing on the other. Then we got the drunken idea that a hot tub would keep us warm all over. But, how will a 10' × 10' × 2' body of water be heated and kept hot? With fire, of course!

This Instructable explains how to build a camping hot tub and is for entertainment purposes only. Safety first! It involves power tools, fire, electricity, and water. Recreation can be very dangerous. I am in no way liable for any damage to vehicles or equipment, loss of life, accidents that may occur, fines incurred, acts of God, and so forth.

Leave your chosen campsite the way or better than you found it! Clean up and don't start a forest fire! Do not cut down trees!

Our goal was to create transportable hot-tub equipment.

Step 1: What You Need
Tools:
- chainsaw
- shovel
- car/truck or generator

Materials:
- 20' × 20' tarp
- 100' of copper coil 5/8" OD (outside diameter)
- hose 5/8" ID (inside diameter)
- hose clamps (get more than you need!)
- washers
- power inverter
- pump 1/12hp utility continuous operation
- large pond pump
- large hose
- rocks (should be on the beach or in the river)
- strong metal baskets (look around at thrift stores)

Step 2: Location
Find a really awesome camping spot, either near a lake or river, preferably within 100 feet or less. Send the minions out to gather wood for the fire. The more the better. We burn a utility trailer load every three hours. The tub needs to be close so it can be filled and refilled as needed.

Step 3: Frame
Caution! Chainsaws are not toys! Cut the logs to equal lengths so they can be stacked, notching the ends. Flatten an area so the logs will not roll out of place. This will begin to look like a log house "foundation"; if there are other groups around, be prepared to answer questions. This frame will need to be two to three feet tall. Get a helper to build a fire. Get another helper to move those neatly cut logs with you.

Tip: Placing a path of lighter logs on the ground makes rolling the big logs easy!

Step 4: Liner
Place the center of the tarp in the middle of the frame. The water will spread the tarp to the outside and fill the holes.

Tip: Place a decent-sized rock in the middle to hold it in place while filling!

Step 5: Pump Setup

To fill this large hot tub, connect the large pond pump to the large hose and power inverter or generator. Caution! If the power inverter is connected to a vehicle and it is the only one there, this is a bad idea as this will likely drain the battery!

Place the large pump in the water with a filter, or else it could and will suck up sand. If this happens, the pump will break. Fill the pool with water.

Tip: Use the smallest vehicle as it will be the easiest to jump and restart.

Step 6: Stone Boiling

Caution! Rocks that are hot will burn! Place rocks in baskets in the fire the minions have prepared. After about 15 minutes the rocks should be hot enough to heat some water.

Caution! Do not place the baskets on the tarp, as it will melt! Use an insulator, like large branches, to keep the baskets off the tarp. Once there is a significant amount of water in the pool, place the baskets in the water. Exchange them in intervals of about 15 minutes. Four baskets of rocks keep everything moving ahead.

Step 7: The Small Pump

Now the pool is full and getting warm from the stone boiling. Disconnect the power inverter or generator from the large pond pump. Prime the inlet hose by placing it in the pool. Connect it to the appropriate side of the pump and test to ensure it will pump water. Connect another hose to the first 50' copper coil with a hose clamp so that there is the proper connection for the pump on the other end. Connect the two copper coils with a section of hose and two hose clamps. Then connect the second copper coil to another section of hose that leads to the pool. Weight the out-to-pump end of the hose in the pool so it always is free of obstruction.

Caution! The copper coil will melt if water does not flow through it whilst in the fire. Prime the hose that goes to the pump, turn it on, and connect it to the hose that goes to the copper coil. Things should be wet but functional. Check the in-to-pool end of the hose to make sure water is flowing freely. Troubleshoot if not. Carefully place the copper coil in the fire while ensuring all rubber connections are at least one foot from any heat, preferably protected.

Step 8: Done!

Things should be warm by now, so go get in and keep the fire and the pump going! Maybe make a new friend! Enjoy the warm water of labor.

Clothing & Accessories

Tie-Dyed T-Shirts

Electroluminescent Wire Clothing

Clap-Off Bra

Turn-Signal Biking Jacket

Chainmail Shirt

R2D2 Heels

Bent Wood Rings

Electronic Motherboard Bracelet

LED Tron Suit

Iron Man Arc Reactor

Soda Can Tab Chainmail

Smelt Your Own Ring

5 Cent Men's Ring

Woven Paracord Bracelet/Watchband

Homemade Bath Bombs

Uber Band

Do-It-Yourself Shirt-Folding Board

There is a thin wall of fabric between the world and your naked body. Take control over what you use to cover yourself with these creative and fashionable projects.

Electroluminescent wire suits are great for being seen at night. And at certain parties. A bent wood ring is a handsome accessory that is simultaneously crafty, inexpensive, and ruggedly attractive. A paracord bracelet might just save your bacon when you find yourself kicking through bat guano after spelunking a little too aggressively.

And there's the old countercultural standby: tie-dye. It's not just for hippies and camp counselors, especially with the clever and unique methods of creating specific patterns.

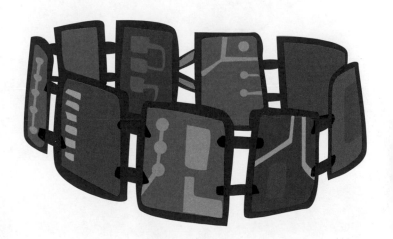

Tie-Dyed T-Shirts

By stinkymum

(http://www.instructables.com/id/
How-to-tie-dye-an-old-white-shirt-or-a-
new-shirt-/)

Take an old white shirt suffering from the "dingies" and turn it into a rainbow masterpiece! I'll show you how.

Step 1: The Shirt, Fit to Be Dyed!

The shirts that work best are 100% cotton, although you can use a 50-50 cotton-polyester blend (however, the results will not be so vibrant). The dyes only bond well with natural fabrics, like cotton, silk, and rayon.

Step 2: Presenting Your Choice of Dyes

You can buy dye kits that come with everything you need in a craft store. They include rubber gloves, rubber bands, soda ash, urea, and complete easy-to-follow instructions. The dyes are already in the squeeze bottles, so all you have to add is warm water (not hot). Other alternatives include buying single packages of dyes, which will come with the necessary urea and soda ash and instructions for mixing. However, you would need to purchase some squeeze bottles separately if you don't have any. Although I have used kits, I prefer to use the Procion dyes as supplied by Dharma Dye. They have a great website where you can buy all you need. However, if you mix the dye powder yourself, always wear a mask so that you don't inhale the powder.

Step 3: The Tools You Will Need for Success

If you are like me and are not using a pre-packaged kit, you will need the following: Procion dye, rubber bands, rubber gloves, squeeze bottles for the dye, urea, and soda ash. Oh yes, don't forget to have paper towels and old rags to mop up the spills. Tie-dying does not have to be messy!

Step 4: Soaking the Shirt

To enable the Procion dyes to bond with the shirt, you need to soak it in a solution of warm (not hot) water and soda ash for about ten minutes. Follow the instructions given with the soda ash so that you have the right mix. Do not use water that is too hot or too cold, and add a couple of tablespoons of common salt to the mix, too! Make sure the mixture is thoroughly dissolved before adding the shirt. The temperature of the water should be about the same as a baby's bath. As the soda ash is slightly caustic, you may want to wear rubber gloves at this point, especially if you have a cut on your finger! After soaking, wring the shirt out thoroughly. The more liquid that you can squeeze out, the more dye that will be able to get in. I usually spin my shirts on the spin cycle of the washing machine. (Note: if you use a brand new shirt, wash it first to remove the newness, which I think they call "size." This sizing will prevent dye from bonding properly, and you may get a streaky effect.)

Step 5: Tying a Rainbow Swirl Pattern!

After you have soaked and wrung out the shirt, lay the shirt on a flat surface. Place it right-side down, as you will then get a sharper pattern on the front of the shirt. Of course, if you want the sharper pattern on the back—well, you know! Place the dowel rod (or your finger, or a wooden clothes pin) in the center of the shirt and start turning it clockwise until the shirt has a nice flat pie shape.

Step 6: Achieving Pie!

This is what your shirt should look like at this stage. Do not allow the shirt to creep up the dowel rod. Make it behave with your free hand. You are now ready to remove the dowel and put on the rubber bands. The trick is to place the bands without disturbing the shirt. However, be careful removing the dowel. You do not want to pull the shirt up in the middle, thus undoing the pie. This part of the process is the most important step of all. Believe me, if you do a sloppy tie you will achieve a sloppy and messy dye and regret it.

Step 7: Join the Band!

With your lovely pie shape achieved, you can now put on the rubber bands. Slip several bands on (see the picture) and then turn the shirt over and put on some

more. This helps it keep its shape. Keep the whole thing as flat as you can. You are now ready to dye!

Step 8: To Dye For

When doing the actual dying bit, you will need to cover your working surface with plastic—a plastic table cloth will work fine. You also need to wear old clothes, old shoes, etc. The dyes will stain your clothes, the floor, the walls, the ceiling, and so forth. So if you are not working outside, please be careful. The dyes are harmless to your skin, but if you don't wear rubber gloves you will achieve red-, yellow-, or blue-dyed hands, which won't wash off for days. Also be ready with the rags to mop up spills. When I mix the dyes, I make sure that the caps are on tight, and I also wipe the screw top and bottle neck to avoid "capillary action." I have also purloined some of my husband's and son's old white socks and cut them down to fit over the bottles, which helps stem accidental leaks. Hint: There is a product called Reduran that can be purchased online from Dharma, which removes dye from the skin instantly so you don't have to suffer "rainbow hand" syndrome!

Step 9: Actually Using the Dyes

Place your shirt pie on a couple of layers of paper towels on top of a paper plate on your plastic-protected working surface. It's less messy and easy to flip the whole thing over when dying the other side. Wear rubber gloves! Just a note: When I tie dye I usually only use three dye colors—fuchsia red, turquoise, and lemon yellow. With these three colors you can make any color you like. To make the rainbow swirl shirt, imagine that your pie is an actual pie chart! Working from the center of the shirt and holding the bottle low over the shirt, dye one third of the shirt lemon yellow. Do not wave the bottle around as you will make a mess! Dye the second third of the shirt fuchsia red, and the final third turquoise.

Do not leave any white spaces showing—the white is hiding within the folds! If you overlap the colors at the edges of each section you will get the other rainbow colors, i.e. green, purple and orange. It's magic! Hint: Always put yellow (or other light-hued dyes) on first. Once you or cover it up by mistake it is changed to something else (either orange or green) and you can't get it back.

Step 10: Turn the Pie Over!

When you have finished putting the dye on the first side, turn the whole thing over. This will be easy to do if you just flip the plate over onto another paper plate with clean paper towels all ready. Throw the first paper plate and towels away and then apply the dye on this second side in a similar manner. If you are making the rainbow swirl, you need to be sure to put the three colors behind the same colors you used on the other side (i.e., red behind red, blue behind blue, etc.). If you don't do this, you will not get a rainbow spiral, but rather a sort of rainbow spider pattern (which is quite nice actually!)

Step 11: Now Comes the Hard Part—Waiting!

After you have finished putting the dye on the shirt, pop it into a zip lock bag and seal it up tight. Put the bag in a warm place and leave it for at least 24 hours! The dye needs this length of time to "prove" and allow the beautiful colors to really bond with the fabric. For you desperate "have-it-knows," you can unwrap after eight hours, but you can also leave it for as long as 36 hours if you are very patient. If you leave it much longer, I have found the colors go sort of fuzzy.

Step 12: Unwrapping Your Masterpiece— Wear Rubber/Latex Gloves!

I love this part! This is the moment you have been waiting for. It's time to unwrap and discover your beautiful (we hope) creation. Take the shirt out of the bag! You can take the bands off first, unwrap, and start running the shirt under a cold water tap, or just run under the tap for a while and then take the bands off!

Beware: If you have never tie dyed before you will be astonished at the amount of dye that pours out as you are rinsing. The water will turn black! Fear not; this is normal. All the dye you so lovingly applied will never bond with the fabric. Enough dye will remain that is well and truly bonded. Keep rinsing until the water runs clear (it may take a while!). Hopefully, if you have done it right, your pattern will be revealed in all its glory. You may now wash your shirt in the normal way in a washing machine (by itself the first

time). I usually wash my shirts two or three times on their own before I trust them with other items.

Step 13: The Moment of Truth

Here's my shirt hanging out to dry. I hope yours is as good, or even better! Enjoy!

Step 14: No White Cotton Garment Will Ever Be Safe Again!

Once you have the tie-dye bug, life will never be the same. Your family members may become paranoid and start hiding their cotton underwear.

Electroluminescent Wire Clothing

By enlighted

(http://www.instructables.com/id/how-to-add-EL-wire-to-a-coat-or-other-garment/)

As a lighted costume designer, I get a lot of questions from people who want to know how to make their own electroluminescent (EL) wire costumes. I don't have time to help everyone individually, so I thought I'd consolidate my advice into one Instructable. Hopefully this will help you understand the steps involved in this labor-intensive process and get you started with your own lighted clothing projects. Rather than describe how to make a single specific design, I am trying to make these instructions fairly general so you can create your own EL wire layout for almost any type of clothing, although many of my example photos refer to lighted coats. Also, since EL wire is very fragile in situations where it is flexed repeatedly, a lot of these tips will focus on methods for improving durability and getting the longest possible life out of the garment.

Note: It's great to be inspired by others' work, but I'd like to encourage you to take things a step further and use these techniques to create your own original designs.

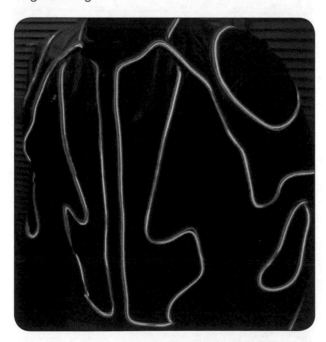

Step 1: List of Materials
- article of clothing to light up (see guidelines in that step)
- sewing supplies: needle, clear thread, scissors
- EL wire (can be a single color or a mix of colors)

- EL wire driver/inverter matched to the total length of glowing wire used in the design
- battery holder and switch (if not included with driver).

If you are soldering you will also need:
- soldering iron
- solder
- wire strippers
- wire cutters
- heat-shrink tubing
- heat gun
- glue, pins, clamps (optional)

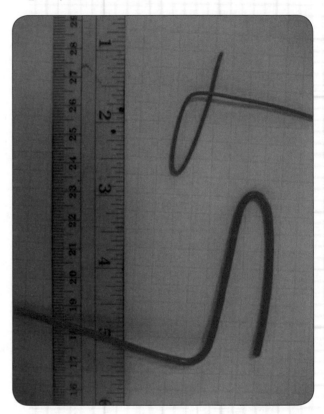

Step 2: Choose Garment to Light Up
Some types of clothing are better suited for EL wire installation than others. Results are usually better when the stiffness of the wire is similar to the stiffness of the base fabric, and the garment does not stretch or flex too much in the areas where the EL wire is installed.

I recommend leather, suede, vinyl, various forms of imitation leather, denim, thick cotton/polyester blends, velvet (non-stretch), faux fur, quilted or padded jackets (like a parka), or any medium to heavyweight fabric that does not stretch. I do not recommended lightweight fabrics or stretch fabrics. In most cases, you don't want the EL wire to be significantly stiffer than the fabric or the wire will dominate the drape of the garment. (One exception would be a ruffled edge on a tutu, for example).

Also, if you bend or fold part of the wire when you wear it or store it, it will retain some of the bend in that location when you want to straighten it out. Over time, these areas are more likely to break.

If you are working with a lined piece of clothing, open up the lining by gently snipping the stitches in an inner seam. Open it enough so that you can access all the places where you will put EL wire.

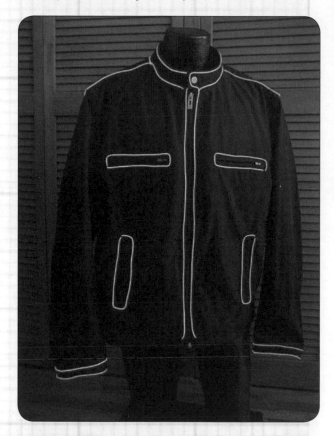

Step 3: Plan the Light Layout

Adding EL wire to clothing can be a good project for a beginner who has limited experience with electronics or sewing. However, you should be aware of the limitations of EL wire when you plan your design. The center core of EL wire is made of solid copper, and like any solid wire it will break due to fatigue damage after repeated bending. On the human body, the elbows, knees, shoulders, and hips undergo the most movement. You can make the electronics last longer by mounting EL on areas that don't flex as much and using stranded insulated connector wire (which can flex) to join the glowing pieces together inside the garment.

Plan the placement of EL wire with temporary markers like pieces of string, pins, or stickers, or make a sketch on a digital photo of the garment. You can follow the seams or add extra lines as desired. Decide which sections can be lit up with a single continuous piece of EL wire and which will require multiple pieces. Then decide what path the wire will take for each section and mark the entry and exit points. To make sharp "T" shaped junctions, you may need to run the wire inside the jacket at some locations.

Step 4: Select and Order the EL Wire and Inverter

Measure the total length of EL wire that you will need, taking into account parts that will be hidden behind the fabric, and add at least 2–3 inches at the end of each piece to allow for stripping and soldering the ends (or sealing the un-soldered ends). If you are not experienced with soldering EL wire, order extra so you can practice. You may need to cut and re-strip the ends multiple times. There are many sources for buying EL wire online, such as coolneon.com and worldaglow.com

Thicknesses:

The various thicknesses of EL wire are thin (angel hair), normal (2.3 mm diameter), and extra thick/phat (3.2mm or 5mm diameter). I prefer normal thickness, high-brightness wire for most applications. The thin wire can be bent into finer shapes, but it is more fragile (better suited for a hat or a tiara, for example). The thick wire is more durable, being protected by a thicker outer plastic core, but it cannot be bent as tightly and may not be suitable for designs with fine details or sharp bends.

Colors:

There are two standard phosphor colors for EL wire: aqua blue (which is white with a clear sheath when off) and white (which is pink when off, due to the addition of a red phosphor in the mix). The other colors (pink, red, orange, yellow, lime green, dark green, dark blue, and violet) are achieved by filtering the aqua light through a tinted outer sheath. Aqua tends to be the brightest, although the brightness can be adjusted when you select your driver.

EL Drivers:

EL wire uses a high-voltage and high-frequency alternating current to activate the phosphor. An EL driver, also known as an inverter, is required to convert your low-voltage DC power from the battery into a high-voltage AC source.

The length rating of the EL driver should be matched to the total length of glowing wire that you want to illuminate, regardless of whether it is wired in series or in parallel. Some drivers will produce a steady glow in your EL wire; others have built-in options for blinking and sound reactivity.

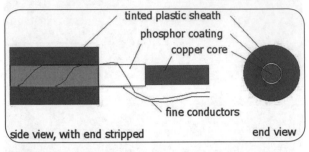

side view, with end stripped — end view

tinted plastic sheath
phosphor coating
copper core
fine conductors

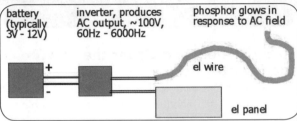

battery (typically 3V - 12V) | inverter, produces AC output, ~100V, 60Hz - 6000Hz | phosphor glows in response to AC field

el wire
el panel

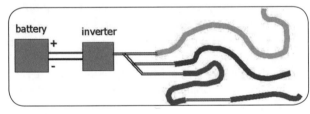

battery | inverter

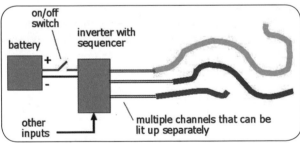

on/off switch
battery
inverter with sequencer
other inputs
multiple channels that can be lit up separately

Step 5: Cut, Strip and Solder the EL Wire Junctions

You can order the EL wire pieces pre-soldered if your design is relatively simple, and in that case you want to skip this step. The sketch below illustrates the method I use to solder EL wire. If you'd like more detail, you can get directions from the places that sell EL wire. For each piece of EL wire in your design, cut the proper length (with at least a few extra inches at each end) and solder the end of each piece to a connector or to a double-conductor piece of ribbon cable that is long enough to reach the driver. The polarity does not matter—either wire can be connected to the center core or the outer wires.

There are many methods for soldering EL wire. For any of these you should end up with a reinforced region with heat shrink tubing covering the junction.

I strongly recommend that you test the wire at this stage, joining the two conductors to an inverter, before it is attached to the garment. This is also a good time to join the pieces together to test the overall brightness and decide whether you'd like to use a stronger inverter. You can achieve a higher level of brightness by overdriving the wire (e.g., attaching a short length of wire to one that is designed for a longer piece). It will burn out the phosphor on the wire faster, but that might not be important for some applications. Under normal usage, EL wire should have 3000 to 5000 hours of glowing life before the phosphor fades to ½ of its normal brightness.

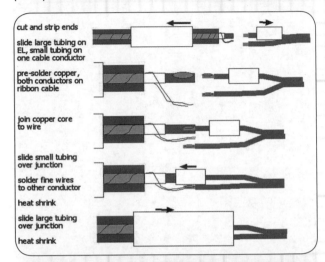

cut and strip ends
slide large tubing on EL, small tubing on one cable conductor
pre-solder copper, both conductors on ribbon cable
join copper core to wire
slide small tubing over junction
solder fine wires to other conductor
heat shrink
slide large tubing over junction
heat shrink

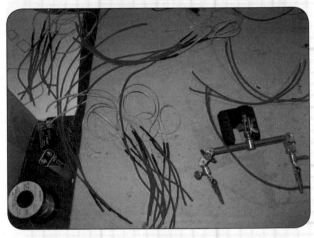

Step 6: Attach the EL Wire

For most projects, the best approach is to hand-sew the wire to the fabric with clear monofilament thread (fishing line). Look for the basic clear kind in one of the lower weights. I typically use the 6lb type, but 4lb and 8lb will also work reasonably well. You can also use standard thread if you don't mind that it will block light from the EL wherever you make a stitch. Make a hole in the fabric where you want to have an entry point. Now, with the connector wires on the inside, pull the EL wire through the hole. When you get to the solder junction and shrink tubing, leave that part inside the garment and position it in a way that can be reinforced. For example, you may want to sew it to the inside of a seam or add glue. It is most important that the area inside the shrink tubing is not going to bend repeatedly—this is the most fragile part of the wire. If you are doing the type of installation where you are running one long piece along an arm or leg, or another line that is going to extend when you flex, then it is better to mount the EL wire in a way that allows the end to slide slightly in and out of the hole.

To sew the wire in place, use a needle that is appropriate for the garment fabric (leather needles have a special piercing point at the end). Thread the needle. As a rule of thumb, a good amount of thread to use is the distance between your hands when your arms are spread out. Shorter pieces will require frequent re-threading, longer pieces tend to get tangled and caught on things. I like to sew with a double strand of thread, meaning the needle is positioned at the halfway point on the piece of fishing line, and the two ends are tied together. A double knot is a good idea. When you start sewing, run the needle between the two threads after the first stitch, to make a better anchor to the knot. This ensures the knot will not pull through the hole in the fabric. Sew along the length of the EL wire with a diagonal whip stitch, using whatever spacing is needed to hold the wire in the proper shape. If the fabric is especially thick or difficult to sew through, you can use a line of topstitching as your anchor. Tie an extra knot in the fishing line periodically (every 5–6 inches), so that if part of it breaks it will not undo the rest of the stitching.

For some materials, strong flexible glue may be a better choice. For example, EL wire can be mounted to a plastic surface (such as a helmet) by hot glue, E6000, or 3M Super Strength Adhesive. Another method for attaching EL wire to clothing is to make a casing or channel with sheer fabric, and slide the wire through there. Or, if you're looking for an extremely easy short cut or a quick temporary attachment, you could weave it back and forth through holes in the fabric, or hold it on temporarily with safety pins, zip ties, or clear tape. When you get to the other end, make an entry hole, if needed. Leave about 2"–3" excess wire at the end. Seal the end with heat-shrink tubing and/or glue and mount it on the inside of the garment, as you did with the leading end.

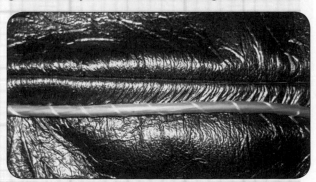

Step 7: Finishing Steps

First, you will need to deal with wire management inside the garment. There should be enough slack for the non-glowing connector wires to reach back to the inverter and battery without being pulled tightly when you move. But you also don't want so much excess wire that it will get snagged when you put it on. I recommend using a big stitch to sew these wires to the seams on the inside of the garment. If your jacket is unlined, this is especially helpful. If your jacket has a lining, it may be sufficient to make some anchor points at key locations where the wire bends, like the armpits. After all the wires running back to the inverter and battery pocket are stabilized, reconnect them as needed. They can be hard-wired to the driver or joined to a plug if you want it to be easy to change it later. Use heat-shrink tubing or other insulators to ensure that you do not short out the two conductors to each other.

Advice for the battery pocket: Use an existing pocket in the garment or add one, if necessary. The pocket should be close to the size of the battery pack. If you will be dancing or moving a lot in the coat, you don't want the battery pack to bounce around too much or fall out. Closing the pocket with a zipper or Velcro can be helpful. Clip a small part of the pocket seam, pass the wire through, and re-sew the seam closed so that the parts don't fall back into the lining. If you do not plan to change the inverter, that part can be hidden in an inaccessible part inside the lining or sewn into a separate closed section of a pocket. Run the wire for the battery connector to that pocket. There should be enough excess wire to easily access the end and change batteries. Many EL drivers run on 9V or 12V. A standard 9V battery is good for many applications. If you want longer battery life with a 9V system, you can also use a 6-pack of AA cells.

Step 8: Other Examples: EL Wire Logos and Shapes

In addition to lighting up the seams of a garment, EL wire can also be bent into shape to create logos and other designs, and can then be sewn or glued to fabric.

Step 9: Other Examples: EL Wire Suits

Here are some examples of EL wire suits.

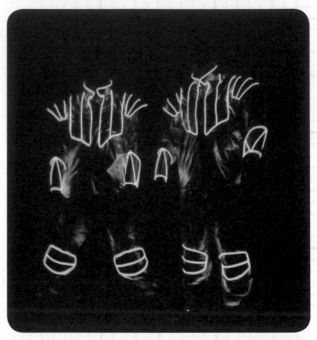

Step 10: Other Examples: EL Wire Hats and Helmets

Hats and helmets can provide a good, sturdy, non-flexing base for EL wire. Cut holes in fabric or drill/melt holes in plastic to pass the wire in and out of the hat at desired locations. A small inverter and battery (9V type, for example), can be hidden in a hat with extra space inside, so those are generally preferred over something tight, like a low-crown baseball cap. The high-pitched whining noise of the EL wire system can be difficult to wear near your ears, although some people don't mind it.

Clap-Off Bra

By randofo
(http://www.instructables.com/id/
Clap-Off-Bra/)

The first time I read about Syrian Lingerie I was quite moved. In the West, we often think of Arab cultures as sexually repressed societies. In fact, it turns out that they are leaps and bounds ahead of us in regards to advancements in lingerie technology. Those of us in Western cultures have a thing or two to learn from the Syrians about gaudy electronic lingerie.

Henceforth, it became my mission to fast-forward lingerie technology in the West. I figured the first step in this critical mission was to replicate some of the advancements made in Syria. The article of lingerie that resonated most with my inner sensibilities was the clap-off bra. I immediately resolved to make my own clap-off bra as a springboard into Western lingerie innovation.

On a quiet morning two years ago, I first set out to make my own clap-off bra. After a long, arduous process, I am proud to present a reliably working prototype.

Step 1: How NOT to Make a Clap-Off Bra

Before I make anything, I always look for existing devices I can model my project on. I knew clap-off bras were available in Syria. I looked all over the Internet to figure out how the Syrians made it. Yet, despite hours of searching, I couldn't find a single instance of a clap-off bra that provided details on the construction.

The lack of reference annoyed me, but I continued my pursuit. My first thought was to use a solenoid. This attempt failed. It got too hot, and I immediately wrote off all electromagnetic solutions as potential burn hazards. In retrospect, this was a horrible mistake.

My second thought was to build a tiny spring-loaded quick-release mechanism. Of course, making a spring-loaded quick-release mechanism is a lot easier to speculate about than to actually build. This attempt ended in disaster, too. I took some time off from the project.

I then partnered with a collaborator. We discussed various possibilities for opening the bra and finally decided upon exploding the bra off. Unsurprisingly, the initial test demonstrated that an exploding button in the front of a bra was going to end in disaster. Yet, this mistake gave us another idea.

We finally decided that we were going to get a large metal button, coat it in nitrocellulose, and create a brief incendiary event that would burn the thread away. Hence, when the thread burns away, the button would fall off and the bra would open. Fortunately, for the poor girl who was going to have to wear this, that approach did not work either. No matter what thread we used, we could never get it to fully incinerate and release the button. This disheartened us and the project was laid to rest yet again.

A year or so passed, and I decided to try an idea that we had discussed in passing but never executed. The fourth iteration involved pulling the pin out of the center of a hinge. By removing the pin, the bra would separate. We initially didn't want to do this because it would involve using a large motor attached to the bra and this didn't seem very classy. Nonetheless, I figured I would give it a go.

I went out and bought the smallest servo motor I could find, and on the first attempt to pull out the pin with the motor, I tore the gears apart and the weak little servo was destroyed. As it turns out, pulling out a pin that runs vertically using lateral force is nearly impossible. Once again, I found myself in overly-complicated mechanical quick-release territory. I consulted Instructables senior engineer and ridiculous clothing expert, Rachel McConnell, and after she surveyed the situation she surmised that my current approach was hopeless. Normally I would just ignore the project for a few more months, but I was hell bent on just finishing the darned thing.

In talking to Rachel about my failures, I recounted the one idea someone suggested to me early on that I had yet to try. Basically, this idea involved using a small electromagnet and a strong rare-earth magnet and polarizing the electromagnet in such a way that it repels the rare-earth magnet. Rachel supposed this would work, and I supposed I would give it a try.

I went shopping for magnet wire to wind an electromagnet, but it wasn't carried in any stores I visited. Fortunately, I had a moment of inspiration. An electromagnet is basically a coil with some metal in the middle. I just needed to find something with a coil.

I tore apart my work station looking for a decent-sized coil of any sort, but to no avail. I finally turned to my coworker and asked, "Hey, you wouldn't happen to have any solenoids or big relays or anything with a coil in it?" He produced a defective 5V DPDT relay. This relay was perfect because it's essentially an electromagnet that controls a switch.

I carefully cut open the DPDT relay and exposed the coil. I stuck a rare-earth magnet to the end and then powered it up and tried to repel it. This attempt didn't work because the magnet was too strong and it'd just reposition itself.

Out of sheer curiosity I checked to see how strong the magnet was with a screwdriver that I had lying around. To my amazement, the electromagnet had a fair amount of pull and was able to lift the screwdriver at 5V. I wondered what would happen if I gave the 5V coil a full 9V. So, I did and discovered that the coil didn't heat up as much as I had expected it to, and the magnet got significantly stronger. It was now apparent to me that the simple electromagnet inside of a DPDT relay, powered at 9V, was going to get the job done.

Now that you know a bunch of ways not to make a clap-off bra, it is time to actually go ahead and start making one.

Step 2: Tools and Materials
You will need:

- a front-opening strapless underwire bra
- black fabric
- small nut and bolt
- Two prototype circuit boards
- an Arduino (w/ATMEGA168 DIP chip)
- 28-pin socket
- Two 22pF capacitors
- Two 0.1uF capacitors
- 10uF capacitor
- 16mhz crystal
- 1K resistor
- 10K resistor
- 100K resistor
- 2N3904 NPN transistor
- 7805 voltage regulator
- 5V SPST relay
- 5V DPDT relay
- an electret microphone
- 9V battery connector
- a spare USB cable
- 1" shrink tube
- threadlocker
- a small grommet
- elastic band
- double-stick tape
- quick-setting epoxy
- ribbons and frills
- sewing stuff
- soldering stuff
- various tools

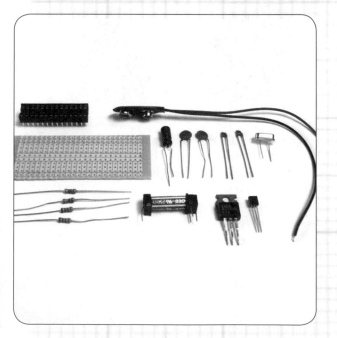

Step 3: Remove the Clasp
Cut the clasp off of the bra using cutting pliers (or similar).

Step 4: Prepare the Electromagnet

Carefully break open the casing for the relay to expose the electromagnet. To avoid damaging the coil, you should start cracking open the case on the side with the switch contact pins. It is okay if the contacts get destroyed, but if you break the coil, then you will need to get a new relay.

Step 5: Prepare the Perf Board

Put your relay into the center of one of the prototype circuit boards and make cut marks around the outline of the relay. These will be used in a moment.

Step 6: Time to Cut!

Cut your two prototype circuit boards down to size. To do this I used a paper cutter. If you don't have a paper cutter, you can also cut them using scissors, but the results won't be as precise.

One board should have a ¼" trimmed off of each long end so that you are a left with a long strip. The other board should be cut to the size of a small square, using the markings you made in the last step.

Step 7: Solder the Circuit

Put together the circuit using the 28-pin socket in place of the ATMEGA168 chip (for the time being). Don't worry about the electromagnet and electret microphone for now.

Step 8: 4-Wire Cable

Take your USB cable and cut off each end so that you are left with a section of cable roughly 6"–8" long.

Step 9: Grommet

Cut a small bow-tie-shaped section of fabric that will fold over the one of the existing sections of fabric in the front of the bra (the part that the clamp was attached to). In the center of this bow tie cut a small opening and fasten a grommet.

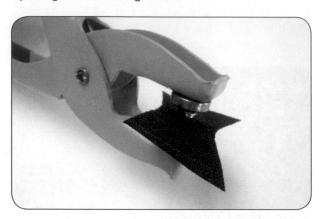

Step 10: Screw It

Insert the bolt through the grommet from the back toward the front. Fasten it with a nut.

Step 11: Sew

Fold the bow tie over the fabric section in the front of the bra that used to hold one side of the clasp. Sew the fabric down to the bra, over the existing fabric. I used a double-backed stitch for extra strength.

Step 12: Cut

Make sure that the nut and bolt are fastened tight. Using a hacksaw or rotary tool, cut the bolt flush with the nut.

222

Step 13: Lock It

Twist off the nut and apply threadlocker to the threading of the bolt. Twist the nut firmly back on.

Step 14: Attach the Cable

Peel back the jacket of the USB cable to expose four colored wires.

Attach these wires to the circuit board as follows:

- Green: 2N3904 transistor ground
- White: junction of 0.1uF and 10K resistor
- Red: SPST 5V relay switch
- Black: circuit ground

Step 15: Program It

Download the .zip file containing the code at http://www.instru-ctables.com/id/Clap-Off-Bra/step15/Program-it/ and upload it to your Arduino board.

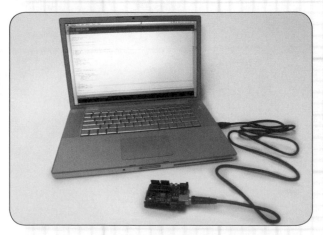

Step 16: Transfer

Transfer the ATMEGA168 chip from the Arduino board to the socket on the circuit board.

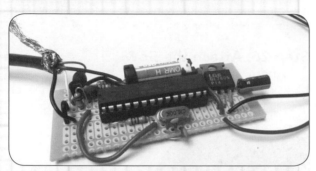

Step 17: Solder the Small Board

Solder the electromagnet and electret microphone to the smaller circuit board.

Step 18: Epoxy

Remove 2"–3" of jacket from the free end of the USB cable. Epoxy the colored wires on the small circuit board, leaving some slack so that you still have some wiggle room to work with when you strip and solder the wires.

Step 19: Solder It Up

Solder the wires to the circuit board as follows:
- White: microphone signal
- Green: microphone ground
- Red: electromagnet coil
- Black: electromagnet coil

Step 20: Sew It Down

Sew down the small electromagnet board to the fabric in the front of the bra to which the clasp used to be attached to (not the one with the nut and bolt attached, obviously).

Step 21: Insulate

Lay down a strip of fabric beneath the long circuit board. It should protrude 1" past the board on each end. Slide the 1" diameter shrink tubing over the fabric and circuit board. Quickly heat the shrink tubing with a heat gun long enough for it to tighten around the board.

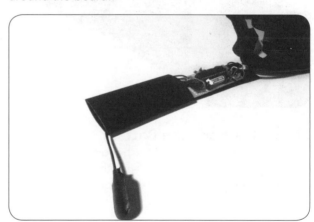

Step 22: Sew It Up

Sew the USB cable along the underside of the bra until you reach the end of the cup. Repeat this stitch several times so it's nice and strong and then stop sewing.

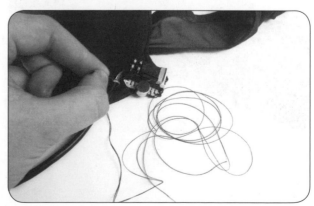

Step 23: Attach the Circuit

Sew the circuit board to the top of the back strap of the bra (attaching it to the top avoids bunching).

Step 24: Attach the Battery

Sew your elastic straps perpendicular to the bra strap at the top and bottom so that it'll hold the battery. When you are finished, slide the 9V battery under the straps.

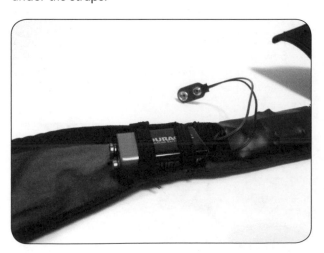

Step 25: Make a Bow

Take your ribbon and make a bow large enough to hide the electromagnet in the front of the bra. If, like me, you don't know how to make a bow, find someone to do it for you.

Step 26: Attach the Bow

Attach the bow to the top of the electromagnet by using strong, permanent, double-sided tape or hot glue. You can sew it on, too.

Step 27: Clasp On. Clap Off

Plug in the battery. Put the bra on as normal using the electromagnetic clasp. When you are ready for it to come off, simply clap twice. If you want to be "modest" about it, you can make your own pasties to wear underneath the bra.

Chainmail Shirt

By mythbuster1633
(http://www.instructables.com/id/How-to-Make-a-Chainmail-Shirt-1/)

In this Instructable I will teach you how to make a shirt of real chainmail. It will take a lot of time and patience but is a very rewarding project when you finish.

Step 1: What You Need

- 1–2 years of time
- a very strong will
- 1200-2000 feet of wire (6000-10000 links)
- 2 pairs of small blunt nose pliers
- a drill (with a chuck)
- ½" or ¼" metal rod
- a Dremel or other cutting device
- a vice or strong clamp
- some 2" × 4" pieces of wood
- 4 screws

Step 2: Making Links

The first step is to be able to make the links of the chainmail. If you have some money you can buy them at theringlord.com as well as at other jewelry stores. If you plan on buying links you can skip this step and the next.

First, you need to build a rig with the 2 × 4s to support the rod (fig 1) that the links will be made on. Attach the three pieces together with the screws. Drill a hole in both sides of the wood big enough for your rod to pass through easily. Now drill a small hole through the rod that your wire can get through. For wire I used a multi-purpose galvanized 16-gauge wire from Lowes. It is sold in 200ft lengths for around $8.

When you have all this assembled, put the rod and drill into the jig (which should be clamped on a table), insert the wire into the hole, and start the drill turning slowly. The wire will wrap itself around the rod, making a nice little spring. Use pliers to pull the wire out of the hole and slide the spring off the rod.

Step 3: Cutting Links

Now that you have the spring, it needs to get cut into individual links. When I started I was using a hacksaw, which did not work very well and took a long time. Then I got a Dremel, which is a rotary cutting tool, and it got the job done very quickly.

To cut the spring, slide it onto another rod of the same diameter and put both in the vice or other clamp. When you are cutting it with the Dremel be sure to wear safety glasses and do it in an area with no combustible gasses.

Depending on the length of the spring it should take around five minutes to cut, and you will then have roughly 40 links that you can start using.

Step 4: Begin Assembly

Now that you have links to start working with, you need to know the pattern to follow. It is a very simple pattern called 4-in-1 European mail, which basically it means that every link is connected to four others. This makes a very strong and, depending on the size of links, very dense fabric. For my chainmail I used 3/8" links, which are really too big to be protective or historically correct. I would recommend using ¼" links instead.

You're going to need a pair of blunt-nose pliers that preferably do not have teeth. First take four links and close them so they lie flat on the table. Then take a fifth link and open it so that you can slide the four other links onto it, then close the fifth link. This is the building block of your chainmail. (Fig 1, 2, 3)

Now that you have the basic building block of the shirt you will need to make many more. To attach them together, line the 4-in-1s up so that the pattern matches. Then take another link and connect the four rings that are in the center. This interconnection creates another 4-in-1 within the first two.

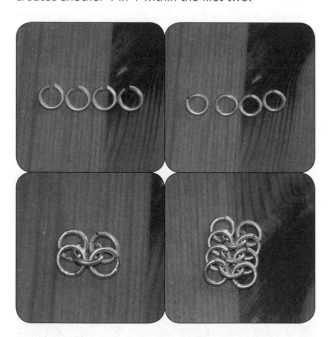

Step 5: How to Make a Chainmail Shirt

Now we can finally start making our shirt. I warn you this is a very long step and will require the most time and patience. First you'll need to make a strip that is one 4-in-1 wide and the length of your waist circumference. Once it is finished, find the middle and put a link there to mark it. Now measure about 4" over on both sides. This will be your head hole, so 8" may be too big or too small. A good way to find out is to measure a T-shirt, but remember that chainmail doesn't stretch so bigger is always better. Mark both sides of the head hole with links and remove the center link. On either side of the head hole you will add rectangles that will be the shoulders. I would

recommend that the head hole be around 20 links, or 6", deep so that it will not slide around too much when you bend forwards.

Now comes the longest part. You have the head hole and shoulders, so now you need to make the front and back pieces. I found the best way to do this is to make strips of the correct length 7–11 rows wide. Just keep adding on rows until it is as long as you want it, probably just past your waist. When you are done it should look like a tunic that fits over your head but has no sleeves and is not connected at the sides. This step will take around 1–2 years (depending on the size of the links and length of the tunic.)

Step 6: Sleeves

Now that you have your chainmail tunic you will need sides and sleeves. I would recommend doing the sleeves first. I made my sleeves 7" wide to make sure that they would not be too tight. A good way to estimate the right width is to measure a T-shirt that fits loosely and then add 2"–3" on that. Now you have to decide how long you want your sleeves to be: anywhere from 6"–18". I made mine T-shirt length, around 6", but it is completely your choice.

Once you have these two dimensions you need to double the width so it goes back and front. Now take a ruler and stretch out part of the mail and count how many rows are in 1" so that you will know how many rows you will need for the sleeves.

You are now ready to make to identical rectangles that will become the sleeves of your shirt. Once they are done, attach the center of the sleeve to the center of the head hole. Do not connect the sleeves at the bottom.

Step 7: The Sides

Now comes the final step: the sides. This step varies for everyone so I will give just basic instructions.

Put on your chainmail tunic and, with the help of a friend, measure the distance between the two sides. Don't pull it too tight across your body or you won't be able to get it on (or off). Depending on how loose you want it to be you can add a few rows to the initial measurement.

Make two rectangles that are that wide and long enough to reach from the bottom of the sleeve to the edge. Go ahead and connect your side pieces.

Finally, you will need a small piece to connect the sleeves at the bottom if they do not already meet. Once again measure and add more if necessary.

When you have these pieces connected all you have to do is attach under the arms. Unfortunately the pattern does not match up here so just improvise: It is not too critical.

You're done!!!!!!

Step 8: Finished!

Congratulations on finishing your chainmail shirt! I am sure that you are very happy now and have a new sense of achievement. This is a very long and, at times, boring project, but it is rewarding like nothing else you have ever done.

R2D2 Heels

By mikeasaurus
(http://www.instructables.com/id/
R2D2-heels/)

These ARE the droids you're looking for! Forget protocol, Droid, and mash up everyone's favorite astromech with mid-heels to create the greatest footwear the Empire has ever seen. These R2D2 shoes are the hottest thing this side of Tatooine and they're cooler than Hoth.

The wide heel of these shoes was removed and replaced with a steel bolt to provide strength and support, but at a fraction of the size. An R2D2 toy covers the heel bolt, and the toes have been decorated with lenses, blue accents, and a blinking red LED to let everyone know just how this droid rolls.

Whether you're dashing to Tosche Station for power converters or just going to the store, these R2D2 heels are sure to give you geek cred faster than you can shut down all the trash compactors on the detention level.

Step 1: What You Need
Here's what I used to make mine:
- MIG welder
- soldering iron
- propane torch
- rotary tool
- electric drill
- rubber cement
- foam glue
- 2-part epoxy (extra strength, not "quick setting")
- white spray paint
- button cell battery holder
- 3V coin cell battery (mine was CR20163)

- 2 identical R2D2 toy action figures (about $8 each)
- white shoes in desired size (mine were free)
- SPST (or SPDT) switch
- 2 5mm red blinky LEDs
- 2 5mm LED holders
- 2 mini flashlights, lenses only ($1 each)
- 1/4" 20-threaded rod
- 2x 1/4" 20 hex nuts
- 2–3mm blue foam sheets ($1 each)
- sunglasses (mine were $1)
- thin-gauge wire
- heat-shrink tubing

Ready to save the galaxy in style? Beep boop beep!

Step 2: Materials and Concept
The idea is to replace the standard heel with a slender support post, then hide that post with hollow plastic R2D2 toys. This will give the illusion that the astromech is holding up the shoe.

R2D2:
The toys I used had electronics inside that allowed them to light up and make sounds when a button was pushed. Since I wanted to retain these features I could not drill straight through; rather, a valley was made in the back of the R2D2 toys that would go around the bolt heel.

Shoes:
I found these brand new shoes for free outside my apartment. How perfect is that?!

Bolts:
Any 1/4" bolt will work, cut to height.

End Caps:
I needed to protect the end of the heel spikes from damaging any floor surfaces when walking, so I modified the existing heel caps to work with my new design.

Step 3: Heel Breakdown
I'm sure all ladies' shoes are manufactured in a similar fashion. Your shoes may be slightly different in construction and may require a different method than the one shown here for modification.

I started by removing the small plastic heel cap with pliers, then bisected the decorative leather sole at the heel and removed the sole portion that was glued to the heel. Making sure not to damage the heel veneer, the white heel covering was peeled back and removed. Set aside this scrap for later as we'll be using it in Step 6 to cover the underside of the shoe where the old heel used to be.

The heel of these shoes were held on with a large industrial cleat that mechanically fastened the heel to the sole and adhesive. The cleat was attached from the top of the shoe under the insole, through the sole, and embedded deep in the plastic heel. It was no small undertaking removing this cleat. It took about 20 minutes to get the heels off. Once removed, the old plastic heels can be discarded. After the cleat and heel are removed it's time to prepare the shoe for welding.

This shoe has a steel shank under the insole for support. The underside of the shank was abraded at the heel with a rotary tool, which will clear away any debris and prepare the surface for accepting a weld.

The heel cleat opening left a jagged edge, which needed to be fixed. I easily cut away excess shoe around the cleat opening and then reinserted the shank-insole back into the shoe to approximately where I was going to weld my new steel heel spike. The new heel location was marked on the steel shank with permanent marker.

Step 4: Cut and Attach Foam and Lenses

I wanted to give these shoes a toe treatment with some elements distinctive to R2D2, particularly his two lenses, blinking light, and blue accents. All these elements are glued to the shoe toe. (Tip: to ensure proper adhesion, select areas of the toe were gently roughed up with sandpaper to remove the high-gloss finish). I will go into greater detail as to how I made each of these elements.

Large Lens:

R2D2 has one large, dark lens. Since my heels will have one of these on both toes, I used a cheap pair of sunglass lenses. The lenses popped out of the frame easily, and I traced a large circle shape using a coin. The circular shape was cut using a rotary tool. I used a strong construction adhesive to affix the large lens to the toe. The adhesive is partially elastic and allows some flex, which will prevent the lens from popping off when being worn.

Blue Accents:

I couldn't find any foam sheets in the blue hue I wanted, but they did have a foam cowboy hat that was the perfect color. I cut off the flat brim and traced R2D2's head accents, then cut them out with scissors. The blue accents were glued onto the shoe toes using a foam glue I found at the craft store. This glue looks like white glue, but is less viscous and sort of melts the foam a little to create the bond. This glue took about a day to completely cure, so masking tape was used to hold the foam in place.

Small Extruded Lens:

I used the focusing lenses of two small flashlights I got from the Dollar Store. The flashlights were broken down and the lenses and black housing were glued to the toe using flexible construction adhesive.

Tip:

Adhering the elements to the toe was very time consuming due to long curing times and the delicacy of work. Each element was done separately and was individually taped or clamped down while glue was curing. Be patient with this part to ensure high-quality results. I do not recommend using fast-set epoxy as the accelerated curing time reduces the effective bond.

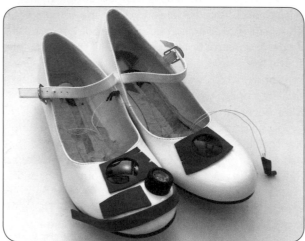

Step 5: Blinky LED circuit

These shoes also have R2D2's signature blinking light for added authenticity. The wiring is a simple circuit that has a switch to operate, one red blink LED, and one 3V coin cell battery to power it.

Switch and Battery:

The battery holder has two prongs on the back, which were lined up on the underside of the shoe next to where the new heel would be located. Small openings were poked into the underside of the shoe to facilitate wiring. The switch was connected to one terminal of the battery holder, and then wires were soldered to the remaining battery terminal and one side of the switch. The wires were fed through the openings, and the switch and battery assembly were then epoxied in place.

LED Holder:

The LED holder I used was polished metal—a perfect addition. However, the threaded mounting neck was much too long and would be uncomfortable to the wearer when installed. I tightened the mounting nut and then shortened the neck using a rotary tool. Backing off the mounting nut ensures the threads are retained.

I drilled through the foam and shoe to create an opening for mounting the LED holder. After I installed the LED holder, I threaded the mounting bracket back on to secure the holder.

LEDs:

I chose to flatten the top of my 5mm red LEDs so they would sit flush when inserted into the LED holder. Using a rotary tool, the LED tops were shaved down to about two-thirds of their original height. The legs of the LED were bent at 90 degrees and wired to the circuit.

Wiring:

After the elements were installed, the excess wiring was glued down using small dabs of hot glue. I also chose to add a small scrap of soft fabric to the inside of the toe to cover the wiring and protect toes from rubbing against any exposed wiring.

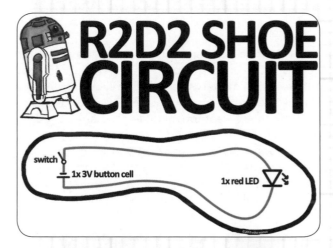

Step 6: Welding and Painting
Welding:

The original heel for this shoe had a wide flange, which helped support the width and weight of the heel and foot. This new design calls for a slender, uniform heel spike and required a platform to support the wearer's weight in lieu of the wide flange.

A small heel platform was made from scrap 1/8" sheet steel. I used an angle grinder to cut out rough rectangles, then rounded the corners until I had a platform that fit inside the insole. The platform was then welded to the steel shank.

The ¼" stainless steel bolts were then lined up and tacked in place to ensure positioning was correct. While the bolt was still just tack-welded on, I made any minor adjustments to the angle of the bolt. It helped to put the insole and shank back in the shoe with the tack weld to ensure the heels were perpendicular to the ground. When alignment was ensured, I welded the bolts in place for both shoes.

Cut Heel Spike to Length:

After welding, the insole and shank were put back into the shoe with the R2D2 toy placed alongside. The heel spike was then cut to be about ¼" longer than the height of where the droid will meet the shoe.

Painting:

After welding, the insoles were masked and the heel was primed and painted with two coats of matte white

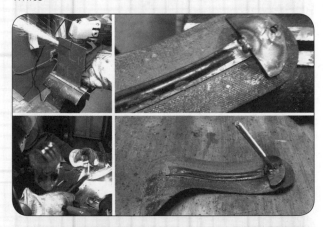

Step 6: Cover Rough Edges and Glue Insole

Remember the heel covering I asked you to set aside in Step 2? We're going to use them here. Using the old heel covering, I covered the underside of the shoe and trimmed to fit. A small opening was then

made in the covering for the new heel spike. Using heavy-duty rubber cement, the painted heel insoles were glued into the shoe form. They were clamped in place and left to cure overnight. These insoles neatly cover the installed wiring.

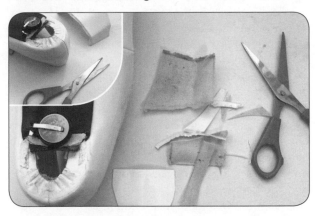

Step 7: Heel Assembly

I decided to reuse the existing heel caps. Since these heels started with a wide heel base and were transformed into a much thinner heel, I was able to make two new heel caps from just one of the originals.

The heel cap was first bisected using a rotary tool. Holding the hex nut with pliers, the nuts were heated using a propane torch. Once red-hot, the nuts were pressed into the plastic of the heel cap, making a cavity the exact shape of the hex nut. I inserted these nuts about three-quarters of the way into the cap. The hex nuts were removed and the plastic and nut were set aside to cool. Using a rotary tool and hobby knife, the edges of the heel cap were cleaned up and the small island in the center of the cavity was trimmed down to allow the threaded heel to be fully inserted. The hex nuts were then primed and painted with two coats of matte white paint.

While the paint was drying each heel cap was then trimmed down and shaped into a smaller, rounded cap, about 3–4mm (1/8") offset from the diameter of the hex nut.

After the paint was dry the hex nuts were epoxied into the heel cap, and the assembly was then epoxied and threaded onto the heel spike.

Step 8: Adding R2 Unit and Installing Padded Insole

R2D2 is cylindrical and doesn't have geometry that lends itself to easily attaching to another cylindrical object (the heel spike). I made a valley in the back of each R2D2 toy by using the shaft of my soldering iron.

Tip: This is a smelly process, make sure you are working in a well-ventilated area.

While the soldering iron is still hot make sure you wipe off the plastic that has melted to it before it burns on there for good. I made these valleys as deep as I could before I hit the electronics and batteries inside. The valley doesn't have to completely conceal the heel, but needs to be deep enough to allow good adhesion between the toy and the heel spike.

Each toy was then positioned in the correct spot on the heel, facing back, and epoxied in place. These were then taped in place and left to cure overnight. Later, the padded insoles were installed with a small dab of rubber cement.

Step 9: These ARE the Droids You're Looking For

With the epoxy set and the padded insole inserted, these shoes are ready for adventure!

All that's left to do is:

- flick the switch where the heel meets the sole to make the LEDs blink,
- press the button on the toy to make R2D2 make sounds and light up, and
- save the galaxy.

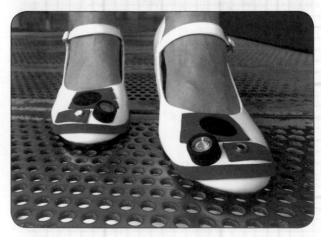

Wood rings are beautiful. They feel warm and have a lovely sheen when finished properly. They tend not to be very durable, though. Often they crack along the grain after continued wear.

Bent wood rings address this problem. Made from very thin layers of wood wrapped with the grain running all the way around the ring (instead of across or through), these rings can stand up to quite a bit of pressure without cracking or breaking.

After a fair amount of experimentation, I've come up with a method of creating bent wood rings that works. I'll also show you how to add a crushed stone inlay.

Some people are now choosing bent wood rings for wedding or engagement rings. They can be pricey. They might take a little bit of practice if you want perfect rings, but the technique is simple and the materials are cheap.

Step 1: Form the Ring Shape
To make the rings, you'll need:
- wood veneer
- straightedge
- thin, sharp blade
- something to hold and boil water
- something finger sized to wrap the wood around
- masking tape, rubber band, or Velcro cable tie to hold wrapped wood in place
- superglue
- various grits of sandpaper
- Dremel (optional)

If you're adding a crushed stone inlay, you'll also need:
- stone to crush
- hammer and anvil or some other device for crushing stone
- epoxy
- toothpick or other small, disposable implement to mix and apply epoxy
- metal file

We bought a sample pack of wood veneer at the local woodworking supply store. It cost $20 and contained more than 20 pieces of veneer, enough to make hundreds of rings. Some types of veneer don't bend very well at all; I had the most success with thin, tight-grained pieces of veneer with the grain running the long way. I'm sure the more difficult woods could be used if they were sanded much thinner.

Using a straight edge as a guide, slice your piece of veneer into a long, thin strip. I've found it works better if I use many light strokes instead of trying to cut through the veneer in one pass. Sometimes the blade tries to veer away from the straight edge along the irregular grain. Lighter strokes helps combat that.

Using a Dremel with a sanding tip, or regular sandpaper, sand down the ends of the strip. You'll want them very thin. If you don't sand them down, a kink will form in the wood as you wrap it. It'll look out of place and will make it difficult to get a tight wrap. It's also easier to hide the seam when the end is thinned down.

If you want to do a crushed stone inlay, slice two thin strips of veneer to fit over the base strip of veneer with enough space between the thin strips for the stone inlay. On the ring in the picture, I simply sliced out the middle of a strip of veneer on one end of the strip, leaving the other end intact so I could wrap the base and overlay of the ring with just one piece. I'm lazy like that. Please look at the picture for reference. I wanted the groove for the inlay deep enough, so I left the thinner strips longer than the base portion.

Some people steam their wood. Some wrap it in wet paper towels and place it in the microwave. Boiling the strips in a pot of water works best for me. Different woods take different amounts of time to get flexible enough. I boil mine for roughly ten minutes. They're usually bendable by then.

I've discovered that a copper pipe is roughly the right size to make rings for my middle or index fingers. I've also learned that a AA battery is the right size to make a ring for my three-year-old.

When the wood is sufficiently flexible, remove it from the boiling water using tongs. It cools quickly, so it shouldn't burn you by the time you get back to the table. Wrap it tightly around the round item of your choice and secure it with masking tape, a rubber band, or whatever you can find.

If you're making a ring with one color on the inside and one on the outside, only wrap the inner portion at this time. Leave the veneer for the outside in the pot for now. If you're making a ring with a stone inlay, make sure to wrap the base part of the ring (the solid portion of the strip) first if it's in once piece. If the thin strips are separate pieces of veneer, leave those in the pot for now.

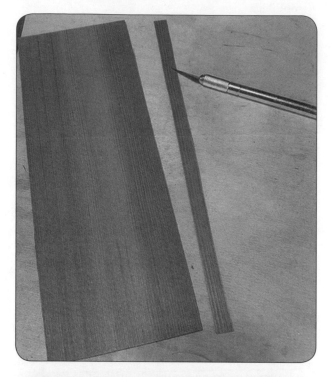

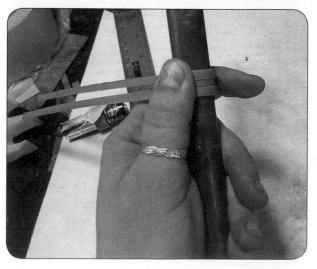

Step 2: Glue

Some retailers of bent wood rings claim that the ring strength comes solely from the direction of the grain. That's not true, in my experience. When these rings are properly made, they're impregnated with cyanoacrylate (also known as superglue). The glue adds a lot to the strength. There's a lot of information out there about cyanoacrylate and woodworking; it's frequently used to finish wood pens because it forms such a clear, shiny, and durable finish.

After the ring has been sitting for five or so minutes, gently peel away the masking tape and let it slowly unfurl. The wood should now form a loose spiral. Starting at the middle, begin wrapping it tightly around the tube again. As soon as you have one loop formed, put a small amount of glue (less than a drop) on the strip of veneer right where the unwrapped part meets the wrapped part, spreading it a bit with the tip of the glue tube. Press the veneer into place firmly. Hold for a few seconds until it will hold together on its own. Be very careful on the first applications of glue. You don't want to glue the ring to the tube you're using. If you're nervous about your skills, you could wrap parchment paper around your tube before wrapping it. I usually slide the ring up and down the tube a couple times when I'm gluing the first layer to make sure it doesn't stick. Keep adding small amounts of glue, spreading it, and pressing the veneer against the lower layer, holding firmly as you work outward in a spiral. Don't skip any areas. The ring is strong and looks best when there aren't any gaps or spots without glue.

Don't wait too long to begin gluing. The water in the wood helps the glue set up quickly. It also helps pull the glue into the wood fibers to hold everything securely together. The wood is less flexible after it dries. You don't want it to splinter on you, and that's very likely if you wait until it's dry before gluing.

It takes a little practice to determine how much glue you need. Too much glue will leak out and stick to everything, including your fingers (ouch). Too little glue will leave gaps in your ring.

If you're adding another layer of wood veneer to your ring, you can now fish the second piece out of the pot of boiling water. Wrap it around the base of the ring and secure it with tape. Wait a few minutes, then glue it to the base layer in the same manner described above. If you're using two thin strips of veneer on the outer layers of the ring to create a channel for an inlay, you can wrap and glue them separately from each other.

I prefer to leave the very outside end of the veneer unglued at this point. Cyanoacrylate likes to turn white when it's exposed to water. If I glue it now, it'll likely leave a white residue when I go to sand the ring and finish it. The residue will be impossible to remove because it impregnates the wood fibers.

When the ring is glued, slide it off the tube and let it sit out to dry. It has to be completely dry before you begin sanding. This can take several hours.

Step 3: Clean Up the Ring

At this point I would glue down the outer edge of veneer. Sand it down, slip a little glue under the edge, and press firmly. Because the outer edge is thin, tapered veneer, I use an implement to hold it in place instead of my finger. The glue will take longer to set this time because the wood is no longer wet. Some woods show the seam more than others. The pearwood veneer I have gets darker edges in places

coated with superglue, even if the ring is finished with that same superglue. The lighter and darker woods I've used (like maple and walnut) don't seem to have that problem. The seam doesn't bother me, but you might not want a visible seam, so you might want to experiment with which types of wood hide seams the best. You could always do some creative cutting and sanding for the outer seam to really blend it with a wood that shows seams. I don't bother to do much seam shaping; I usually can't even find the seam on my maple or walnut rings once they're finished.

Use the Dremel to smooth the edges of the ring, but don't use it for sanding the rest of the ring. Use sandpaper to smooth down any sharp corners at the edges of the ring. If you have trouble getting sandpaper inside the ring, you can use a small file. Sand and smooth the edges of the groove if you're doing an inlay.

Proper sanding will make a huge difference in the finished ring. Use a full range of sandpaper grits and don't skip any. I use sanding blocks from 60 grit to 320 grit, then switch to my micro-mesh sanding sheets. The micro mesh really matters if you want a smooth, glossy finish. You only need to sand up to the 4000 grit in the micro mesh before finishing. Sanding beyond that isn't necessary. The finish needs a small amount of roughness to grip onto, and you'll be using the higher grits to sand the finish, anyway.

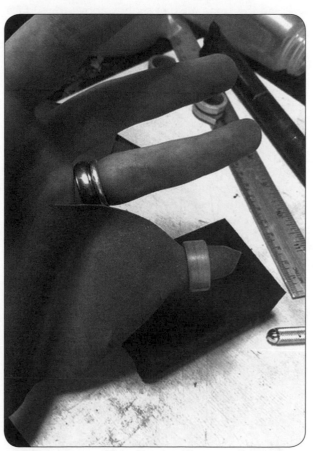

Step 4: Add Inlay (Optional)

If you don't want to bother with a stone inlay, skip to Step 5.

If you want spots of crushed stone in your ring, take a grinding bit on a drill or Dremel and drill holes into your ring. Don't drill all the way through; just make cavities that you can fill with the crushed stone.

We bought some cheap rocks in various colors from the local rock shop. None of them cost more than a dollar.

Use a hammer and anvil or whatever else to smash your chosen rock into powder. Fold a piece of paper in half lengthwise. Unfold and fold crosswise. Unfold. This will create valleys that make it easier to keep your powdered stone where you want it. Dump your crushed stone in the center of the paper where the lines intersect.

On a separate small piece of paper, squirt equal portions of both parts of the epoxy. Mix them thoroughly with your toothpick, trying to avoid adding a lot of air. Pour on a little of the crushed stone and mix. Add enough stone that you won't have empty clear spots in your epoxy when it's in the ring, but not so much that the epoxy can't hold everything together.

Press the stone mixture into the recesses of your ring with your toothpick. Squash it in carefully and thoroughly. After you use the toothpick, put a little petrolatum on your fingertips to squash it in further. Scrape off as much excess as you can while still keeping the stone mixture slightly above the surface wood in the ring. You'll save a little time if you also scrape the epoxy off the surface wood as much as you can while it's wet.

Read your container of epoxy to see how long it has to cure before sanding. The small print on my package stated that it took eight hours before it was usable and 24 hours for the full cure. I'm impatient. I waited an hour or two. You should probably wait longer,. although I didn't have any problems with my rings.

It would take forever to sand down the excess stone mixture with sandpaper, especially if you use the types with a less durable grit. I used a large metal file to get most of it, then refined it with sandpaper.

Work your way back up the grits of sandpaper. Make sure the stone portion and the wood are now flush with each other.

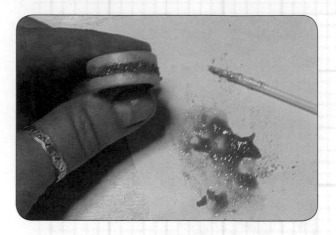

Step 5: Finish the Ring

There are lots of different types of finishes. I will discuss a few of them here.

I've heard good things about layer upon layer of a drying oil, such as tung oil, but I've never tried it. I am fond of shellac. It's hard to go wrong with edible bug excretions. (You don't believe me? Check your candy labels for shellac, resinous glaze, or confectioner's glaze.) Shellac doesn't leave a very durable finish on a ring, though. It flakes off pretty quickly with continued wear.

Some people prefer to finish their wood rings with beeswax and olive oil. The oil and wax should be reapplied regularly and won't be as glossy as other finishes. They leave a really nice, natural feel to the wood, though. I love using olive oil and beeswax to finish a ring made of solid olivewood. Olive oil and beeswax do not fill the pores in wood. When choosing a finish, consider the effect you want, including whether or not you want to fill all the pores to make the surface completely smooth.

My own personal opinion is that cyanoacrylate is the best finish for bent wood rings. It's durable, water resistant, and already used throughout the ring. It's sometimes difficult to work with, however.

Before you add any finish, look closely at your ring. You might see some pale or dark streaks, depending on the color of your wood. These are pores in the wood, and they're likely filled with fine sawdust from sanding your ring. If you don't get rid of the dust, it'll get stuck in the finish and leave your ring dull and dirty looking. Find a cotton swab, a buffing pad, or a very soft cloth. Wipe your ring down, making sure to get as much dust out of the pores as you can. Sometimes you need to use a cloth with very fine fibers or a damp cloth to get all the pores cleaned out. If you do use a little water, let the ring dry completely before you apply a finish.

Find tweezers or some implement to hold the ring if you feel a bit clumsy like me and don't want glue on your fingers. Carefully squirt out a small amount of superglue onto the ring (about a drop or less). Spread it around as much as you can with the tip of the glue

tube or a clean cotton swab. Hold the ring away from your face and let it dry. Do not blow on it. The moisture from your breath can cause the glue to turn white. If that happens, you'll have to sand it all off and start again. If you touch it before it's dry, the moisture from your fingertips can also turn it white. Once it's dry, add glue to another area of the ring. Continue until the ring is all covered, inside and out. The glue will look less shiny and smooth once it dries. That's okay.

It's now time to sand. If the coating is particularly rough, I might go as low as my 320 grit sanding block and then work my way up with the micro mesh. If it looks relatively smooth, I'll usually just use my micro mesh to sand it all the way up to 12000 grit for a high-gloss finish. Inspect the ring carefully for things like white spots or dull spots where there is no glue. Sand down and redo any white spots. Add glue to any bare spots and sand smooth.

Some people add several layers of cyanoacrylate. Some people layer it with boiled linseed oil. I used one layer of cyanoacrylate to finish my three-year-old son's ring. It's holding up really well so far, even after playing in the sand and washing his hands. Wood rings will last longer if properly cared for. Scratches should be sanded with fine sandpaper and refinished to protect the wood from moisture. Ideally, they should be removed before swimming, showering, or washing dishes.

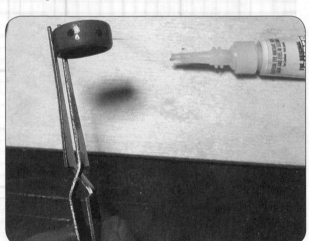

Electronic Motherboard Bracelet

By II.13

(http://www.instructables.com/id/
Motherboard-PCB-Bracelet/)

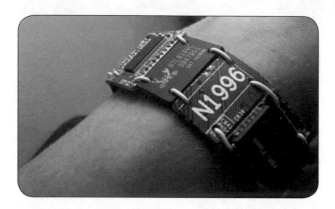

This bracelet is for the geeks and also for looking funky.

Step 1: Tools and Supplies Needed

- drill
- drill bits
- hacksaw–or similar
- file (I used a hand-saw file)
- pliers (cutting and small long-nosed)
- dust mask
- 1 computer motherboard
- wire (telephone wire and thick copper wire that is the size of the earth wire for house wiring)

Step 2: Measure Your Wrist

You will need to measure your wrist (or the wrist of the person it's for) so you know how many PCB pieces to cut. I am using a metal tape measure, but a seamstress's tape measure would be easier to use.

Step 3: Cut Up the Motherboard

It is easier to cut up all the pieces you need and refine them before doing all the easier things. You will need a dust mask when cutting up and filing the motherboard pieces. Although it most likely won't kill you breathing in the PCB dust, it will not do any good and could possibly destroy your lungs. Cut strips out of the motherboard that contain your choicest electrical components in the width that you want for your bracelet, and then cut those strips up into segments. After you have cut the pieces, washing them in water will remove most of the dust.

Step 4: File Pieces

File the pieces so that the edges are smooth . A sharp file will cut the PCB very fast, so just be careful you don't file away too much.

Step 5: Drill Holes

Now all the PCB pieces need to be connected together. Drill four holes in each piece using a 3.5mm. drill bit. Please take care while drilling, as I snapped a drill bit twice (shhh). Try and drill the holes as close to the edge as possible without going so far that when in use the chip is in danger of coming off. Also, try to line up the holes so the holes of different chips are in a straight line.

Step 6: String Them Up

After the holes have been drilled, I recommend you wash the pieces again to remove any dust. I used some telephone wire (a single strand) to hold the bracelet together, which comes in a variety of different colors! If you are using elastic you don't need to follow the next step, just tie the elastic so there are no ends.

Step 7: Create a Hook

If you are using wire to connect all the pieces then the bracelet needs to be joined at the ends somehow. I used some thicker wire as a hook for joining the ends of the bracelet.

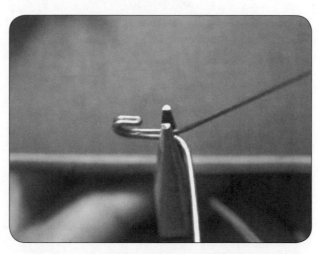

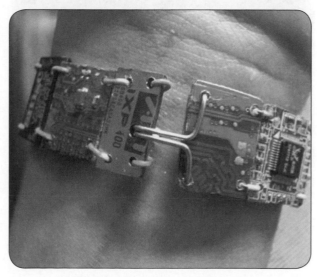

LED Tron Suit

By sheetmetalalchemist
(http://www.instructables.com/id/LED-lit-Tron-v20-suit/)

Costumes rule. Glowing costumes rule even more. By following this Instructable, you'll have the knowledge and ability to make an LED-lit garment that looks just like the ones in the Tron movies.

My goals in making this costume were to make a robust, easily washable, waterproof, Tron-style suit that was energy efficient in order to minimize battery weight and hardware bulk. To do that, I had to dodge the commonly used EL wire implementations and switch to LEDs.

Even if you aren't interested in making a Tron suit, I would highly recommend reading the section on lighting implementation. I did not individually stitch each LED with conductive thread. Instead, I used a combination of silicone-coated LED strips and faux leather to produce a beautiful, diffuse light without seeing those pesky LED points.

Step 1: Other Lighting Options— Why Not Use EL Wire?

Most Tron-ish garments are made with this stuff called EL wire or EL tape (which is based on the same technology). Although EL technologies are great for a lot of reasons, I feel that they aren't very well suited to wearable apps. I built an old-school Tron suit using EL wire and found the following problems with it:

- EL wire is super fragile! Bending it too tightly or repeated bending motions (i.e., wrapping around body joints or placing into a washing machine) will cause the EL wire to fail. And when you try to repair any EL wire damage, you quickly find out that EL wire repair isn't pretty.

- To repair EL wire, you splice in solid non-glowing wire to the broken sections, which completely destroys the effect of a single, unbroken line.

- EL wire is pretty dim! You won't be able to see EL glow at all during the day, which leads to the next problem—

- EL wire looks lame if it's not illuminated! You can get fancy and do some work to hide EL wire, but in general, unlit EL wire looks like just that— wires on the outside of a garment. So, if it's not glowing, its generally pretty ugly.

- You need an AC inverter for mobile applications! EL wire runs on AC current, and any battery pack you can buy will be DC. Therefore, you need to add more bulky hardware, and there are more things to break while wearing your creation.

In an effort to dodge these issues, I decided to use LEDs to light the suit instead. They are harder to implement, but the results are worth it.

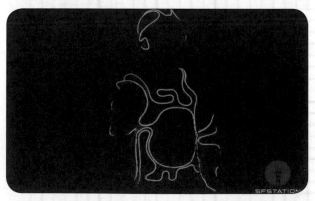

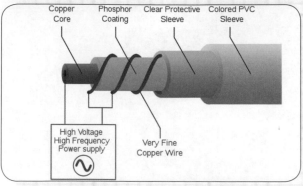

Step 2: Clothing Layout

I'm not really a clothing design expert, so I made this suit by attaching laser-cut faux leather to a store-bought undergarment instead of sewing everything from scratch.

Your undergarment needs to have the following characteristics in order to work for this project:

- You want an undergarment that is pretty much form fitting (I got one that was a size too small for me on purpose).
- You want something that can diffuse light well and absorbs very little light.
- It is recommended you use something with flat seams on both sides of the garment. This will make your life much easier when it comes to attachment of the light-blocking material.

These requirements pretty much limit your search to lightweight athletic performance base layers. For the record, I ended up using an REI Lightweight Polartech Power Dry Base Layer as my undergarment.

For the overlay material, you need something that is going to be completely opaque to very bright LEDs, yet laserable. This limits your choices pretty much right off the bat to some sort of synthetic leather (which stinks since it is still kind of spendy). I used some home decor fabric made from polyurethane.

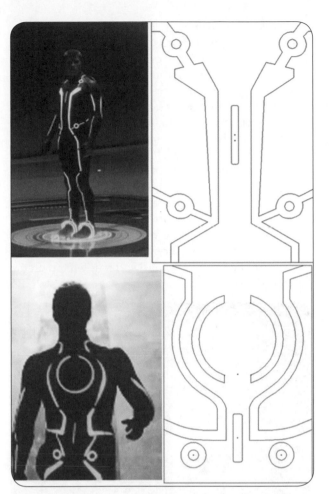

Step 3: Designing the Laser Vector Paths

Based on watching a few of the trailers for the new Tron, I got a decent idea of what the new suits should look like and drew some front/back views of my design. I then turned these concepts into single pieces of vector art to be cut using Illustrator. You can download the .zip file of all the pieces from this Instructable's project website!

Step 4: Resize the Vector Paths to Fit Your Shirt

The vector paths created in the previous step were not made using a de facto shirt pattern in order to make them as easily scalable and widely applicable as possible. Therefore, in order to resize the paths downloaded in the previous step, you only need to make two measurements and do just a teensy bit of math. Don't worry about being super precise with the measurements; the patterns are designed to be a bit big, then trimmed down to size once they are on the garment.

First, measure the width of the shirt from side seam to side seam and write that down. If your shirt doesn't have side seams, lay your shirt out as flat as possible and measure its width. If you shirt has curved side seams, measure the longest width (should be just below the arms) and the shortest width (should be right by your belly), then average the results. This will be the "width" in the math bits below.

Next, measure the height of your shirt. Measure from the absolute bottom of the shirt (like where your legs come out of it) to halfway down one of the shoulder seams (see image; the shoulder seam is tough to see so I outlined part of it in red). Write this number down. This will be the "height" in the math bits below.

Now for the math. The patterns I provided are sized for a shirt that is 24" wide and 26" high. Therefore, if your shirt is only 22" wide, you should make the width of the patterns 22/24 of their original size. You can use a bunch of different programs to do this (if you don't have one, try GIMP. Its free and available for any platform).

Now, do the same thing for the height. If your measured height is only 21", then you need to make the patterns only (21/26) of their original size. Make sure to get enough leather to make your outfit when buying materials—realize there is a fair amount of wastage here. I used about 1½ yards to make my shirt using the 24" × 26" patterns.

At this point, you should have some .dxf vector paths that fit your shirt primed and ready to rip on the laser. Let's start the cuttage!

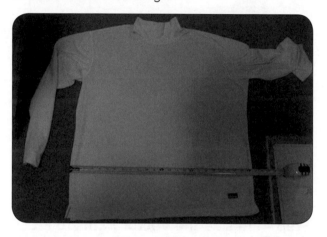

Step 5: Laser Cut the Opaque Leather

If you're using the same fake leather that I am, you'll realize that you can get amazing cuts on this stuff with the laser—no overburn, fast speeds, and no jagged edges. To do the cutting, I used the following parameters on an Epilog Helix 45W laser:

Speed = 70% of max

Power = 50% of max

Frequency = 500Hz

When you are done, you should have enough pieces to assemble a Tron suit horizontally on a table.

Step 6: Attach the Lasered Leather to the Undergarment

Now that you have a whole bunch of leather pieces, all you need to do is get them on the garment. I did the attachment using a heat-fusible adhesive called stitch witchery. It's simple to use—you cut a piece to length, place it between the two pieces of fabric, and put an iron on top. You only need to apply the stitch witchery on the edges of each piece of leather.

I would recommend attaching in some logical pattern so you can make sure you are aligning everything properly. I started with the pieces cut from the vector pattern "front center," then added "front left" and "front right," then the "upper back" and "lower back pieces."

While you are attaching away, keep in mind that the patterns aren't going to match your shirt perfectly. You'll need to trim away excess leather from the neckline and the shoulder pieces for sure. These are easy to see and easy to trim. You can't wrap the side panels around the arms—instead, you'll need to cut the panels when you reach the arms.

You'll need to test fit, test fit, and test fit some more while you are doing the attachment of the leather. Since the shirt is skin tight, it probably has some spandex in it and therefore stretches a lot. Leather doesn't stretch at all. Therefore, you're going to need to purposely cut some sections of the garment to allow for the underlying spandex to move without ripping the leather layer on top.

Step 7: Cut and Attach Leather for the Arms

You'll notice that I did not supply any laser patterns for the arm leather. Given the differences from shirt to shirt on how the arms attach to the rest of the garment and the differences in sleeve lengths from size to size, I figured I'd leave the arm design simple and just cut straight pieces of leather from the scrap to cover them. I suggest you do the same!

To do this, I cut two long, rectangular sections of leather to match the sleeves. Then I cut the side closest to the body of the shirt at an angle so I'd have another straight patch of undergarment to light (see picture).

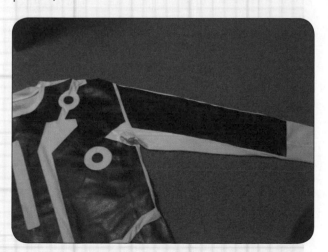

Step 8: Picking Some LEDs for the Lighting!

Now that you've got a shirt that looks like a beautiful leather-clad Tron dude, you're going to need to light it with LEDs. Rather than stitch individual LEDs to the shirt, I decided to use flexible, waterproof LED strips to make my shirt. This takes away a lot of the stitching hassle and also makes the shirt very easily repairable and upgradeable. If for whatever reason a section of LEDs fails, it can be removed and replaced with a low cost and time investment.

Now, when using LEDs and trying to diffuse them enough so you can't see individual light points, the only thing you need to worry about is space! Anything you can do to increase the space between the LEDs and the cloth of the shirt, the better the diffusion you'll have and the more you can light with fewer LEDs (more power and heat efficient).

Therefore, diffusion becomes the next big reason to use flexible LED strips instead of individual LEDs, since they will stand off from your body a bit. If you couple this with a super tight shirt, you'll create a "tent" where the LED light can shine (see pictures). LED strips are thick enough to create a reasonably sized tent to look awesome. However, if you use too loose of a shirt, you won't get this tent effect, and your shirt won't glow!

So, what did I use in the end? I used White Silicone Encapsulated LED Strips from Oznium. I picked these for two reasons. First, they were much more flexible than any other LED strip I could find. Second, since silicone is clear, you can get a lot of side diffusion out of these LEDs (a picture of the strips is below). I needed a total of eleven of them for my outfit.

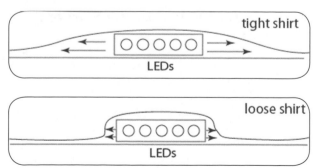

243

Step 9: Cut the LEDs to Size

Now that you've got your LED strips in hand, you'll need to cut them to size and position them on the shirt. Your LEDs should be placed just underneath the opaque leather (because you don't want to see any of those nasty LED points). The LED strips I was using could be cut every three LEDs (about 2"). See the images to see the LED layouts I used. I included kind of a crappy squiggly line so you can see where the leather on the front side of the garment is. I would highly recommend you label the LEDs as you cut them, as well as labeling their positions on the garment. They will start to all look the same after a while!

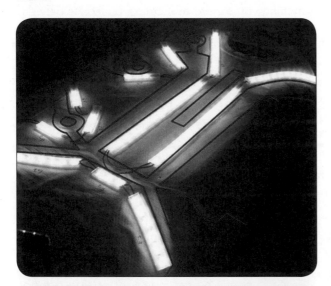

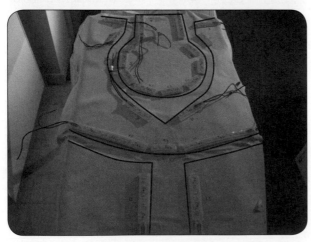

Step 10: Add Velcro to the Shirt and the LEDs

Layout done? Check. LEDs cut? Check. Now, all you've got to do is attach them to the shirt! I ended up using Velcro to do this. Not only does it add a little more height to the LED strip (thus increasing the amount of "tenting" you'll get—see step 8 if you forgot already), but it makes washing and replacement a breeze. If you are scared your electrical work isn't stable enough to take a washing,

then just take the LEDs off when you wash and reapply later! If an LED strip breaks, make a new one, slap some Velcro on the back, and stick it to the shirt! Simple!

I used sticky back Velcro, so I didn't need to apply an adhesive between the Velcro and the silicone LED strip. I needed about 11 feet of it to do the entire shirt. I affixed the other side of the Velcro to the shirt using the same heat-fusible adhesive that I described earlier.

I affixed the LED strips so the LEDs would be facing my body. This also helps to increase the distance between the LEDs and the diffuser fabric, producing a smoother glow. See the image below for the order in which I affixed everything.

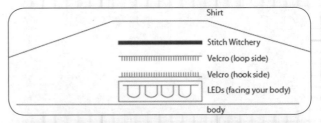

Step 11: Solder and Hot Glue the LED Strips

Okay, now you should have a shirt that has a bunch of disjointed LED strips stuck to it. Chances are, you had to make a bunch of cuts, and you need to resolder. Thankfully, if you are using the same strips I am, each cut end of the LED strip is clearly marked with a + and - pad. Pretty much, all you need to do now is solder all of the + pads together and all the - pads together. Do a little planning—you want to minimize the number of times a wire crosses a white section (the wire crossings can generally be seen). Also, in order to only use one battery connector, the strips need to be connected in a single loop.

These connections are kind of tricky—not only are you soldering a wire to a surface-mount connection, but it's a surface-mount connection that can flex! If you've never done surface-mount soldering before, check out a tutorial before you start.

Since these connections are going to come under a fair amount of abuse, we'll have to add hot glue on top of every single joint for strain relief. Trust me, if you don't do this, one connection or another will break within an hour of you putting it on. So just do it.

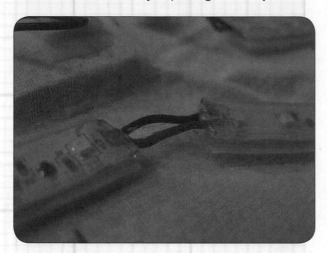

Step 12: Add a Battery Connector and a Sweet Battery

To size your battery, you need to know how many volts and amps your particular LED strips are using. If you are using mine, they are 12V strips that use 130mA per foot. I'm using about 11 feet of LEDs, which means that my whole setup uses 1430mA at 12V.

Battery capacities are usually listed in Ah (amp-hours) for a given voltage. Ah are just amperage requirements multiplied by time. In other words, to keep a 1.43A system lit for 1 hour, we'd need a battery capacity of 1.43Ah at 12V.

For this setup, I'm using a LiPo battery, which has a 6.2Ah life at 12V. It's waterproof, shockproof, and fits snugly inside of a hip pocket. Using this battery, I can run my setup for about 4½ hours continuously. If you want yours to run longer or are okay with a shorter life, scale your battery appropriately!

My battery uses a trail-tech connector to discharge. You want to solder the red wire to the "+" side of your first LED strip, and the black wire to the "-" side of the LED strip.

Step 13: Power It Up!

If you've done everything properly, you should now have an amazing-looking suit! Use your Tron suit to do something epic, like defending your living room from evil forces headed up by the Hawaiian breeze fan and folding chair behind you!!

I didn't have a lot of time to make a great Halloween costume this year so I decided to do something relatively simple that was still eye catching and cool. My Arc is kind of a cross between a MkI and MkII version. There are some things I'd change on the next version (and I'll point them out) but overall I'm pretty pleased with it.

The reactor is attached to an old heart rate monitor strap and is powered by a 3-volt battery pack that just slips into my pocket. It's lightweight and comfortable to wear for several hours at a time. In the photos, you can see how bright it is—it easily shines through my T-shirt under normal office lighting conditions and is very bright at night.

Follow along and see how it's made.

Step 1: Tools and Materials
There are a few necessary tools:
- soldering iron
- Dremel tool
- drill bits
- metal snips/shears
- jeweler's saw (or some kind of saw to cut metal and plastic)
- needle-nose pliers
- wire cutters
- files/sandpaper
- glue gun

And for materials:
- thin brass sheet
- plastic sheet (I used Delrin)
- clear acrylic sheet
- copper wire—22ga and 24ga thickness solid wire
- sheet metal—22ga thickness (.025in., or about .5mm, thickness)
- PCB (printed circuit board)—at least 4" square (Radio Shack sells some that measure around 4½" × 6")
- several small bolts—I used 10ea 2.5mm bolts and 3ea 3mm bolts w/nuts
- 3 volt battery
- 11 ea. NTE30027 surface mount LEDs
- battery hook-up wire

Please note: Be careful cutting sheet metal as the edges can be very sharp and it's easy to cut yourself.

Step 2: Start with the Backplate
The first thing I did was draw up a general plan to see how everything would fit together. The outer diameter of the Arc Reactor is 4", so if you print the plan photo to that scale it will g help you get everything lined up correctly. All the measurements used in the drawings are in inches, and they are really just to be used as a guide. I just eyeballed everything as I was making it. By no means are they meant to be exact measurements. The most important thing is getting the proportions correct so everything will fit together during the final assembly.

The easiest way I found to cut out all the parts was to draw the patterns on paper and then glue the patterns to my sheet plastic or sheet metal using rubber cement. I then cut the patterns out with a jeweler's saw. Next I filed all the edges and smoothed them with sandpaper.

Let's start by making the outer ring/backplate assembly. Begin by cutting a 4" diameter disc from PCB material. There are two copper traces cut (or etched) into this, as well as a couple of solder pads on the center so you can solder down the LEDs. There are 11 LEDs—10 for the clear ring and one for the center lens. The LEDs I used are a surface-mount type. Despite this, they are pretty easy to solder to the copper traces. The LEDs sit directly under a clear acrylic ring and are spaced 36 degrees apart—just make sure they are all facing the same direction! I simply connected the LED copper traces to the center solder pads and then drilled two small holes. I next soldered some wires from the back of the board to my 3v battery.

The outer ring was cut from a thick plastic sheet—I used Delrin because it cuts well and is pretty durable. A good substitute would be a ½" MDF sheet. I should have painted the ring silver but I ran out of time. There are ten 2.5mm Allen head bolts evenly spaced at 36 degree intervals around the ring. I just drilled a pilot hole then drilled a countersink for the bolt head so it would sit just below the surface of the ring. I threaded the holes for the bolts, but you could probably just shove them in there with a bit of glue.

The outer ring is glued to the PCB backplate with a hot glue gun. Then I ran a bead of hot glue over the LEDs and the copper traces. This will protect the LEDs, help diffuse the light, and keep the circuit from being shorted out when the remaining parts are installed.

Now you need a lens for the center. I made mine from acrylic sheet, but you could use just about any kind of lens or clear plastic part that would fit. The thing to remember is that if it is too tall then it will come into contact with other parts later on, so watch the height. I used a Scotch-brite pad on the lens to help diffuse the LED light.

Next, an old heart rate monitor strap was glued and screwed to the backside of the backplate. The two screws went through the PCB and into the outer ring, helping to hold everything together.

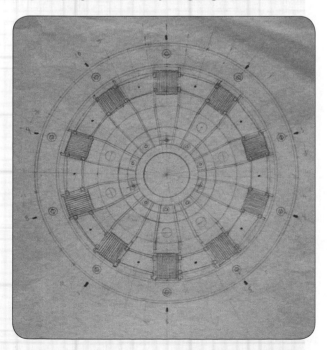

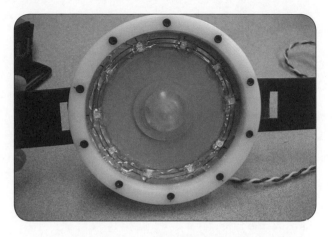

Step 3: Make the Inner-Ring Assembly

Now we have to make the inner ring. This is a clear ring that is held by a frame (which I call the lower spider frame). First cut the inner ring from clear acrylic sheet and rub it with a Scotch-brite pad (steel wool would also work).

Now comes the tedious part—there are 20 arms that need to be cut out, bent, and then placed around a central ring to form the lower spider frame. The dimensions on this are not critical, but you have to constantly check the fit so that it will fit into your previously constructed backplate assembly. You also have to make sure that the clear ring will fit into the slots cut into the spider arms.

The distance from the outer edge to the opening of where the large notch is approximately .08 inches. The trick is that you will have to adjust the fit of this to your acrylic ring as well as to the outer ring. You want the spider to essentially fit snugly into the outer ring. Then fit the acrylic ring to the spider. I can guarantee that you will probably have to do some trimming to get everything aligned properly, because the spider is so difficult/frustrating to make. I had to trim nearly every opening to get everything to fit properly.

The easiest way to trim the openings in the spider is to use a small sanding disk with a Dremel tool to carefully trim them to fit the acrylic ring. The acrylic ring doesn't have to be a perfect fit, as it's held in place by the copper wire wrapped around it.

I cut both the central ring and spider arms from 22ga sheet steel using sheet-metal shears and a jeweler's saw. A Dremel tool would also work and would come in handy cleaning up all the rough edges. The finished arms were then welded to the central ring. The center bottom ring was then cut from steel sheet and welded to the spider frame assembly—note how it is positioned. I was short on time so I left out the additional slots. The bolt holes were threaded for 3mm bolts.

As a substitute for sheet steel you could make the parts from brass or copper sheet, or even from thin plastic sheet that you could just glue together, but plastic wouldn't be as durable.

Now you have to make ten little brass tabs. These sit on top of the clear ring after it has been placed into the spider frame assembly. They are then wrapped with 22ga copper wire. Make sure when you wrap the wire that it doesn't stick too far outside the spider-frame arms. Make sure to check the fit with the backplate assembly—mine is just a light friction fit. The brass tabs should be about the same width as your clear ring, and the four little tabs should just barely stick out over the edges of the spider arms. The last step is to solder some short 24ga copper wires to the tabs.

Step 4: Make the Top-Ring Assembly

The top-ring assembly is made just like the spider-frame assembly—it's cut from 22ga steel sheet, but you could also use brass sheet or plastic. I oxidized my steel assembly to get the black finish, but a Sharpie pen or black paint would also work. There are three 3mm bolts that go through the spider

and slotted ring; there is a nut on the backside so the assembly stays put when everything is put together.

There is a central ring that is made from aluminum, but it could also be made from plastic that is painted silver. It's held on with some thin copper wire and a few dabs of glue from a glue gun.

The last element is a coil of copper wire that has been formed into a ring. I used wire that was coated red—you could use a marker to color the wire. The wire was wound around a drill bit, formed into a circle, and then glued together with a glue gun. The coil ring is then placed around the bolts.

Step 5: Testing and Final Assembly

Plug in your battery and make sure all your LEDs light up. Then mount the center of the top-ring assembly to the inner-ring assembly by lining up the three bolts and tightening them until the bottom of the top-ring assembly sits just above the inner-ring assembly. You can add a dab of glue to the bolts to make sure they don't come loose.

Now press the entire assembly into the backplate assembly—note the orientation, making sure everything is aligned correctly. If the fit is really loose, you can put a couple dabs of glue between the wrapped copper wire sections and the backplate to hold everything together.

That's it! Now go finish your Iron Man armor suit.

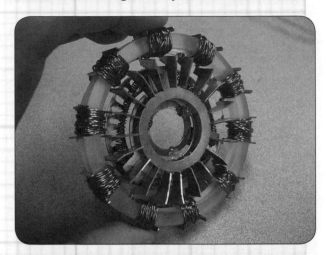

Step 6: New-Style Reactor

This is a new reactor based on what I believed the Iron Man 2 movie reactor would look like based on early screen shots. Notice that it now has eight segments instead of ten. It is constructed in a similar manner as the original reactor, except that it is made from stainless steel and aluminum instead of plastic. This particular pair of reactors were built for a custom Iron Man–theme motorcycle, so they had to be able to withstand heat and vibration. They measure four inches in diameter and one inch deep.

The first thing I did was make a simple model in Sketchup to get an idea of what the finished reactor would look like. Note that there are slight changes between the model and the finished reactors. The first thing I made were separate circuit boards for the LEDs. These are different from my original reactor in that they have 100ohm resistors connected to one side of the LEDs to protect the LEDs from burning out. The circuit boards now have wires soldered to them and are then bolted to the stainless backplate with small hex-head brass screws.

The spider is made from stainless steel that is welded together. There are four small brass hex-head bolts that are threaded into each section of the spider and then soldered together to keep them from coming loose. The lenses were turned from clear acrylic and then the outer lens was inserted into the spider. Then the wire wrapping began. The wire wrapping takes forever since it's pretty hard to keep it straight. There's about 50 feet of wire in each reactor.

The outer ring is turned from thick-wall aluminum tubing using a lathe, and there are four holes drilled and threaded into the back side so it can be mounted to the stainless steel backplate. There is also a thin lip machined into the front of the ring—this will hold a clear protective lens on the finished piece.

The center piece is also turned from aluminum. There is a lip machined into the back side to fit the small brass screen. The back side is also drilled and threaded for two Allen-head screws so it can be bolted to the stainless backplate. The screws go through the center lens to hold it in place, and the center aluminum piece fits into the stainless spider. There are also several small bras hex-head screws that hold the stainless spider to the back plate.

Next, the outer ring and clear lens are bolted in place. The clear lens slides into the outer ring from the back and gets a bead of clear silicone to seal it to the outer ring. This assembly is then fitted to the backplate.

Since these reactors were built for a motorcycle, they needed to be able to take 12v input power and output no more than 4v. To accomplish this I used a power supply circuit from Adafruit (www.adafruit.com). The power supply is adjustable and can accept up to 20v input—it's a really easy-to-build kit that works great.

These reactors were a lot more work to make than my original reactors, but I think they came out nice. All in all there are 26 stainless steel parts, 32 laser-welded joints, 40 soldered joints, 3 acrylic lenses, 2 machined aluminum parts, 50 micro-sized brass hex-head bolts, 6 Allen-head bolts, 50 feet of copper wire, 9 surface-mount LEDs, 9 surface-mount resistors, 2 circuit boards, and 1 brass mesh piece in each reactor—whew!

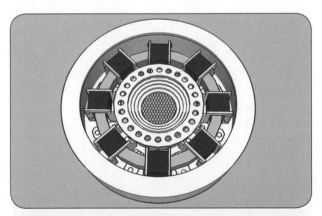

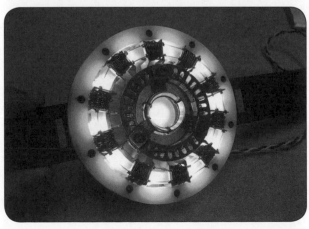

Soda Can Tab Chainmail

By quixotiCfluX

(http://www.instructables.com/id/Genuine-chainmaille-from-pop-tabs/)

It turns out that constructing a genuine European 4-in-1 chainmail weave using only soda can tabs is very easy and makes a really great-looking piece of mail. As an added bonus, you don't have to worry about having a quarter mile of wire on hand to attach them together.

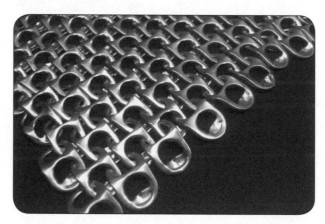

Step 1: Assemble Your Supplies

You are going to need lots and lots of soda can tabs. Don't give yourself renal failure trying to drink tons of soda by yourself. Spread it out over weeks and enlist the help of your family, friends, workmates, or maybe even the local recycling center!

Here is what you will need:

- cutters
- staple remover
- old key
- non-mangled soda can tabs (however many you need—1000 is a good start)

Step 2: Prepare the Tabs

You will need to prepare the tabs for weaving. Bend the collar down from the "top" side of the tab using the tumbler side of the key. Then use the back of the key to continue bending it down against the back of the tab. Lay the tab face down and push the metal down flat.

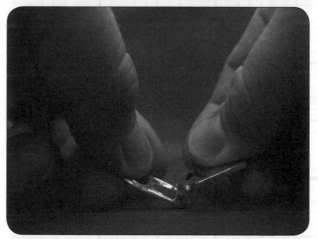

Step 3: Cut

Now that all your tabs are flat and consistent, you need to cut and crimp them. Cut them in the very middle of the pull part of the tab or, for a stronger connection, on the rivet side. Choose whichever side you prefer, just be consistent.

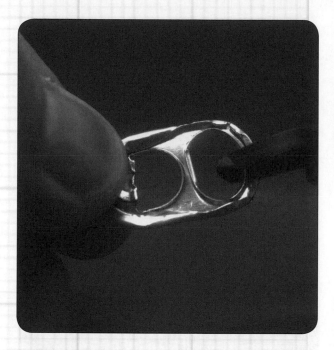

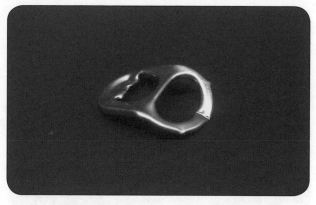

Step 5: Repeat

Keep making the links. You can do them all at once or in batches. Either way, it's pretty easy to make them.

Step 4: Bend

The tabs will need to be bent slightly so they will lay together properly. This step is where the staple remover comes in. It gives the tabs just the right amount of bend. Put the tab in cut-side first and close the tool down so that one side holds the cuts and the "bridge" is over the metal edge on the other side. Press with your finger and bam! You're finished.

Note: If you are using cutters, you can bend the tabs first if you want; if you are using scissors you have to cut them first.

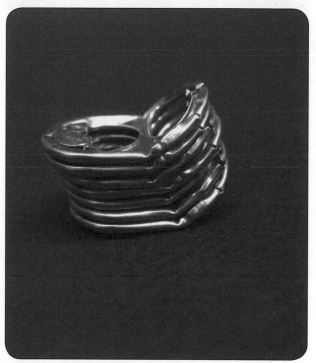

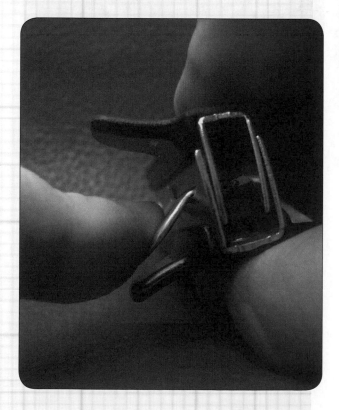

Step 6: Weave

Now that you have a massive pile of tabs ready, you can begin weaving. The first picture shows four links woven together in the traditional European 4-in-1 style. The next photos show the proper order in which to connect them. Holding one tab by the back, with one hand, take another tab with your free hand. Push the back of the second tab through the cut on the first tab from the bottom so that it is on one side.

After they are connected together do the same with a second tab but on the opposite side. The fourth tab you put on will connect the two "shoulder" tabs together. Connect the fourth tab so that the second and third are laying one on each side. The back of the tabs should always end up on the bottom side of the weave.

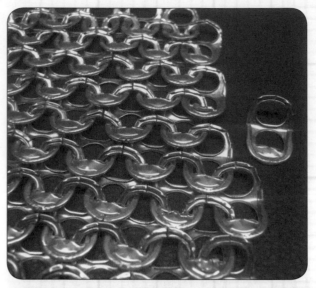

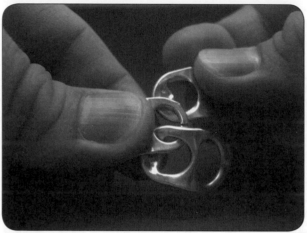

Step 7: Continue Weaving

Keep doing this until you have reached the desired size. I won't go into detail regarding how to make a specific garment or item, but I will give you some tips on weaving. This pattern allows for a couple of different "fabric" geometries you can work with.

The first is the diamond geometry—each link is connected to three others. The second is the square—each link (except those on the edges) uses the pattern's full 4-in-1 connection. As your swatch gets larger it might be easier to flip it over to continue weaving because you will need to handle the main body less as you attach new links.

Smelt Your Own Ring
By Mrballeng
(http://www.instructables.com/id/Smelt-Your-Own-Ring/)

Caution! Melting pennies will release zinc oxide fumes, which cause flu-like symptoms. Use a well-ventilated area with power-assisted ventilation to avoid breathing in fumes during this project.

This project is a ring made from pennies. You will smelt the copper coating off, leaving you with zinc. Pennies minted after 1983 are all made like this.

You don't have to have a lathe tool to do this. You can hammer the ingot flat and follow the nickel ring instructions. It's surprising how light the ring will be. My wedding ring is the same size and weighs 8 grams. This ring weighs in at 3 grams.

Step 1: Smelt

> smelt 1 (sm lt). v. smelt-ed, smelt-ing, smelts.
> v.tr. To melt or fuse (ores) in order to separate the metallic constituents.

I placed ten pennies on a spoon and heated them with a propane torch. The spoon was held with locking pliers, which was held by a wooden clamp. Once the zinc liquefied I removed the copper with a metal probe .

I then poured the liquid zinc into a section of ½" pipe and let it cool off.

Step 2: Cut a Ring Blank

Here I machined the ends off the blank then drilled a hole through it. I chucked the same drill bit into the lathe. Next I wedged the blank on by placing a plastic bag over the bit. Finally the outside was machined.

Step 3: Size the Ring

To expand the blank I hammered it over a pry bar. I started out with a small bar then moved up in size as the ring expanded. To get to my ring size I eventually had to hammer over a ½" socket bit. Of course, once you get to your size, simply stop hammering.

Step 4: Polish

I evened out the ring with a file and then spun it on a ½" socket bit. I then sanded it with 1000 grit followed by 200 grit sandpaper. Lastly I buffed it on a buffing wheel.

5 Cent Men's Ring

By Mrballeng

(http://www.instructables.com/id/Mens-5-
Cent-Ring/)

I'm going to show you how to make a men's ring using a nickel.

Step 1: Mark the Center

Center the coin in the carpenter's square, and, using a razor blade, score a line in the center. Rotate the coin 90 degrees and score another line. Where the lines cross is the center. Now use a punch to mark the center. This helps you in the next step.

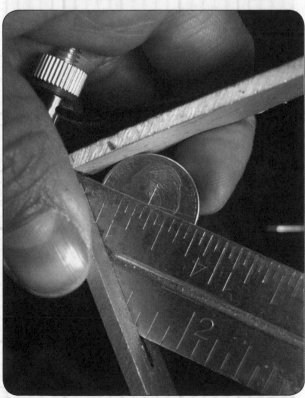

Step 2: Clamp and Drill

Clamp the ring. Drill through the premarked center. You can progressively drill a bigger hole until it will fit on the mandrel you're using. Or, you can just use a 3/8 spade bit like did. I used a pry bar as the mandrel.

Step 3: Hammer

Place a large hammer on a flat surface to serve as an anvil. Next, place the coin over the mandrel. Using a small hammer, hammer the edge of the coin at a 45° angle. As you hammer, rotate the mandrel and apply slight pressure towards the anvil. The ring will form a cone shape. Continue to hammer until the cone forms a cylindrical ring.

Once you have the ring shape you can continue to hammer, causing the ring to expand in diameter. This is where you check it against the measurement of the finger it's being made for.

Important: As you move the ring up the mandrel, flip it around. This helps to make the cone a cylinder.

Step 4: Mount the Ring

Find a socket bit just barely smaller than the ring. If you can't find a socket that's just right you can use a smaller socket and wedge something between the ring and socket. I use paracord when I need to. After you press the ring on the socket, use a nut and bolt and secure it through the female end. The protruding end of the bolt will be used for mounting in the drill press. Place a smaller coin under the socket while you tap the ring on. This leaves an even spacing to true the edges up. Mount the assembly in the drill press and spin it round. You will shape the bottom side first.

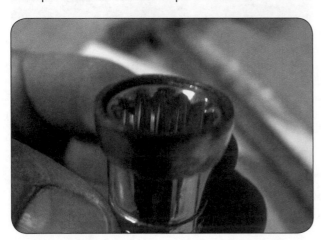

Step 5: Shape

With the assembly spinning in the drill press, use progressively finer sand paper to make the ring its final shape. I start with 80 grit, then 400, then 2000. Spray the 400 and 2000 grit sand paper with water. This prevents the sand paper from getting clogged with metal particles. Again, this gets hot! And don't breathe the metal dust.

Flip the ring as needed. Use polishing compound to buff it to a shine. Now that the outside is nice, time for the inside. Be careful not to mar the ring. Use the wood clamp to remove the ring from the socket. Flip the ring over and press it back onto the socket. Make sure you use a soft work surface when you hammer the ring on and off. I used the clamp itself.

Step 6: Smooth the Inside

Take a larger drill bit and tape a piece of 1000 grit sand paper to it. Roll the paper around the bit with the direction of spin for the drill press. Smooth the inside and any sharp edges.

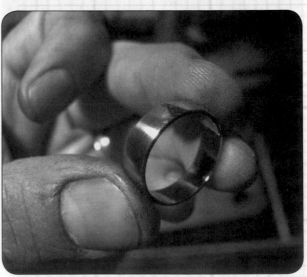

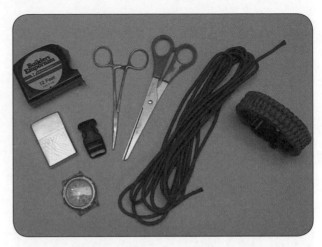

This Instructable will show how to make a paracord bracelet or watchband using a weaving method.

Step 2: Measuring the Paracord

Measure about 20 inches from one end of your length of paracord. This is where you'll attach one side of the side-release buckle. You'll end up with a shorter section of paracord on one side of the buckle, and a longer section on the other side. This longer section is what you'll be working with. The shorter end will be tucked in when finishing the bracelet/watchband.

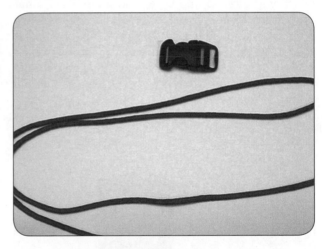

Step 3: Add the Watch and Adjust for Wrist Size

If you're making a watchband, this step is the point at which you'll take the strands of the paracord and run them over the watch pin, under the watch, and over the other watch pins. Then loop the paracord around the other buckle end twice.

At this point, you'll measure the distance between the buckle ends for your wrist size. The distance should be equal to your actual wrist measurement. The weaving process will stretch the original spacing of the bracelet/watchband by approximately an inch after tightening.

Don't include the prong section of the buckle in your measurement. It is snapped into the catch end of the buckle when worn and isn't used in figuring the wrist measurement.

Step 1: Supplies
- approximately 10 feet of paracord
  - Paracord can be found at local Army/Navy stores or at various online sources
  - The actual amount of paracord that will be used depends on your wrist size. My wrist is about 8½" inches, and I used 8 or 9 feet after finishing the bracelet/watchband. Using 10 feet is a safe estimate for most folks, since having too much cord is better than coming up short when making your project.
- scissors
- lighter
- tape measure
- hemostats or manicure scissors
- watch
- A 5/8" side-release buckle. I used a 5/8" ITW Nexus contoured side-release buckle, but you can use other less expensive ones like those found at Creative Designworks.

If making a watchband, the watch needs to have about 5/8" space between the lugs (where the watch pins go) so that five strands of paracord will fit.

Now bring the cord ends back through the watch pins alongside your first pass and around the starting buckle end. If you're just making a paracord bracelet, you'll just be going from one end of the buckle to the other without adding the watch.

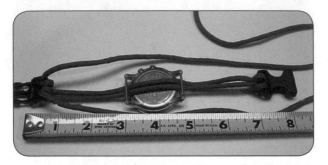

Step 4: Begin Weaving

Now begin weaving the long, working end of your paracord. The shorter end will be left out until it's time to finish the bracelet/watchband, when it will be tucked into the weave.

This weaving process is called weaving with three warps. You'll be going around the outer cord with your working strand, under the center two cords, which you treat as one cord, and around the other outer cord. You weave it back over the center two strands and around the outer, continuing this process back and forth. Try not to leave too much slack as you go in order to keep the weave uniform. Every couple of weaves, tighten your work by pushing the weave up towards the starting buckle end.

Step 5: Threading the Watch

Once you've reached the point where your watch will be centered, push the watch tight against the woven cord and bring your working strand through the pin alongside the other cords under the watch and back through the other pin.

If making the bracelet, there's no watch in the way so just keep weaving.

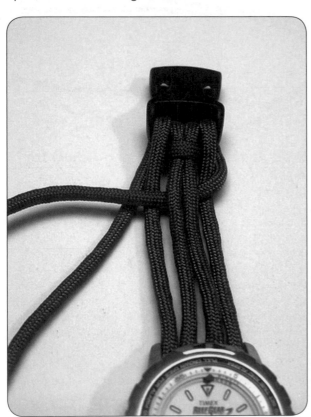

Step 6: Continue on the Other Side of the Watch

Continue weaving the paracord, keeping a uniform look and tightening as you go. A pair of hemostats can help work the cord around as you get close to the buckle end.

Step 7: Finishing Up

To finish up, take the working strand around one of the outer cords so it's coming through the underside of the bracelet/watchband.

Check for a good fit on your wrist at this point. If it's too loose or too tight, untie, adjust your starting measurement to correct, and try again.

Take your hemostats or manicure scissors and work them through about three of the center weaves, towards the buckle end, as pictured. Grasp the working strand and pull it back through the center weaves. Trim the end of the strand with your scissors and burn the end to prevent the cord from fraying (only for a few seconds). Then tuck it under the weave. Now do the same with the shorter end of cord and you're finished!

If you measure again, you'll see that the finished length is about 1 inch longer than the starting length. This will vary depending on your tightening of the weave as you go, but the difference should make for a loose, comfortable fit. Enjoy!

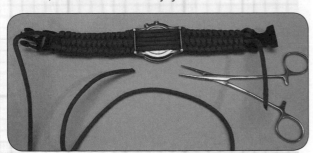

Step 8: Maintenance
Cleaning:

A nylon/paracord bracelet or watchband can get dirty and smelly after a while. To clean it, use an old, soft-bristle toothbrush to scrub the strands with soap and water in the sink. Hopefully your watch is waterproof. If not, just be careful while scrubbing, then let the bracelet or watchband air-dry overnight.

Paracord Shrinkage:

Paracord may shrink as much as 10 percent to 12 percent (especially black and Kelly green paracord), so it's recommended that you soak the cord first before manipulating it. It's the inner strands that shrink, not the outer sheath. Type III 550 mil-spec paracord has the best reputation for not shrinking. I've mostly used the mil-spec type paracord, so if it's shrunk on me, it's not noticeable.

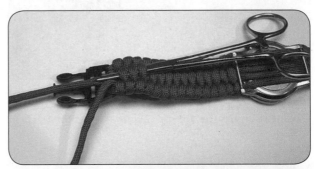

Homemade Bath Bombs

By SoapyHollow
(http://www.instructables.com/id/
How-To-Make-Bath-Bombs/)

Everybody loves bath bombs. It is like taking a bath in champagne, only without the show tunes and chorus boys. They are fairly simple to make, keeping in mind that the strangest things can make a batch go weird: humidity, room temperature, oil viscosity, the moon rising in the seventh house of Aquarius—they are a mysterious wonder. For this recipe, I am using ingredients that are pretty common in most areas. Essential oils can be found in small amounts at places like health food stores. Craft stores often carry essentials and fragrances. Just make sure that if you buy fragrance oil, you are buying "body safe" oils and not stuff for candles or oil warmers. Let's start with a basic recipe in two parts.

Step 1: What You Need

Dry ingredients (by weight, as measured on a scale):
- baking soda
- 8oz. citric acid
- 4oz. corn starch
- 4oz. salts (in these pictures, I used Dead Sea salts, but mineral salts work too and are easier to find and significantly less expensive)

Wet ingredients:
- 75 tablespoons water
- 2 teaspoons essential or fragrance oil (for these I used a Ginger Peach)
- 2½ tablespoons oil (I used cherry kernel, but any light vegetable oil will work)
- a few drops of food coloring (your color will look very dark in the emulsion but will be light in the fizzies, so as to not leave rings around the tub. For this batch I used one drop red and two drops yellow. The final result will be a very light peach.)

Step 2: Blend the Dry Ingredients

Begin by putting all of your dry ingredients into a big bowl. Glass is best because it is non-reactive. Whisk or pestle those pesky clumps out. You want a fairly smooth consistency throughout the entire mix.

Step 3: Mix Liquids and Blend Dry and Liquids Together

Blend your wet ingredients together. I usually use a small jar to shake it up. Don't worry about separation too much; you are not going to get a full emulsion. Then, while whisking, slowly add small amounts of the liquid to your dry ingredients. Here we see my faithful Igor prepare to pour.

Step 4: Try to Avoid Creating Volcanoes

If the mixture starts to foam, you are adding the liquid too quickly. Instead, quickly whisk the reacting ingredients into the nonreactive part and you should be able to stop the reaction. I add about a teaspoon at a time. When all of the wet ingredients have been added, you should have a mixture with the consistency of slightly damp sand. It should clump together when you squish it.

Step 5: Mold Quickly

Once your mixture is together, you have a pretty limited amount of time in which to get it into molds. To create the giant Soapy Hollow Ball of Bath Doom, I use round Christmas tree ornaments that were designed to be filled with goodies. To do a three-dimensional bomb like these, you pack each side, then overfill a tad at the center and press the two sides together. It takes a little practice to get a feel for how much filling you need, so don't get discouraged if your first few fall apart. Here we see Igor holding a filled ball and wondering about child labor laws.

Step 6: Unmold and Let Dry

You don't need to leave them in the mold for very long—in fact you can tap them out as soon as you fill them. These are four bombs we made with this batch. You can use all sorts of things to make your bombs: muffin tins, ice cube trays, candy molds, Aunt Magnolia's denture case . . . whatever makes you happy. This batch didn't make quite enough for five bombs, and the humidity levels made the batch start to puff up, so I quickly stuffed what was left of the batch into my "bath cookies" mold.

Note: When using things like silicon trays that surround the seltzer mix, or any mold with a lot of details, the mix must stay in the mold until dry, or it will crumble when you try to take it out. Once they are completely dry, store bath bombs in an airtight container or bag. High humidity will make them activate. Because we used oil and water and no preservatives, you want to use them within about six months, assuming you can keep them for that long. Igor demands payment in immediate fizzy baths, but you may have better luck actually getting to use yours. When you're ready to use one, just drop it into a warm bath and relax.

261

The uber band is a soft, expandable money clip made from durable industrial elastic. It allows simple access to all your cards and cash while keeping them tightly in place both in and out of your pocket.

Step 2: Measure and Trim

The first thing you'll need to do is trim down your elastic to about 4½" long.

Step 1: Materials and Tools

Uber band is pretty easy to make.

All you need is:

- approximately half a foot of 2" thick industrial elastic
- thread color of your choice
- a sewing machine (not pictured!)
- measuring tape or ruler
- fabric sheers
- A little pair of sheers for cutting thread
- 1 straight pin

Step 3: Defray

Now that you've got the appropriate length of elastic, finish the edges so they don't fray over time. I used an overlock stitch to finish the edges, but a zigzag stitch will also do the trick.

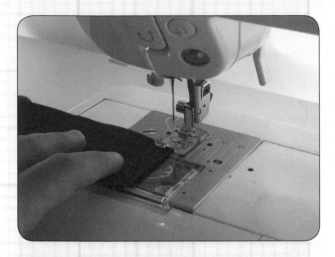

Step 4: Pin and Sew

After defraying your edges, fold the elastic in half so that the two ends meet. Pin it about half an inch away from the ends. This step will help ensure that they stay aligned when making the seam. Make a straight stitch just to the inside of the existing overlock or zig-zag stitch to join the two ends together, making sure to go over your stitch twice at both beginning and end.

Step 6: Stretch and Stuff

You did it! Stretch your uber band over the top of your cards and cash and fall in love. To easily find a card in the middle of the stack just place your thumb and index fingers on either side to spread them apart and pick the card out without having to remove every card. The extra thickness of the seam provides a perfect spot to tuck back and insert cash. Enjoy!

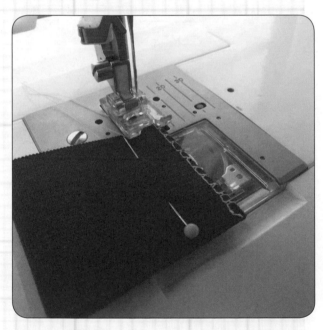

Step 5: Flip

Next, just flip the elastic inside out so that the seam becomes hidden.

Do-It-Yourself Shirt-Folding Board

By DIYHacksAndHowTos
(http://www.instructables.com/id/
Shirt-Folding-Board-from-Cardboard-
and-Duct-Tape/)

If you are like me, you want to spend as little time folding clothes as possible. In retail stores, they speed up the process by using a folding board. A simple hinged board dramatically reduces the time that it takes to fold a shirt while maintaining a perfectly uniform fold. To implement this brilliant idea in my own home, I designed a simple DIY shirt-folding board out of cardboard and duct tape.

Step 1: Materials

The materials that you need for this project are cardboard and duct tape. More specifically, you need six pieces of corrugated cardboard that are each at least 9" × 12" (23cm × 30.5cm). I found pieces of the appropriate size in the form of three shipping boxes that I had in my garage. The duct tape can be replaced by any other kind of tape. However, there is just something iconic about a project that is made with nothing but cardboard and duct tape.

The only tools that you will need are a sharp knife (such as a box cutter) and a ruler or yardstick (optional).

Step 2: Cut the Cardboard to Size

You need six rectangles of cardboard to form the base of the folding board. The dimensions of the cardboard pieces will determine the dimensions of the folded shirt. 9" × 12 inches (23 cm × 30.5 cm) is a dimension that is commonly used in department stores for large shirts. Alternatively, you can just fold a shirt to whatever size that you prefer and use that as a template.

Measure and mark the outline of six rectangles of your chosen size. Then carefully cut them out with your knife. Try to keep the sides as even as possible.

Step 3: Tape the Panels Together

Lay out the panels in a grid of three wide by two high as shown in the picture. Space them out so that there is a gap of about ¼" between each panel. This gap lets the panels easily fold and move while in use.

On both the front and back sides, tape each of the panels on the top row to each of the panels adjacent to it, as shown in the picture. Then your shirt-folding folding board is complete!

Step 4: Use the Folding Board

Now you are ready to fold some clothes.

1. Place a shirt face down centered on the board.
2. Fold one side panel over and back.
3. Fold the other side panel over and back.
4. Fold the bottom center panel up and back.

If all went well, you should have a perfectly folded shirt in a fraction of the time.

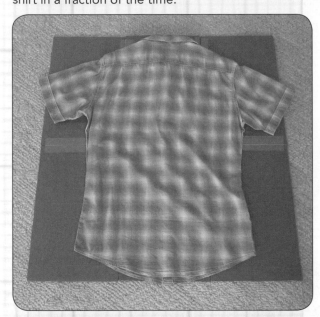

Reuse

Do you have access to old CRT computer monitors, dead mice, or old floppy disks? If so, you can turn those pieces of trash into treasures worthy of displaying in your home or at the office. These projects will guide you through each step of the way, whether that means eviscerating a mouse or simply pulling the guts from a toaster.

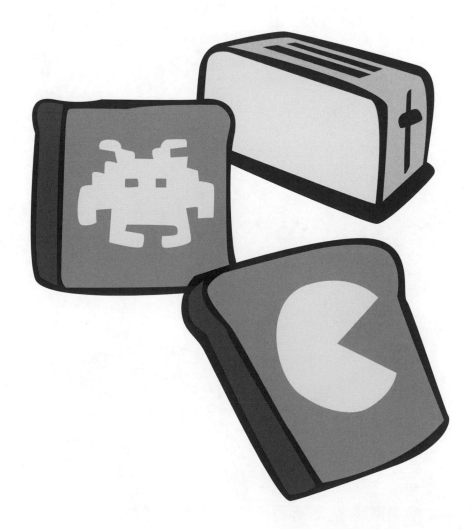

Hacked travel-size (hardware) mouse + taxidermied (wetware) mouse = Mouse Mouse! Fully functional and furry!

Step 1: Acquire Mice

Obtain a small, travel-size (hardware) mouse. This one is a wired mouse that is way too small to use comfortably every day, but perfect for going inside of a mouse. Obtain a similarly-sized (wetware) mouse. These are commonly available fresh or frozen from pet stores or any other place that sells reptile food. It's easier to fit a small object into a large mouse than a large object into a small mouse, so err on the side of caution. You can always fill extra space with cotton balls.

Step 2: Dissect (Hardware) Mouse, Part 1

Disassemble your mouse. The mini travel mouse didn't come factory ready to get put inside of a taxidermied mouse. (What were they thinking?) Thus, you'll need to take your mouse apart and see what's inside. Take off the spring-loaded cable retractor by taking out the screw and then pop the two halves apart with a screw driver. Remove the little plastic nub that was on the wire so that the wire will thread smoothly through a hole in the (wetware) mouse. Next, grab a marker and draw lines around all parts of the plastic mini mouse housing that aren't essential.

We needed to slim our (hardware) mouse down to fit inside the (wetware) mouse. We used a rotary tool to remove sections from the front of the buttons and the rear sides so that the (hardware) mouse would fit between the (wetware) mouse's shoulders and hips.

Remove as much plastic as necessary to make your mouse fit, but take care not to damage the circuit board. The pseudo-ergonomic styling is really for decoration—you can't make a little mouse like this ergonomic, so go ahead and trim it down to the size of the circuit board. Make a new slot in the back of the (hardware) mouse for the cord—we need to relocate it to the back to fit with the (wetware) mouse tail.

Step 3: Dissect (Hardware) Mouse, Part 2

To pass the USB cord through the tail hole in the (wetware) mouse, we had to remove it from the circuit board. This is done by desoldering the connections using a soldering iron. It's easy to do once you have done it before, so maybe practice the method a bit before you give it a shot on the actual mouse. Before you take things apart be sure to write down what wires go into what mounts on the circuit board so that you will be able to put things back together correctly. Using a soldering iron, gently touch the tip of the iron to the ball of solder holding the wire in place. After a second or two the solder will melt and the wire will come free. Leave the ball of solder attached to the circuit board—you can use it to reattach the wires later on.

Step 4: Shave (Wetware) Mouse

Grab a pair of tweezers, your fingernails, a razor, or some wax and remove some fur from your (wetware) mouse's belly. This is where the optical sensor will peek through at the end of the process, so you'll need to clear the fur out of the way. We started with a sharp scalpel, then moved on to tweezers and fingernails, as they are easier to use and less likely to damage the skin. Your mileage may vary—go with what works.

Step 5: Dissect (Wetware) Mouse

Disassemble your mouse. Take your mouse apart using the techniques described in my previous Mouse Taxidermy Instructable. You should now have a bag of mouse skin; discard the innards. Remove the tail if you want to run a cord through the opening instead. Wrap and wire the legs as described for a bit of support, but cut off the wire ends—we'll just

269

let the legs hang loose around the Mouse Mouse body. Prepare a head-only form and attach the eyes.

Step 6: Assembly, Part 1: Reconstitution

Run the cable through the tail hole and re-solder the four wires onto the surface of the circuit board. Refer to the How to Solder Instructable if you need a refresher on surface-mount soldering. Once the wires are in place, plug it in to make sure everything works. Reassemble the shell and circuit board and hot glue the pieces in place. If you've trimmed any bulky edges of the casing away, you'll want to wrap them in plastic to keep the mouse skin away from the circuit board. We used folded-over kitchen plastic wrap and hot glued the edges to the sides of the casing.

Step 7: Assembly, Part 2: Integration

I inserted the mouse head form just like in the Mouse Taxidermy Instructable and trimmed the wires so they wouldn't interfere with the rest of the project. We inserted the (hardware) mouse into the shoulders first, then pulled the tail region around the back. It was a tight fit— next time we'll find a fatter mouse, as it's easy to fill extra space with cotton balls! Skin is stretchy, though, and so long as you keep it moist the mice should integrate nicely. Sew up the back opening, starting near the tail and working towards the head. Leave a space for the scroll wheel—it won't work properly covered in fur! Tack the skin down around the scroll wheel with a bit of superglue, taking care not to gum up either the buttons or the scroll wheel. I usually apply the glue with a tool, either a pin or a piece of wire with a small loop on the end.

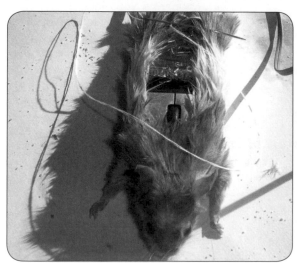

Step 8: Optical Sensor

If you've got an albino (wetware) mouse, its skin might be clear enough for your optical mouse to work directly through the dry skin. Our mouse had a bit of pigment, so it was necessary to remove the skin flap. Thankfully we had already shaved this area, making the process much easier. Make sure your completed Mouse Mouse is dry first, or the skin may pull and warp as it dries! Use your X-Acto knife or scalpel to carefully trim a hole for the optical sensor to peek through, then add just a touch of cyanoacrylate (tissue glue, aka superglue) to the edges of the skin. This will toughen the skin edge and fasten it to the plastic around the sensor. Use a tool (I used a bent piece of wire) to apply the glue, and do so sparingly—you don't want to drop any on the optical sensor!

Step 9: Completed Mouse Mouse!

Now plug your Mouse Mouse into your computer and test things out! Ours worked perfectly—I was really quite surprised by how well it turned out. The buttons and scroll wheel worked beautifully, as did the cursor movement after we trimmed the belly skin away from the optical sensor. You may need to trim a bit of fur around the edges of the scroll wheel or optical sensor, but otherwise it's a wrap! Keep in mind that this mouse isn't meant for heavy-duty computer use—it's a functional work of art and should be saved for stylish installations and special occasions. Using the Mouse Mouse on a daily basis will likely cause shedding (the mouse) and repetitive strain injury (your wrists), so we really can't advise it. Of course, it's really damn cool—every nerd who's any nerd should have one!

So you've embarked across the unknown to reach Alaska—the land of mystery and intrigue. Your mind is racing full of Jack London adventure novels and various wildlife scenes from the dozens of National Geographic episodes you consumed in the months leading up to the trip. You find yourself looking out the window of a small yet reliable Cessna 127 as it soars delicately through the wild blue sky. Below a thin layer of misty cloud, you're able to see a bit of lush Alaskan tundra—truly a modern-day Eden. If all goes well you'll catch a glimpse of a pack of majestic grey wolves in search of their next prey, or perhaps a herd of the noble bull moose standing confidently in a field of indigo wildflowers.

Everyone on the plane is ecstatic, conjuring a bit of that excited nervousness one feels just before touching down in a new and strange land. Little do these passengers know that in ten minutes time this very plane will be nothing more than scraps of bloody metal littering the landscape, the beauty and destruction posing as complete paradox. The bull moose with their grand antlers will look on indifferently.

You are the only survivor. You find yourself a little bruised, having received only a few cuts, but to your surprise, you are relatively unharmed. After the shock, you experience sheer panic, then an unusual sort of levelheadedness. One question permeates your thoughts: "What now?"

There's nothing left. Everything is charred and burned beyond recognition, all except the cellphone in your pocket. The screen is cracked and it won't turn on. It's broken, yet not useless. It simply needs to be pried apart.

Here's how you can turn your cellphone into a survival tool.

Note: In this demonstration an Android phone is used; however, I've also done the exact same experiment with the T-Mobile Blackberry 10 phone. The parts may vary from phone to phone, but the core concepts remain the same.

Step 1: Useful Parts
- speaker
- LCD screen
- metal divider
- wire
- circuit board
- battery

Step 2: Fire Starting
You will need:
- the battery
- wires (see arrows)
- kindling from environment

Process:

This process is quick, so have all components close at hand. First, touch the wire to the positive and negative nodes on the battery. Almost instantly, the wire will become hot. This is when you'll add the kindling. By touching these materials together, the kindling should ignite. However, you should be warned that the wire is likely to disintegrate in only a matter of seconds so you will only have one shot per wire (a Brillo pad works really well too, so keep one in your backpack).

Step 3: Cutting Tools
You will need:
- the circuit board
- the metal divider
- a rock from environment

Process:

Take one edge of the circuit board and sharpen it against a stone. Break off the metal mount by folding it back and forth while creasing it with the rock. These items can then be used as rudimentary cutting tools.

REFLECTION

Step 4: Signal Mirror
You will need:

• LCD screen

Process:

Every phone screen is composed of multiple mirror-like layers. To use the mirror as a signaling device, hold it up just below your eyes with one hand, and with the other make a peace sign.

You'll then line up the mirror so that it's reflecting light onto your two fingers. While keeping the light on your fingers, align the rescue craft (plane, vehicle, train, etc.) between them.

Step 5: Creating a Compass
You will need:

• speaker
• steel wire (or a needle, or a seconds hand from a watch)
• leaf from environment
• puddle of water in environment

Process:

Extract the magnet from the speaker. Straighten the wire (needle, seconds hand, etc.) and rub one end against the magnet for a few seconds. This end of the wire is now magnetized.

You'll then place the wire on the leaf, making sure it's able to float in a puddle of water. The wire and the leaf will align so that the end you rubbed will point north.

Step 6: Survival of the Fittest

Feel like an Eagle Scout yet? Now that you're essentially MacGyver of the Alaskan wilderness with merely a phone, a few rocks, and a leaf, your chances of surviving are much greater. Safe travels and don't forget your phone at home… you never know!

Computer Monitor Cat Bed

By AlpineButterfly
(http://www.instructables.com
/id/Make-a-Cat-Bed-from-a-
Computer-Monitor/)

You've seen old TVs and monitors out on the curb everywhere as they get replaced with flat screens. But what to do with the old monitors!? Trash 'em? Bad idea, as they have all kinds of lead and stuff in them that you really don't want in your ground water. Recycle 'em? Hard to do sometimes, and doing so may even cost you a couple of bucks, but it's certainly worth it if you go that route!

My cat and I like to reuse 'em and recycle them!

Step 1: Find a Monitor

Old monitors and TVs are pretty readily available these days—just ask a few friends, post it on your Facebook page, look out for one on freecycle, and Goodwill always has a stash! Cats seem to like to be cozy, so pick a monitor that's not too big and not too small. I generally use monitors between 15 and19 inches.

Step 2: Dismantle Monitor

Note of caution: Monitors and TVs can hold a charge in their capacitor for a number of months. It is entirely possible to shock yourself. If this part seems daunting, take your monitor to a TV repair person. I'm sure they will be happy to help. Some old TVs have slightly more fragile glass and also have an implosion hazard. I am not an electrician—I will simply show you what I do.

You will want an extra cardboard box for the bits. Gloves, flat-head screw driver, Phillips-head screw driver, ¼" nut driver, something you can cut wires with, and some extra wire or alligator clips. I also suggest you grab a pair of safety goggles.

TVs and monitors aren't very different from each other in terms of dismantling, but the ¼" nut driver is particularly useful for the old TVs; you won't likely need one for a monitor.

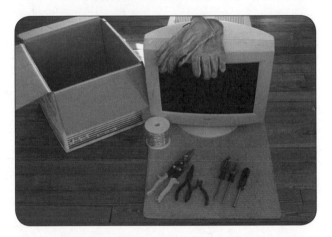

Step 3: Taking It Apart

Every monitor I have come across dismantles a little bit differently, so I'm going to give you the theory, hoping you will know that you may have to apply it a little differently in each case.

Place the monitor face down, which makes life easier in the long run. Remove the stand on the bottom of the monitor (your cat may not appreciate rocking back and forth). They often have a plastic slot that you have to press before they will slide off. I have encountered one that I actually had to rotate to remove.

Find all the screws and unscrew them. (Save these outside screws to reassemble it when you're done.)

Find all the plastic tabs. On many monitors, there are little plastic tabs you have to find to pop open the outer case. They are sometimes in the back near the outlet cord. Other times, they are in the seam between the front of the monitor and the back.

Do a jiggle test. This is my scientific term for making sure you've found all the screws and plastic latches. Jiggle test repeatedly until you find all the screws and tabs. The two halves will then separate easily.

Separate the tube from the front. Unscrew, cut, and jiggle until the tube comes off.

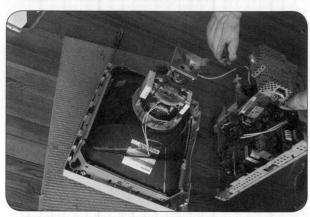

Step 4: More Screws to Remove

You may find your monitor has an inside silver casing. (If not skip to the next step.)

Find screws and remove. Similar to the last step, you simply want to remove this casing. It may be in one piece, or in a couple. Just keep finding screws and removing them. Jiggle test to find all of them.

Step 5: Taking Out the Tube

Caution. This is where you need to be a little more aware of electricity and implosion hazards. If you have an old TV and would like to ensure there won't be an implosion, check out the second image. If it's not old (around 30 years), don't worry about it, because sometimes breaking the tube means it can't be recycled.

Find a friend. Okay, I'm a wuss—even though my husband has kindly explained electricity and hazards to me multiple times, I always find a friend who can watch and dial 911 in case I shock myself. I haven't even gotten a spark yet, but better safe than sorry. I put on my gloves and don't stand in puddles.

So that I can ground the capacitor, I make a tool by connecting a wire (or alligator clips) to two screw drivers. Drag the tool around to try and ground the electricity. I then drag my screwdriver tool over the circuitry on the one side and under the rubber hood that connects to another wire on the other. I move around, touching one side to anything that looks of consequence, and the other to grounds, framing, anything that looks like it could conduct electricity. So far I have not encountered any sparks, but I often have monitors in my attic for ages! This is the step where I would expect to encounter sparks if there were going to be any.

Separate the tube from the circuit board. Any screws I still see, I unscrew. Wires that connect from the back of the tube to the circuit board get pulled or cut. Jiggle test until you've found all the screws, connection points, and wires.

Sometimes I find cool things in this step (springs, colored wires) and I save them for other projects.

Step 6: Taking out the Circuit Board

Okay , so now we have our plastic frame pieces, but it still needs a bottom. The bottom is still attached to the circuit board, so we will need to find all the little screws that keep that in place and remove them. They are all over and often hidden under other things, so look closely. Jiggle test and unscrew away.

Some of the boards are puzzled together with the metal frame, so be on the lookout for pieces that slide out or flip open.

Step 7: Reassemble

Puzzle the pieces back together and use the exterior screws (the ones we first took out) to reassemble the monitor shell.

Take a break. You could stop here, put an old sweater in, and you would have a perfectly happy cat with a rather cool cave. I would, however, recommend cleaning the monitor and recycling the insides.

Read on to learn how to make the interior pillow and how to paint it.

Step 8: Recycle the Insides

Okay, we have a lot of leftovers. This stuff can be recycled and should be recycled. But sometimes it's hard to figure out where, and many recyclers don't even take monitors and old TVs. It often costs a few bucks ($8 to $20), but it can be more if it's a bigger item. But that's totally worth it for an awesome cat bed. (And it does a little bit to help the Earth.)

Some resources:

• in the US: http://www.ecyclingcentral.com/
• where I go (cause they're cool folks, and they can tell me where it goes): http://www.eendusa.com/

Step 9: Creating the Pattern for the Pillow

If your cat is going to be totally happy with an old sweater, no need for a fancy pillow so skip ahead to the cleaning step. But do remember that cozy pillows keep cats oh-so-warm and happy.

You'll need:

• scrap paper
• tape
• scissors
• a pencil

Tape pieces of paper together to get the approximate width and depth of the monitor. Cut off the excess in the front. Draw the pattern. Once all the paper fits in, you can loosely fold and draw along the edges of the monitor to create a pillow pattern.

Cut out the pattern. Following the lines you drew, cut out the pattern. You can place it back in to see if it fits or if you need to make adjustments.

Step 10: Sew the Pillow

Get Fabric:

Return to the attic to check out your fabric stash. I'm using an old fleece sweatshirt, but any fabric will do. If you are not using a knit (fabric that stretches, like your T-shirt), cut out the pattern with zig-zag scissors or run a zig-zag stitch around the edges to keep them from fraying.

Cut Out the Pattern:

Lay the pattern down on your fabric, pin it in place, and trace ¼" to ½" out from the pattern (this will be your seam allowance). Cut out (through both layers of fabric) along the line you just drew.

Measure Out the Circumference:

Measure out the circumference of your pieces, but be a little liberal, as it's always easy to cut some away and nearly impossible to add.

Cut Strips:

You are going to want to cut 3" strips of fabric until their total length is longer than your circumference. These will be the sides of the pillow, giving it some height. So, for example, in my pattern the circumference was 60". I'm cutting five 3" strips that are each about 12" long to total 60".

Sew the Strips:

Putting right sides together, sew the strips together until you get one long strip. (It should be at least 60 inches in my case.)

Pin the Long Strip:

Pin your long strip all the way around one of your pattern pieces. Be sure to pin it with the right sides together.

Sew the Circumference:

Sew all the way around your piece, about ¼"–½" (your seam allowance). Cut off any of the excess strip at the end, leaving ½" to fold in later.

Pin on the Top:

Pin the last piece all the way around, attaching it to the other side of the long strip. Be sure to make sure right side is facing right side.

Sew the Circumference of This Side:

Sew all the way around your piece, about ¼"–½" in (your seam allowance). Be sure to leave a hole at the end so you can turn the pillow inside out and stuff it.

Cut the Corners:

Cut away excess fabric at the corners, making sure you don't cut the seams!

Flip It Inside Out:

Through the little hole you left, flip it inside out. Through the same hole, stuff the pillow (until your cat is happy). Hand sew the last little hole closed and place the pillow in the monitor. Admire.

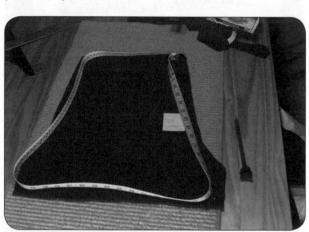

Step 11: Clean the Monitor

If you would like to paint the monitor, you will first need to clean it. Mind you, you will probably want to clean it anyways.

To clean for painting you will need:

- soap and water or regular surface cleaner
- Goo Gone for the sticky stuff that somehow is on every second-hand monitor I've found

- paint thinner to prep for some of the plastic paints
- rags

Clean with the Goo Gone first and get all the sticky tape and sticker residue off the monitor. Then for any dirt and dust I use plain old soap and water or surface cleaner. Finally, I wipe it all down with a little paint thinner.

Some parts of the monitor I don't want to paint. I usually like keeping the monitor info intact, and sometimes other little areas. Use painter's masking tape to cover that up. And if you plan on just spray painting the outside of the monitor, tape up the vent holes on the back and the top from the inside so the spray paint doesn't float in.

Step 12: Painting and Accessorizing the Monitor

Only some types of paint will stick to the plastic.
Spray Paint:

I have found plastic spray paints to be excellent and fairly easy to find at big home improvement stores; however, you have a limited range of colors.
Paint Pens:

Awesome for fun and small areas. I don't like the smell, but the adhesion is great, and you don't need to wait to be able to go outside in order to paint and work on it.
Sharpies:

These are really neat for transparent effects, but don't expect the color to last forever with these; they will fade with UV light over time.
Plastic Primer:

I have long been looking for ways to paint with acrylics on my monitors, and this seems to be the best solution. The plastic primer (also available in a spray can) seems to give the surface enough tooth for the paint to hold on to. This is fairly hard to find though, and I can only find it consistently on the Internet.
Model Paints:

The little paints you can buy for painting model airplanes and such also work quite well on the TVs and monitors.
Gluing Accessories Onto the Monitor:

2-part Epoxy and E-6000 seem to work well for gluing things on to the monitor. I find I sometimes need to use painter's tape to tape things down while it sets.

Step 13: The End

That's all folks. I hope you and your cat (or other pet) thoroughly enjoy.

Retro Art Toaster Mod
By 5Volt
(http://www.instructables.com/id/Mod-a-toaster-and-have-retro-art-toast-for-breakfa/)

Yes, I've been caught by the toast-modding wave and made my own. Just some aluminum or stainless steel and a regular toaster can do the trick.

Step 1: Safety

Before starting, you must be absolutely aware that this thing is powered from the mains and as such it could kill you and cause damage or injuries. If you are not really skilled at mains-powered electric devices and related safety building practices and are not well aware of the risks, you are urged to have a friend help you with this project. Also, as a general rule, when you are working on dangerous things always have someone next to you instructed on what to do if something goes unexpectedly. The main issue here is to make sure that the metallic parts of the prongs and shapes in no way come into contact with the electric heaters of the toaster. These notes are not just to scare or bother anyone—I absolutely do not want fun to turn into grief.

Step 2: Parts
Just a few parts are necessary:
- aluminum "flashing" from the roofing department of a home improvement store (about 1mm thick)
- paper template
- paper
- glue
- scissors (or a laser cutter, if you have one)
- a ruler
- Dremel or similar (not necessary, depends on shape's complexity)
- small fine file
- hammer and wood block
- toaster
- bread slices

Step 3: Measure

The basic idea is to place the aluminum shape inside the toaster prongs so as to block the heat to some extent, resulting in a white shadow silhouette of the shape on the bread's browned surface. You can use my template, but you are invited to do your own also. The shape comes with flaps to be wound around the steel structure of the prongs. To do so you must be sure that the size is correct so as to make the flaps at the correct distance. Measure the distance at which you will tuck the flaps. Now, with your drawing program, resize the template so as to make the distance between the two flaps of each shape the exact length between the prongs you just measured. Print the template.

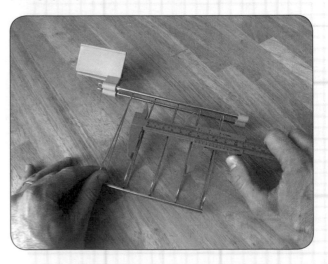

Step 4: Glue

Cut the shapes out; there is no need to be precise. Glue the shapes on the aluminum sheet. You may not need to wait until the glue is dry. Just make sure it does not move easily.

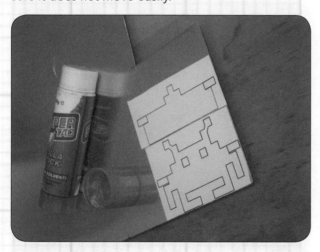

Step 5: Cut

Using the scissors start cutting out the shapes. Some parts of the shapes you may want to finish with a Dremel or similar. You may need to file the edges.

Step 6: Remove the Paper

Now dip the shapes into water to dissolve the glue and remove the paper.

Step 7: Attach the Shapes to the Prongs

Attach the shapes so they are inside of the prongs. Try to think it through before bending, as aluminum is fragile and the flaps will easily break after a few repetitive bends.

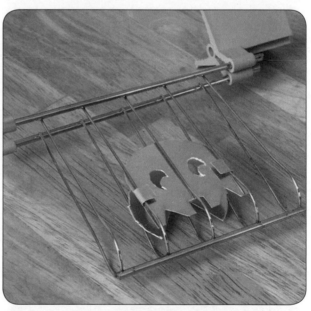

Step 8: Final Words and Advice

Use plain aluminum or stainless steel only: Do not used painted tin, as the heat would transfer paint or finishing onto your meal! Try to avoid elaborate shapes; details will not show up. The toaster makes the difference: The larger the heating resistance the more uniform the drawing will be; try smaller bread slices or larger prongs (and toaster). When you are tired of a shape, just remove it and do another one. Actually, you don't need a toaster at all—just lay the aluminum shapes on a pan and put your bread slices on it, or, even better, use a press toaster. You can also print a slice of meat. Buon appetito!

Floppy Disk Notepad

By 1up

(http://www.instructables.com/id/Floppy-Disk-Notepad/)

Have you ever had way too many unused floppy disks and needed to write something down at the same time? Here is a solution that solves both of these problems at once: a miniature notebook made with floppy disks. Geeky and stylish!

Step 1: What You Will Need

You don't need much for this project, and what you do need, you should already have.

You will need:
- 6–8 sheets of paper
- something to cut the paper with
- a pen or pencil
- drill with assorted drill bits
- two floppy disks
- clamps
- stiff wire or small chain links
- soldering iron (only necessary if you're making your own chain links)

Step 2: Make a Template

Unless you have floppy-disk-sized sheets of paper readily available, you'll need to cut your own sheets of paper. This is not as tedious as it sounds. First, we need a template. Lay the floppy disk on one sheet of paper and trace around it. Draw a couple of lines inside the template on the left and right sides, about .5cm in. Do the same for the bottom, too, then cut it out. This is so the paper is just a little smaller than the floppy disk. You don't have to do this unless if you don't mind the paper coming out the sides.

Step 3: Cut the Paper

Stack six to eight sheets of paper on top of each other, lay the template on top, and cut away. Cut out as much paper as you like, but just know that the more paper there is, the bigger the chain link has to be. I cut just enough for it to be similar to a cheap little notepad. I won't run out of paper soon, but when I do, I can simply cut more paper and put it in.

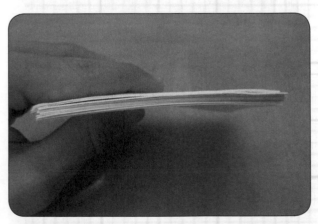

Step 4: Stack and Drill

Once you have all the paper you would like, lay one floppy disk face down. Put your paper on top of it, then add the second floppy disk, face up. Place the top edge of the paper close to the top edge of the floppy disk. Mark where you are going to drill the holes and put a some small marks there. Put the clamps right below the drill spots to reduce vibration and provide a cleaner hole. With everything in place, drill small holes in the designated spots, through the paper and all. Then take a bigger bit and drill a hole big enough to give your chain links just a little room to move around. The purpose of the smaller hole is to act as a pilot hole and to make sure that when you drill the big hole, the drill bit goes where it's supposed to.

Step 6: Love It

Now use it. Draw a keyboard inside. Take orders at the Geek café, or show it off to all your friends. Just have fun with it! If you run out of paper and you don't want to make a whole new notepad, just cut some more paper, desolder or unbend the rings, and add the paper.

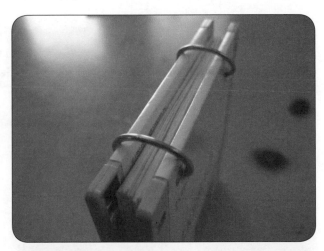

Step 5: Make Chain Links and Solder

If you have pre-made chain links that are the right size, great! Stick 'em in, bend them shut, and you're good to go! For the rest of us, though, we'll need to make our own chain links. Cut two pieces of wire a few centimeters long to become the chain links. You'll need more if you have more paper, but always try to get a little more than you think you might need. You can cut more off, but you can't put it back on. Bend the wires into circular shapes, but leave the gap big enough so you can put them through the floppy disks and paper. Put the open chain links through the whole thing. It'll be easier if you leave the clamps in place to hold everything together. Bend the wires shut and shape them so that they are more circular. Solder the wires together, and you're done! Try not to make the chain links too big, or everything will move around too much, and don't make them too small, or nothing will move at all.

Audio/Visual

If you're into making noise or taking pictures, these projects have you covered. Learn to make your own whistles, a giant xylophone made from 2x4s, or a guitar made from trash. You can also learn to use kites to perform feats of aerial photography, make a flash diffuser from a cigarette packet, or create beautiful time-lapse photos.

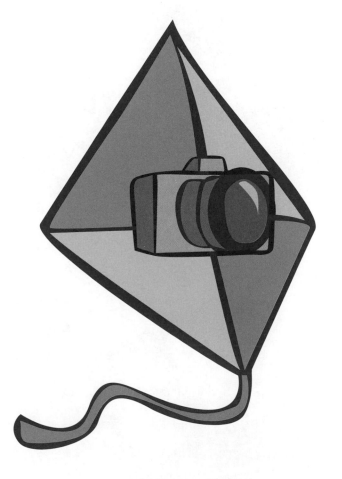

Animal-Shaped Clay Whistles
By alaut
(http://www.instructables.com/id/Bear-Whistles-Bird-Whistles-How-to-Build-Sculptu/)

There is something magical about taking a soft piece of earth or clay and making it whistle. This Instructable will walk you through the steps of making a clay whistle.

Step 1: What You Need
You'll need clay and a few tools:
- soft earthenware clay
- popsicle or other similar flat, wooden stick
- sharpened pencil
- palette knife or other small carving knife
- needle tool; used to remove bits of clay from the airway of the whistle; scoring when attaching pieces of clay
- round tool for making tone/note holes

- carving tools; small ribbon tools and stamps for decoration/ texture

Step 2: Forming the Whistle
Begin with a round ball of clay. The size will determine the tone of the whistle—the larger the piece of clay, the larger the chamber, the lower the tone.

Cradle the ball of clay in the palm of one hand, pressing the thumb of your other hand into the ball to open up the clay. Press until you feel pressure against the palm of the hand holding the clay.

With your fingers on the outside of the ball of clay and your thumb on the inside, begin pinching and turning the ball of clay, working from the bottom towards the top and thinning the wall of the chamber as you go. The goal is to turn and pinch in such a way that the wall of the whistle is about 1/4" thick or thinner and even on all sides.

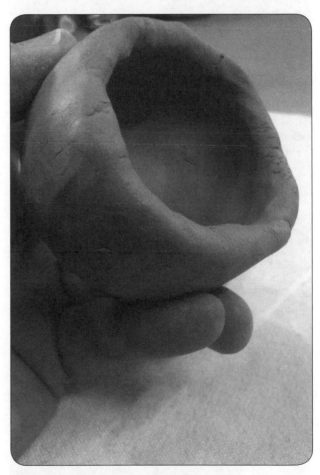

Step 3: Closing the Chamber
Alternating between pinching and smoothing, slowly work on the opening of the chamber until it is closed and the form is sealed.

Note: You can use a small piece of clay to fill the hole, if needed.

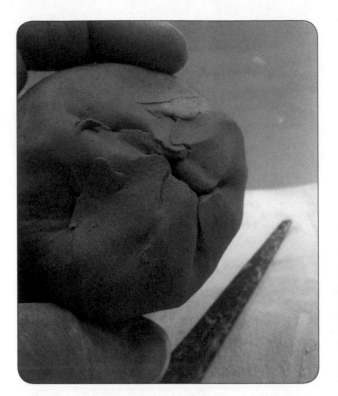

Step 5: Making and Attaching the Mouthpiece

Roll out a coil of clay about the diameter of your finger one inch long. This will be used for the mouthpiece. The mouthpiece will be attached so it lines up with the flattened bottom of the whistle.

Score the two pieces of clay where they join with a needle tool and smooth the mouthpiece onto the body of the whistle.

Note: This is the time to trim the length of the mouthpiece if it seems too long.

Step 4: Tap the Hollow Ball/Chamber on the Table

The bottom of the whistle needs to be flat. This will enable you to add the mouthpiece and create the bevel that a whistle requires in order for it to make sound. Gently tap the hollow ball of clay on the table until the bottom is flat.

Let the clay firm up for about 25 minutes. In a hurry? You can dry your piece with a hairdryer, for five minutes. Why? The next step will be to attach the mouthpiece and alter the chamber so your whistle whistles. Clay that is too soft will be difficult to work with.

Step 6: Making It Whistle! Part One— Making the Sound Hole

Part One: Making the Sound Hole/Beginning the Bevel

Use the sharpened end of the pencil and insert it so it creates an opening along the inside wall of the chamber. Push the pencil in far enough to create a sound hole that is the diameter of the pencil. Then tilt the pencil back, away from the mouthpiece and rock it from side to side to begin creating a bevel.

Step 7: Making It Whistle! Parts Two and Three

Part 2: Making an Airway in the Mouthpiece to the Chamber

You will take the popsicle stick and insert it into the center of the mouthpiece and push it straight back into the chamber of the whistle. You should be able to see the wooden stick through the sound hole you just made with the pencil.

Keep it horizontal.

Part 3: Finishing the Bevel

With the popsicle stick still in place, take your palette knife, and carve the bevel. Work to make it a sharp angle (see close-up direction below).

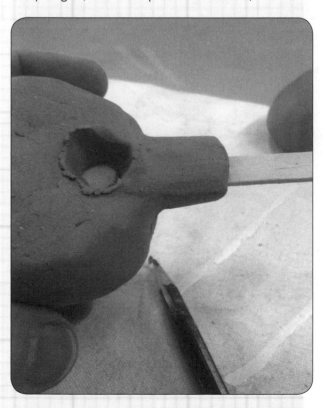

Step 8: Making It Whistle . . . Almost Done!

When you have a bevel carved, pull the popsicle out of the airway. Clean any small bits of clay that block the airways. Gently blow into the mouthpiece of your whistle to see if it makes sound. It whistles! Congratulations! You can go on to the next step.

No sound??? Keep your chin up . . . this is very common the first few times you make a whistle. Insert the popsicle stick into the mouthpiece again to clear any clay that might be blocking airways. Remember that the stick needs to go straight back into the whistle. You might need to make the bevel sharper.

The sound is weak or airy? Check again for any clay that might be blocking the airway. Play around and adjust until you get a strong, clear sound from your whistle.

Step 9: Decorating and Sculpting Your Whistle

After creating the basic form of your whistle and getting it to make sound, you can sculpt and embellish the form.

A few suggestions:

- Add pieces of clay to create bird and animal whistles.
- Create texture by pressing into the clay with various objects.
- Carve designs and patterns with small knives or ribbon tools.

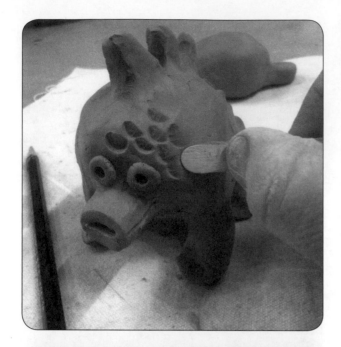

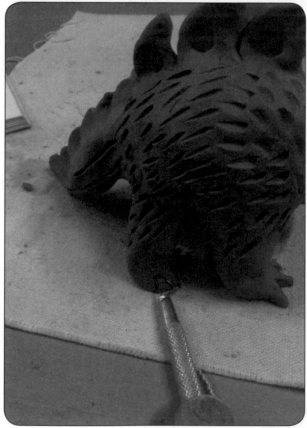

Step 10: Adding an Additional Tone or Note

You can add an additional tone and make your whistle a two- or three-note whistle by making additional holes on either side of your whistle. Use a pencil or similar-sized dowel and drill a hole in the side of your whistle; this will allow you to play two or more notes. Additional holes can be added, depending on the size and shape of your whistle.

Step 11: Last Steps . . .

Earthenware clay is allowed to dry slowly over about a week. Immediately after finishing your whistle, cover it loosely with plastic. After a day or so, uncover your whistle and allow it to finish drying.

Firing:

Earthenware clay is traditionally fired or bisqued in a kiln to make it more durable. After the bisque you may want to paint or glaze your whistle. Use care around the bevel and airway of the whistle.

The whistles shown here were made with cone 10, white stoneware clay. After they were bisqued, an iron oxide/colbalt stain was applied, and they were fired a second time to cone 10 in a reduction gas kiln.

Additional Resources:

Hall, Barry. From Mud to Music; making and enjoying ceramic musical instruments. The American Ceramic Society. 2006

Ellis, Mary. Ceramics for Kids; Creative Clay Projects to Pinch, Roll, Coil, Slam &Twist. Lark Books. 2004

Moniot, Janet. Clay Whistles: The Voice of Clay. The Whistle Press. March, 1990.

Mary Stone—Vermont Whistle-maker: http://www.marystonewhistles.com/

My blog: http://anniepots.com/

This xylophone consists of three 2" x 4" x 8' kiln-dried boards (don't use pressure-treated boards, as they are bad for kids), about 15 feet of rope, some staples, and a wooden dowel. The total cost is under $10, and it can be made from start to finish, including clean up, in about an hour. I made this for free from scraps I had on hand. I built this using a lot of guesstimation, so please feel free to do the same on yours as well.

Step 1: Measuring, Cutting, and Sanding

I made nine "notes" on this xylophone, so all of my measurements will be based on that. The "notes" were cut starting at 36 inches, and the next one was two inches shorter, and so on (36, 34, 32, 30, 28, 26, 24, 22, and 20 inches). After all of these pieces were cut, I ran the belt sander over each piece, smoothing them out and rounding over the edges. I cut the 2 x 4s as follows: 36 inches, 34 inches, and 26 inches; 30 inches, 24 inches, 22 inches, and 20inches; 28 inches and 32 inches. The first two equal 96 inches exactly, so when cutting, split the line to get it close. You could break them up differently to get better measurements, but that is not necessary.

Step 2: Assembly

Next, I measured and marked the center of each "note." I then started at the 20" piece and measured out 2" from the center, making a mark for

where the rope will be stapled. For the 22" piece, I measured 3" from the center and continued adding one inch from center to the next-largest piece. Find the middle of the rope and leave about one foot of slack to tie the xylophone off. Start stapling the rope at the marks on the first "note" and leave 1½" of space between notes as you staple. (Why 1½"? Because that's what the scrap wood is). Make certain the centers are kept in line. Don't cut the ends at the long side, as they will be used for tying up the xylophone, too.

Step 3: Tie It Up and Play

Now you just have to find somewhere to hang the xylophone. We have ours on the porch so that we can play even when it rains. This winter I'll install hooks in the playroom. When you hang it, the angle and droopiness of the xylophone will have an impact on sound, so play around with it to get the best sound from yours. I sanded down the dowels and used them as mallets, but you can use whatever is handy. Have fun—my daughter loves hers.

Trash-o-Caster Guitar

By gmoon
(http://www.instructables.com/id/
Trash-o-caster/)

During a recent storm, I found this abused electric guitar on the curb, buried in snow. Lacking all the electrics except the jack, I resolved to bring it back from the brink. I've always wanted a Strat, or something similar. That sweet single-coil sound is something a Gibson man can't get.

Disclaimer: By following this guide you will refurbish a junk instrument into something decent. However, some choices in this project (type of paint, etc.) are choices a professional guitar technician would not make; meaning, don't use these techniques on a vintage collector's instrument or it'll lose significant value.

Stratocaster, or Strat, guitars are made by Fender. This Peavey is Strat-like, although both Peavey and Fender might be insulted by the reference.

Step 1: Is It Worth Fixing?

Ask other musicians, check online. Do people like the Predator? The general consensus is Yes! Although it's a starter guitar, the playability is high. Other questions you should ask are: Is it modular? Can the neck be removed easily? One positive—despite the current fashion of locking tuners, the tuning machines on this particular guitar are solid, quality equipment.

Step 2: Second, Can It Be Fixed by an Amateur?

After scoping it out, here are the problem areas:

• bad finish/paint (was partially restored by previous owner)
• pickguard missing
• no electrics
• needs pickups, pots, switches, wiring, etc.
• missing string guide on peg head
• back cover (over tremolo springs) missing

All of these fixes are doable, but is it worth it? Although mine was abandoned, it still had a full set of strings! Tune yours and see how it plays. Is the neck straight? The action playable? Mine sounded kind of alright, but on further examination I noticed that the bridge pivot studs had cracked the body in two places. No wonder it wouldn't stay in tune!

I had no idea how this guitar was damaged, unless the pole pivots/studs were replaced at some point, but this is fixable, too! Fortunately, the bridge itself fits perfectly in the routed cavity and appears to be original. Of course, each discarded instrument will have unique problems. Give yours an honest assessment before beginning the project.

Step 3: Parts and Supplies
Equipment:
- power sander (vibrating will do)
- files
- high-speed rotary tool (Dremel)
- clamps
- soldering iron and solder
- miscellaneous screwdrivers
- drill and bits

Parts/Supplies:
- new string guide
- new tremolo springs
- new jack
- new electrics

EBay to the rescue! You can purchase an entire pickguard/pickup assembly with all the switches, pots, and wiring for cheap!

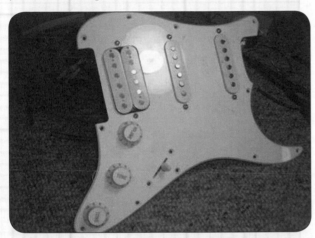

Step 4: Parts and Supplies, Continued
- epoxy (I used West System, but any will do)
- paint, clearcoat (acrylic)
- sandpaper (both regular 100–320 and wet/dry 400–1000 grit)
- rubbing compound
- spray-mount glue (Duro, Elmer's, 3M)
- rubber cement
- foil (heavy-duty aluminum or copper)
- guitar polish

Step 5: Repair the Body at the Bridge
Without this step the guitar will never stay in tune because the bridge will constantly sag toward the nut.
- Remove the studs.
- Prep the wood by roughening and drilling holes into the cracks so the epoxy can fully saturate the crack.
- Apply epoxy and clamp with a bar clamp.
- After allowing two full days for the epoxy to harden, file smooth for fit with a rat-tail file. Now pound in the studs for a friction-fit.

Step 6: Reshape the Pickguard
This Strat shape won't fit on a Peavey guitar, so the pickguard needed shaping with a high-speed grinding tool. I used a Dremel tool for the job. Most of the pickguard mounting holes in the body needed filling. I used bamboo skewers fixed with wood glue. When it was dry I sanded it to be flush with the body. The new holes in the pickguard itself were made by first drilling a pilot hole of the correct diameter, then creating the conical shape with a counter-sinking bit. Do the drilling by hand because it's less likely to damage the instrument.

Step 7: Dismantle Guitar for Painting

The guitar I found had been partially refinished, as you can see in the picture. Yet most of the finish had been sanded off, and it had been sealed at least twice (on the second coat the bridge and jack plate had been left on!). The blonde finish was nice, but the laminates had been sanded through in several places so the effect was not ideal. It was better to repaint. All hardware, neck, and so forth must be removed before painting.

Step 8: Painting Prep

Shaping:

Due to defects in the previous finish, parts of the guitar needed shaping and smoothing. A combination of a sander, sandpapering by hand, and filing did the trick.

Initial Sanding:

At this point a sanding sealer should be used. Since the guitar had been clear-polyurethaned at least twice, I skipped this step. Pits and dings can be filled with a wood filler. Use progressively finer grades of sandpaper, up to 400 grit, for the sanding stage. A vibrating or orbital sander works well.

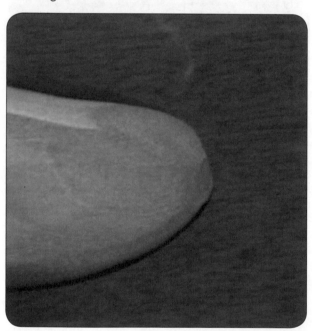

Step 9: Painting

Volumes could be written regarding painting guitars. We'll keep it simple in this project.

Disclaimer: Use a mask when painting, especially indoors.

Painting:

For my needs, a fast-drying acrylic from a spray can works fine. If this were a $10,000 collector's item, then a compressor/gun/lacquer wouldn't risk the guitar's integrity.

- First, securely hang the body from the hole drilled within the neck mounting section as pictured. Don't worry, that's why the hole is there!

- Make sure the body is clean and free of dust.
- Spray successive coats of color, following the instructions on the spray can for drying time between coats.
- Wet-sand the body once some density is built-up (four or five coats should be enough).
- Follow the color with a couple coats of clear acrylic paint.

Finish Sanding:

When working at this stage, always lay the body on a few layers of cloth, like old towels. It helps to keep the work stationary and prevents scratching on the underside.

- Now wet-sand, starting with 400 grit paper and moving up through at least 800 grit.
- Wipe often with a clean damp rag and check your progress.
- Be especially careful on the edges and corners, as it's easy to sand through the paint. If you do sand through, it's necessary to touch up the error by hand. Wet-sand, apply clear paint, and sand again. That's lots of extra time and work, so just keep a light touch on the edges!

Rubbing:

Use a rubbing compound to restore the gloss that the wet-sanding has dulled. There are many types—I used an automotive compound. Crest toothpaste can be used as a finish compound.

Step 10: About Pickups

The pickguard on this guitar came fully loaded with three pickups, but not good ones. However, if the guitar sounds halfway decent and plays well, the pickups can always be upgraded! Cheap pickups usually sound a bit thinner with more treble. Since that's quite different from my Gibson, I was cool with it, but, if you're a veteran de-Fender then you might hate the sound. To quickly compare good vs. not-so-good single-coil pickups

Better pickups generally have more coil winds, which result in more power and a somewhat mellower sound. Most use cylindrical Alnico magnets as posts.

Cheaper pickups have fewer winds and have a thinner and somewhat harsher tone, but there is more treble from the skimpier coil. A pair of cheaper (but strong) ceramic bar magnets are used to magnetize the steel posts. Not all pickups with the ceramic bar pair are cheap, however.

If you don't change strings every three weeks you probably can't tell the difference once you filter and amplify. I had one vintage single-coil from the mid-'70s and tried it in the guitar. Unfortunately the impedances weren't well-matched for the phasing mix, so I reverted back to the newer pickup.

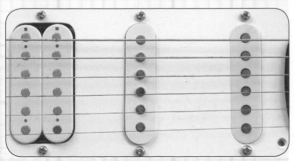

Step 11: Shielding and Wiring

Most guitars, especially those with single-coil pickups, need additional shielding to prevent noise and hum. Factory shielding just doesn't cut it.

Shielding Basics:

- Remove the existing wiring, knobs, etc. Be sure to save all the parts.
- Cover the backside of the pickguard with foil. Use spray-mount glue and heavy-duty aluminum or copper foil.
- Same with the routed cavities of the guitar body. Spray-mount could work here, but rubber cement is easier to control. The bridge/string ground can be attached directly to the foil with a screw so it won't need to be desoldered every time the pickguard is removed.
- Separate the shield ground from the main ground. Connect to main ground at only one point (to remove any ground loops).

Wiring:

Take several photos of the existing wiring before beginning this step. If you screw it up, you can always start from scratch.

Once the wiring is finished, tidy up the jumble with plastic zip-ties. It not only makes it less confusing, but it seems to help the noise ratio (maybe my imagination). Every guitar has a different wiring schema, so I won't go into detail on actual connections. The Internet is filled with wiring options for various guitar makes and models.

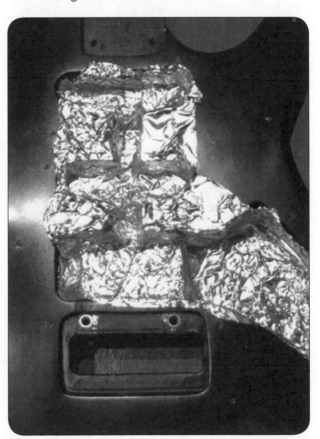

Step 13: Replace Missing String Guide

The high E string kept popping out of the nut when bending notes. Replacing the string guide solved the problem. I left the second guide off. Guitar techs advise not to use it if it won't cause problems. If you're aggressive with the whammy bar it might be helpful.

Step 12: Reassemble

Carefully put the guitar back together.

I did it in this order:

- Reattach the neck. Begin by advancing screws partway for alignment, then clamp the assembly together (backplate, body, and neck), firmly but gently so no gap forms between body and neck. Tighten screws.
- Solder output jack to electrics on pickguard.
- Install pickguard.
- Reinstall bridge at posts. Flip it over and insert the tremolo springs. I prefer three, minimum, but four is better.
- Add the knobs and other small parts you removed when shielding the pickguard.

Step 14: Scope the Results

Stand back and take it in your work This still needs some guitar polish, new strings, and a bit of tweaking

Step 15: Play It!

Well, what else would you do? I played my restored guitar through an old 'Decca solid-state practice amp, no filtering, at half volume

Well it's the start of the rainy season again in Vancouver, which means I get to bust out my brand new, globular Dome Umbrella! But you know, as useful as umbrellas are, I don't think they've quite reached their full creative potential. That's why I decided to take a tip from Brown Innovations and start off the season with my latest Mattraption™, the umbrelAudio™ Unidirectional Umbrella Speaker!

Note: Mattraption and umbrelAudio are registered trademarks of Matt Co.

Step 1: Abstract

If you've ever been to a music store or library then you've probably seen one of these objects hanging from the ceiling. Devised by Brown Innovations, the Localizer Sound Dome speaker is a parabolic unidirectional speaker that's able to direct audio, such as music, to one specific location. This, in turn, creates a localized sound area for the listener, creating an incredible atmosphere.

My build is pretty much the same, except I'm using a Dome Umbrella instead of a plastic bowl because the double function of an umbrella makes it so much more useful. Plus it's just cooler.

Step 2: Materials and Parts

Most of the parts I used came from two places—Target and Home Depot. The rest of them came from spare things around my household that were either broken or unwanted.

Materials:
- dome/bubble umbrella (has to be this kind)
- battery-operated speaker (important: It must have a flat side where you can attach the copper wire)
- small length of copper wiring (around 1cm thick)
- a 3/8" to 1" direct burial ground clamp
- assorted lengths of earphone/speaker wire (optional)
- nylon thread
- hooks (optional)
- heat shrink

Tools:
- hot glue
- metal hammer
- pliers

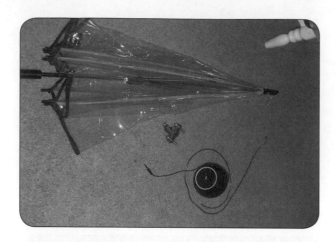

was only five inches and certainly not long enough, so I extended it to around four feet long.

Using your soldering iron and broken/spare earphone wires, cut off the earphone parts and connect a long strand of earphone wires together, leading from the speaker to the banana jack at the end. Remember to use the heat shrink to protect your solders.

Note: The reason I made my strand so long was because I planned to hang my umbrelAudio and wanted to use it from any point in my dorm room. You do not have to make it this long.

Step 3: Drill a Hole

Before we start anything, drill a hole beneath the Ferrule (end cap) of the umbrella. This will be of the utmost importance when we hang it up later on.

Step 4: Preparing the Speaker Mount

The first major part in this project, after you've accumulated all of your materials, is to begin creating the mount for your speaker. The way this is going to be connected to the umbrella is using the copper wire and brass ground clamp. In this step we will construct the copper wire mount.

First, using your pliers, bend the copper wire into a zig-zag shape with at least three curves. This will be used to attach to the flat side of your battery-operated speaker. Now use your metal hammer to pound the bent copper wire until metal can be placed flat down. Finally, hot glue it to the speaker.

Step 6: Connecting It Together

Now that you've finished creating the parts and soldering the wires, it's time to put it together! If you've done the previous steps correctly, this step shouldn't be difficult.

Attach the brass clamp to the thick copper wire, using a screwdriver to tighten the screw bolt. Next, attach the brass clamp to the metal umbrella rod. Hand tighten the clamps together as you do not want to bend the umbrella rod. Make sure that the speaker is placed at least five inches away from the top of the umbrella to maximize the sound space of the umbrelAudio.

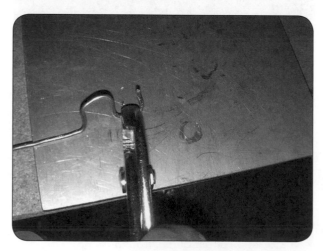

Step 5: Soldering the Wires

In this next step we can begin rewiring and soldering the speaker wire itself. Considering how long your speaker wire was originally you may not need to do this step. A good length should be around one to two feet long. My speaker's input wire

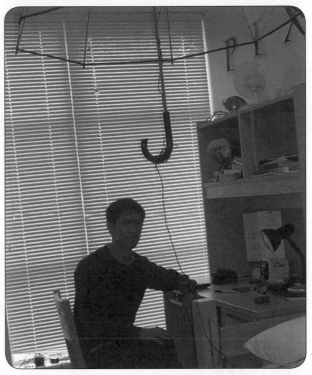

Step 7: Optional: Hanging It Up

Finally, in order to get that true Cone of Silence feel, find a suitable place to hang up your umbrelAudio on the ceiling. Using rubberized metal hooks, I was able to hang mine on my dorm room's lighting fixture, as you can see in the pictures.

Step 9: References

For more information about Sound Domes and how these devices work, please visit Brown Innovation's website for their complete line of unidirectional speakers. For another glimpse at musical umbrellas feel free to take a look at the Oto-Shigrue, devised by Yusuke Kamiyama and Mai Tanaka. They are currently sold at a hefty price of $100 each.

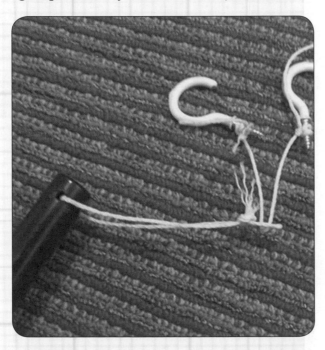

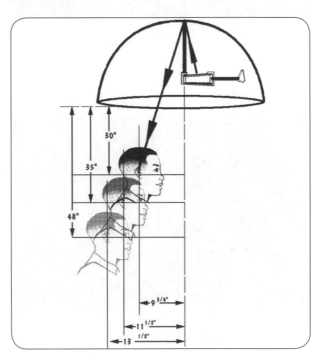

Step 8: Finished

Alright, you are now finished with creating an electronic umbrella speaker—the umbrelAudio! You now have the coolest, most waterproof speaker apparatus available! Now go give it a test listen in the rain.

Ever wanted to take indoor photos at night, but hate the washed-out look your built-in flash creates? I've often been at a pub and found the regular flash to be a bit of a pain. Thanks to a little drunken curiosity and an attention-span problem, I created a flash diffuser using only an empty cigarette packet.

Step 1: Equipment Needed
- SLR with built in flash
- cigarette packet
- pocket knife

Step 2: Quit Smoking

This will not only provide you with the empty cigarette packet, but it will improve your health, make climbing stairs easier, and probably save you enough money to buy a real external flash unit. If you don't smoke, I'm sure your friendly neighborhood chain smoker will provide you with an empty.

Step 3: Removing the Foil

Remove the foil from inside the pack, taking care not to tear it. Once the foil is removed, reverse it so the shiny side is facing inwards. Then reinsert the reversed foil into the packet. This provides a reflective surface with which to bounce the light out of the box. Note: With some brands of cigarettes, you can skip this step as the foil is already facing shiny side in.

Step 4: Attach to the Camera

This one's pretty obvious. Feel free to adjust the angle of the packet's lid to differ the angle of the flash spread. Also, experiment with the position of the box. Reversing the box may also help. The more upright your flash unit and the lower the ceiling, the better the results will be.

Step 5: Results

Here is a before and after shot to demonstrate the difference. These shots were taken in a fairly dark place with relatively high ceilings. No way will this replace a $400 external flash unit, but it is improvement on what you already have using something that you can probably find on the floor the next time you're at a pub.

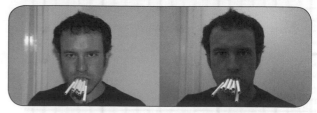

Long-Term Time-Lapse Photography

By fpound

(http://www.instructables.com/id/How-to-make-a-long-term-time-lapse/)

A single, standard battery in a DSLR camera will suffice for making most time lapses, but what if you want to capture a time lapse for a week, a month, or an entire season while being far removed from any source of power? Well, for a recent documentary called Watershed, produced by Kontent Films, I did just that. I built four time-lapse camera rigs that ran, unassisted, for up to four months.

I made this camera at Techshop in San Francisco, where there were lots of tools available, but it can also be built at home with no problem.

Step 1: Gather Materials

Materials:

- I made suggestions for possible options, not necessarily the items I used. Please be smart and take measurements and look at reviews etc.
- Camera. I chose to purchase used Canon 20D cameras through KEH. You want something solid and high quality, but remember, megapixel count isn't super essential because the likely final output is HD video.
- Lens. As with all pictures, the better the glass the better the time lapse. But I'd also recommend not going too crazy—balance your risk and benefit. I chose a cheap zoom lens from KEH so I could change the shot as needed from where I was able to place the cameras. If you know what your shot is beforehand, a prime lens in this situation might be appropriate.
- Media card. Get a big one because you don't want to run out of space!
- Intervalometer. Depends on what model of camera you choose. I'd definitely recommend not skimping here; just get the one made by Canon so you don't have to worry about it (my knock off failed on me).
- Battery. How long do you want this time lapse to be? We used a car battery (really, just a slightly larger RV battery) for our rigs. They didn't run out of juice, so we don't really know how long they would have lasted. Probably a lot longer. Try to find a battery that isn't built to deliver massive amounts of power all at once (starter battery), but one that's used to releasing a small charge (like a battery used for RV appliances, or what they call a marine battery) We were able to get one for cheap at a place that recycles old batteries.

- Battery case. A plastic shell for the car battery that can be purchased at West Marine or other places. It's not technically waterproof, but it does help keep the rain off the electrical components while still allowing it to off gas in extreme weather. It's also helpful for attaching various components. Make sure it's the right dimensions for the battery you get.
- Dummy battery. It goes in your camera in the battery slot and has a cord that extends out. You can make your own if you know how (read all of my instructions before you build), or you can do what I did and buy a cheap AC adapter for the camera.
- Voltage converter. Your camera operates on around 7 volts of DC power, whereas a car battery runs on an average of 12v DC (household power is 120v AC). Look for a variable DC converter that takes 12v power and makes it something close to 7v (7.5 works fine). Again, higher quality here is better.
- OR a voltage converter, dummy battery combo. This guy in England makes really high quality ones for about the same price. I only found out about them after I had placed the cameras. If I were doing this project again I'd use these.
- Pelican case. This case is a standard water- and weatherproof case for your camera. You don't need the foam if it makes it cheaper.
- Mounting plate. It's not essential, but it certainly makes mounting your camera easier.
- 20 amp fuse
- Electrical connectors of the appropriate size (terminal ends, butt splices, etc.)

- Large-diameter PVC pipe for the lens snout. I purchased at Home Depot. The interior diameter needs to be bigger than the diameter of your lens.
- Clear UV lens filter. This filter covers the opening in the PVC pipe, making it weather-proof. It can be purchased at a camera store; bring in the pipe to make sure it fits.
- Epoxy, or some sort of really strong, really gooey substance to fill up holes and hold some things together.
- Silicone moisture packets
- Mounting hardware (screws, bolts, nuts, washers, rubber washers, brackets, etc.) and miscellaneous scrap wood
- Velcro

Tools:
- wire-cutting and splicing tools
- multimeter
- large-diameter circle cutter (slightly smaller diameter than exterior of PVC pipe)
- drill
- wrench
- file

Step 2: Plan

Once you have all your materials, you should start to map out how they'll all fit within the case. It tends to get crowded in there, so careful planning is a must. For balance, I put the camera's lens roughly in the center of the Pelican case. With this established, make sure that there will be enough room for the voltage converter and the intervalometer on either side.

Consider leaving enough room for the camera mounting plate, mounting hardware, etc. The picture shows the placement of the different items in the case. If I were building this camera again, I'd trim off a lot of the wire and make it nice and tidy inside.

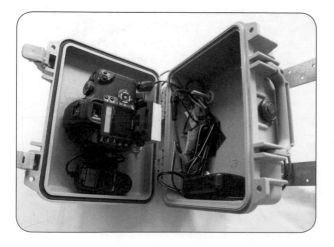

Step 3: Hardware

I can't tell you exact measurements or show you pictures of every step of this process. Yet, with the age-old advice of measure three or four times and cut once, you shouldn't have any issues. Using a circle-cutter drill bit that's a tiny bit smaller in diameter than your PVC pipe, cut a hole in the front of your Pelican case. I used a drill press, but a handheld drill would work fine. File away at the hole until the pipe will fit in snugly.

Mount the camera. Attach the Manfotto quick-release plate to a small piece of wood with a screw. Then attach that to the Pelican case with two 90° angle brackets, a couple of bolts, and rubber toilet washers to make it more waterproof. Make sure the height is correct so that the camera and lens are properly positioned in the large hole.

Cut the PVC pipe so that it extends not much more than ¼" to ½" beyond the end of the lens. The beauty of the quick-release plate is that you can slide the camera forwards and back some to ensure a good fit, but at a certain point the camera won't slide any farther. Just know that the farther the lens is from the end of the PVC pipe, the more risk there is for reflections and vignetting. If you care about aesthetics or camouflage, spray paint your pipe to match the color of the Pelican case. Use the epoxy/silicone sealer to secure the pipe in place.

Attach the clear UV filter to the front of the lens pipe using some of the epoxy. Be careful, because the case is probably front heavy at this time and a direct nose dive will shatter the glass. I speak from personal experience, unfortunately.

Attach mounting hardware to the back of the pelican case. I used long bolts through the back of the case that connected to flat metal brackets. With nuts and washers (some rubber ones for waterproofing) this became adjustable to suit the needs of mounting the case to trees, posts, rocks, and so on. Drill a hole in the back of the case for the wires to the battery.

In some installation configurations, you'll want the battery box to be directly attached to camera box to act as a stabilizing weight and anchor. Drill four holes in one of the long sides of the battery box matching the position of the mounting hardware on the Pelican case. To give it rigidity and an anchor point for the mounting bolts, I used two pieces of wood (approximately 8" x 10") on either side of one of the battery box's longer walls with the same hole pattern drilled into them. Also, you might want to drill holes in the battery box's walls and lid so that you can use a couple of zip ties to secure the lid.

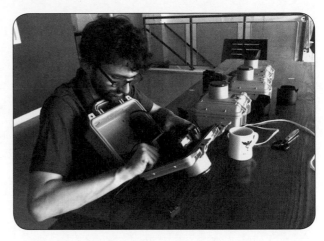

Step 4: Electrical

The diagram below is more of a wire diagram than a circuit diagram. I'm not an electrician and don't really know how to draw these things. But my diagram does explain the basic setup. Your car battery has two wires coming off it (remember, red's hot [positive], black's not); put an inline fuse in to the positive wire. Both wires come off and go into the voltage converter. Wires come out and attach to dummy battery wires and then go into camera.

Be careful. At 12 volts, risk of electrocution is fairly minimal as I understand it, but you can melt a wrench if it makes contact with the two terminals on the battery. You can also fry your camera, I'm sure. And make sure you don't cross your wires. As I said above, red = positive, black = negative. Sometimes consumer electronics don't have red wires, but they have a white stripe on a second black wire instead.

Cut your wires. Cut the black box off the dummy battery if you're using an AC adapter.

Strip the insulation off the last quarter inch of each wire. I used butt splices to hold the wires together, but a wire nut will also work, though it might take up more room inside the case. Try to get connections that are the right wire gauge. Too fat and the wires will fall out; too small and they won't fit.

Attach terminal connectors to the wires that will attach to the battery. Pass the other end through the hole you drilled in the back of the case. Install the fuse. You might as well keep that inside, so make sure you have plenty of wire to connect the camera box to the battery box. A couple of times I placed the camera about six feet away from the battery box to aid in mounting the thing, so plan accordingly.

Attach these two wires to the wires going into the voltage converter. Then attach the other side of the voltage converter to the dummy battery wires (if you got the astronomizer kit, which I recommend, your setup will be a lot easier).

I kept the extra wire coiled in the case, but if you wanted to trim off your excess, it would make for a much cleaner rig. You can use the Velcro to secure the voltage converter to the side of the case. It'll keep it from rattling around and disturbing the camera.

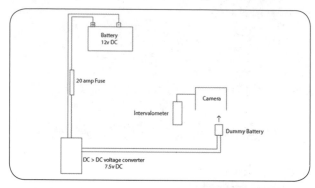

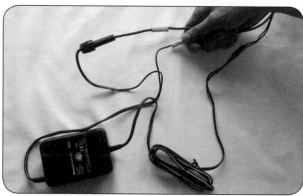

Step 5: Moments of Truth

Turn on your camera. Hopefully you don't smell smoke or see sparks. If your camera does work, congratulations—you're almost finished! Mount your camera on the quick-release plate. Plug in the intervalometer and Velcro it to the side of the case as well. I wouldn't try and trim these wires. You'll just have to live with them in there. Plug up any holes with epoxy or silicone as this box will need to survive the elements.

Test the rig before you commit to a multi-week time lapse. I ran mine for a few days on my roof to test both the length and the weather durability of the rig. I learned a lot from those experiments.

Step 6: Ready to Place

Particular care must be taken when placing the camera. First, you need to figure out what subject matter you'll be capturing and what angle will best accomplish that. For example, we at Kontent Films knew we wanted to cover the annual snow melt in the Rocky Mountains, but we needed to decide how to photograph it. We knew we needed to photograph an area that would experience spectacular change, not subtle change. We chose two very different locations to accomplish these goals. One camera was placed on a hillside overlooking a snow-covered landscape miles away; the other was in a small, snow-filled ravine down which flowed an ice-covered creek. When the snow melted in both shots, we knew (okay, hoped) that the change would be dramatic and informative.

When you're ready to place your camera, you'll find that precise placement and mounting will be difficult, but it's the key to success. We traveled with several different mounting options and used a few on location. The default set up was of the camera box attached solidly to the battery box. We used this configuration to place the rig on the hillside and also inches from the edge of a 300-foot cliff overlooking Lake Powell. We covered both cameras with rocks for camouflage and to protect them from the wind.

Our other mounting arrangement was to attach the camera box in a tree and run wires to the battery box resting on the ground (or itself mounted to a tree separately). Attach the mounting bolts on the camera box to the flat metal brackets. With long bolts, nuts, and washers, you'll be able to subtly adjust the position of the camera by lengthening and shortening the bolts and connecting the camera and battery boxes. Then, using long wood screws, attach the brackets (and camera box) to the tree, post, or anything else that's suitable.

Once mounted, you'll want to double check your shot. Set your intervalometer to a short interval. Close the case, take a few pictures, and then open the case back up and take a look at what you just took. If you like what you see, great! If not, adjust the position and framing as needed.

Focus and zoom are especially tricky, depending on the type of lens you're using. Once you've dialed that in, tape the lens so it can't accidentally adjust. Again, take test shots of your focus and zoom before sealing the case up for good.

Set your intervalometer to the desired interval. It could be once an hour, once every 30 minutes, every 5 minutes? The decision is a combination the size of your media card, the size of the pictures you camera takes, and the length of your time lapse (in video time and it real time).

Once you close it up for good, I'd suggest waiting during your interval and listen closely to the case to see if you can hear the camera click. It's smart to write down the time of day and come back to check in on it the next day or even every couple of weeks.

I heard a that a component of the Extreme Ice Survey's long-term time-lapse rigs malfunctioned, and when they came to check on them six months later, they'd captured no images. Now, I'm not saying they weren't fastidious in their double and triple checking, but you can to avoid a little heartache of your own by making sure everything is working properly before you leave the camera for good.

Step 7: Security

Now, you'll probably wonder, Won't my camera be vulnerable to thieves as well as the weather? That was the most common comment I received when I was making these. We planned ahead and prepared this little laminated note to try and convince a potential vandal or thief to move along. I think it's enough to stop curious people. We also locked some of the cases and left some unlocked. We figured that in high traffic areas, casual hooligans would be less likely to try and open a locked case, whereas in the middle of nowhere, vandals would be rarer, and in case they did find the camera, a little padlock wasn't going to stop a determined thief.

We also included a self-addressed, stamped envelope inside the case pleading with a potential thief to send back the media card so that our work wouldn't be completely for naught. Luckily, when we returned to the cameras they had not been tampered with at all, and my trust in humanity prevailed.

> ### TIMELAPSE PHOTOGRAPHY PROJECT - PLEASE DO NOT TOUCH
>
> Hello and thank you in advance for not disturbing my set up. My name is Forrest Pound and I am experimenting with a way to capture the flows of the river through long term time-lapse photography. The equipment is quite sensitive to movement and disturbance, so please do not touch or otherwise disturb. About a month of my hard work went into building this camera, please take this into consideration. I will return for all of this shortly, and remove any trace of its existence. In case of problems or emergency, please contact me at 7 questions.
>
> Thank you

Step 8: Ingesting and Editing

I'm not going to spend a lot of time on this section because I don't think this is the time or place, but I did want to mention a couple of things. When setting out to do a longer-term time lapse, consider what the end product will actually look like. We set the intervalometers on our rigs to take pictures every twenty minutes for months. That resulted in a lot of images. If we were to lay all those out together, we'd get day-to-night to day-to-night to day-to-night, etc. It'd be a little nauseating to look at. We chose to select only images taken at a specific time, 6 p.m., for example. That way the sun was always roughly in the same spot (we shot around the summer solstice, so daily sun position didn't change as much as it would have around the equinox).

Once we'd selected our images and weeded out a few that were too different from the others (lens covered in snow for instance), we took them into After Effects for a little sweetening—exposure balancing, color correction, stabilization, and, in a few instances, sky-replacement masking. I know, I know, a blasphemy for purists, but honestly, if it comes down to a shot looking good being included in the project, I'd choose a slight digital manipulation that helps to convey the concept and enhances the story any day.

Step 9: Good Luck

An image shot on a different time scale from everyday life, whether it be super slow motion or time lapse, can have a profound impact on a person's perspective of the world around them. Some of the most inspiring shots I've ever seen are time lapses that explain a natural process. When I see clouds forming and colliding in the wake of a mountain I understand a little piece of the mystery of weather. A beautiful nighttime shot with the stars making their circle around the North Star does more to explain astronomy and our place in the universe than any physics text book could.

With a long-term time-lapse camera, we can stretch the human conception of time even further. I used these long-term time-lapse rigs to shine a light on processes that happen too slowly to notice in our daily lives.

I envision these long-term time-lapse rigs being used for art and for film, of course, but also for scientific observation like the Extreme Ice Survey or, in our case, to document the Sonoran Institute's efforts to re-water the Colorado River Delta. They could be used where there is a need for consistent observation and understanding of a plot of land and the intricate systems within it—a farm, ranch, or garden, for instance. The observation of remote building projects is a common use, but ultimately, these cameras can be used to satisfy the curiosity we innately have about the world around us.

This design is a good start, but there are many different variations that I could imagine. The first and most obvious would be to scale down the size of the battery and add a solar- or wind-based power source to supplement the battery. You could use different cameras for an especially small rig.

Good luck making your long-term time lapses and have some fun with it!

Kite Aerial Photography (KAP)

By mikeasaurus
(http://www.instructables.com/id/Kite-
Aerial-Photography-KAP/)

Design and manufacture your own mechanical intervalometer trigger for your old digital camera. In this project we'll see how to make your own camera trigger from recycled, reused, and re-purposed materials, many you may find laying around your home!

Prologue

One starry, sleepless night, my mind wandered. I had a vision of floating upwards; all I was able to grab before my feet left the ground were my sunglasses and camera. I was carried to the sky, photographing my way upwards. I had broken into the stratosphere when. . . . It was over.

I was inspired to create my own aerial photographs. Since I am not familiar with the methods of making my trigger from 555 timers, I needed to make a mechanical trigger. As a twist I would use recycled and repurposed materials and combine the trigger with an old, abandoned digital camera to take photos from my kite.

While electronics may be second nature to some, to others (myself included) they are a mystery. I did not want wiring or programming to be a deterrent, so for this project this element is removed entirely. In addition, I wanted a design that would not compromise the camera housing. This rules out opening the camera to solder on a trigger.

My guidelines for this project were:
- use as much recycled content as possible
- budget of around $50
- able to function with any digital camera
- no special camera function (or special plug)
- no specialty knowledge (e.g., no electrical/ Arduino/555 timers, etc.)

With these ideas laid out, I was set to take some aerial photography and maybe have an adventure along the way. Enough talk, let's build!

Step 1: The Kite

Research pointed me toward a few possible options for achieving the required height. The original idea was to use a balloon filled with helium to generate the lift. This idea is still good; however, I wanted to make something portable, and riding the bus with a giant balloon isn't a great way to make friends (or is it?). Instead, I opted for the more passive method of a kite. Kite design is everything. There are countless varieties of kites, and luckily there are a few that lend themselves well to this application. I suggest doing your own research to determine which style fits your needs best. I chose a design that was simple, easy to fly, able to achieve lift in any wind, and large enough to accept a payload. The Delta Conyne satisfies all my criteria. With a little sleuthing you may find dimensioned plans online that you can use to build your own. As I was on my way to find materials to make my kite (rip-stop nylon and wooden dowels), I happened upon a kid's store nearby that had the exact kite I was looking for, in the size I needed (6' or more, or 1.8m or more, from wingtip to wingtip), and on sale! The kite cost $30. The remainder of the budget was spent on the line. The only downside is that the kite is pink.

Step 2: The Trigger—Materials
Objective:

Battery-operated motor turns a toothed cam, which depresses a plunger to activate a camera shutter—a basic mechanical intervalometer.

Method of Attack:

Since electronic timers were out, I had a blank slate for how I wanted to approach assembling the trigger. After a brief review of my options, I discovered that there are unlimited ways of making a trigger assembly. This is just one. Actually, this one in particular had maybe too much thought put into it. I wanted the largest possible audience to participate.

It was time to get dirty and creative. I compiled a few collections of CD spindles to free up a spare. The paint sticks were free from the hardware store. The pen and pushpins were liberated from the tyranny of the office supply closet. The toy bunny was a gift from my sister, to which I thank her by mutilating said gift. As for the cassette? VHS is a relic from a bygone era best forgotten. There will no tears shed for its fate.

Almost everything used for the trigger was recycled, found, or free:

- CD spindle
- clicky pen
- push pins (around 30)
- paint sticks used for mixing paint nuts
- butterfly nuts
- washers
- 90° angle bracket
- 3 50mm (2") steel mending plates
- VHS cassette
- electric motor from kid's toy
- camera mount (from old tripod)
- plastic tubing (can use washers or plastic spacers instead)

Tools needed:

- glue gun
- hobby knife
- pliers
- screw drivers
- safety goggles (seriously)
- rotary tool (optional)

The methods used are specific to the materials on hand; your project may differ, so improvise as needed.

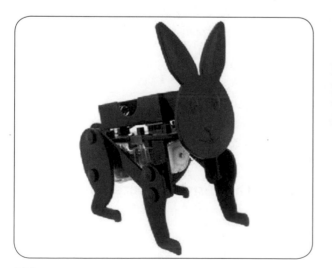

Step 3: Material Modifications

A few of the materials I used required minor modifications to allow this assembly to work.

Paint Sticks:

These act as the spine of the assembly. The wood is soft, light, and workable. Since I wanted the assembly to be used with any camera, it needs to be adjustable. Simply mark out an elongated rectangle on the paint stick and use a hobby knife to cut through. Paint sticks can be found free in your local paint store.

Push Pins:

The pins will act as teeth for our motor to grip on to. These push pins have plastic heads, which are not needed. The heads can be easily removed with a set of pliers. During operation, the teeth may catch on the motor; this problem was solved by grinding each tooth with a slight angle, allowing the motor to slip into the grooves of the teeth easier.

Camera Mount Nut:

Most mounts will have plenty of thread to allow a firm grip between your camera and the mounting surface. However, you may need to add a small collar (or washers) to the threads for a snug fit.

Clicky Pen:

In the interest of having a smaller assembly I chose to cut the pen down to size. Originally the pen measured 20cm (8"), and was reduced to around 7.5cm (3"). It's vital that the pen's clicky mechanism still works. It should be a stubby, operable, pen.

Step 4: Trigger Assembly—External

The idea was to use the spinning motion of a small motorized toy to operate the shutter of my camera. However, mounting the motor directly to the camera was out because the motor for the toy turned too quickly and would have spun about ten times between shots, which would have shaken the camera too much, producing jittery shots. Since stability is an issue, I needed something that slowed down the pace of that tiny motor. Sticking to the idea that I wanted to keep this project out of the realm of wiring and electronics, I was left with slowing the rotation of the motor to a speed that would allow shots to be taken at the intervals I wanted.

First, I stripped the toy to just the motor and a gear that had been attached to the rear legs of the bunny. A portion of the CD spindle was cut away, allowing the turning part of the motor to be placed inside the spindle, while the housing and battery were outside the spindle. The motor and housing were glued to the top edge of the spindle as shown. Next, a small oval was cut about 90° from the motor opening, allowing the pen to be inserted and then glued in place. The pen tip is what will trigger the shutter on our camera, and this will need to be pointing out. The clicking portion will be operated by the rotating cam inside the spindle.

you've got the teeth spacing and cams set properly, as there is not much you can do to modify this once you have it assembled. Your only option may be to dismantle and start the inner workings again, so be patient.

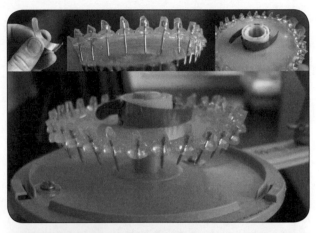

Step 5: Trigger Assembly—Internal

For the "guts" of the trigger I created a cam to rotate around the spindle and trigger the clicky pen. For this I busted open an old VHS cassette and used one of the tape spools. The inside diameter of the spool was a snug fit on the spindle, so the VHS spool opening was widened a little to allow it to spin freely on the spindle. Then I hot glued the modified push pins to the outside rim of the spool, forming the teeth that would step the spool forward, eventually engaging the cam with the pen. The cam was made from a small metal tongue found inside the VHS cassette. The tongue is bent to fit around the cassette spool, with the tapered end sticking out. The cam was then glued to the inner wheel on the spool and bent into position. A small piece of tubing was used between the spool and the spindle to achieve the proper height needed to allow engagement between the motor and the teeth. This was by far the most difficult step; take your time and make sure

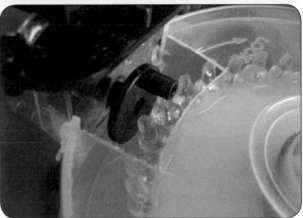

Step 6: Closing the Assembly

The top of the CD spindle conveniently screws to connect with its base. To ensure the motor engages with the toothed spool, a piece of large-gauge tubing should be placed under the spool. The size of the plastic tubing collar is important. It's not enough the teeth will not engage. If it's too tight the spool will not turn. I estimate a tubing length of 25mm (1"). Luckily the tubing is forgiving and has some give, just don't overcut or you will need a new collar.

Step 7: Kite Streamers

I may have scored a deal on my kite. However, streamers were not part of the package. As a requirement for flight, kites do not need streamers. However, flying without them is like driving a car with no steering wheel—a bad idea. Streamers act much like the fin on a weathervane, keeping your kite angled towards the wind and allowing for maximum lift. Streamers are nothing more than a means of adding drag to your kite (windsocks function the same way and can be used instead of, or in combination with, streamers). I decided to make my own using everyone's favorite unnecessary grocery item: the plastic shopping bag.

The original intent was to use an unaltered bag as a sock and just tether it behind the kite, acting like a parachute. While this worked, it looked ridiculous. My kite was made fun of by all the other kites for looking frumpy and trashy. I told my kite it was prettier than all the other kites, and that being pink is much more eye-catching than the flashy streamers on the other kites out that day, but it was no consolation. That night I stayed up and made my very own streamers. Two shopping bags make one streamer: Cut down the sides of the bag, lay flat, and cut into strips. Gather the ends from one side and tie off with string. For the Boy Scouts in the back section, try adding a lengthened loop during your tie-off so you can attach the streamers easily to the kite.

Step 8: Putting It All Together

Mounting Camera to the Rig:

By adjusting the slider and swivel arm, the camera can be placed directly under the nib of the pen. I have found the most success by turning on the camera and engaging the shutter slightly, thereby only requiring the slightest increase in pressure from the pen to complete the action and take a picture.

Attaching the Rig to the Kite:

I aimed to make my rig as light as I could; however, the heaviest load will be the camera itself. My camera was about three times heavier than my rig, so the entire rig with camera weighed less than 700g (1.5lbs). If you have a strong, consistent wind you can mount the rig wherever you choose. In many instances, though, you will need to get the kite in the air before attaching your payload. Through trial and error I determined that there is a threshold of turbulent air from the deck to around 15m (50'); past this the air seems to move faster and smoother. This was my marker.

The assembly is hanging about 15m (50') from the kite, around the threshold mentioned. In the picture you can see that the rig is suspended between two points on the line. This was an attempt to add stabilization by allowing the rig to swing independently of pulls in the line. The solution is to have a cradle capable of suspending the rig and allowing it full travel regardless of any fluctuations or turbulence; however, I was not able to complete a more comprehensive stabilization cradle for my rig. See the last step of this Instructable for links to more information on cradles.

Step 9: A Word on Line

Consideration was taken as to which line to get with this kite. While my kite isn't the largest on the block, it was going to be under stress not designed for your average flyer due to the payload. If I had any hope of keeping my camera and rig in one piece I was going to need a line that was light enough to be lifted but strong enough to withstand stress on the line. My first line was a nylon composite purchased at a dollar store, which snapped on the third outing. The good news is that the camera rig wasn't attached yet. The bad news is that it snapped while I had 60m (200') of line out. I was in a downtown city park. It's quite a feeling watching your new favorite toy sailing away. The kite flew just like a paper airplane, catching rogue wind and slowly drifting farther and farther away from me. Turns out it landed around 550m (1800') away. I managed to find it in an alleyway. The remainder of my budget was spent on new fishing line. I bought a high-stress fishing line at a hardware store for around $20. The line was rated for 50lbs of stress (a fisherman friend tells me this is, in fact, not high-stress, as they make lines capable of up to 150lbs+). If there is more than 50lbs of stress on the line the kite is just as likely to break as the line, so there is no need to go higher in this case. Before you go flying, a good idea is to measure out your line into measured intervals with markings (I used 10m, or 30', intervals). This way you can estimate the height of the kite by how much line is let out.

Step 10: Flight (Finding the Right Conditions)

I hate waiting. It's hard to have a project ready for testing and then having to wait for conditions to be favorable. During assembly construction the sunshine was bright and the wind was brisk. The first week after the assembly was complete the weather was nothing but rain. The following week had no wind. Finally, after a few days of frantically running around the park trying to tow the kite higher, my legs had had enough. It was time to find a different approach. Realizing that springtime weather is fickle at the best of times, instead of waiting for wind I decided to go find it. Being near a coast, I knew some of the best winds are where land meets water, and since I was ready for a vacation anyways, I made a trip to the real west coast of Canada. You can see where the landscape has been visibly altered by the intense winds off the Pacific Ocean. If I couldn't find my wind here, this project would never get off the ground. Pun intended.

Step 11: Aerial Photographs

The day the kite flew the winds were well over 20km/h (12.5mph) with a consistent direction—the conditions were perfect! The kite held, so did the line, and so did the little toy motor.

Empirically I've determined the following:
1. minimum windspeed required with no payload: ~4km/h+ (2.5 mph+)
2. minimum windspeed required with payload: ~17km/h+ (10.5 mph+)

The entire rig held up well under the punishment of crashing more than a few times. Eventually the motor snapped off and the rig was no longer operable. At the time I had over 400 shots from the air (and one partially corrupted file that must have been taken while crashing). Once home I was able to organize the photos. Sadly, due to the lack of a leveling and stabilizing rig many of the shots were too blurry, and in some cases were unrecognizable. Approximately 30 were of a quality I would be comfortable sharing.

Step 12: Final Thoughts and Further Reading

Stability:

As you may have noticed, my rig is attached directly to the line itself. In kite aerial photography terms this is nothing shy of barbaric. There are sophisticated rigs out there (for sale and handmade) that use a series of strings and pulleys and are designed to level the rig and add stability, ensuring quality shots.

Further Reading:

There's no shortage of people who have attempted homemade kite aerial photography. Get on Google and start reading. Use a wide range of references to make your kite. Following in someone else's steps is sometimes boring, so be creative and try out our own ideas!

Amplifier Dock

By timwikander

(http://www.instructables.com/id/Amplifier-Dock/)

This amplifier dock is a passive amplifier and docking solution for the iPhone and iPod Touch that utilizes the shape and material of an ordinary ceramic bowl. Designed for disassembly, the ceramic bowl may be reused, steel hardware may be recycled, and hardwood/ wool felt may be left to biodegrade. This was my first project as a 2013 Artist in Residence at Instructables.com.

Step 1: Materials and Tools

The material count and skill level necessary to make this project are both pretty low. That being said, you will need access to a pretty decent wood shop.

Materials:

- ceramic cereal bowl about 6¼" in diameter and 2½" high
- 2 10-32 thread, 1" length flat-head Philips machine screws
- 2 10-32 thread wood tee nuts
- small piece of 1/8" thick wool felt, at least 2½" sq.
- block of hardwood you can cut down to 16" x 2.3" x 3/8"
- a dime

Machine Tools:

- wood planer
- table saw
- chop saw
- belt or disc sander
- drill press

- drill bits
- Forstner bit
- countersink bit

Hand Tools:

- pencil
- calipers or tape measure
- block sander
- medium- and fine-grit sandpaper
- clamp
- wood glue
- craft glue
- mallet or dead-blow hammer
- X-acto knife
- metal ruler
- masking tape
- Philips-head screwdriver
- awl

Step 2: Plane Hardwood Block to 3/8" Thickness

The hardwood clamp, which holds onto the front lip of the ceramic bowl, is composed of three parts: the base, a spacer, and the cap. All three parts are the same thickness, so you can make them from one 3/8" piece. First order of business: plane to 3/8".

Step 3: Cut to 2.3" Width

The hardwood clamp is meant to create a flowing line directly to the point at which it touches the iPhone/iPod touch, which is why it's measured to 2.3", the precise width of an iPhone or iPod Touch. Use a table saw to cut your 3/8" piece to a 2.3" width.

Step 4: Cut the Base, Spacer, and Cap

Use a chop or miter saw to cut your block into the three separate pieces, which will become the base, spacer, and cap—6" for the base, 2.3" for the cap, and 1" for the spacer. Make sure to account for blade thickness when measuring and cutting your pieces.

See the technical drawing for the coming measurements and cuts.

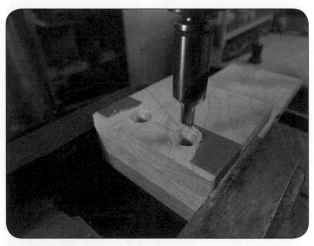

Step 5: Countersink Base for Tee Nuts

Use the technical drawing to mark holes on the bottom of the base. Now you're ready to grab your Forstner bit and carve out a small countersink using a drill press. This will make the head of those tee nuts nice and flush with the bottom of the base.

Step 6: Drill Out the Base

Now you're ready to drill out the holes for the tee nuts to slot through. Use a 1/4" bit here.

Step 8: Drill Through All

Okay, you're finally ready to drill through all three pieces and make the holes for the machine screws. A 3/16" bit will do the job. Line it up, nice and easy.

Step 9: Insert Tee Nuts

You're all set to make metal meet wood. Insert your tee nuts into the bottom of the base one at a time, making sure to position them so that the prongs face as far from the front edge as possible (this will prevent splitting). Use a mallet or dead-blow hammer and a piece of scrap wood to hammer the tee nuts until they sit flush with the bottom of the base.

Step 7: Countersink the Cap

Being mindful of the grain, take your three pieces and sandwich them together with some masking tape. Transfer them into the vice (base-side up) with a piece of scrap wood underneath.

Use a small bit to drill a pilot hole all the way through from base to the cap. This will save you from having to measure again onto the cap.

Now flip your wood sandwich right-side up, get your countersink bit, and carefully drill out countersink holes in the cap for the flat-head screws.

Step 10: Glue Spacer to Base

It's coming together now! Put a little bit of wood glue on the underside of the spacer and position it onto the front of the base. Go ahead and stack the cap on top, insert the machine screws, and see how it looks!

Step 11: Curve the Corners

It just so happens that the .36" radius you'll need is about the same as that of a U.S. dime. Grab the nearest dime and trace around the four corners of the cap and rear two corners of the base. Use a belt or disc sander to carefully sand down your corners. Remove the cap to hit its rear corners.

Step 12: Sand It Smooth

Use a block sander and hit the curves, edges, and surfaces with medium- or low-grit and then fine-grit sandpaper until you get a nice smooth finish. Leave the edges on the spacer square to maintain a seamless transition between the three stacked pieces.

Step 13: Cut Wool Felt Square

Using a sharp X-acto blade, and with the cap as a template, cut out a rounded 2.3" square from your wool felt.

Step 14: Glue Wool Felt to Cap

Use craft glue to attach your rounded wool felt square to the bottom of the cap. The wool will act as a bushing between the cap and base, creating a nice tight grip onto the lip of the ceramic bowl. Wait a few minutes for the glue to bond.

Step 15: Poke

Use an awl, or similarly pointy thing, to poke holes through the wool from the cap.

Step 16: Assemble, Dock, Amplify!

You're all set! Grab your ceramic bowl, slide it in between the base and the cap, and tighten the machine screws until they sit flush to the cap. Enjoy!

Play

Rockets, toys, and games are fun. These projects will show you how to make small devices capable of launching office supplies, board games designed for inebriation, and even DIY prescription swimming goggles.

These projects are cheap fun, and you and your kids will get several hours of amusement from these. (Except for the drinking games. Save that for the grown-ups who are children at heart.)

Tiny Catapults

By pariahcycle
(http://www.instructables.com/id/
Tiny-Catapults/)

Construct your own miniature siege engines!

Step 1: What You'll Need

- a couple of old, worn boards
- a ½" diameter dowel
- a short piece of a 2" x 2" board
- a length of thin rope
- 2 1" wood screws
- ½" drill bit
- ¾" spade bit
- drill or drill press
- table saw, circular saw, or handsaw
- miter saw, miter box, or motorized miter box
- scissors
- screwdriver
- lighter
- pencil
- roll of tape
- ruler
- miniature enemy

Step 2: Preparing Your Boards

First, use your table saw to cut your boards into two 7½" x 3½" rectangles. Once you've completed this, tape the two boards together with the broad sides touching. Then, with your pencil, mark the two longer edges "Top" and "Bottom" and the two shorter edges "Front" and "Back." Measure 1" up from the "Bottom" and 2" from the "Front" and draw an X. Next, measure 1" down from the "Top" and 3" from the "Front" and draw another X.

Now, with your boards still taped together, measure ½" up from the "Bottom" and ½" from the "Back" of the board and draw a V. Flip your taped boards over and draw another V in exactly the same place on the other side.

Last, measure 3½" from the "Front" and 1½" inches from the "Bottom" and draw a T. Do the same on the other side.

Fit your ½" bit into your drill. Drill the Xs all the way through. Drill the Vs to a 4" depth. Drive a screw into each of the Ts so about ¼" sticks out. These screws will be important when you begin building the catapult in Step 6. Separate the two boards. They should look like a mirror image of each other.

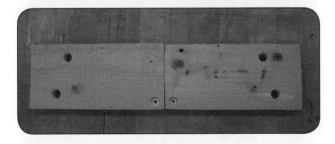

Step 3: Preparing Your Dowels

Next, use your miter saw to cut your dowel into two 5¼" lengths and one 4¼" length.

Step 4: Creating Your Catapult Arm

Cut your 2" x 2" board to a 7" length. Cut one end into a triangle shape, as pictured. With your ¾" bit, drill a ¼" deep hole on the end opposite and the side perpendicular to the triangular end. Drill a ½" hole toward the triangular end.

Step 5: Rope

Next, use your scissors to cut a 26" piece from your length of rope. If you're using braided nylon or another synthetic like I am, you'll have to use your lighter to melt the ends so they won't fray.

Step 6: Assembling the Parts

Now that you have all your parts, you can start to assemble your catapult. Tie a knot in each end of your 26" piece of rope. I prefer to use a knot called a double half hitch for this step. Then attach it to the screws you inserted in Step 2. Now, pass one of the 5 ¼" dowels through the ½" hole on the triangular side of your catapult arm. Fit each end into the lower holes on the sides. This dowel will be a pivot for the arm. Use the catapult arm to twist the rope around the dowel, as shown. There should be a fair amount of tension. Slip your other, longer dowel into the upper holes in front of the arm to maintain the tension in the rope.

Finally, notch the shorter dowel into the shallow holes you drilled toward the back, and you're done. You now have a functioning mechanism with which to wage minuscule siege warfare!

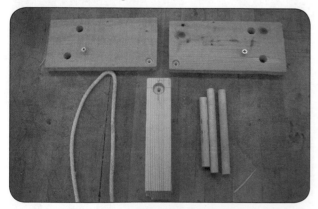

Step 7: Embellish

Don't stop there though. Embellish your creation!

Bullet Bill is a character that has appeared as an enemy in almost all of the Super Mario games from the very beginning. There are a few varieties, as their look and behavior have changed over the years. Like me, I'm sure you've been killed by Bullet Bill many times.

I thought it would be neat to build a life-size Bullet Bill model rocket, as it provided all sorts of great challenges. I ended up building two versions, both of which I thought were beautiful in many ways, and they taught me a lot of new tricks.

Version 1 is covered briefly in steps 1–3. I began this first attempt with most of the planning focused on how to create a lightweight, visually accurate model of Bullet Bill. I didn't think much about its flight-worthiness until it was complete. At that point, I knew it surely wouldn't fly well, but thought, Well, let's just go shoot this off and see what happens.

It didn't end well.

For version 2, which the photos show here, I applied the building techniques I learned with version 1 but paid closer attention to giving it a shot at actually flying. It was scaled down a bit, and built (somewhat) more like a real model rocket.

Step 1: Version 1—A Quick View

This is a quick view of version 1. Both versions were built from foam core, cardstock, thin painters' masking paper, and lots of glue. Version 1 was 19" tall and 12" in diameter (without the fins attached).

Construction details were very similar for both versions, and will be covered fully in steps 4–14.

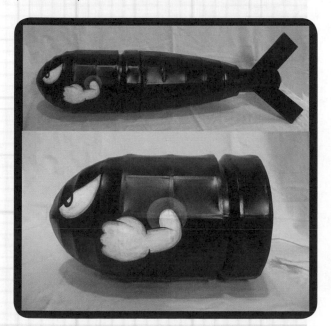

Step 2: Version 1—Finished Details

I was quite proud of the finished result of this rocket and was tempted to not even shoot it off, knowing the likely consequence.

For both versions, the launch rod goes directly through the middle of the rocket, and a cluster engine setup is used.

Step 3: Version 1—The Results

I launched this off of a small cliff with the hopes that the extra space below would allow a little more time for the chute to open. No such luck.

Step 4: Version 2—Homemade Rocket Tube

After all the work for version 1 and the awful launch, I was surprised at how quickly I wanted to get back to this. I couldn't go down like that!

I began version 2 by making a homemade paper tube. I've been making my own rocket tubes for a few years, and I'll be honest—it's tricky and can be messy and frustrating. But it is also very rewarding.

I figured out this method through a lot of trial and error. I found that using a straight piece of PVC works best as a blank. I cut out strips of brown craft paper and roll one tightly onto the blank. This is taped in place at the ends of the paper strip, making sure the edges of the strip don't overlap each other and the entire strip sits snugly on the tube.

A second strip is painted with white glue (or wood glue) that has been watered down, about one part water to four parts glue. This is carefully rolled over the first strip, being sure to cover the seams. Three or four layers of craft paper can be done, although for this I only did two. Each layer needs to be quickly rolled and pressed into place. The paper is extremely porous and the glue bonds the paper almost immediately, so you only get one chance. I've tried all sorts of other adhesives, and only white and wood glue have worked for me.

A final layer is added in the same manner, except using painter's masking paper instead. This type of paper is thinner and less porous than the craft paper and makes finishing much better. It is sealed with a coating of the watered-down glue and then lightly sanded with 220-grit sandpaper.

The paper tube is cut from the PVC and is slid off to dry. If you spread the glue thinly and evenly and don't stretch the paper too much, the tube will dry straight. If not, you'll have a warped and worthless tube, which I have made many of!

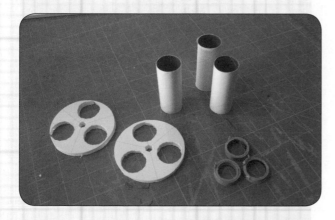

Step 5: Engine Mounts and Fins

The engine mounts were made using foam core and store-bought tubes that fit the size engines I was using (D- and E-size).

Fins were made with ¼" balsa. When gluing things like wood and paper, it's always best to put a thin layer on both surfaces, wait a few seconds, and then put them together. Once each fin was dry, fillets were added with more glue.

The most useful tools for this project were a circular protractor for laying out angles, scientific calculator for figuring radii and such, metric rulers, X-acto blades, cutting mats, and a couple of good compasses.

Step 6: Bullet Bill Nose Cone

In version 2, Bullet Bill is the nose cone. This was made with a skeleton of foam core, just like version 1. The design was laid out on paper, carefully cut out with X-acto blades, and pieced together like a puzzle. This was all glued together with regular white glue. Once the glue was dried, I used a sharp utility blade to shave off the square edges of the circular pieces on the dome.

If you just want to make a lightweight model of the Bullet Bill character, it should work well for you. Cut out the cross-section piece and use it as a stencil to trace and cut out six pieces from foam core. Match a compass up to the plans to determine the various distances needed to lay out the circle pieces. Use a protractor to lay out where the notches will go to fit the cross pieces. Study these pictures carefully to see what you need to do. It will be challenging, but you'll get it!

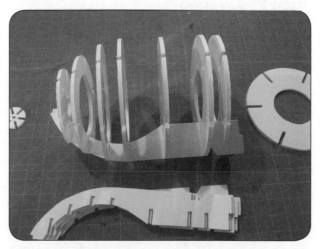

Step 7: Nose Cone to Tube Transition

The bottom of the nose cone had to receive the top of the tube snugly, but not too tightly. This should, in theory, pop off when it's time for the parachute to come out and bring the rocket safely back to the ground.

This area was made with light cardstock.

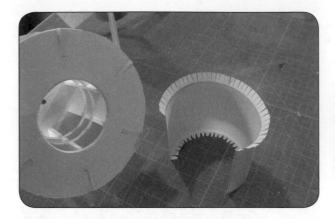

Step 8: Bullet Ridge

The ridge on the bullet was made with pieces of cardstock that were carefully measured, cut out, and glued in place.

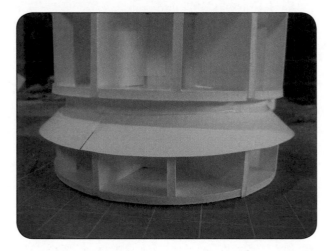

Step 9: Covering

I found that painter's masking paper is a great covering for this type of model. Each piece of covering is cut out separately, painted entirely with watered-down glue, and quickly glued in place. As the glue-wash dries, the piece of covering stretches and becomes tight. A light coating of glue over the entire surface helps strengthen the covering.

Step 10: Rocket Body

The rocket body was made of foam core and was built directly onto the tube and covered in the same manner as the nose cone.

Step 11: Painting

A few coats of primer were used to seal up the paper and make it ready for the final coat of paint. The rocket was painted with two coats of flat black spray paint.

Step 12: Details

I made some stencils to help me lay out the details for the rocket. The details were painted on with craft paint, and the rocket received a light coat of lacquer to seal it up and make everything shine.

Step 13: Parachute

The parachute was made from rip-stop nylon. I hit the edges with just a touch of flame to melt them and keep them from fraying.

Step 14: Launch Preparation

I did some balance tests and determined that I needed to add about 2oz to the nose to make this flight-worthy. I cut out one of the panels on the nose, added the right amount of weight, and patched it up. The final flight-ready weight was just a little over one pound.

The parachute, wadding, and nose cone had to be prepared for launch with the launch rod in place. Three D-size engines were used.

The launch pad is homemade, and the launch controller is a modified Estes cheap-o that I hook up to my cordless drill battery. For cluster engine launches, I have an octopus-like attachment that works very well.

Step 15: Final Thoughts

Bullet Bill version 2's flight was fantastic. The rocket flew straight, and it flew high.

The parachute failure just killed me, though. It was due to a stupid, avoidable oversight in the design. When the chute deployed, it went straight into the nose cone, and there it stayed. If I had built a paper cylinder of some kind inside the back of the nose cone, it would have prevented the chute from being shot up inside of it and getting stuck.

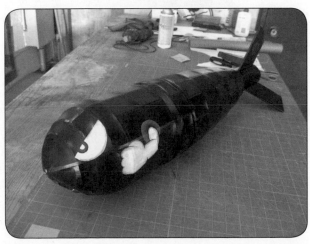

Homemade Bound Book

By KaptinScarlet
(http://www.instructables.com/id/How-to-bind-your-own-Hardback-Book/)

The art of book binding is an ancient craft, but actually it is not very difficult to do. With almost no practice you can get really awesome results. If you are on the lookout for fun craft projects or quick ways of making nice presents and gifts, then this could be the project for you. I know that there are other Instructables on the art of book binding, but this project is meant to be a simple and quick project that will result in a book that looks like it has been professionally made without the need for any special equipment.

All you will need is: about 32 A4 or U.S. letter-sized sheets of paper to make a half A4 (half U.S. letter-sized book), although small books can be made, as can ones with more pages. You can use tracing paper, thick or thin paper, and, of course, colored or even preprinted paper. You will need PVA (Elmer's white glue) or a rubber fabric adhesive. A glue gun would help with one of the stages, but is not mandatory. You also need some stiff or corrugated cardboard and some fabric or leather—any old stuff will do for the cover. I used the fabric from some old trousers that were being thrown out. You could use a bit of leather, some old curtains, cushion covers, etc. I'm sure you get the idea.

Step 1: Stack Your Paper Neatly in at Least Four Piles of Eight Sheets

You are going to be binding your paper in eight-sheet folios. Of course, you could do more or less. I have found eight sheets to be a good number. Since you are folding the paper in half, each sheet is going to make four pages of your book—this eight-sheet stack is going to make 32 pages. Your book should have at least four of these eight-sheet folios, which will therefore make 128 pages. You can use plain paper or paper upon which you have already printed something.

Step 2: Fold Each Stack in Half

As neatly as possible, and keeping the paper as lined up as possible, fold each pile of eight sheets in half cross-wise.

Step 3: Unfold the Paper and Turn Over

Making sure you keep the paper nice and straight, unfold each stack of eight sheets and turn it over.

Step 4: Staple the Pages Together

I have a long-arm stapler, but if you don't have one of those, just do the following: open your stapler, place the upturned paper stack on top of an eraser (positioned where you want to staple, which will be about 2" from the edge of the page, exactly on the crease) and slowly but firmly push down on the stapler until you have stapled the pages. Turn over the pages and pull off the eraser, then fold over the staple ends with the blunt end of a dinner knife or your thumbnail, being careful not to break it or stab yourself. Repeat at the other end of the crease so that each page has just two staples in it. If you, like me, have a long-arm stapler, simply staple the eight-sheet stack in two places.

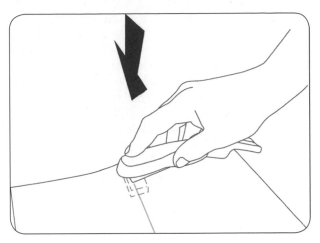

Step 5: Glue the Binding onto the Folios

You are now going to make the heart of the book. You have made at least four of the eight-sheet/32-page folios, and they need to be stuck together. First, cut a piece of thin fabric the same length as the page height and about five times the thickness of all the folios held together. Hold the folios tightly together and all lined up. Either get a friend to help or clip the folios together using giant paper clips or bull dog clips (or even a rubber band I guess). When they are all nicely aligned apply glue to just the spines of the folios. You can use white glue for this (this was what white glue was originally made for), but you must be careful not to let it drip down in to the gaps between the folios. Alternatively you can use hot glue for this part. Again, hot glue is used in the book binding industry, so it is perfect for the job. Before it has a chance to set, quickly turn over the wad of folios and glue them to the piece of fabric so that some fabric sticks out beyond each side (i.e., it is not glued to the pages)

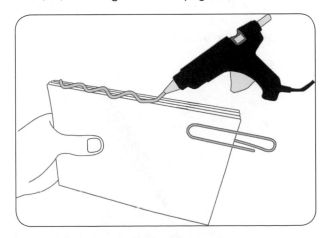

Step 6: Trim the Bound Folios

You may be able to get your bound pages trimmed by a paper cutter at your local print or copy shop. Failing that, you can trim the folios a tiny bit yourself. Beware that the first time you do this you might end up making more of a mess of the edge of the paper than if you had just left it. It takes a bit of practice and a sharp craft knife or scalpel (definitely NOT something for children to do on their own). If you want to trim, then the most important edge to trim is the edge opposite the binding, because when the paper is folded over all the pages get to be slightly different lengths depending on where they are in the folio stack. The trick is to hold the rule very steady and make many repeated cuts, being careful to cut in the same groove. Try to ensure that at each cut the paper on at least one layer is cut from edge to edge. If you have access to a proper paper cutter that can cut through paper stacks (i.e., at work or at school) then this is the time to use that, as it will give you the most awesome finish). Trimming is by no means necessary. Trimming or not, you have now finished the paper part of the book and it's time to move on to the cover.

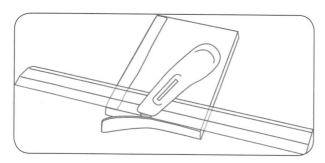

Step 7: Mark and Cut Out the Cover Boards

Place the bound folios on a piece of stiff card so that the bound edge lines up with one straight edge. Then draw round the paper, allowing about ¼"/5mm border on the three other edges. Cut the card out, and then cut a duplicate. Using corrugated cardboard as the cover is fine, as is thin foam core (foamboard), but the best kind of card is the stiff card that is used as the backing for drawing and sketching pads.

Step 8: Make the Book Spine

Loosely assemble the bound paper and the covers. Press them together and then measure their combined thickness, noting it on a piece of scrap paper. Cut the spine so that it is the thickness of the covers and the paper together and the same length as the height of the book covers.

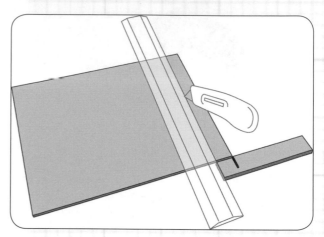

Step 9: Mark and Cut the Material

Position the book covers and the spine on the reverse of your chosen fabric or leather and mark out so that there is a border of about 1"/25mm all around. Cut out the material. As already mentioned, you can use any material you want, although very thick material will be difficult to fold and glue. I used material from a pair of trousers.

Step 10: Glue the Cover Board and Spine in Place

Using white glue or rubber cement, smear an even coating over the boards and place them face down on the wrong side of the material (i.e., the side of the material that you don't normally see, which has the pattern the wrong way round, etc.). Make sure you stick them neatly in a row so that they are aligned with each other and straight. Also make sure that there is a gap of about one or two thicknesses of the card you are using between the spine and each of the cover boards to allow the flexibility needed for the book to close.

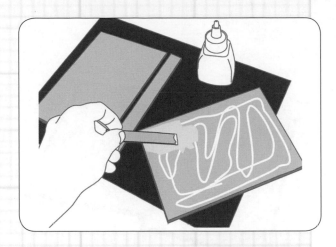

Step 11: Finish the Edges of the Cover

Smear an even layer of white glue or rubber cement round the edge of the boards and fold over the material to cover the edge, working on one edge at a time. Do opposite ends first and then fold the other ends over on top so that all the folds go the same way. If you are using thick material, you may well have to cut away some of the material that is going to be hidden under the fold over to stop the corners from getting too bulky.

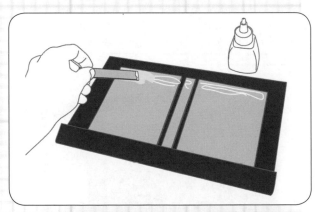

Step 12: Glue the Paper into the Covers

Things are starting to shape up now. Smear some white glue (or rubber cement) in two stripes down the middle edges of the cover boards, being careful not to get any glue on the spine board. Then place

the bound paper wad so that it is centrally resting on the spine board and only the thin cotton "wings" are glued to the cover boards. The spine should not be glued to the bound paper wad, although you should make sure that the paper wad is glued to the cover boards right up to their edges, because this is the joint that makes the book strong and stops the page block from falling out of the cover. It is best if you wait for this part to dry before moving on to the next step. It is probably a good idea to leave the book lying on its back with the paper supported by to food cans while it dries. If you leave it to dry closed, bits of it might stick together that you don't want sticking together.

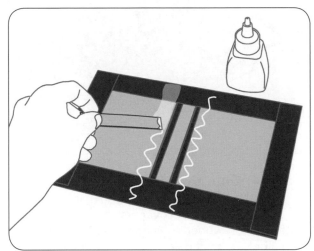

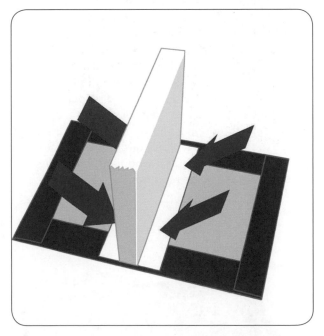

Step 13: Cut Out Your Lining Paper

Your book is nearly finished. Functionally, it is already a hardback book; however, the next step will make it look like a real book and will cover up all the bits of folded -over material. For the lining paper you can use almost any type of paper. Traditionally, marbled paper was used. Now you can make this yourself or buy it in sheet form from most good craft shops. Or alternatively, you can use a bit of old gift wrapping paper, or even just plain old brown packing paper. Be as creative as you can here—the lining paper is like the lining of an expensive suit in that it is hidden until it is revealed by someone opening it. Ideally you want the lining paper to be a fraction smaller than the paper wad's height so that you can line it up neatly, and twice as long as the paper wad's width so that it covers the inside of the hard cover (see next step).

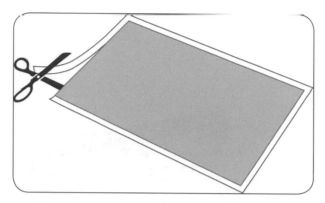

Step 14: Glue the Lining in Place

Fold the lining paper sheet in half crosswise. Smear the inside of the cover and the first page with white glue or rubber solution glue. Carefully place one half of the folded lining paper on the glued first page so that it lines up neatly with the edge of the paper. Then, making sure that it goes in to the corner of the joint between the paper and the cover, fold the liner out and glue it to the inside of the cover so that it covers up all the folded over material and the inside of the cardboard covers. Repeat for the back of the book. That's it—you're done! If the first paper goes a bit wrinkly as it dries out, wait for at least a day for it to dry really thoroughly and then iron over the page using a medium iron. It won't get all the wrinkles out, but it will make the page a whole lot flatter. Just try to use less glue for the next book.

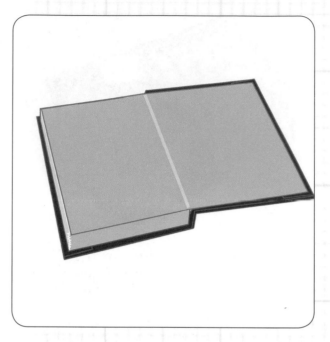

Step 15: Experiment and Make Loads of Different Books

Make books as presents, make them for school, and make them for friends. I made the jeans one with a pocket after my niece suggested that I use the pockets from the trousers for pens and stuff. It seems to work rather well. See what you can come up!

Full-Size Do-It-Yourself R2D2

By BrianH
(http://www.instructables.com/id/Full-Size-
R2D2-on-a-budget/)

This is a prop I built for a Star Wars party. I didn't want to spend a lot, but I did want it to look cool. I know that there are some incredibly talented folks who put years of effort into making the awesome R2D2 and other droids, but I wanted something inexpensive and I only had a few months until the party. So rather than use sheet metal and fiberglass, I used mostly cardboard and drywall joint compound. I also used a lot of stuff that I had in my junk box.

Step 1: R2D2 Frame and Covering

Once I found the overall dimensions of R2D2, I was able to calculate the size of each piece based on photos found online. R2D2 is about 43" tall, and the body is about 18" in diameter (not counting the legs).

I acquired a few refrigerator boxes at a local retailer and got to work. I created a frame for the body and then wrapped the cardboard around the frame. This is a bit tricky. You'll need to soften—but not drench—the cardboard by spraying it with water and letting the moisture soak through the layers. When it's sufficiently soft, you're ready to wrap it around the frame. Apply hot glue to the edges of

the frame and attach the softened cardboard sheet to it. I recommend that you get some assistance with this step. It has a few inconsistencies, but we'll compensate for that later.

Step 2: Cutting Out and Assembling the Legs

The legs are also made of cardboard, so I drew an outline on the cardboard and cut out a total of four identical pieces. I left a lot of extra cardboard at the bottom since I wasn't quite sure what I wanted to do with the feet. I then assembled the legs with several long strips of cardboard, softened as before and wrapped around the sides of the leg. Patience is key; you have to allow time for the softened cardboard to form to the shape that you want. I'm getting better with the use of the hot glue gun!

To help keep the two halves of the leg separated by the proper distance, I tacked in a 2" x 4" piece of lumber temporarily between the two halves of the leg. I later ended up gluing a 2" x 4" in permanently, but it was oriented so that when assembled with the body, I could put a long wood screw through the wood and securely attach it to the body, which had another piece of wood glued into its inside.

The cardboard, however, has the unmistakable look of cardboard. I decided to cover the legs and the body with drywall joint compound and sanded it flat. This covers a number of goofs and bumps.

Step 3: The Body—Altering My Plans

My inspiration for creating this project was partially from an R2D2 promotional Pepsi beverage cooler that I saw while doing a Google image search. The body of the beverage cooler went all the way to the ground, which makes sense for the cooler and was a simpler design. This is what I intended to do, but I changed my mind and decided to make it more like the real R2D2. I cut off the bottom, sliced about 30 angled "fingers" in the bottom, and folded them toward the center to form a bevel that looks more authentic.

Step 4: Building the Head

My first thought was to create the head out of paper maché applied to a balloon, but I was unable to find a properly sized balloon that matched the diameter of the body, so I decided on a ribbed design. This was similar to the way I made model airplane wings when I was a kid. Unfortunately, I forgot to take a picture before I put on the paper maché, so you'll have to imagine what the ribbed cardboard looks like.

The downside of the ribbed method is that the ribs show through. It is going to get several coats of drywall joint compound to make it more spherical. In hindsight, I should have spent more time looking for a balloon. The ribbed method never got perfectly spherical.

To give the paper maché more strength, I coated the inside with a layer of expanding foam. Between the cardboard, hot glue, paper maché, and a lot of drywall joint compound, the head is getting rather heavy.

Step 5: Smoothing the Body and Adding Details

The body has now taken form and is covered with the drywall joint compound. I used a very wide strip of sandpaper attached to a piece of wood to make the body smooth and uniformly shaped. I spray painted the body white to seal the joint compound. I found a drawing of R2D2's body detail, so I printed it out and attached it to the body so that I could make the appropriate marks where the boxes would go. I made a few masks for spray painting and covered up areas that were to remain white. A sharpie and a straight edge were all I needed to draw the outlines.

Step 6: Spray Painting R2D2's Head

After getting R2D2's head smooth, I spray painted it metallic silver. The spray paint is very silvery, but I later found that it's not as durable as other spray paints; even removable tape leaves a mark on it. I laid out the design details and sprayed on the blue, then carefully removed the tape when it was dry.

Step 7: Adding Details to R2D2's Head

R2D2's "face" is a focal point, so I wanted to add some carefully crafted pieces. R2's "eye" is made from a lens from a dollar store plastic magnifying glass. In the movies, it always looks like a black void, so I spray painted the back side of the lens black and placed it into a recessed hole in its frame. The frame is made from a scrap piece of MDF (medium density fiberboard). I like MDF since it cuts well and is easily smoothed.

The red/blue circle was made from a scrap of PVC pipe, and I attached a translucent piece of Plexiglas to the PVC. So how does one make it blink?

At the dollar store I found a flashing LED gadget that contained three colored LEDs. I gutted the gadget for its circuitry and installed it into the PVC tube. But since I only wanted red and blue, I removed the green LED and added another red LED in its place. And, finally, it's time for the projector that R2D2 uses to project the memorable holographic image of princess Leia saying, "Help me Obi Wan Kenobi, you're our only hope." Okay, so mine doesn't project anything, but I used a short piece of metal tube from a discarded vacuum cleaner and a fishing bobber painted grey.

Step 8: Attaching the Legs

Next step—attaching the legs. Since the little droid may end up in storage at some point, I wanted to make sure that I could easily assemble and disassemble it. I decided to make the legs removable, yet sturdy enough to hold the load. As I mentioned earlier, I glued some solid pieces of wood on the inside of the body and on the inside of the legs. This way, I can run a couple of long wood screws through the legs and into the body. After the screws were in, I covered up the holes with a piece of decorative trim.

Step 9: Final Assembly

The head was designed to simply slide on the top of the body, and it's ready to go. I was concerned that R2D2 would be a little top heavy and possibly fall over, but it appears that the large feet keep it steady. Now all that's left to do is install a MP3 player with some amplified speakers and some appropriate sound effects.

Recently I was invited by a couple of friends of mine to their home. They have an awesome collection of classic G.I. JOE action figures. Some of them were damaged because the inner rubber band that put them together was broken. Luckily, they kept the parts. Then I took one of the apparently good figures and I accidentally broke its rubber band. Now I have in my hands the legs, hip, and chest of another dead JOE.

Although I was ashamed, my friends told me I didn't need to blame myself. After all, it was normal age damage on the classic JOEs. Maybe one day they would buy some rubber bands for the action figures. Or maybe not.

I didn't want to leave without making amends for my destruction. But what could I do? I didn't have any rubber bands, nor did I have my Dremel or Sonic Screwdriver. So I used something everybody has: a condom. It worked so well my friends asked me to fix other figures. It's a simple solution that can give a new life to your old G.I. JOEs. You can even use expired condoms.

And here I am, using condoms to repair some old toys.

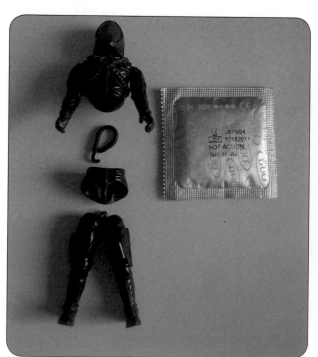

Step 1: Materials

You will need:

- a classic G.I. JOE action figure, with the inner rubber band broken
- condom
- scissors
- tweezers (or anything for grabbing the rubber band, like a paperclip)
- small screwdriver

Step 2: The Condom

First, transform the condom into a rubber band. Unroll it and cut the base ring off. Wash it.

(CAUTION: Please, for God's sake, use a NEW condom. The rest of the condom will become useless for its original purpose. So please again, PLEASE! Don't try to use it).

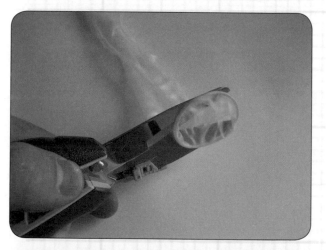

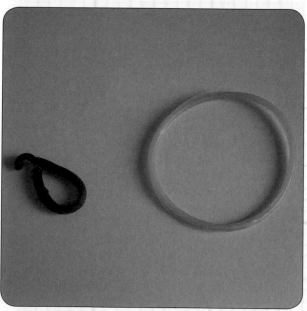

Step 3: The Torso

With the screwdriver, remove the screw. Remove the chest. Watch out for the correct position of the arms.

Step 5: Arm It Again

Put the rubber band in the center of the chest. Make another loop to reduce the elasticity. Put on the head, arms, and chest and screw it closed. It's done.

Step 4: The Legs

Hook the condom's rubber band (use it in two loops) on the legs' hook and pass it across the hip.

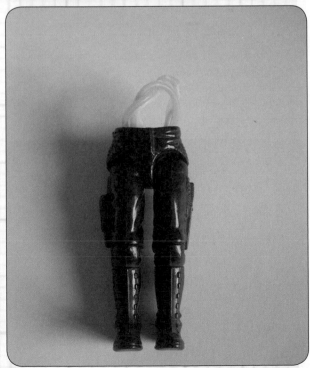

I provide childcare in my home for three toddlers, and I've noticed that they really love board books with flaps that open. So I made three customized lift-the-flap books for them. This Instructable will explain how to make your own and give some tips on how to make the process a little easier.

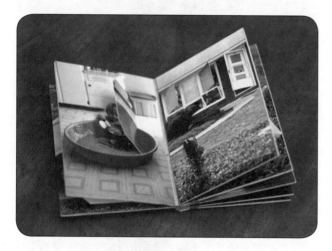

Step 1: Edit Photos

Before assembling the book, you need to create two prints for each page. During Step 2 you will cut through the top layer to make a flap that will reveal someone (or something) on the layer underneath. This is easiest to do with a photo editing program that supports multiple layers (Photoshop Elements 2.0 worked fine for me). Note that I only printed the first two images. The second two are just to help explain how to use multiple layers for alignment. I found it helpful to cut the windows out of the top layer and place them on a separate layer in Photoshop. That way I could hide the layer with the windows temporarily while I dropped my images of mom, dad, girl, and the squirrel onto a layer under the top layer for scaling.

Since the windows are cut out and hidden you will be able to see the people through the openings and scale them to fit. Then you can turn the layer with the windows and doors on and off to test the flaps. Once you have made the two layers for each page, and a front and back cover, you can print out all your prints—either at home if you have a photo printer or at your local print shop. (I printed mine over the Internet via the one hour photo center at Walmart.)

I would recommend a matte finish, which won't show fingerprints as quickly as glossy will.

Step 2: Cut an Old Board Book to Size

On your way to pick up your photos at the print shop, swing by your local thrift store and get a board book to use as a base. The book should be at least 4" x 6" in order to fit the prints. I cut mine down to exactly 4" x 6" using a saber saw with a fine blade. You could also use a utility knife to cut one page at a time. I spray painted the binding black to hide the old book title. As another alternative (which I'll probably try on my next book) you could glue the photos onto individual pieces of cardboard and then bind it yourself, or take it to a print shop and get it spiral bound. Using an old board book as my base spared me from dealing with binding the thick pages, but it ended up making it difficult to close the book due to the extra thickness of the four prints between pages. This isn't all bad though, because it makes it much easier for a toddler to turn the pages since they stand apart.

Step 3: Cut the Flaps

This is the trickiest part of the project. Take an X-acto knife or razor blade and carefully cut three sides of your doors and windows to make flaps. Make sure you have a good, sharp blade in the knife and use a metal straight edge to make straight lines. Wouldn't a laser cutter be handy for this task?

Tip: It's a good idea to plan your book before you start cutting so you know which images will be for left-hand pages and which will be for right-hand pages. Then when you are cutting the flaps, always put the uncut edge toward the inside of the book. That way the flaps will automatically close when the book is closed. If you put the uncut edge toward the outside of the book (or top or bottom) you will tend to have problems with the flaps getting squashed or pressed into the open position.

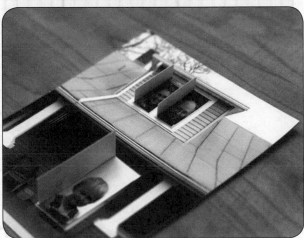

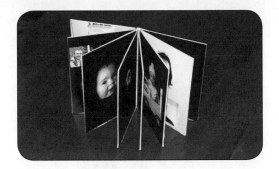

Step 4: Glue the Prints onto the Board Book

Once you have all your flaps cut, you can start gluing the prints onto the board book pages. The bottom layer prints can just be sprayed and then attached to the board book, but the top layer prints will need to be protected with low-tack masking tape or other shielding to avoid getting spray glue on the flaps. (You obviously don't want to glue your flaps closed!) I supported my prints on wire mesh. If you just laid them directly on newspaper and then sprayed on the adhesive you would tend to have problems with the edges of the prints sticking to the newspaper.

Tip: I used 3M Super 77 multipurpose spray adhesive. Don't spray a print and then immediately try to glue it into the book. You will get glue on your fingers and then on the print, and it will be much messier and more difficult than necessary. Instead, lay out all your prints and spray them all at once, then wait five minutes for the glue to partially dry. After five minutes the prints will still stick very well to paper but will hardly stick to your fingers at all.

Step 5: To Finish

The most important and final step: Leave the book fanned open with all the flaps open overnight to dry completely. The last thing you want at this stage is to glue your flaps shut or to glue entire pages together. One other minor detail I added was a title on the binding. I just printed out some text on my laser printer, cut it down to a narrow strip, and then used clear packing tape to attach it to the binding. I also used the spray adhesive to attach single prints (no flaps) to the front and back covers.

By the way, if the whole process of making two layers and cutting the flaps sounds too complicated, you can still make a fun custom book for a toddler by making single prints in Photoshop (like image 3 on Step 1) and just gluing those onto a board book.

Photo Block Puzzle

By noahw
(http://www.instructables.com/id/Photo-Block-Puzzle/)

These photo blocks make a great gift for a loved one or friend and are a fun way to interact with your favorite photos. At home in your hand, on the coffee table, or displayed on a shelf, they call to be played with and enjoyed. This particular 3" x 3" block layout displays as few as 6 and as many 54 different photos, but you can scale the project up and make more blocks to display even more photos and make the puzzle harder to assemble.

This project took only a few hours to make, would be great to build with kids or first-timers in the shop, and was a great custom gift for the holidays.

Step 1: Dimension Wood on Table Saw

The photo blocks were made from an old fir 4" x 4" post that was sitting outside in the shop yard. Using a table saw, we cut the 4" x 4" down to approximately 3" x 3". You can choose whatever size you'd like, as this method is totally scalable—just make sure that the length, width, and depth of the blocks are the same so you end up with perfect cubes.

Step 2: Cut Cubes on Chop Saw

Trim the cubes to their final dimension size on the chop saw. We set a simple maple stop block in place on the saw so that every cut would be exactly the same. Our photo puzzle was made from nine 3" x 3" x 3" blocks to form a single 9" x 9" surface when assembled.

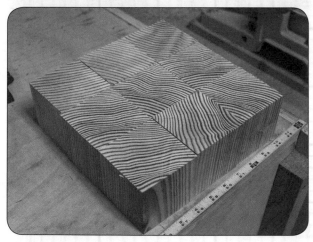

Step 3: Clamp and Sand

Once you have all of the blocks cut to size, clamp them together using some straight edges (we used some scrap steel square tube) in their assembled form. Place a board on top of the assembled puzzle and level any blocks that misaligned in the clamping process with a dead blow or rubber mallet. Next, sand the top surface of the blocks to eliminate any small imperfections—120-grit paper is sufficient, as the wood will be getting a covering later on and won't be a finished surface.

little more varied—i.e., nature scene, up-close face shots, group shot with people—make an easier puzzle since each face of the cube is obviously different then the next.

Step 4: Number and Rotate Five Times

Once the top surface is sanded, mark all of the blocks on that side with the same number, rotate each block to a new un-sanded side, and repeat the whacking and sanding process. Repeat this process five more times so you get to all six sides of the blocks. Once fully sanded, set the blocks aside and head to the computer.

Step 6: Print

Print your photos on high-quality photo paper. We had access to an 11" x 14" photo printer to print the large 9.25" square photos. If you don't have access to a large printer, make your blocks smaller or have your photos printed at the drug store on their commercial machine capable of handling the larger size.

Step 5: Size Photos

Select six or more of your favorite photos that you'd like to display. For this particular project, we chose to display five large photos on five sides and then have the sixth side be a composite of individual, smaller photos.

Crop and adjust your photos in Photoshop. When you are cropping, make sure to crop a slightly larger area of the photo than the area of your photo blocks, which gives you enough printed photo to have a little wiggle room when gluing and trimming to the final size once they are affixed. We cropped our large photos to 9¼" x 9¼" and our smaller individual photos to 3¼" x 3¼".

Tip: If you are going to print multiple photos per page, make sure that the resolution of your cropped photos are all the same in Photoshop.

Keep your puzzle block audience in mind while selecting your photos. Similar photos for each side make for a more difficult puzzle. Photos that are a

Step 7: Cut Out Photos

Cut each photo. There's no need to be dead-on with this step, as each picture will get trimmed to size later on.

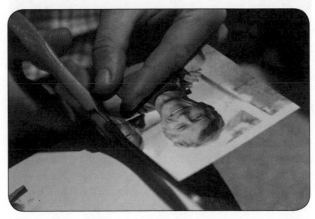

Step 8: Glue— Small Photo Method

To attach the photos to the wood blocks we used Aleene's Tacky All-Purpose Glue, which can be found at most craft stores. This product works exceptionally well to bind paper to wood and can be watered down to your desired glue thickness. We definitely recommend watering down the glue from its rubbery concentrated state to something that paints a bit more easily. Paint the glue directly on to the block using a brush.

For the individual photos (smaller photos) we placed the photo face-up directly on the block and positioned it to the portion of the photo we wanted displayed. Press firmly down on the photo to ensure a good glue seal. When performing this step, make sure all of the individual photos are placed on the same number on each block—this is important later for the larger puzzle photos.

Step 9: Trim to Size—Small Photo Method

Once the glue dries, flip the block upside down on a clean surface to avoid scratches to the photo. Using an X-acto knife or box cutter, trim the photo to the size of the block. Be careful not to cut into the block itself. This process takes just a tiny bit of practice, but is easy to get the hang of.

Step 10: Cut Large Photo

Cut the large photos out from the print job.

Step 11: Glue—Large Photo Method

For the larger photos, place the photo face down on a clean surface and paint glue on to the back of the photo. Place a selected side of the blocks down onto the back of the glue-covered photo. Make sure all of the blocks are straight in relation to the photo as well as tightly nestled against each other. You should have a border around the nine blocks when you are done. Let the blocks dry like this, allowing the weight of the blocks to keep the photo flat as the glue dries.

Step 12: Trim— Large Photo Method

Now that your puzzle has dried, you can trim off the border of the large photo using either an X-acto knife or box cutter.

Please note, you will cut apart the blocks in the next step, this is only to remove the border.

Step 13: Cut Blocks Apart

Once the border is removed, you can now carefully flip the blocks over so that the large photo you just glued is displayed face up. Using your X-acto knife or box cutter, carefully cut in between each block by starting at one end where you can see the distinct separation between blocks and allowing the knife to follow in between the blocks for each cut. The groove between blocks should guide the knife on its path so you get nice clean cuts. Repeat steps 10 through 13 for each of your large pictures until all the sides of the photo block puzzle are covered.

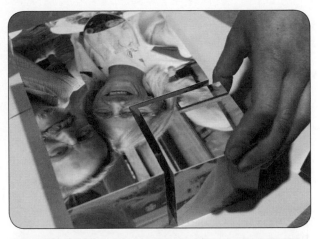

Step 14: Optional Clear Coat

Clear coating is something that you might want to consider before using your photo blocks. It will help to protect the photos from wear and tear. We chose not to clear coat our photo blocks simply because these are pretty light duty and were gifted to a grandmother, rather than, say, a toddler. Clear coatings should be applied either between steps 6 and 7 after the photos are printed or on the finished blocks as a final step.

While there are many professional-quality clear coats for digital prints, a simple coat or two of Krylon Crystal Clear will suffice. Flat or glossy, the choice is, of course, yours.

Cy-Barbie!

By M. C. Langer
(http://www.instructables.com/id/
Upgrading-an-abandoned-Barbie-into-a-
CYBARBIE/)

I'm not the most popular man when it comes to Barbie dolls. I'm on Mattel's Black List and am hated by my female cousins. (Good thing they haven't seen my failed attempts.) One day, I was walking at my favorite flea market when I found some old and abandoned Barbies with damaged hair. One of them even had arms from another Barbie. It's redemption time!

I bought two Barbies. One of them I decided to transform into an awesome Barbie so I cleaned and repaired her body. I made futuristic new clothes and gave her a radical hairstyle. Oh, and a brand new mech, Power Loader style, for kicking some serious butt! And the other Barbie? Well, old habits die hard . . .

Step 1: Materials

Do you remember every time I said, "Always have junk in stock"? Well, that's where you'll get most of your materials:
- a wireless phone base
- PC joysticks
- a saucepan handler
- Walkman headphones
- airplane headphones
- damaged toys
- a pump handler
- the electromechanical caterpillars from an R/C car (if you have the whole R/C car, much better!)
- 1 Barbie

- Sugru (depends on the clothes you want for your doll)
- 2 big LEDs.
- 2 DPDT lever switch
- 1 simple switch
- iron angles
- red and black wire
- screws and bolts
- tin soldering

Tools:
- Dremel rotary tool
- tweezers
- screwdrivers
- scalpel
- pliers
- wire cutters
- screwdriver kit
- soldering iron
- superglue

And don't forget:
- If you don't have it, replace it!
- Use protective equipment (dust mask and goggles).
- Beware of drilled and soldered hot surfaces.
- Work in a well-ventilated area.
- Always have junk in stock.
- Enjoy!

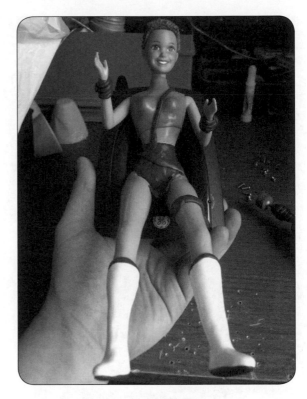

Step 2: Extreme Makeover

First, you have to clean Barbie with water, a sponge, and dish detergent. Cut her hair, too. For the clothes, I used Sugru, orange, black, and white colors. I used soapy water for a better texture.

Try to make a mini-skirt with Sugru for your first time. Now, we have our Futuristic Fashion Barbie.

Step 3: Starting the Mech

Take the phone base, open it, and remove the circuits. You will only need the plastic case. Keep the case screws in a safe place. You will need them to close the case later. The front part of the base will be the mech's cockpit where the Barbie will sit. Keep it disassembled. Take the back part of the case and attach the pump handler (it will be the spine and shoulders) and a printer piece on top (Barbie's headrest).

Step 4: The Arms

For each arm you will need the following plastic parts:

Arm:
- 1 joystick handler (disassembled)
- half saucepan handler
- 1 iron angle

Pincer:
- 1 oven knob
- 2 cash register pincers (or something who look like pincers)
- 1 toy car wheel

Attach the pieces on the way indicated in the pictures to make the two arms.

Step 5: Fixing Arms and Lower Pillar

Attach the arms on each side of the pump handler. On the lower side of the base, attach the pillar (I used one piece from a PC joystick). The pillar will join the body to the locomotion mechanism (the caterpillars). It's much better if the pillar is hollow because you will need to pass some wires through it.

Step 6: The Cockpit

You will need the front part of the phone base, the Barbie, the diadem of the Walkman headset, and two airplane earphones. Sit the Barbie on the front part. Use a screw to fix her to the chair. Cut the diadem in half and put each half on each of Barbie's shoulders as seat belts. Fix them with screws. The ear parts of the earphones will be the controls. Remove them from the rest of the headphones. Screw each one to iron angles and on each side of the seat, within reach of Barbie's hands.

Step 7: Locomotion

Important: If your caterpillar R/C car still has a working R/C (or you have a R/C system available for installing in the caterpillar), then keep the R/C (or install it) and just attach the pillar to the car and the base front part (seat) to the body. I only found the car without radio control so in Step 8 I will show how to make a simple motion control for the mech's back.

Open the mechanism and remove the remainder circuits. Connect long wires to each motor and to the battery pack. Pass them through holes on the back part of the car and then introduce them into the pillar towards the mech's back. Attach the pillar to the car, close the car, and attach the seat to the mech's body.

eight, but I use only six). Now you have your very own Barbie ready to roll with kick-butt action!

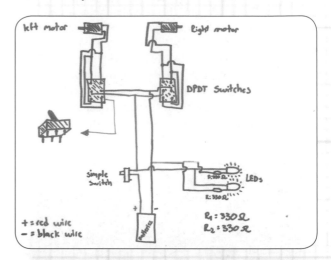

Step 8: Electronics and Controls

We will make a simple motion control with the three switches. The simple switch will energize the whole system, lighting the LEDs. The two DPDT lever switches will control the way the mech will move. First "program" the motion turning the DPDT switches, and then turn on the simple switch. Right switch controls right caterpillar, left switch controls left caterpillar.

DPDT Motion Options:

- Both switches up: Forward
- Both switches on the center: Off
- Both switches down: Back
- Right switch up/down, left switch on the center: Forward/Back motion to the left
- Left switch up/down, right switch on the center: Forward/Back motion to the right
- Right switch up, left switch down: Counter-clock spinning
- Right switch down, left switch up: Clock spinning

Install the control on the back, add more weapons, and insert the batteries (the battery pack has room for

Blacklight BattleShots

By kaptaink_cg

(http://www.instructables.com/id/Ultimate-Blacklight-BattleShots/)

Beer pong is overrated and has become a bit passé. I have been searching for a drinking game with a bit more strategy and panache. Although I only recently learned of the drinking version of the old Battleship board game, it has apparently been around for a while. However, all of the adaptations I've seen have left a lot to be desired. And so I set out to create the ultimate Battle Shots game: portable, black-lit, magnetic, and spill-resistant. Enjoy!

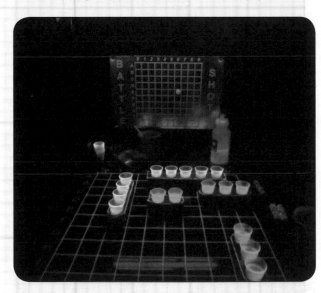

Step 1: Materials, Supplies, and Tools

Materials:
- 4' x 8 'x ½" sheet of plywood
- 2" x 12" x 3' plank of pine
- 2' x 4' x 1/16" sheet of transparent acrylic (Plexiglas) OR two 2 'x 2' x 1/16" sheets
- 12" x 16" steel sheets
- 24" blacklights
- small hinges
- #10-24 3/4" Machine Screws
- four #10-24 lock nuts
- door handle
- medium U-shaped staples
- small bungee
- 100 3/4"Ø magnets
- 50 1oz. neon shotglasses
- 9 1½" wood screws
- sheets of sticky-back black felt

Supplies:
- various fluorescent acrylic paints
- 3 cans grey primer
- fluorescent spray paint
- can black spray paint
- can black furniture paint
- package transparent sticky-back paper
- tube clear bathroom caulking
- roll 1" painter's tape
- finishing nails
- electrical tape
- wood glue
- wood putty
- parchment (or wax) paper
- gin and tonics

Tools:
- patience
- razor blades
- drill with various bits, including a countersink bit
- 1 ½"Ø Forstner bit
- wire strippers
- screwdriver
- hammer
- measuring tape/carpenter's square
- T-square or ruler
- iron
- syringe
- table saw
- router
- putty knife
- sander
- band saw
- corner clamps
- laser printer

Step 2: Print Out Plans and Templates

Visit this Instructables' website to download the PDF files. Print two copies of the Stickyback_8x11.pdf on the Transparent sticky-back paper. Print two copies of the 11x17Sheets.pdf on (preferably) heavy 11x17 sheets. Print one set of the Layouts.pdf on regular 8 1/2"x11" paper.

Step 3: Build Lower Boards

If you have a single 2' x 4' sheet of Plexiglas you will need to cut it in half. Take your carpenter's square and a razor blade and score it to where you want it to break. Be sure to score it deeply. Placing it on an edge beneath the score line, bend one end of the acrylic down and it should snap. You can see from the photos that I didn't score it well enough and my break wasn't a straight line. Fortunately I was still able to use both pieces.

Remove the film from one side of the acrylic only. Take the large grid-layout sticky-back sheets and apply them to the exposed side of the acrylic. Using a sharp razor blade, remove all sticky-back sheets, leaving only the lines and lettering.

Using multiple thin coats, spray paint all of the exposed acrylic black. After the paint is no longer tacky, but before it has fully cured, remove all of the remaining sticky-back paper. You should be left with crisp transparent lines and lettering.

Choose the fluorescent colors you want and begin painting over all the transparent areas. It's rather difficult to paint on Plexiglas. At first I had to use multiple coats, laying down as much paint as I could with each pass. Later I discovered painting the gridlines was much easier when I used a small syringe.

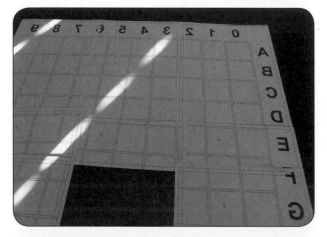

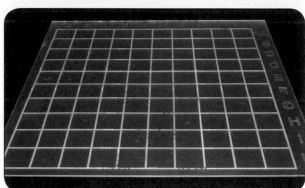

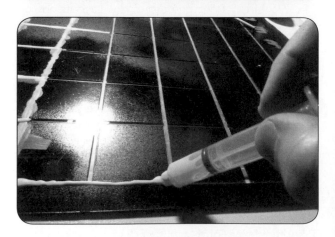

Step 4: Build Upper Boards

Take the two smaller grid layouts that are printed on the heavy 11" x 17" paper and place them on the steel sheets face down. Align them as accurately as possible and secure in place using tape.

Set the iron to the highest setting with steam turned off. Begin ironing the paper to the metal applying even pressure and heat. Check it periodically to see which areas need more attention. A perfect toner transfer isn't necessary, just enough to help align the tape we will be using to build the grid.

Lay down strips of 1" painter's tape following the grid guidelines on the metal sheet. Next, using a T-square and razor blade, cut lines through the tape at the horizontal guidelines. Remove the excess tape and you should have a grid made up of square pieces of tape. Next, lay down the remaining stickyback pieces, aligning them with the tape grid. Using a sharp razor blade, remove the black lettering.

Next it is time to paint it. Lay down a very thin coat of primer first. After about 15 minutes you can start laying down your next few coats of fluorescent spray paint. I had originally planned on using white spray paint for the upper boards, since white usually reacts very well to blacklight. I learned that for some reason most spray paints don't react well to blacklight unless they are fluorescent. Again, before the paint has fully cured, remove all of the tape and sticky-back material.

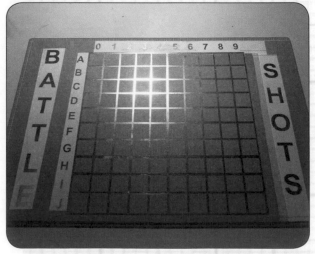

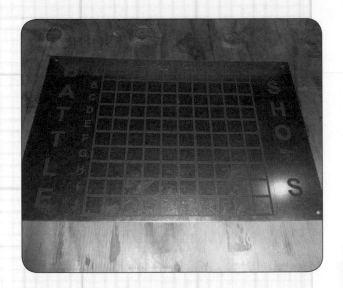

Step 5: Build the Enclosure

All of the enclosure pieces are made from a single sheet of plywood as you can see in the layout sketch. When you buy the wood, see how many of the cuts you can have made at the store. The rest will have to be cut with a circular or table saw.

Mark a centerline on the four side pieces and drill three evenly spaced countersunk holes. Using the corner clamps, align the center piece with the middle of one of the side pieces. Drill guide holes into the center piece, run a bead of wood glue between the pieces, then affix with screws. On the top and bottom corners, hammer in a few finishing nails to keep the edges from separating. If you have a centerpunch or something similar, it's usually a good idea to recess the nail heads a bit.

Locate the door handle on the center of the top piece and install. Drill a 1/2" hole (for the power cords) on one of the side pieces about 1½" down from the top. It should be centered and cut into the center board at least ¾". Next, install screws as needed for mounting your blacklights.

Take the two metal sheets and line them up back to back. Drill a hole in each of the corners to accept the #10 screws (it helps to secure the pieces together at each corner with tape). Position one of the metal sheets on the center sheet of the enclosure and then drill through the wood at each corner hole.

Using a router and a 1/16" round bit, router all edges of the box and lower boards except for the joint where it will be hinged (see photo).

Patch all screw and nail recesses with the wood putty. Paint with two coats of primer. The first should be very light. After the second coat dries, give it a light sanding with 100-grit sandpaper, then paint with at least two coats of black latex furniture paint.

After the paint has dried, install the blacklights. You will need to cut the cords and then rewire them together so that one plug feeds both lights. Next, install the metal sheets.

Finally, attach the lower boards using the small hinges. Ensure these are as straight as possible so it will close properly. I had originally planned on putting small latches on top to hold the lower boards closed, but since I was unable to find exactly what I wanted I settled for a lower-tech solution—two staples and a small bungee. Drill small pilot holes for the staples so the wood won't split when you hammer them in. Locate as shown in the photo.

Finally, attach the Plexiglas sheets to the lower boards using the clear caulking. Try to keep the caulking near the edges so that liquids can't seep underneath and damage the paint.

Step 6: Paint the Markers

Take all of the magnets and paint with two coats of the primer. I found a long steel post that made painting these much easier.

After the primer has fully dried, paint 36 of the magnets with red or orange fluorescent paint. (Hit!) Paint the remaining magnets with blue or white. (Miss!) If you are brushing on the paint, it helps to lay a sheet of wax or parchment paper over a metal cookie sheet and place the magnets on it. It will keep them from sliding around when you try to paint them.

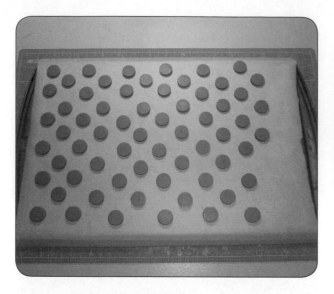

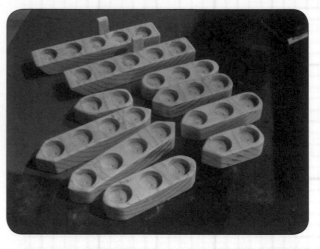

Step 7: Build the Boats

Using a table saw, cut as many 2" wide pieces from the 2" x 12" board as you can. Due to imperfections in the board, many of your pieces may be unusable. Cut the boat templates from the remaining sticky-back sheets. Starting with the larger boats first, find suitable pieces and affix the templates to them. Take the 1½"Ø Forstner bit and cut out each of the holes on the templates. Drill down approximately ½" (the depth of the bit).

Next, using a band saw carefully cut out the shape of each ship. My band saw skills are sadly lacking so I had to smooth them out a bit using 60-grit sandpaper. This is also useful for rounding all of their edges.

Paint with two coats of primer. Once the primer dried I decided to add a little glow-in-the-dark pinstriping. Using the painter's tape, mask out the lines you want to paint. Once the pinstripes are on, remove the tape and then cut out pieces of felt to attach to the bottom of each boat.

Step 8: ATTACK!

Turn off the lights, plug it in, and you're ready to play! For the shots I chose to go with Gin and Tonics. They aren't overly strong and they glow under the black light! Mix one part gin with two parts tonic water. It's also a good idea to announce the rules before the game begins. Ships can only be placed horizontally or vertically, not diagonally. Have fun and be safe! "You drank my Battleship!!"

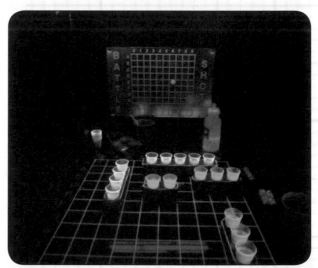

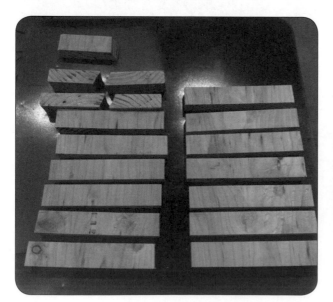

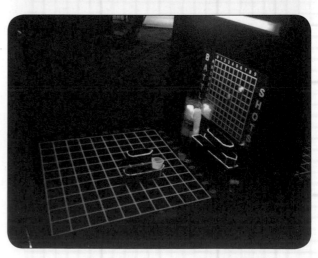

Modular Origami Sculptures

By joettle

(http://www.instructables.com/id/
MAKALU-modular-origami-sculpture-
6-woven-pentago/)

Makalu origami is one of the five Himalayan peaks of origami folding, but don't let that deter you—it is a relatively easy model to fold.

Step 1: What You Will Need

- patience
- good music
- 15 squares of paper

This is a relatively sturdy model and holds together well with no glue or attachments. Okay, let's jump right in!

Step 2: Music and the Paper

Okay, first things first: Good music! You want something that's slow, mathematical, interesting, and not too distracting.

Okay, paper! Cut your squares in half accurately. You should have 30 rectangles with 2" x 1" dimensions. No rocket science here.

Step 3: The Folding Begins!

If you are using colored paper, start with the white side up. Valley fold your paper in half lengthwise. Valley fold means to fold the two sides towards your face, making a valley. Mountain fold means to fold the two sides away from your face, making a mountain. Do this again, folding your paper accurately into quarters.

Step 4: Guideline Creases

Valley fold the bottom right corner over, as if you were folding the paper again into eighths, but only fold the bottom centimeter or so. Unfold. This is called a guideline crease; it is used as a marker for later on.

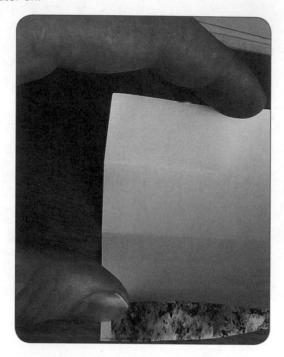

Step 5: More Guideline Creases

Valley fold the top right corner down and the bottom left corner up to the middle. Unfold. These are also guideline creases. For the first few fold the whole way, but as you get the feel for it you will notice that you only have to crease a small area to use as a guideline. Fewer creases equals a more elegant model.

Step 6: More Folding

Valley fold the bottom left corner up until it just touches the guideline crease you just made. Make sure that the corner of the crease is exactly at the previous guideline fold you made. This isn't difficult—check the photos. Repeat on the top end.

Step 7: Folding Continues

Fold the edges in to the middle. It should look like this.

Step 8: More Complex Folding

Open the top right corner and reverse the corner along the existing creases so that it lies open. Fold the model flat again so that it looks like the photo. Two out of the three creases necessary here are already in place. Repeat on the bottom left. Fold the model in half once this is done. Crease the top and the bottom where your new folds cross the midline (about where my thumb and middle finger are in the picture).

Step 9: A Valley Fold

Valley fold the bottom bit up along the level that already exists there. This is self-explanatory if you are doing it.

Step 10: A Mountain Fold

Mountain fold (away from you) the little white bit on the left side of the model around to the other side of the model, hugging the edge as closely as you can. It should look like this. Repeat on the top side.

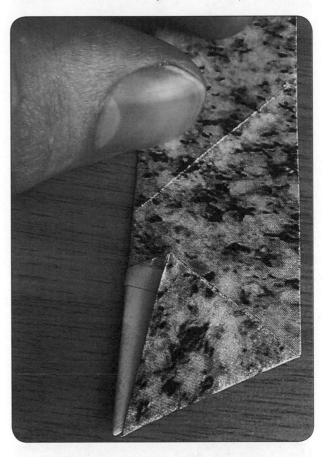

Step 11: The Model Is Done

Unfold the last two folds you just made; your model should look like this. Tuck your flaps in where they belong. Well done, the model is done. Make another 29 (groan).

Step 12: The Fun Begins

Okay, you're over the hump, now on to the fun stuff! If you made it this far, well done. This is where it gets cool! You have made the pieces, now to put the puzzle together. Put two pieces end-to-end and tuck their flaps into one another as shown. You will notice that the pieces are not flat when they are put together. Once they are properly and neatly tucked in, pinch the top edge to secure them.

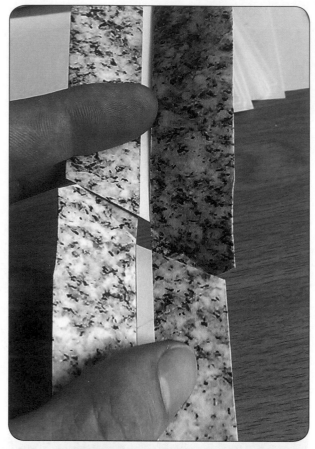

Step 13: Create a Pentagon
Put five of these together in a pentagon. Well done, first pentagon done!

Step 14: Make Another One
Make a second pentagon and loop it into the first one, then arrange them as shown in the photo. (This is important. Hold them like this.)

Step 15: Connect Your Pentagons
Make a third pentagon, and loop it into the first two. Notice the triangles where the three pentagons meet: This is important.

Step 16: Make a Fourth Pentagon

The fourth pentagon: the hardest one to put in. As you put it in, you will notice the triangular pattern as it crosses the previous three. There is a rule: Each pentagon must intersect each other one once and once only. This isn't very helpful. Try to figure it out from the photos. Look at the pattern at the base (first photo); you should see this at the top as well. Where you had one triangle, you now have two. The first three you put in relatively upright; this one you must put in at an angle.

Step 17: A Fifth Pentagon

The fifth one is a bit easier; by now you will start seeing where the pieces go. Here it is easier to put the pentagons in in segments of one or two pieces, attaching the pieces once they are in place. You can see this is what I have been doing.

Step 18: Final One!

The last pentagon is easy; you will see where it has to go—just follow the symmetry. I made the last one golden, as it adds a nice contrast. This pentagon you will have to put in piece by piece. Well done! Put it in a spot where people can admire it.

Homemade Prescription Swimming Goggles

By engineerable

(http://www.instructables.com/id/ Prescription-Swimming-Goggles-for-12-See- Underw/)

Wearing your glasses in the water is a sure way to end up having to buy a new pair, and contacts tend to pop out when swimming. I don't wear glasses, but lots of my friends do, and I have seen many a pair of expensive glasses lost into the deep blue yonder or the murky abyss.

We came up with this simple and great idea to make prescription goggles for only $12 (the cost of the goggles), saving $$ compared to buying a pair from the optometrist or dive shop. If you have an old pair of prescription glasses, you can probably make a pair of these for cheap and in only a few minutes.

Not only do these work well for swimming, but they are also especially useful if you're doing a water sport, like surfing, kayaking, bodyboarding, or kitesurfing where, if you're like me, you will end up doing a face plant.

So you're not going to look like a rockstar wearing these, but if they are carefully made, no one else will notice that the lenses are glued on. Only with thicker lenses do you notice because of the distortion, which is visible with regular glasses anyways. Although, who wears swimming goggles to look cool? They're all about functionality, and what's more functional than not only keeping water out of your eyes, but also being able to see clearly?

Step 1: Materials

The materials you will need to make the prescription swimming goggles are:

- Pair of old prescription glasses that you don't use anymore. The prescription just has to be good enough to see, not read.
- Pair of swimming goggles. The Boomerang Goggle from Speedo worked the best of any goggle I found. $12 at Target, probably available elsewhere too.
- Use silicone adhesive. It remains more flexible, seals better, and makes a stronger bond than five-minute epoxy.
- Fine-grit sandpaper
  I said it was simple, right?

Step 2: Remove Lenses from Your Old Glasses

Use an eyeglass screwdriver (usually a small flathead screwdriver) to remove the screw that clamps the frame around your lenses. If the lenses are held in the frame without screws, they may just be popped out by hand.

Step 3: Test Fit the Lenses onto the Goggle Frames

The size and shape of the lenses may determine what pair of swimming goggles will fit the best. First, put the goggles on and hold the lenses up to the goggles to check if you can see well with them. Ideally the lenses should be close to the same distance away from your eye as the eyeglass frames originally held them, and this quick test will determine if you will be able to see well with them once they are glued on. The lenses should at least overlap the frame of the goggles on the left and right sides. This is the minimum amount of glue area that you will need, as shown in the pictures of the clear goggles below.

In this case, the top and the bottom edge will be open, allowing water to flow freely between the glasses lens and the goggle lens. This is probably the easiest and most reliable solution. If the lenses overlap the frame all the way around, as shown in the pictures of the pink goggles, then the glue can be applied all the way around. This will created a sealed space between the glasses lens and the goggle lens.

There needs to be as little moisture trapped in the space as possible to prevent fogging, so this should be done in a dry place, or you can apply some anti-fog to the lenses on the inside of the space. Also, the glue needs to be properly applied to prevent leaks. If you are going to buy a pair of goggles, you may want to remove the lenses from your old glasses first, take them with you to the store, and see if they would fit well over the goggles.

Step 4: Note: Curved vs. Flat Lenses

You may have to glue the lenses on differently depending on whether they are very curved or flat. If the lenses are very curved, as shown by the clear goggles in the pictures below, then you should only apply glue at the edges where the lenses touch the goggle frames. This is the preferred method because you don't have to worry about leaks. If the lenses are flat and fully overlap the goggle frames, as shown by the pink goggles in the picture below, then you can apply glue all the way around. This is risky, because you may end up with leaks. I therefore highly recommend putting a temporary spacer between the lenses and the goggles to allow for a 1mm to 2mm gap and only applying glue to the edges, leaving a space at the top and bottom to allow water to flow through.

Step 5: Sanding the Surfaces in Preparation for Gluing

The edges of the prescription glass lenses that overlap the goggle frames need to be sanded for better glue adhesion if you are using plastic lenses. Using the fine-grit sandpaper, lightly sand around the edge of the lenses (on the inside surface) where they will be glued to the goggles. You should also lightly sand/roughen the goggle frames to which the sanded edges of the lenses will touch. This will help the glue adhere to the goggles.

Step 6: Glue the Lenses to the Goggles (Very Curved Lenses)

Follow these instructions if your lenses are very curved.

1. Apply the glue on the edges of the frame where the lenses will overlap the goggles. The top and bottom is left open for water to flow through. Put just enough so that there will be a good

bond between the frame and the lens.
2. Position the lenses onto the frames and hold in place until the glue hardens. It should only take a few minutes.

Step 7: Glue the Lenses to the Goggles (Flat Lenses)

Follow these instructions if your lenses are almost flat, or overlap all the way around the frames.

1. Apply the glue all the way around the edges of the frame where the lenses overlap. Put just enough so that there will be a good bond between the frame and the lens. I made the mistake of putting a little bit too much the first time and making a mess.
2. Position the lenses onto the frames and fill in any gaps with adhesive. Make sure that there is a watertight seal between the lenses and the goggles.
3. Hold the lenses in place until the glue hardens. It should only take a few minutes.

Step 8: Finished! Now Go for a Swim!

After leaving the goggles alone overnight so that the adhesive can fully cure, you are ready to go for a swim and test them out.

Workshop

Vacuum-Cleaner-Built Skateboard

DIY Stubby Screwdrivers

Stained-Wood Pixel Art

DIY Terrarium

Wooden iPhone 5 Case

Copper Rose

DIY Knife-Sharpening Kit

Yes, you can build your own skateboard deck or stubby screwdrivers. Those projects, along with the instructions for bending your own copper rose, staining wood to create pixel mosaics, and sharpening knives, will teach you the basics of operating average workshop tools and leave you with cool and, more importantly, useful products to display or play with.

Vacuum-Cleaner-Built Skateboard

By gregorylavoie
(http://www.instructables.com/id/Use-a-Vacuum-cleaner-to-build-your-own-Skateboard/)

This Instructable is a step-by-step description of the process behind building a skateboard deck, which includes making a bending mold, building a bag press, and squishing/cutting plywood into the shape of a skateboard. These instructions are for a specific type of board but are intended to be easily modified to make any type of skateboard, longboard, or bent plywood project, for that matter.

Being a skateboarder and a constructive individual, I always fantasized about making my own custom-designed skateboard. Now I can make as many skateboards as I want, and you can too! Follow these steps. I suggest reading all of the instructions before starting the project!

Step 1: What You Need
Materials:
- scrap cardboard
- pencil
- 1 4' x 8' sheet of ¾" spruce plywood
- 2 5' x 5' sheets of maple veneer
- hand-held jig saw
- 1 liter of wood glue
- 8 12" wood clamps
- wood rasp
- sandpaper
- masking tape
- 20-gauge thick vinyl sheet (or waterbed bladder)
- contact cement
- duct tape

- 2-part 5-minute epoxy
- vacuum cleaner with hose attachment
- ¾" plastic conduit pipe
- dowel that fits in conduit pipe
- plastic mesh from dishwashing scrubber (the one that looks like a mesh donut)
- rubber mallet
- skateboard trucks, wheels, and nuts and bolts
- grip tape paint
- Optional (but helpful): a hand-held belt sander

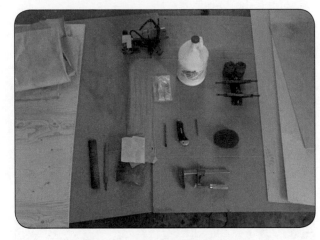

Step 2: Building the Mold
The mold is what the plywood is squashed against, forcing it to take the curvy shape of the skateboard. It will be made from stacked cross-sections of the spruce plywood.

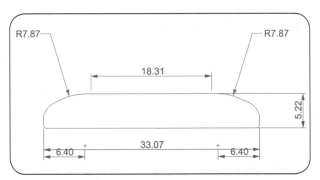

First create a cardboard template of the mold cross-sections and use it to trace out 15 versions onto the spruce plywood sheets. Cut out the cross-section layers, then glue the layers together and squeeze with clamps; wipe off the excess glue that squeezes out.

Once dry, remove clamps and use rasp or belt sander to remove any differences in the cross sections so the surface of the mold is smooth.

Mark off the area for the inner concave where material needs to be removed. Make a template of the desired inner curve so you know exactly what material needs to be removed with the rasp or belt sander. Refine the surface of the mold first with the coarse and then with the smooth sandpaper.

357

Step 3: Making a Bag Press

A bag press is basically a giant Ziploc bag with a connector where you can attach a vacuum. A bag press works on the principle that nature resists a vacuum. Therefore, if you suck all the air out of a container, it will squeeze in on itself creating a press that is excellent for bending things onto a mold.

1. Take two 3' x 4½' sheets of vinyl plastic and apply a liberal coat of contact cement glue on both sheets along the two long edges and one of the short ends.

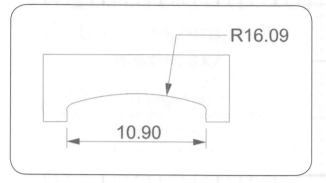

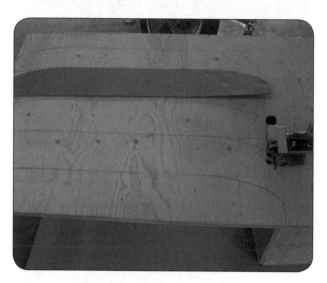

2. Allow the glue to dry for 45 minutes.
3. Starting with the back edge, press glued edges together. Be careful not to create ripples.
4. Once the back edge is pressed, work up the sides to the open end of the bag.
5. Once all surfaces are contacted, apply force to the tops of glued areas by rubbing with a spoon or a rolling pin. You can then add extra reinforcement by folding strips of duct tape over the edges to strengthen the seal and plug any leaks.

Now you'll need something that will suck the air out of the bag. I used a vacuum cleaner with a hose attachment, which worked fairly well. You also need to figure out some way of attaching the vacuum to the bag. I used a plastic tube that hooked up with the hose attachment.

1. Create a hole smaller than your connector pipe (but large enough that it can be forced through) in the middle of the top layer of the vinyl sheet.
2. Then force the pipe through from the inside of the bag out so that it is almost all the way though.
3. Mix up half a tablespoon of 5-minute epoxy and place liberal amounts of the glue in the trench between the plastic pipe and the vinyl from inside the bag.

Now you need to create a giant zipper to seal the bag.

1. To do this take a plastic ¾" conduit pipe and a dowel that fits not quite snuggly inside it.
2. Cut the pipe and dowel so they are a little longer than the opening of the bag.
3. Then cut a strip out of the conduit lengthwise so the cross section of the pipe is a "C" shape. The cut can be made with a sharp X-acto knife, or I used a mini circular blade in my Foredom tool. To make sure the cuts are straight, it helps to first use a marker to draw guide lines where you want to cut.

4. How the seal (zipper) works is that the "C" shaped tube goes on one side of the opening of the bag and the dowel goes on the other side.
5. Then the sandwich is squeezed together by hitting the dowel with the rubber mallet, forcing the dowel and vinyl inside the C-tube, creating an airtight seal.
6. More or less material may need to be removed from the "C" cross-section if the dowel will not snap into place. I suggest making a small test zipper with extra dowel and conduit pipe to determine the exact shape needed before making the real one.

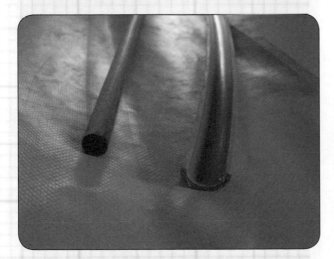

sheets should have the grain going lengthwise (easier to bend the short way) and four should have the grain going widthwise (easier to bend the long way). Be sure to sand off any chipping on the edges so that the wood is smooth.

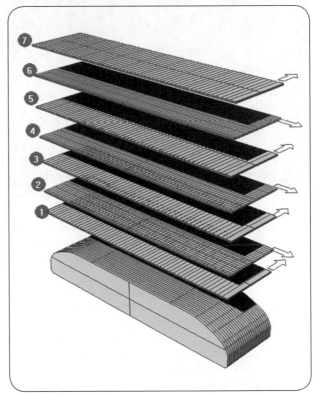

2. Take layer one (grain going widthwise) and apply a coat of wood glue over the surface all the way to the edges. Place layer two (grain going lengthwise) on top and apply glue over the surface all the way to the edges. Place layer three (grain going widthwise) on top.

Step 4: Make a Skateboard

Now you are ready to make the skateboard.

1. Cut seven 34" x 11" sheets of the maple veneer (the sheets need to be larger than the final board because there will be waste wood formed on the edges from the bending process). Three of the

3. Now stack the three glued layers so they are centered on top of the mold. You can put four tabs of masking tape on the edges of the wood

to make sure it does not slide around when you put it in the bag.

4. Take a large, mesh dishwashing scrubby, unroll it, and cover the mold and wood veneers with the mesh. This will allow air to flow around the mold and be sucked into the vacuum easily. You do not want to have any trapped air pockets. Slide the finished compilation of the mold, the glued veneers, and mesh into the center of the bag-press and close the seal. Hook up the vacuum and turn it on. Keep the bag from sucking itself under the maple veneers by pushing the tips of the veneers down when you turn on the vacuum. As the air is removed the bag will force the wood to conform to the mold. Once all the air is out, gently hit the inner concave with the rubber mallet to help bring in the curve.

6. Once the curved board is dry, make a paper template of the shape you want the board to be and trace it onto the curved wood. Carefully cut out the shape with a scroll saw. Refine the shape with files and sandpaper and round all the edges.

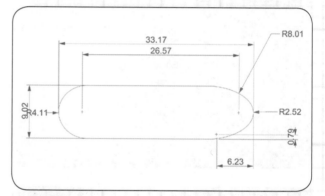

5. Let the wood press for at least four hours before opening the bag and removing the bent board. Remove the mesh and masking tape. Now repeat the last steps to apply the final four veneers on top of the three first ones.

7. Locate where you want your wheels attached and mark the location for the holes with a pencil on the bottom of the deck. Drill the first hole then screw the truck in place. You can then

use the holes in the truck as a guide to drill the next holes, guaranteeing they will line up properly. Once the holes are all drilled, remove the screws and use a countersink on the tops of the holes so that the screw will lie flush with the board.

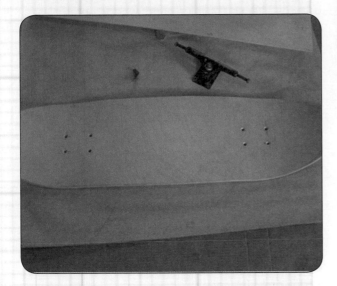

8. At this point you can paint and seal the board to help protect the wood and make it the color you want.

9. The board itself is complete. Now you just need to apply the grip tape. Don't peel all the backing off the roll and just stick it on because this will create bubbles. Instead start at one end and peel off only a little backing at a time, working it down as you go.

11. Take an X-acto knife and run it around the edges. If there are any little pieces remaining you can use the sandpaper and sand them off. Next feel out where the truck holes are on the top and stab/trim them out with the knife. Now attach your trucks and wheels, and you are ready to go.

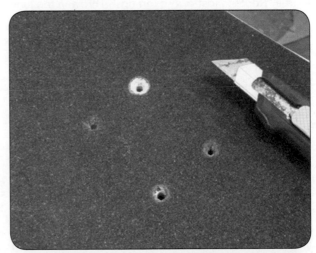

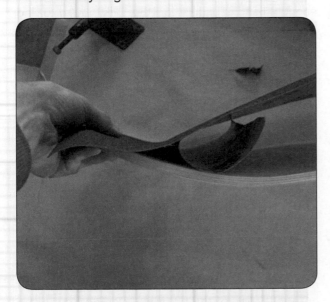

10. Once the grip tape is on, you need to trim it to match the edges. Take an old piece of sandpaper and rub the excess grip tape on the edges; this step will soften the edges and leave a mark were you need to cut.

DIY Stubby Screwdrivers

By pocmarck
(http://www.instructables.com/id/
DIY-Stubby-Screwdrivers/)

Anyone who works with their hands knows that you can never have too many tools. In that pursuit you inevitably wind up with multiples of certain accessories. Two socket sets, three multi-meters, and more crescent wrenches than one person could really use. Most multi-attachment screwdrivers will even give you an assortment of bits: straight blade, Phillips, hex, etc., with doubles of the same size. Over the years I've had three screwdrivers (ChannelLock, Kobalt, and Craftsman) that each came with its own collection of bits. I finally had to start a collection cup to hold them all. So what do you do with these extras? Replace lost or broken tips? Throw in the junk drawer? How about making another set of tools to round out your collection?

Stubby, or low-profile, screwdrivers help for the really tight spaces: low clearance, cramped quarters, you name it. But why buy them? You can easily make a set that'll allow you get to all the tight spaces with just the right driver bit. And in the process you'll have a nice set of durable screwdrivers to round out your ever-growing collection. Drop them, step on them, lose them, find them in again 20 years. If you choose the right materials, these drivers will out-last you.

This is actually a quick and easy project. I was feeling spontaneous when I made mine and it only took about 20 minutes to make four. That's including interruptions. You could easily make a set of 8–12 in an hour.

Step 1: Material Matters

As this is a set you'll wind up using for years to come, go wild with the design. I used materials I had on hand. A simple dowel rod provided a cheap and easy-to-finish handle. I think it gives the screwdrivers a nice rustic or antique look, but you can use whatever you have on hand: wood, metal, plastic, dice, bottle caps, nuts, stones, 3D printed anything. Just use whatever suits your fancy. These instructions will show you how to make the wood handles that I made.

Materials Needed:
- screwdriver bits (various sizes and types)
- 1" dowel rod
- paint or wood stain (optional)

Tools Needed:
- ruler
- marker
- hacksaw
- sandpaper (various grits)
- ¼" drill bit and drill
- small socket
- vice
- drill press (optional)
- belt sander (optional)
- bandsaw (optional)

Remember to use your eye protection. It's going to take a long time for science to replace the Mk.I eyeball. Be safe and have fun.

Step 2: Handle With Care

Take the dowel rod and start marking out 1" increments on it. Cut it at these lines until you have enough handle blanks for the bits you're giving homes. If you are using a hacksaw, clean up the ends with some sandpaper or the belt sander. To make the handles easier to grip and put force on, I sanded the sides into a rough octagonal shape. Give the whole thing an once-over with light-grit sandpaper to smooth out the rough edges.

Mark the center of the handle on one of the ends. This is where the bit will be installed. For now set the handles aside. One possible upgrade would be to "dish" out the tail end of the handle. Use a large drill bit and make a shallow depression in the end. This helps you center some pressure on the bit's tip while installing or removing screws.

Step 3: Bits and Bobs

Most screwdriver bits are machined out of hexagonal bar stock. Measure the length of the hexagonal part of the bit. Mine averaged out to be ½" from the base to the beginning of the machined end. This will be the depth of the hole in the handle.

Take your ¼" drill bit and mark ½"inch on the end. The ¼" size should ensure a tight fit of the bit in the wood handle. You may have to experiment with drill bit sizes depending on the material you chose to use. Install it in the drill.

Step 4: Putting Holes in Things

Secure the handle in a vice and begin drilling. The line on the drill bit will be the "end-stop" of the hole. Once the line is level with the end of the handle, you've gone as far as you need to. You can play with the depth of the drill to make a higher or lower profile screwdriver.

Step 5: Getting a Handle on Things

Take the newly drilled handles over to the vice. This is where you'll need the socket. The bit should fit in the end of the socket so only the hexagonal part sticks out. Seat the bit in the socket and press the bit down onto the handle. Give it a few light taps with a hammer. You can drive it all the way with the hammer but the vice is more consistent and is much easier. Place the socket-bit-handle sandwich in the vice and screw it down. Once the socket contacts the handle, stop tightening. Pushing the bit into the wood will provide a very tight fit without the need for glue. Pull

it out of the vice and revel in your work. Complete the other bits in your collection and get to work in those tight places.

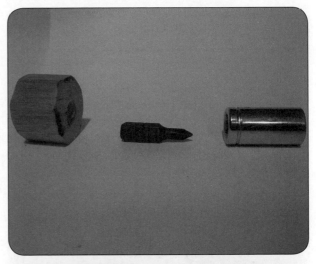

Step 6: Parting Thoughts

The last step is to put a finish on the handles. I'm going to leave the wood on mine unfinished as they will likely get oiled down plenty at work. If you choose wood for your screwdrivers, you might consider a nice wood stain or some paint.

Stained-Wood Pixel Art

By 8bitwood
(http://www.instructables.com/id/Stained-wood-pixel-art/)

I am going to show you how to make a piece of pixel art out of stained wood. The organic nature of the wood adds a nice touch to the blockiness of the pixel sprite. In this example I am going to make a sprite from Zelda on the NES, but these same techniques can be used to create any sprite.

Step 1: Materials

- wood for the pixels (I use select pine from the local Home Depot)
- a table saw in case you need to rip the wood down to a smaller width
- a planar to make sure every strip of wood is identical
- a chopsaw to cut the pixels
- clamps are a big help for cutting the blocks and gluing them together
- wood stain
- foam brushes for the stain as well as sealant
- sealant! I used a high-gloss finish
- wood glue. I use Titebond II wood glue
- a nice big straightedge for the gluing process
- time and patience. You're going to be cutting a lot of blocks of wood. Make sure you are mentally prepped!

The first thing you need to do is create a template of the image you want to create. Here I have an image of Link from Zelda on a grid. I just went into Photoshop and gridded out the sprite based on images from the game. You will notice that I used this pattern to figure out how many of each colored block I'd need, as well as to plan out the grain pattern. I like to create a checkerboard pattern with the wood grain because I think it makes the piece more interesting. Once you have your pattern and know exactly how many blocks you'll need you can move on to the next step.

Step 2: Cutting the Wood

So you have all your materials gathered. Great! Time to start cutting wood. Determine exactly how big each pixel square should be in inches. I've made pieces that use ½" pixels and some that use 2½" pixels. Figure out what size you will need and cut all the blocks at once. Resetting the planar/chop saw for another run of pixels that match your first set is a real pain since the blocks need to be precise. If a block is off by even half a millimeter, throw it out!

For this sprite piece I needed to make 1" blocks. My pine strips were 1½" wide so I needed to cut them down a bit. Rip them to be just a bit wider than your target width; the planar will take care of the rest. Once you have the ripped boards, run them through a planar to make sure that every single board is the exact same width. Now you have a bunch of boards that are all identical.

Next step is using the chop saw to cut the boards into pixel squares. It's easy! I used a 2" x 4" piece of wood and clamps to setup a stop on my chop saw, then I cut test pieces. If you can take two pixels, turn one 90 degrees so it is off-grain and then fit them together and feel no difference then you are good to go! Start cutting! I cut four boards at a time and I double check the length of the pixels every few cuts.

I cannot state enough how important it is to continually check the cuts. If a piece is even a hair off that will mess you up when gluing.

Step 3: Prepping Wood

Now you have a big pile of wood blocks that are all perfectly square. Before putting the blocks together you have to color the wood. You should have your template image ready to go—just look at the colors and decide what you want. For the Link piece I used green stain, Red Mahogany stain for the brown, Golden Amber stain for the Triforce, and bare wood for Link's face and hands.

From your template, count the number of blocks that you will need for each color and then group the blocks into piles. It is always safe to add a few extras to stain just in case you need them. Stain the blocks of wood per stain instructions. Don't forget to stain the edges that will be showing! Let the pieces dry for at least a day.

After a day you now have your pixel blocks colored and ready to glue together!

Step 4: Putting It All Together

The big day is here! It's time to glue the blocks together. The important thing here is to take your time and make sure everything is straight so it will all line up!

I laid down a long sheet of butcher's paper on a workbench. The blocks will be glued on top of this paper (but not glued to the paper). At the edge of the workbench I clamped down a long metal straight edge over the paper. The paper should be able to slide forward and back under the metal straightedge.

Lay out your first row of blocks that form the top of your image. Add a bit of wood glue on the right edge of each piece, except the last one in the row. Now press them all together while making sure they are lined up with the straightedge. Let the blocks dry for a minute. Now pull the paper away from you, and the first row of glued blocks should move with it, freeing up space for you to use the straightedge on the next row of blocks. After gluing the individual blocks together in the next row, glue the top of the second row to the bottom of the first row, so then you'll have two rows glued together! I use blocks of wood to press them down and make sure everything is connected. Keep going all the way down the sprite!

Keep at it and take your time. When you're finished you will have your sprite glued together! Great job! Let that dry for at least a day.

Step 5: Continuing to Put It All Together

Here are more shots of the piece coming together.

Step 6: Finishing Touches

So now you have a glued-together sprite that is all dry. Pick him up and remove the paper backing. There will probably be some glue back here, but no worries—no one is going to see this side. It's time to finish the piece. These steps are all optional, but I like to seal the piece, paint the back, and mount a support on the back.

I put several coats of Clear Gloss Sealant on the pieces. It makes them look much better. Be sure to seal the edges too! After sealing I turned the piece over and cut out a strip of wood to make a support structure for the piece. Here you can see the simple pieces glued down to the back. These make the piece stronger and also make the piece pop off the wall a bit, which I think looks great.

I like to use a router to cut a groove in the bottom of a horizontal support. This is what I use to hang the piece on the wall (screw head slides into groove). Then I paint the back black to finish it off, and that's it! You now have a classy stained-wood pixel piece!

DIY Terrarium
By noahw
(http://www.instructables.com/id/DIY-Terrarium/)

This DIY terrarium makes a great gift, was assembled in a matter of minutes, and looks really beautiful. Glass globes are now readily available at garden nurseries, and air plants, like the Tilandsia that we used in this terrarium, are even carried at Home Depot during some seasons. I think at one point these plants were harder to locate, but now they're becoming quite common. Terrariums are simple to make and maintain and are perfect for hanging next to a desk, bed, or by the kitchen window where they can be admired and enjoyed.

To make a terrarium you will need:
- glass globe to house the terrarium—this can be purchased new or can be a repurposed glass jar or bowl that has a pleasing volume
- sand
- activated charcoal
- well-draining potting soil
- various mosses
- small sticks or bark
- minerals, shells, or stones
- small plants well suited to terrarium life
- air plants like tilandsia or another bromeliad you like
- succulent, if you like, although it's not recommended to mix succulents and plants due to different watering requirements—we did anyway
- a nice hook or string to hang it by
- spray bottle or mister

Step 2: Sand Layer

The first layer in the terrarium is a thin layer of sand or pebbles for drainage. We chose sand because Long Island, where the terrarium was constructed, is literally one giant pile of sand, so if you dig down a bit it's readily available, and free. Small pebbles might look nicer.

Find a small cup, scooper or funnel to load the sand into the terrarium. It doesn't take much; one cup of sand is probably more than enough.

Step 3: Activated Charcoal Layer

The next layer to put in is activated charcoal or activated carbon—they are the same thing. This is the stuff from your Brita water filter or fish tank filter. If you've got that, toss it in there. Otherwise, you can buy small amounts online or skip this step entirely. I just happened to have a whole lot of activated charcoal lying around for a future project, so we took a ¼ cup or so and added it in.

My sister and I devised a simple cardboard chute to deliver materials precisely where we wanted them in the terrarium. The chute, plus a push stick or brush, works much better than the dump method.

The activated charcoal layer keeps things "fresh," or so I've read.

Step 1: Materials

The materials for a terrarium can usually be purchased at a local nursery or hardware store. There are online retailers for most of these items and specialty retailers who specialize in exactly these kinds of supplies.

yourself some room to be creative with what little space remains.

Step 4: Soil Layer

Next, put in an inch or two of well-draining soil. I mixed some potting soil with succulent soil to achieve a good blend. You don't need much, as the plants themselves come with a soil clump that will likely allow them to survive on their own for quite a while.

We found the paintbrush to be very helpful in moving the soil around. If you were making a larger terrarium or working with one that had a larger hole, I think positioning plants and soil mediums would be much easier, but, alas, we liked the look of this globe and did our best.

Step 5: Large Features

We're breaking a cardinal rule of terrarium building and including both a plant and a succulent in the same terrarium. Generally it's thought that the small plants well suited to life in a terrarium require different living conditions then succulents. I, however, am a non-conformist and chose to break this rule.

The living plant we chose was hearty and strategically planted at the back of the terrarium where it's likely to remain moister. We positioned the succulent on a little hill of soil so it would drain first, as well as located it closer to the opening, which is likely to be a dryer environment. I'm sure it won't take too long for terrarium experts to correct my potentially fatal mistake, but we really wanted to combine both plants and succulents in a single terrarium.

It can be easier to position the plants before filling the terrarium with soil, and then backfill the space between the root balls of the plants. You can also simply dig small holes and plant normally. Both methods worked well for us, but the bigger the plant, the more sense it makes to put it in before the soil and then add the soil around it.

Don't overcrowd the terrarium with large elements; there's quite a few additional small elements that we're adding, so it's important to leave

Step 6: Small Features

We used a pair of long-handled tweezers to position additional items inside the terrarium. Chopsticks also work well.

We added in a hearty dose of a few different types of dried, ornamental mosses, a mineral that my mom really likes, and a small stone egg.

We also included some dried pieces of tree bark from some trees that were shedding this past fall. This was followed up by inserting a small "air plant" called Tilandsia. These plants don't need to be planted in the conventional sense—they require no soil and simply extract their nutrients and water from the air. They are perfect candidates for terrariums.

Finally, we added in some colorful shells that we had collected at the beach (wash them thoroughly as they may introduce salt to the tiny ecosystem, and plants and salt don't get along well) and a small little set of thorns that had come off of a cactus that I used to own that had died.

Step 7: Maintenance

You've got to water the terrarium from time to time—once or twice a week depending on location and weather conditions. We set my mom up with a dual watering system—the regular water can that services most regular house plants and then a special mister that's designed to spray down living things like the air plant. A regular spray bottle from the drug store will work just fine; we just wanted to class the gift up a bit.

Maintenance on the terrarium is pretty easy. Simply hang it in an area that receives moderate sun, but not direct sun if possible, and make sure you water it once a week. If it's looking really wet in there, or if mold or a swampy odor develops, you're definitely over-watering. If the plant parts start to wilt, they you're likely under-watering.

Wooden iPhone 5 Case

By strooom

(http://www.instructables.com/id/Wooden-iPhone-5-Case/)

The contrast of a high-tech phone against the natural look of solid wood makes this an impressive case. Wooden cases can be bought at web shops, but of course it's much more fun and rewarding to make a case yourself.

Just as the iPhone is a precision device, manufacturing this case will require precision.

With basic tools and minimal materials, you can build a really impressive case for your phone!

Step 1: Warning

Before you begin, I must warn you about a few things:

- An iPhone is a delicate object and doesn't really belong around the dust in your woodworking area. Keep it covered and to the side when it isn't needed for measurements or proofing.
- When working with glue, make sure everything is dry and clean, especially your hands, before touching the phone.
- Throughout the construction, you will need to measure, try, and proof with the real phone. Be very careful to not scratch the display as you're building the case.

    Tip: If you are still unsure about using your actual phone for this Instructable, you can make an iPhone dummy, which is a wooden piece with the same iPhone dimensions.

Step 2: Tools and Materials

Tools:
- caliper
- router with straight 12mm router bit
- sander (belt sander for rough work and an orbital sander for finishing)
- jig saw with precision-cut saw
- clamps

Materials:
- A piece of solid wood, preferably a nice piece of tropical wood. I used Bamboo.
- Some fabric from a pair of old jeans

Other:
- wood glue
- contact glue
- CAD drawing with iPhone 5 dimensions

Step 3: Building the Jig

Precision routing cannot be done freehand, so you'll need a jig to support your movement. A jig is a self-made support tool that enhances the capabilities of other tools.

Usually they are built from scrap materials, and the quality of those materials affects the life expectancy of the jig.

The jig shown in the picture is one I use regularly when routing small pieces of wood.

Step 4: Routing the Piece

The case will be assembled from two wooden halves that will be glued together at the end. The two halves are symmetrical, but one will have an extra opening through which you can push out the inserted phone.

1. Mount the bamboo in the jig (see image). I used two wooden wedges to keep the bamboo in place. Make sure the wedges don't run away from the vibrations of the router.
2. Adjust the guides so that you will route a rectangular area out of the center. This area should measure 130mm x 62mm and be 4.5mm deep. Remember that you can always make this cutout wider and deeper but not the other way around.
3. Cut the piece down, lengthwise, to almost its final size. The last millimeter will be trimmed on the belt sander.
4. Route an extra opening on one piece that will allow you to push out the phone with your index finger. This opening needs to be slightly wider than the width of your index finger

    Tip: Regularly clean your work area, as even tiny chips of wood can make your work inaccurate.

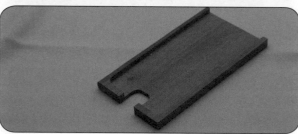

Step 5: Testing the Dimensions

The most difficult aspects of this project are making sure the phone slides in and out with ease to prevent scratching and ensuring a snug fit so it doesn't randomly fall out.

Both objectives can be reached by adding a piece of fabric to the inside of the case. In Step 3 we made each half-shell 4.5mm deep, resulting in a total of 9mm of space. The iPhone is 7.6mm, so we can add 1.4mm of fabric. I used some jeans, of which four layers (two on each side of the case), provide the right friction.

This will take some experimenting. Tentatively stack up all the parts—first the under shell, then the fabric, phone, fabric, and upper shell—and join them together with small clamps. Then test the friction by sliding your phone in and out. Take your time and, again, be careful not to scratch your phone.

When you're confident that the friction/protection is perfect, glue the fabric to both halves of the wooden shells. Excess fabric should be hanging outside of the shells; it'll be cut later. I used an extra dummy piece of MDF to press the fabric in place while the glue dries.

After the fabric has been glued, cut away 2mm of the excess from the entrance of the case.

Step 6: Gluing

Use a flashlight to check the inside of the box after assembly for any dripping glue. Make sure it dries long enough to avoid getting wet glue on your phone.

Step 7: Sanding and Finishing

Sand the box down to its final size. Start with P80 grain on the belt sander and then finish with P400 by hand.

Oil the outside with wood oil and be careful not to get it inside the case, where it'll grease the protective fabric. Again, let everything dry well before inserting your phone.

Copper Rose

By SanjayBeast

(http://www.instructables.com/id/Copper-
Rose-an-everlasting-flower/)

Here's a step-by-step guide to making a rose out of sheet copper and steel/brass rod. Of course, this is not a definitive guide, so feel free to adapt and change as you go along. This is a fairly simple metalworking project, as there is no welding of any kind involved, which can sometimes dissuade beginners.

Step 1: Go Forth and Gather!

Most of this is fairly crucial to the project but should be in your toolbox anyhow:

Tools:

- scribe and center punch (I actually made myself a set from some old, thick nails, but I also use some I found in my toolbox)
- ruler
- cordless drill/drill press/Dremel/hand drill (as long as it can take a 5mm [3/16" or thereabouts] drill bit, you're good)
- drill bits: 5mm (3/16") and 3mm (7/64") for use with above. Other sizes are always handy.
- tinsnips/jeweler's saw/pneumatic press (essentially, something to cut your copper with. I found these to be excellent, but use whatever suits you the best.)
- rubber/leather/wood mallet (to flatten out your copper without marking it)
- metalworking file (for removing rough edges and cut marks. Dirt cheap and common at DIY stores)
- cross peen hammer (you know the end of the hammer head you always thought was for use with tacks? Well, it's not.)
- anvil/metal block (for hammering on. I bought a 10cm x 10cm slab of steel and use that.)
- propane torch/forge/brazing hearth (a heat source, capable of annealing copper. You can get

away with using a cook's blowtorch or a gas hob, but I invested in this as I do a lot of metalwork at home.)
- pliers—needle-nose, locking, rounded (for manipulating the metal. I daresay you have at least needle-nose pliers lying around, and you can manage with just them.)
- M6/M5 dies (optional; for cutting the thread. If you can't get your hands on some, I'm providing a workaround as they are slightly obscure. A full set will cost a bit, but they don't wear out quickly and are very useful.)
- cutting fluid (optional; this helps to make a nice, clean thread as well as prolongs the life of your tools)
- metalworking vise (ideally with some softgrips so you don't mark your work as much)
- ballpeen hammer (with a rounded head to make rivets)
- wire brush (one with a toothbrush-sized head works best)
- sandpaper (100/220/500 grit)
- steel wool
- buffing wheel/attachment for drill &buffing compound (optional)

Right! Now that you've worked your way through that rather long list of tools, we can move on to the materials you'll need.

Materials:

- 50mm x 225mm of 1.2mm/16oz copper sheet (If you can't get hold of this locally, there are plenty of suppliers online. Alternatively, reclaim some copper by opening out some old copper tubing and flattening that out.)
- 2 steel M6 hex nuts (very common and very cheap. Keep a couple spare, in case something goes wrong.)
- 200mm of 6mm or 3/16" silver steel rod (you can use mild steel rod [cheaper, and more common] but silver steel is harder; while this makes it more difficult to work as cutting threads takes longer, it also means that the thread is much neater and better for what you're going to use it for. Now that I've made lots of roses, I recommend using smaller diameter steel as it is more aesthetically pleasing. However, the pictures in the guide are old. Use 4mm steel and an M4 die if you want to go for something prettier and only slightly less strong.)
- OR, if you haven't got access to a set of dies:
- brazing rod/brass rod of a smaller diameter, around 4mm (This is for the workaround step. Brass is one of the few metals that's really soft enough to be cut without using a die, but more about that later. You can find this in most hardware/ironmongery-type places, or online.)
- 2 steel M3 hex nuts

Finally, we can begin work.

Step 2: Mark Up

So you've gathered your equipment and your materials. Now, turn on some of your favorite music, grab a drink, and get to work on this first stage.

Take your copper sheet. Remove any protective plastic so that you are faced with a clean sheet and mark one edge every 50mm (about 2"). Repeat on the other side. Using your scribe and a ruler, draw lines across the width of your copper to divide it up into four 50mm x 50mm squares, with one 25mm x 50mm rectangle left over.

In the photos, I'm going to be making two roses (to demonstrate the normal method and the workaround method), so don't worry if what you're doing doesn't match up exactly, though everything should be obvious enough. (It doesn't really matter how you do this, as long as you end up with four 50mm squares and one 50mm x 25mm rectangle)

In order to find the center of each piece, join the corners up with a ruler and, using a centerpunch and hammer, mark where the lines join. These dents allow us to drill the holes we need without the drill bit slipping too much. Then, using your 5mm (3/16") drill bit (3mm [7/64"] if you're using brazing rod, as that's roughly how thick it is), drill holes in the center of all of your pieces. I tend to use my 2.5mm bit to drill pilot holes first, as I don't want to wear out my 5mm bit too quickly, but it's up to you.

Go slowly and make sure your work is firmly clamped to a piece of wood to stop the copper bending. I improvise a good clamp by using some cheap g-clamps and my 'anvil,' and that helps to secure the metal without leaving marks. File off any rough edges from the drilling.

Step 3: Cut

Using your tinsnips/preferred method of cutting, cut out all the pieces so you end up with four 50mm squares and one 50mm x 25mm rectangle. Using a file, remove any sharp edges or cut marks. You should be left with your copper blanks ("petals"), each with a hole in the center. Check that your rod ("stem") fits cleanly through.

Cut all the corners off each blank. You want to remove enough copper so that you end up with something that looks like the photo.

For the square pieces, make cuts from the center of each side towards the center that come to about 5mm from the hole. Much closer and the copper will break at these points; any less and it'll be hard to shape the petals. If you're using good tinsnips, the copper will naturally bend up.

Remove the corners that you have now exposed, to create four individual petals. File all those new cut edges to remove any tool marks. Then, use your soft mallet to hammer the copper flat. It doesn't matter if the petals overlap slightly, we'll sort that out later.

For the rectangular blank, make a tiny cut from the center of the long edge towards the hole, giving the same 5mm clearance around the hole. Then, remove the corners you've created to make two triangle-shaped cuts. Again, file the cut edges and hammer flat.

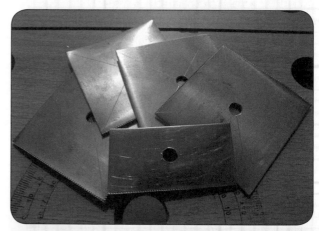

Step 4: Hammertime

Grab your crosspeen hammer and turn it over so you're using the flat (regular) side. Using firm, regular strikes, hammer the edges of each petal thin on both sides. You want to make them so that they can be easily curled at the edges. It doesn't matter that much if you mark the copper, as we're just about to start texturing it.

Now, flip the hammer over so you're using the crosspeen head. Begin to strike the edges of the petals to create a series of radial indents that all point towards the center of the petal. This gives each petal a nice texture. Don't worry about texturing the center of each petal, as it won't be seen. It's important to be brave here and strike quite forcefully.

Only do this for one side of each blank—there's not much point in doing it to both sides, and by trying to do it to both, you'll end up flattening out the other side.

Undoubtedly, your petals will now be slightly overlapping due to the copper being spread out over those cuts you made. This will prevent easy shaping, so you want to remove that overlap. Simply use your tinsnips to make those cuts again, in the same places, and the overlap will drop off. The petals should be nicely separate.

At the end of all this, you should end up with five petals almost ready to be assembled. Now to make them soft...

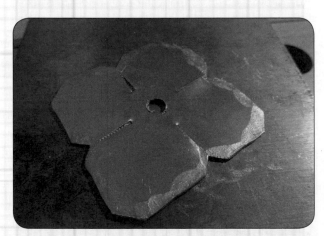

Step 5: Annealing

A quick word about copper and work hardening: Copper is one of a few metals that the more you work it, the harder and more brittle it becomes. This isn't great for us, as we want to bend all the petals and shape them a lot without them breaking. Fortunately, copper is very easy to get back to its malleable, soft state via a process known as annealing.

To do this, heat your copper with your torch/ furnace until it is an even cherry/brick red, noticing the amazing color changes that occur along the way. If you've never done this before, do it in the dark so you can easily tell when the color changes. It's quite

difficult to melt copper by accident. Just don't heat it unevenly or leave it in the forge too long, and you'll be fine. Maintain that red color for a couple of seconds, and then either leave it to cool or immerse it in cold water. Surprisingly, quenching it like this actually makes it easier to clean as lots of the oxide flakes off in the water.

The more times you do this, the easier it is to judge when the color is just right and how long it takes to heat it to that state. Practice and you'll be doing it in no time!

Clean your copper up with a wire brush and some sandpaper (I go all out and use my burnishing wheel, even though it makes the shaping trickier) and set it to one side. This is the last time you can clean/ polish up the middle parts of the petals, so take the time to get them looking nice. Alternatively, you can leave them in their oxidized, reddy/brown state— that looks nice too. The petals are done, so begin work on the stem.

Step 6: Stem and Threads

Taking your length of steel, grind a slight bevel on one end using a file or an electric grindstone, if you have one. This is to get the die to grip the steel and makes it easier to start cutting the thread.

Take your M6 die and liberally paint the inside of it with cutting compound. This makes life a lot easier. Secure your length of rod with some softgrips in a vise and start to cut your thread. If this is your first time, I cannot recommend enough practicing this over and over again; it must have taken me four goes to learn exactly how to cut threads, and a bad thread cannot really be salvaged. I recommend going one turn clockwise, then half a turn back, then one turn forwards, then half a turn back, etc., as this helps keep the thread neat. If you're using silver steel, this can be quite tough work, so take breaks and go carefully. You want to end up with about 50mm (2") of thread on the end of your stem.

Take one of your hex nuts and screw it on to the thread you just made, until it reaches the bottom. Make sure to tighten it as much as possible (I use my locking pliers to get a really good grip). You want to get a nice, secure platform for those petals to sit on. If you wanted to, you could run some JB Weld (or any other liquid weld) into the threads on the nut beforehand so that it glues in place, but I never bother.

Now, skip ahead to Step 8.

Step 7: Alternate Method

(Ignore this if you did get some dies, and continue to Step 8)

So for those of you unable to get your hands on a set of dies, we're going to improvise. The aim of this is to cut a thread using your hex nut (steel) on the softer stem (brass). I'm assuming you use brass rod of roughly 3–4mm and a hex nut that's a size too small.

Take your brazing/brass rod and file/grind a point on one end to allow the nut to slip on easily to get it started. I actually put some cutting compound on the inside of the nut, just to see if it would improve its cutting ability, and it seemed to improve how well this worked.

Then, using either a spanner (tough) or a socket wrench attachment for an electric drill (easy), tighten the nut onto the rod while steadily applying downward pressure. It'll be very hard going by hand, so I highly recommend the latter method. Eventually, you'll notice that the nut is beginning to cut a thread—continue until you have about 30mm (1") of thread on the rod. I actually remove the nut at this point and replace it with a fresh one, but you can leave the original one on. You're done!

While this will work, it doesn't give a high enough quality product for me, as the thread you cut is very rough and weak. You could use JB Weld to affix the nut, or solder (silver solder) it in place for a stronger join.

Step 8: Assembly

So you should now have all your copper blanks and a stem with a nut on it. Assembly is not as simple as you might think, however.

Having cleaned your blanks to your satisfaction, take your first square and thread it onto the stem. Take your next one and repeat, but align it so that its petals cover the cuts in the square below, and only overlap slightly with the petals below them, like this the photo.

This is very important: If you don't do this right, you won't be able shape the rose later. Take the next square, and align it with the first. Then, align the fourth with the second. Finally, simply thread the rectangle on top—it doesn't really matter about alignment, though I place it in line with the third out of habit.

To finish off, thread your second hex nut on top and tighten it down so that the petals begin to buckle slightly and the nut is tight. Don't tighten too much, as you could damage the copper. Make sure to keep all the petals in their correct alignments. After the next step, you can't change where they are.

Step 9: Riveting!

I'm going to assume that you now have roughly 20mm/1" of threaded stem left on top of your last nut. Using a hacksaw or a file, trim this down to about 4mm or ¼" and clamp your flower securely in some softgrips.

Now, take your ballpeen hammer and begin forming a rivet. Once you have done this, you cannot change the arrangement of the petals. To do this, forcefully strike the edges of the stump of thread, using a regular vertical hammering motion, until it starts to mushroom and form a rounded half-sphere. Continue striking until the bottom edge of this rivet is flush with the top of the nut, locking the nut in place.

Awesome! So close to finishing!

Step 10: Shaping

The last step, but maybe the most fun, is shaping. Yet it's the hardest to get just right.

Pick up your round pliers (so you don't leave grip marks) and get to work.

Begin by taking your rectangle and folding one of the petals up and around the rivet. It can be very useful to start at the part of the petal that is closest to the stem, and work outwards - that applies for all this shaping. If at any point the metal becomes unworkable, stop—you can't force it. Simply anneal that section of the copper (by tactical application of a blowtorch, for example) and keep going. You really don't want to break one petal now.

Repeat with the other petal of the rectangle, but form it around the first petal to form a bud. Now, use your pliers to bend up, shape, and curve the next 16 petals to your liking. I can't really be much help here, as it's all down to what your idea of a rose is. However, I can tell you what I do. I normally bend and curve the first eight (top two layers of squares) quite severely upwards and inwards, to form a larger bud. I then steadily reduce the angle of the bends for the next two layers, to make it so the bud is opening out.

Finally, curl the tops of your petals outwards to expose the texturing you worked on, and crinkle the edges. This step really makes a huge difference.

And that's it! Apart from some cleaning and finishing, you're all done! Congrats!

To clean up any oxidation from annealing, use a wire brush followed by sandpaper. Wire wool also works well to get into all the nooks and crannies you've now made. Either burnish the steel/brass with sandpaper to get it to gleam, or leave it dull. Both look nice and complement the rose.

At long last, you can apply a spray of clear coating (I hate the stuff, so don't bother—it will make the color last, but adds an unnatural gleam).

Step 11: Fin. (and extras)

Phew. Take a step back, breathe in, and admire your creation.

Now that you're done with that, how about some modifications!

- Add a sepal (star bit underneath a flower) from brass sheet
- Cut leaves from copper, texture as before, and braze onto stem
- Texture stem with ballpeen hammer
- Insert ball of cotton wool soaked in rosewater into innermost bud, to make it scented

DIY Knife-Sharpening Kit

By Quad89

(http://www.instructables.com/id/DIY-Knife-sharpening-kit/)

Most knife-sharpening kits that you can buy can damage or scratch your knife. The professionals always recommend using a set of sharpening stones, such as Arkansas stones, whetstones, or waterstones. However, these stones often run around $40, and even more for a good-sized one. These stones also have the problem of developing a bowl shape after repeated use, which in turn requires you to buy another stone—a flattening stone. As you can guess, buying these varieties of stones becomes extremely expensive.

The knife-sharpening kit that I made is capable of making a knife sharp enough to shave with, utilizes easily obtainable parts, and never goes bad or develops bowl-ing problems. Some quick repair or maintenance and the knife-sharpening kit is as good as new, with minimal costs.

Step 1: Materials

So the basic idea behind this is that you will be attaching sandpaper onto bathroom tiles in order to create DIY sharpening stones. Simple and it works. The best part is that you can easily replace the sandpaper whenever it gets old.

Materials Needed:

- container of acetone—around $10
- spray adhesive—$10
- a variety of high-grit sandpaper—$3/(pack of 5 sheets) × 5 packs = $15
- cotton cloths (or cut up an old T-shirt)—free

- rubber bumpers (optional)—$3
- smooth bathroom tiles—$0.80/tile × 5 = $4

The high-grit sandpaper can be found at automotive stores or in the automotive section at Walmart. For those who don't know, the higher the grit number, the finer the sanding. You'll want 800-, 1000-, and 2000-grit sandpaper. 200- to 400-grit sandpaper would be used for a really dull, dinged up, and damaged knife that you want to remove nicks from. Though at 200 grit, you may as well use a Dremel with a grinding bit. While 2000-grit sandpaper will give you a knife that you can shave hairs off with, if you are sharpening a straight razor and actually plan to shave with your blade, you may need to order higher-grit sandpaper (4000 grit).

You'll want as large (long) of these sand paper sheets that you can find, and then get the smoothest bathroom tiles that you can find that will fit these sheets of sandpaper. The sandpaper sheets that I found were 3.5" x 9", and the tiles I found were 4" x 8".

Everything else on the list can be found at a Lowes or Home Depot. The cotton cloths can be found in the painting section.

Step 2: Prep/Cleaning

You'll want to do this in a relatively clean area with no wind. I chose to use my bathroom because it seemed like the best place. Though, word of caution—don't stay in an enclosed area with an open container of acetone for very long, and turn on a vent as soon as you attach the sandpaper sheets.

First, get your cloth rag and put a little bit of acetone on it and clean the bathroom tiles. You want to make them clean and free of any fuzzies. Give them a few minutes for the acetone to flash off of the tiles.

Step 3: Attach Sandpaper

Setup an area where you can spray the adhesive. Spray both the bathroom tile and the back of the sandpaper sheet and attach them. After messing around with this sharpening kit for a while, I found that I preferred the sand paper to be on the edge of the tile, as shown in the third picture, but you may just have to try it to find out what you like best.

After you have attached the sandpaper to the tile, quickly get your cotton with acetone on it and remove the spray adhesive from the rest of the tile.

Then place something over it that won't attach to spray adhesive or could be easily removed (wax paper, plastic, etc.) and put a large flat weight on it to compress the sandpaper sheet onto the tile; let it sit and cure. I used a sheet of plastic from a package of computer paper, placed a book on top of it, and then put 20lbs from a weight set on top of it.

Rinse and repeat for each set of sandpaper that you use. Use a sharpie to label each tile. Remember, when you are sharpening there will be water on these, so you don't want to have to turn them over to see which sharpening tile you are using.

Let the spray adhesive cure for an hour or two before you start using these sharpening tiles to sharpen your knives.

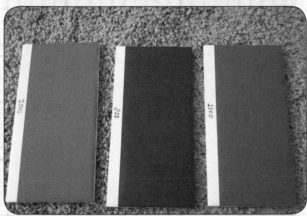

Step 4: Results/Conclusions/Suggestions

I recommend putting some of those little rubber bumpers on the bottom of the tiles so that you can stack the tiles without worrying about damaging the sandpaper sheets. It also has the added benefit of making it easier to sharpen your knives without the sharpening tile moving.

As I mentioned before, while trying out this sharpening kit, I found it more convenient to have the sandpaper flush with the edge of the tiles and to have the excess sand paper cut off from the tiles.

If the sandpaper ever becomes damaged or old, it's easy to replace. Just peel the sand paper off and remove the adhesive using the cotton cloth and acetone. The spray adhesive seems to be acetone-soluble.

If, after you've sharpened your blade using the 2000 grit, you feel that it is still not sharp enough, you could get some higher-grit sandpaper, or you could lap the blade a few times using an old belt or an old pair of blue jeans. Just cut up some blue jeans and lap the blade like you would see a barber do with a straight razor.

Important: Recommended Sharpening Method

So I used this sharpening kit to sharpen my kitchen knife set and learned some things doing so. If you don't know how to sharpen a knife using a sharpening stone or whetstone, watch some YouTube videos on how to do so. When you are sharpening using this kit, you only want to pull the knife back as you sharpen it —as in don't push the knife, sharp edge first, forward to sharpen it. This will prevent damage to the sand paper and extend its life.

Use water as a lubricant. Sharpening stones often require you to use some kind of oil or soapy material, sometimes water. Since the sandpaper is wet or dry type, just use water—that's what it was made for.

Final Thoughts:

So I've used this sharpening kit to sharpen all of my kitchen knives, my pocket knife, and a bayonet and have been very pleased with the results. After sharpening 75% of those items, I had to change the sandpaper on the 800, 1000, and 2000 grit because they received some damage while I was learning the above recommend sharpening techniques. The 800, 1000, and 2000 will be your most used grits/tiles. Anything less than that is used more for major repair.

Remember: Be careful with sharp objects! Don't cut yourself. I'm not responsible for any damage to yourself, others, creatures, or objects.

Storage

Invisible Book Shelf

Tetris Shelves

Framed Vinyl Records

Rope-Bridge Bookshelf

Adjustable Bookshelf for Angled Walls

Concrete Lightbulb Wall Hook

Cardboard Waste Tower

Like most furniture, storage solutions are painfully dull or expensive. These projects will help you find a middle ground between customized works of art and functional shelving to keep your stuff organized.

The invisible bookshelf always impresses guests, and the Tetris bookshelves will keep your knick knacks together until the whole shebang gets launched into space along with the Kremlin. (For those of you who have yet to beat Tetris, sorry for the spoiler.)

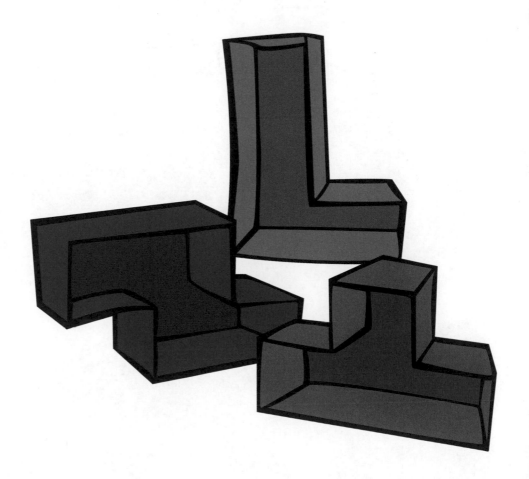

Invisible Book Shelf

By dorxincandeland
(http://www.instructables.com/id/Invisible-Book-Shelf/)

Cast levitation level 7 on your books (make them float)!

Step 1: What You'll Need

- book
- good-sized "L" bracket
- carpet knife
- pen
- small wood screws (of the flat-headed variety)
- large wood screws
- tape measure or ruler
- glue
- a stack of books for weight

A friend at work gave me a stack of Stephen King books that were collecting dust in his garage to make shelves with. My previous two shelves were made out of free books that my public library was trying to get rid of. Use a book you don't mind never reading again.

Step 2: Measure Twice, Cut Once

Measure the halfway point and make a mark. Set down your bracket at the mark, draw an outline, and measure again. Cut out a hole deep enough that the bracket will sit flush with the book's surface. You are doing this to the back or bottom of the book, the part that will be visible in the finished product.

Step 3: Don't Put Away the Carpet Knife Yet!

Use your knife to make a notch for the "L" bracket so the book can sit flush against the wall.

Step 4: Screw Stephen King!

. . . or at least place your small wood screws to secure the "L" bracket in place, and then put one on each side, toward the edges of the book, to secure the pages of the Stephen King (or other) book together. Hanging the bracket over the edge of a desk, chair, or counter is helpful. The pages will try to rise up the screw as you insert it, so make sure you're putting some pressure on them to keep them in line. If this part is not done correctly the end result will show the pages as wavy and will tip off the viewer that something is amiss. The picture shows me using a cordless drill, but I found that doing it by hand was much more effective.

Step 5: Glue and Apply Pressure

The glue will hold the bottom cover of the book in place, and the screws will hold the pages together. Put the stack of books on top of the whole deal and wait overnight.

Step 6: No, Seriously. Wait Overnight

Did you think I was kidding?

Step 7: Attach It to the Wall

Use a large wood screw to attach the whole mess to the wall. Find a stud first.

Step 8: Load It Up!

Put some books on it to cover your handiwork. Make sure you put enough books to cover the bracket—don't leave it like this picture.

Step 9: Forget That It's There . . .

. . . and wait for the crazy looks on people's faces when they notice it and can't figure it out.

Tetris Shelves

By HicksCustomFurniture
(http://www.instructables.com/id/Tetris-shelves/)

Having seen a bunch of examples of these that other people on the Internet had made, I took a crack at my own take on the idea.

Step 1: Stuff You'll Need
- table saw
- steel rule
- squares
- knife
- router and dovetail bit
- dovetail jig
- wood glue
- paint
- 12mm MDF—8' x 4f' sheet
- 3mm MDF—6' x 2' sheet
- dust mask/goggles/ear defenders

Step 2: Design
When you think about it, each Tetris block can be broken down into four equal squares. I decided each square would be 160mm2 and 150mm deep (good for CD's).I took to AutoCAD and drew up some plans.

I chose to use 12mm MDF, which would be backed with 3mm MDF. The joints would be dovetailed to make them nice and strong. Dovetailing is not that hard when you've got a router and a dovetail jig. Once I was happy, I wrote all the measurements down as a reference sheet and took to my little workshop.

Step 3: Cut MDF to Size
I gathered up all the bits of 12mm MDF I had left over from other projects and cut it into 150mm strips with a table saw. I reckon you'd have enough to make a full set of 7 blocks from an 8' x 4' sheet.

I marked out the lengths, allowing for a bit off each end, and ticked them off my reference sheet as I worked. It's a good idea to have a few extra lengths handy, as the occasional screw-up is pretty inevitable.

They then got cut to length on the table saw using a template piece for each length to ensure they came out the same.

Take your time with this. If your pieces aren't spot on it'll have an effect on the angles later. Then, with a couple of passes through the table saw, I cut rebates for the back panel into each piece.

Warning: Use the blade guard on your table saw! I only took mine off briefly to cut the rebate for the back panel.

Step 4: Cut Joints
I then labeled which pieces were to go next to each other. It can get confusing so it's good to mark, cut, and glue one block at a time.

Then I set up the dovetail jig, testing and tweaking it with some offcuts until the joints were coming out just right. I chose to use 6mm dovetails.

Then came a long day of cutting joints! Make sure you're fully covered in protective equipment, like gloves and safety glasses, as this stage is very dusty.

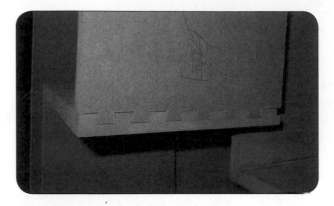

Step 5: Glue Them Together

I used Resintite wood glue. Just use plenty of clamps and keep checking that everything's square. For the more complicated shapes, you'll want to do the gluing in a few phases. Maybe make a jig to help you along too.

You'll have a little bit of play in the joints before you put the back panels on, but it can't hurt to get them as accurate as possible now. Scrape the excess glue off the inside joints now, as sanding it off later will be a nightmare.

Step 6: Back Panels and Filler

Simply cut the back panels to fit each piece. I measured the channels on each block and copied it onto some 3mm MDF using squares and suchlike. Get it as square and accurate as possible, as the back panels will hold the cube in shape.

3mm MDF isn't the toughest material, so with a bit of persistence I got through it with a knife and a straight edge. Then I glued them in place, wiping the glue off the inside. Once that was dry I rubbed in a good amount of filler, and then it all got a good sanding.

Step 7: Paint

Before painting I gave each surface a wipe with a damp cloth to get the dust off. Then I gave each block a couple of coats of primer, sanding with 240-grit sandpaper after each coat.

I went for the "Tetris worlds" color scheme, as all the other versions have a magenta (pink!) block. I thought I'd give spray paint a chance, as I found it hard to get a smooth finish with brushes on my first set.

Basically spray from about six inches away and perpendicular to the surface and wear a good quality mask. It's better to do lots of thin coats instead of fewer thick coats.

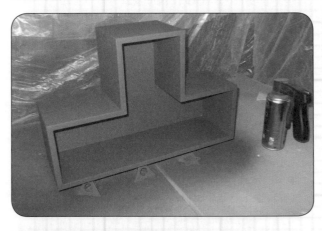

Step 8: Finished!

And there we go! The long piece came out more green than cyan, but other than that, I'm really pleased with them and, added to my old set, they're well on their way to making it to the ceiling!

Framed Vinyl Records

By bonzo363

(http://www.instructables.com/id/Hang-Up-Your-Old-Vinyl-Records/)

A few months ago I came across a huge load of my dad's old records and decided to hang them up on an empty wall in my room.

Step 1: Getting the Tile Trim

At Home Depot I found an employee who recommended using some plastic tile trim for the project. I picked up about ten pieces of 1/4" x 6' of QEP Black Plastic Tile Trim, which ended up running me only about $30— much cheaper than any of my other options. The tile trim also has very convenient holes, through which I put standard wall screws to hang the trim.

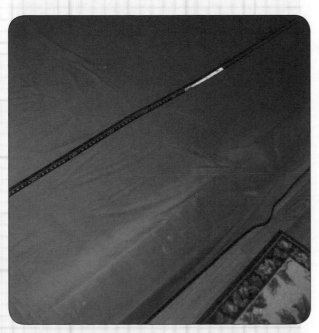

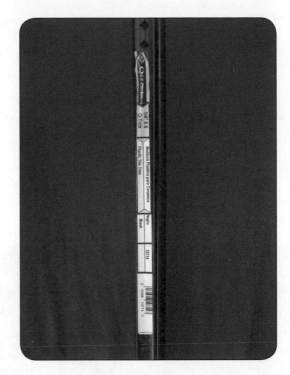

Step 2: Hanging the Trim

Next, I hung the first layer of trim, using a level at the top, with about five to six wall screws across the length of the 6' piece. After that, I took three of my records and pushed one in at the near end, one in the middle, and one at the far end of the piece of trim. Then, I took the next piece of trim and stuck in into the bottom of the records and screwed it in. I did this to accurately measure the space needed in between each layer of trim to hang the records. I repeated this process for each row of records I wanted.

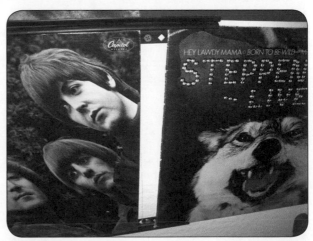

Step 3: Hanging the Records

Last, I gathered all of my records and slid them into all of the rows of tile trim that I'd hung, and presto! I have a cool collage of some really awesome old records on my wall that has been up for at least four months now. But what's the best part? If you get sick of the records, simply slide them out and put some new ones up. It never gets old and always looks great.

Rope-Bridge Bookshelf

By *fungus amungus*
(http://www.instructables.com/id/Rope-Bridge-Bookshelf/)

The rope-bridge bookshelf lets books have a relaxed home when they're not being read. It can be rough being opened and left in all sorts of locations during the reading process, and the books have earned a nice break.

Step 1: Supplies
Materials:
- STATLIG board from IKEA
- EKBY BJARNUM shelf-holder pair from IKEA
- paracord
- steel washers

Tools:
- miter saw
- drill press
- lighter

Step 2: Chop
Using the miter saw, cut the wood into several pieces. With the board I had I got:
- Two 2½" pieces
- Eleven 2" pieces

Step 3: Drill
Using the drill press, I drilled out pairs of holes in all of the pieces. I clamped a couple of pieces of wood to the drill press to make sure that all of the holes would be aligned correctly.

Step 4: Start the Paracord
Cut off two lengths of paracord and singe the ends with your lighter to prevent fraying. Tie a knot in one end and start feeding it through the pieces of wood.

To make the knots extra secure, use the lighter to melt the knot into a gooey mass.

Step 5: Washers
String the cord through all of the pieces of wood, using the steel washers as spacers. I used three for each gap.

Step 6: Add the Bracket
Use the included hardware that came with the EKBY BJARNUM to attach the bracket to the wood.

Step 7: Hang It Up!
Find a nice spot for your bookshelf and install it! I used a few drywall anchors to keep everything nice and secure. Now find some books that deserve a nice rest and put them down on it.

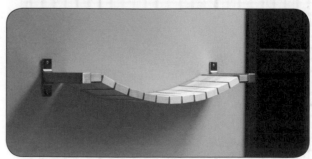

Adjustable Bookshelf for Angled Walls

By joteach
(http://www.instructables.com/id/
Adjustable-bookshelf-for-angled-walls/)

Since angled walls and roofs are hard to make shelving systems for, I have made a bookshelf to utilize this mostly lost space. You can adjust the bookshelf to every angle by adapting the bolts and setting the angle right. If you want to, you can also put it on a regular wall wherever you want or on a flat surface. Of course, you don't have to use it for books; you can put any stuff you want in it.

As we had to move the bookcase several times to take pictures, I didn't secure it to the wall because that would make too many holes in my walls. Therefore you can see my hand on most of the pictures. The system is not expensive—I only had to buy wood and bolts/screws. The whole build took just a few hours. It is extremely convenient!

Step 1: What You Need
Materials:
- long pieces of wood
- 8 screw bars (30cm each)
- 16 iron nuts

Tools:
- drill
- saw
- some sand paper to finish the edges

Step 2: How It's Done
Cut the wooden pieces to the right size. Drill the holes for the screw bar. Assemble and attach the wooden pieces to the screw bars. Tighten the bolts. Finish the corners with sand paper.

Concrete Lightbulb Wall Hook

By whamodyne
(http://www.instructables.com/id/Concrete-
Lightbulb-Wall-Hook/)

This will provide you with an excellent excuse for driving a lag bolt into your wall—more specifically, the Concrete Lightbulb Wall Hook. Functional yet stylish, it gives a nice industrial design feel wherever you mount it.

I've been playing around, trying to make a concrete lightbulb. Why? Because I find the contrast of blending a new material like concrete in an everyday shape like a lightbulb to be a great design element. So, while messing around with these guys, I realized this would be a great excuse to drive lag bolts into my wall for hooks, which I was in need of. By embedding a lag bolt into the concrete lightbulb, I could make a wall hook that was useful enough to handle anything I wanted to hang off it. Thus, this project was born.

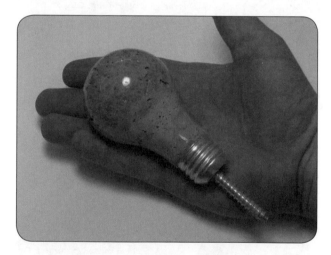

Step 1: Tools and Materials

You will need a work area where a little sand and concrete mix or glass shards is not an issue. Make sure you have a small brush and dustpan available at all times. Normally you wait until the end to shatter the lightbulb, but it can happen at any point in this process. Be ready for cleanup from the very start.

Tools:
- pliers
- wire cutters
- screwdriver
- carbide scribe
- plastic tub to mix the concrete in

- scrap of wood to mix the concrete with
- plastic spoon
- measuring cup and measuring spoons
- old toothbrush
- coffee stirrer and plastic cups you "borrowed" from Starbucks
- gloves and safety glasses
- miscellaneous items like Sharpies, some rags, etc.

Quikrete Mortar Mix:

"Concrete" is a mix of cement, water, and aggregates. My research showed that a sand mix, aka mortar mix, is good when using a smooth-surfaced mold like the inside of a lightbulb. It gives a very high shine when cured. A sand mix is different from your generic concrete in that the aggregates don't have any gravel, just various sizes of sand. I decided to do it with mortar mix instead of your standard bag of generic concrete.

I got the ten-pound bag at the local home improvement store for $2. This is enough to do over a dozen lightbulbs. I could have purchased the 60-pound bag for $7 at a much lower cost/volume, but this project really doesn't need that much.

Lightbulbs:

Just get the cheapest standard sized incandescent lightbulbs you can find. I got mine at Walmart—a pack of four for 77 cents. Can't beat that with a stick.

Water:

You'll need about 4 tablespoons. I kept a bottle of water nearby on the bench and refilled it from the tap when needed.

Lag Bolt:

I'm using a 5/16" lag bolt that is 3½" long. 5/16" was the largest lag bolt I could fit into the lightbulb without cutting off the head. I didn't want to do that because the head gives the bolt a lot of grip when embedded in the concrete. With a lag bolt 5/16" in diameter, I can drill in the wall a ¼" hole to get a good balance between grip and ease of installing. In other words, it turns easily into the wall yet holds really well.

Step 2: Hollow Out the Light Bulb

With practice this becomes quick and simple. A lot of the time you are poking around inside the lightbulb trying to break off the internal glass bits. Do this over a trashcan and shake the lightbulb often out over the trashcan to get rid of the glass shards. Wear safety glasses at all times. More than once some glass flew up toward my face when I was doing this.

First, grip the metal circle that has a blob of solder in the middle at the bottom of the lightbulb with your pliers and gently pry it up from the dark purple glass insulator. This is pulling a wire in the middle that you want to break, so just pull it off.

Once that is done, take your carbide scribe and, over a trash can, pry into the hole you just made in the purple glass insulator and break up that purple glass. You want to remove all of the purple glass insulator from the lightbulb body. I use the scribe to start some cracks and lift off a section of it, and then I follow up with the screwdriver to get the rest. Turn the lightbulb upside down and shake out all the glass bits that have fallen inside. Inside there is a small glass tube that pokes up into the glass insulator. You might or might not have already broken that off by now. If not, just lever the screwdriver against it until it snaps loose. Empty into the trashcan.

Now you have a hole in the bottom of the lightbulb. At this point I take my pliers and gently bend over the metal tabs on the inside of the hole so there is no "lip" on the inside. Later when you have broken up the rest of the inside pieces, there won't be anywhere for the bits to catch and stay in the lightbulb when you shake it out. There should be a wire visible inside, soldered to the side of the metal screw piece.

Take your wire cutters and cut the wire as close to the side of the bulb as possible. Now, the inside has a glass cylinder you need to break off, then you need to clean up the edges to finish the job. Take your scribe or screwdriver and insert it into the lightbulb until it meets resistance. Tap it gently until something breaks. Then, using the screwdriver, lever against the side of the lightbulb to clean out whatever remaining glass bits are left. You want the neck of the lightbulb to be clear from the hole all the way down the body. Turn the bulb over and shake it out one more time to get rid of the last of the internal glass pieces floating loose.

Take a toothbrush and, while dry, push it into the lightbulb and start loosening up the dry white powder, especially in the neck of the bulb. Don't worry if you can't get the stuff the toothbrush can't reach at this point. I found the bulb cleans out easier if you do loosen up the white powder in the neck before it gets wet.

Now take it over to the sink and add a little soap and water. Scrub around with the toothbrush and shake the bulb to get the water everywhere. Pull out the toothbrush and then wash out the soapy water from the bulb. At this point, it will be all nice and clean inside without any soapy residue. Set it aside to dry out. Now it's time to mix up the concrete.

Step 3: Mix Up the Concrete

This is the part that's more art than science. I've found that in the small batches this project calls for, it's very easy to add too much or too little water to the mix. When you are mixing an entire 60-pound bag of concrete, being off a teaspoon on the water doesn't matter that much. When you are mixing up just a cup of concrete, that teaspoon starts to matter.

Mortar mix, when cured in a glass mold like we are using, gives a very nice gloss surface. The lower the amount of water you use, the smoother and more glass-like the surface is, and the stronger the resulting cured concrete is. However, the smaller the amount of water you use, the harder it is to have it fill in the gaps on the sides, and it leaves lots of holes and divots. Getting the mix liquid enough to spread out but not so liquid that it loses its strength is one of the issues on the water-to-dry mix ratio. Finding the correct compromise between these two issues is really a matter of practice and personal taste. I would suggest you play around with it in multiple bulbs if you are interested in getting the best result you can. The ratio I've found works well is about 1¼ cups of the mortar mix and a hair under four tablespoons of water.

Measure out a little less than four tablespoons of water and put that into your plastic tub. This is more mortar mix than you need to fill a lightbulb, but there is always some spillage, and trying to reduce the amount means even more accuracy on the water measurement. This is a good amount to start with.

Slowly mix in the mortar mix a little at a time. Let a little bit get wet, and then a little more, then a little more, while stirring the whole thing. It's a bit like making biscuit dough at this point, but you're pouring the dry into the wet instead of the other way around. The consistency should be good enough that the mortar mix wants to stick together in one large clump, but it isn't sopping wet. If you feel you need to add more water or mortar mix to get it correct, then go for it. Just do it a little bit at a time. A small amount of either material makes a large impact at this stage.

Once it's at a consistency you like, keep stirring nice and slow for a few minutes. You want everything to be thoroughly wet. Important: At this moment the clock starts and you have 30 to 45 minutes to finish the lightbulb before the mortar mix starts to harden. Once you have thoroughly mixed up the mortar mix, bring out the lightbulb and start filling it up.

Step 4: Start Filling Up the Lightbulb

You are working on a time limit at this point as the mortar mix starts to set. If you can get it all done in 30 minutes or so, it should be fine. Put your lightbulb into a small plastic tub with the hole pointing upwards. When you are adding the mix there is always spillage, and you don't want that all over your work area. I put a little bit of sand in the bottom so it will stay straight early on; once you add a few spoonfuls of the mortar mix it stands up straight on its own.

Take a plastic spoon and scoop up a level amount of the wet mortar mix. Holding the end of the spoon over the hole in the lightbulb use your finger on the other hand to push it down into the hole. Some will spill over the edges of the hole—that's okay. You made almost twice the volume of mortar mix as will go into the lightbulb.

After four or five spoonfuls into the lightbulb, you want to vibrate it so the mortar mix liquefies and spreads out evenly on the inside. Shake it back and forth to make it liquefy. If there is an air bubble visible on the side that just won't fill in no matter how much you shake it, tapping it repeatedly with your fingertip moves the bubble up and the liquid towards the tapping.

Repeat these steps, a handful of scoops and then much shaking and tapping to fill in the gaps and make it all liquid-like, until you reach halfway up the neck of the bulb. At that point it's time to add the lag bolt.

Step 5: Put in the Lag Bolt and Finish Up Adding the Mortar Mix

Before putting in the lag bolt, mark off with a Sharpie where 1½" is from the pointy end so you know how far to push it down. Put the lag bolt into the mortar mix. Because the lightbulb shape has some undercutting with the mold, the mortar mix wants to clump up in the middle of the bulb and not grip the sides. You can use the head of the lag bolt to tap down the pile in the middle of the bulb so it starts filling in all the gaps.

Keep adding mortar mix around the lag bolt to fill it up. Holding the lag bolt firmly to make sure it does not rattle, keep shaking the bulb and tapping the sides to fill in gaps and liquefy the mortar mix. Take a coffee stirrer you "borrowed" from Starbucks and use that to tap down the mortar mix. You want to keep adding the mix, tamp and fill, tamp and fill.

Finally, the entire bulb is all done and you are tamping on the top. You want the mortar mix to be level with the top of the hole but not sticking out in a bulge. When you are all done, put the lightbulb with the lag bolt pointing up in a spare plastic cup. The ones I used were also borrowed from Starbucks.

Take a rag and clean up the metal threaded part of the lightbulb as well as you can—you don't want the mortar mix drying on it. Set this to the side for at least 72 hours to let the mortar mix cure. I normally write the date it was made on the glass with a Sharpie so I can keep track.

Step 6: Crack the lightbulb

Let the mortar mix cure for at least 72 hours. A few days more is a good thing. This is the part where you are breaking up the lightbulb glass into little bits and pieces. Glass will be flying in all directions, so wear safety glasses and at least one glove (like in the pictures) at all times!

Over a trash can, hold the bulb in the hand that has a glove on it. I've tried to use gloves on both hands at this stage and didn't have the fine control I wanted. You might be able to do it. Taking a hard metal object, start striking the side of the lightbulb. I'm using my carbide scribe. The glass will start to crack and form spider-web fractures. Keep hitting. Eventually small pieces will fall and/or fly off of the bulb.

When you have formed a good number of cracks around the bulb, take a toothbrush and scrub it vigorously over the entire bulb. This will brush any glass grit or loose pieces free and into the trash can. Then take your carbide scribe (or awl or sharp nail) and start to pry up the edges of the glass left on the bulb. Some of it will come off in large chunks; some of it will come off a little piece at a time. Try to aim for the trashcan but know that it won't all go in there; some of it will pop up and go in any direction. If a large piece of glass doesn't want to come up and doesn't have any cracks in it, beat it with the metal object some more to create the spider web.

Every so often take the toothbrush and rub down the lightbulb to get rid of any ground-in glass or loose bits. When all the glass has been removed from the lightbulb, take your scribe and carefully go around the neck of the bulb where the metal met the glass. Make sure there are no loose glass shards under the lip of the metal. Shake and tap the bulb to see what comes loose.

When you are done, take a shop brush and run it over the entire bulb one more time to get any glass grit or loose pieces out of the holes in the concrete. It's done! The mortar mix often leaves pits and holes even with all that shaking and tapping you did, but I think it adds a bit of character to the whole thing and makes each one you do unique. Feel the glossy, smooth glass finish on the bulb and see how it reflects the light. Now it's time to mount it!

Step 7: Mount It on the Wall

Now that you have this killer Concrete Lightbulb Wall Hook, it's time to mount it into the wall. The steps here are fairly simple. First, find the stud. This needs a wood stud in the wall. There are multiple ways to find a wood stud—I'm using a cheapie stud finder.

Then, drill the hole. Using a ¼" drill bit, drill a hole 1½" deep into the wall. Finally, screw the hook in. The hole is big enough that you can screw it in, but the bite is good enough that it can hold just about anything you want to hang off it—heavy overcoats, small children, whatever strikes your fancy.

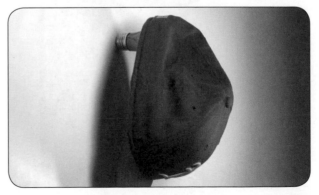

Cardboard Waste Tower

By dontstop1990
(http://www.instructables.com/id/
Cardboard-Waste-Tower/)

I made this Waste Tower when I moved into my dorm room at college and got fed up having such a messy trash and recycling situation. I designed something to elegantly separate trash from both paper recycling and plastic/metal recycling. Having just moved to New York City, I was inspired by the efficiency of building upward. So I decided to make the Waste Tower.

I designed the Waste Tower to hold standard-size office waste bins. This is one of those projects that is pretty self-explanatory. I could give you the dimensions and layout to cut the cardboard exactly how I did, but I didn't keep those notes, and you will probably learn something planning it on your own.

Step 1: What You Need
Materials:
- cardboard
- tape

Tools:
- box cutter or X-acto knife
- something to cut on: a piece of cardboard works but one of those cutting mats is preferable.

CONVERSION TABLES

One person's inch is another person's .39 centimeters. Instructables projects come from all over the world, so here's a handy reference guide that will help keep your project on track.

Measurement								
	1 Millimeter	1 Centimeter	1 Meter	1 Inch	1 Foot	1 Yard	1 Mile	1 Kilometer
Millimeter	1	10	1,000	25.4	304.8	—	—	—
Centimeter	0.1	1	100	2.54	30.48	91.44	—	—
Meter	0.001	0.01	1	0.025	0.305	0.91	—	1,000
Inch	0.04	0.39	39.37	1	12	36	—	—
Foot	0.003	0.03	3.28	0.083	1	3	—	—
Yard	—	0.0109	1.09	0.28	033	1	—	—
Mile	—	—	—	—	—	—	1	0.62
Kilometer	—	—	1,000	—	—	—	1.609	1

Volume									
	1 Milliliter	1 Liter	1 Cubic Meter	1 Tea-spoon	1 Tablespoon	1 Fluid Ounce	1 Cup	1 Pint	1 Quart	1 Gallon
Milliliter	1	1,000	—	4.9	14.8	29.6	—	—	—	—
Liter	0.001	1	1,000	0.005	0.015	0.03	0.24	0.47	0.95	3.79
Cubic Meter	—	0.001	1	—	—	—	—	—	—	0.004
Teaspoon	0.2	202.9	—	1	3	6	48	—	—	—
Tablespoon	0.068	67.6	—	0.33	1	2	16	32	—	—
Fluid Ounce	0.034	33.8	—	0.167	0.5	1	8	16	32	—
Cup	0.004	4.23	—	0.02	0.0625	0.125	1	2	4	16
Pint	0.002	2.11	—	0.01	0.03	0.06	05	1	2	8
Quart	0.001	1.06	—	0.005	0.016	0.03	0.25	.05	1	4
Gallon	—	0.26	264.17	0.001	0.004	0.008	0.0625	0.125	0.25	1

conversion tables

Mass and Weight						
	1 Gram	1 Kilogram	1 Metric Ton	1 Ounce	1 Pound	1 Short Ton
Gram	1	1,000	—	28.35	—	—
Kilogram	0.001	1	1,000	0.028	0.454	—
Metric Ton	—	0.001	1	—	—	0.907
Ounce	0.035	35.27	—	1	16	—
Pound	0.002	2.2	—	0.0625	1	2,000
Short Ton	—	0.001	1.1	—	—	1

Speed		
	1 Mile per hour	1 Kilometer per hour
Miles per hour	1	0.62
Kilometers per hour	1.61	1

Temperature		
	Fahrenheit (°F)	Celsius (°C)
Fahrenheit	—	(°C x 1.8) + 32
Celsius	(°F − 32) / 1.8	—

also available

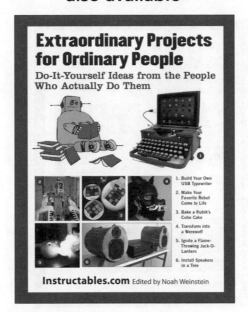

Extraordinary Projects for Ordinary People
Do-It-Yourself Ideas from the People Who
Actually Do Them

by Instructables.com, edited by Noah Weinstein

Collected in this volume is a best-of selection from
Instructables, reproduced for the first time outside of
the web format, retaining all of the charm and ingenuity
that make Instructables such a popular destination for
Internet users looking for new and fun projects designed by real people in an easy-to-digest way.

Hundreds of Instructables are included, ranging from
practical projects like making a butcher-block countertop or building solar panels to fun and unique ideas for
realistic werewolf costumes or transportable camping
hot tubs. The difficulty of the projects ranges from beginner on up, but all are guaranteed to raise a smile or
a "Why didn't I think of that?"

US $16.95 paperback ISBN: 978-1-62087-057-0

also available

How to Do Absolutely Everything
Homegrown Projects from Real Do-It-Yourself Experts

by Instructables.com, edited by Sarah James

Continuing the Instructables series with Skyhorse Publishing, a mammoth collection of projects has been selected and curated for this special best-of volume of Instructables. The guides in this book cover the entire spectrum of possibilities that the popular website has to offer, showcasing how online communities can foster and nurture creativity.

From outdoor agricultural projects to finding new uses for traditional household objects, the beauty of Instructables lies in their ingenuity and their ability to find new ways of looking at the same thing. *How to Do Absolutely Everything* has that in spades; the possibilities are limitless, thanks to not only the selection of projects available here, but also the new ideas you'll build on after reading this book. Full-color photographs illustrate each project in intricate detail, providing images of both the individual steps of the process and the end product.

US $16.95 paperback ISBN: 978-1-62087-066-2

also available

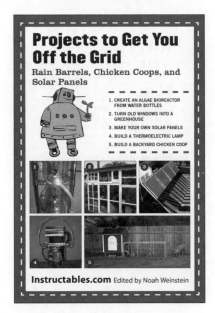

Projects to Get You Off the Grid
Rain Barrels, Chicken Coops, and Solar Panels
by Instructables.com, edited by Noah Weinstein

Instructables is back with this compact book focused on a series of projects designed to get you thinking creatively about thinking green. Twenty Instructables illustrate just how simple it can be to make your own backyard chicken coop or turn a wine barrel into a rainwater collector.

Illustrated with dozens of full-color photographs per project accompanying easy-to-follow instructions, this Instructables collection utilizes the best that the online community has to offer, turning a far-reaching group of people into a mammoth database churning out ideas to make life better, easier, and, in this case, greener, as this volume exemplifies.

US $14.95 paperback ISBN: 978-1-62087-164-5

also available

Practical Duct Tape Projects

by Instructables.com, edited by Noah Weinstein

Duct tape has gotten a reputation as the quick-fix tape for every situation. However, did you know that you can use duct tape to create practical items for everyday use? Did you also know that duct tape now comes in a variety of colors, so your creations can be fun and stylish? Originating from Instructables, a popular project-based community made up of all sorts of characters with wacky hobbies and a desire to pass on their wisdom to others, *Practical Duct Tape Projects* contains ideas from a number of authors who nurse a healthy urge to create anything possible from duct tape.

Practical Duct Tape Projects provides step-by-step instructions on a variety of useful and fun objects involving duct tape. Guided through each endeavor by detailed photographs, the reader will create articles of clothing, tools, and more.

US $12.95 paperback ISBN: 978-1-62087-709-8

also available

Backyard Rockets
Learn to Make and Launch Rockets, Missiles, Cannons, and Other Projectiles

by Instructables.com, edited by Mike Warren

Originating from Instructables, a popular project-based community made up of all sorts of characters with wacky hobbies and a desire to pass on their wisdom to others, *Backyard Rockets* is made up of projects from a medley of authors who have collected and shared a treasure trove of rocket-launching plans and the knowledge to make their projects soar!

Backyard Rockets gives step-by-step instructions, with pictures to guide the way, on how to launch your very own project into the sky. All of these authors have labored over their endeavors to pass their knowledge on and make it easier for others to attempt.

US $12.95 paperback ISBN: 978-1-62087-730-2

also available

Office Weapons
Catapults, Darts, Shooters, Tripwires, and Other Do-It-Yourself Projects to Fortify Your Cubicle

by Instructables.com, edited by Mike Warren

Bored in your office? Did your coworker just prank you and you're wondering how to get him back? Is your boss constantly stealing your paperclips and you don't know how to keep his mitts away from your desk? *Office Weapons* gives you the complete step-by-step instructions for thirty different daring office pranks. Check out these simple but effective weapons fashioned from office materials and be prepared next time someone borrows your special stapler or leaves the copy machine jammed.

These projects are made by the best in the business; the office workers who actually need them! They say necessity is the mother of invention; leave it to the Instructables community to put that theory to the test!

US $14.95 paperback ISBN: 978-1-62087-708-1

also available

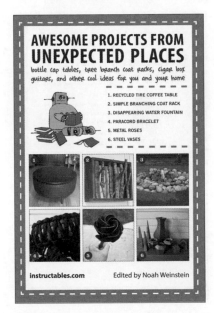

Awesome Projects from Unexpected Places
Bottle Cap Tables, Tree Branch Coat Racks, Cigar Box
Guitars, and Other Cool Ideas for Your and Your Home
by Instructables.com, edited by Noah Weinstein

The term "crafting" used to call to mind woven baskets topped with bows, braided friendship bracelets, and painted angelic-faced figurines. Thanks to Instructables.com, crafting has shed its wings—and its ribbons—and has become a pastime appreciated by both men and women.

After reading *Awesome Projects from Unexpected Places*, readers will no longer panic when a coveted watchband breaks. Instead, they will coolly use a woven paracord to replace the band with little effort. When the living room needs a bit more life, crafters will rise to the occasion and deliver Dalí-inspired melting clocks, geometric cut-paper table lamps, and eco-friendly lights.

US $12.95 paperback ISBN: 978-1-62087-705-0

also available

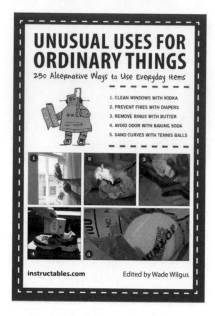

Unusual Uses for Ordinary Things
250 Alternative Ways to Use Everyday Items

by Instructables.com, edited by Wade Wilgus

Most people use nail polish remover to remove nail polish. They use coffee grounds to make coffee and hair dryers to dry their hair. The majority of people may also think that the use of eggs, lemons, mustard, butter, and mayonnaise should be restricted to making delicious food in the kitchen. The Instructables.com community would disagree with this logic—they have discovered hundreds of inventive and surprising ways to use these and other common household materials to improve day-to-day life.

Did you know that tennis balls can protect your floors, fluff your laundry, and keep you from backing too far into (and thus destroying) your garage? How much do you know about aspirin? Sure, it may alleviate pain, but it can also be used to remove sweat stains, treat bug bites and stings, and prolong the life of your sputtering car battery. These are just a few of the quirky ideas that appear in *Unusual Uses for Ordinary Things*.

US $12.95 paperback ISBN: 978-1-62087-725-8

also available

Amazing Cakes
Recipes for the world's most unusual, creative, and customizable cakes

by Instructables.com, edited and Introduced by Sarah James

With Instructables.com's *Amazing Cakes*, you'll be able to make cakes shaped like animals, mythical creatures, and vehicles. They may light up, breathe fire, or blow bubbles or smoke. They may be 3D or they may be animated, seeming to move of their own free will. Whether they're cute and cuddly (like a penguin) or sticky and gross (like a human brain!), these cakes have two things in common: They're (mostly) edible and they're amazing!

Instructables.com authors walk you through each step of the process as you cut plywood for cake bases, hardwire figurines for automation, and mix nontoxic chemicals for explosions and eruptions. The photos accompanying the step-by-step directions provide additional information about the processes.

US $12.95 paperback ISBN: 978-1-62087-690-9

also available

Meatless Eats
Savory Vegetarian Recipes from around the World
by Instructables.com, edited and Introduced by Sarah James

"Originating from Instructables, a popular project-based community made up of all sorts of characters with wacky hobbies and a desire to pass on their wisdom to others, *Meatless Eats* is made up of recipes from a cast of cooks who demonstrate their culinary savvy and flavor combinations.

Meatless Eats gives full step-by-step instructions for creating delicious vegetarian dishes that even die-hard carnivores will crave. Written by cooks who can't get enough of veggies, each recipe contains pictures for an easy follow-along guide, even for those who spend little to no time in the kitchen. Discover your inner vegetarian with these mouthwatering recipes."

US $12.95 paperback ISBN: 978-1-62087-697-8